THE PULITZER PRIZE STORY II

COMING HOME
Pulitzer Prize for Feature Photography, 1974

SLAVA VEDER'S PHOTO FOR THE ASSOCIATED PRESS OF A VIETNAM WAR PRISONER'S HOMECOMING

THE PULITZER PRIZE STORY II

AWARD-WINNING NEWS STORIES,
COLUMNS, EDITORIALS, CARTOONS,
AND NEWS PICTURES, 1959–1980

Edited, with Commentaries by John Hohenberg

93-1354

New York
COLUMBIA UNIVERSITY PRESS

Library of Congress Cataloging in Publication Data
Main entry under title:

The Pulitzer prize story II.

Companion volume to the 1959 work: The Pulitzer
prize story, edited by J. Hohenberg.
Includes index.
1. American prose literature—20th century.
2. Caricatures and cartoons—United States.
3. Pulitzer prizes. I. Hohenberg, John.
PS647.N4P8   070.4′31   80-16880
ISBN 0-231-04978-1

Columbia University Press
New York   Guildford, Surrey

9 8 7 6 5 4

For Jo Ann

CONTENTS

ILLUSTRATIONS

ACKNOWLEDGMENTS

This book is the product of my 22 years as administrator of the Pulitzer Prizes at Columbia University. From 1954 to 1976, as the representative of the University and the Pulitzer Prize Board, I was privileged to oversee the day-by-day operation of the nomination and selection process, to become familiar with the problems in both areas, and to form many close and enduring friendships in the profession as well as in the academic community associated with it.

I am grateful to Columbia University, its Graduate School of Journalism, the Pulitzer Prize Board, and the Pulitzer Prize Administrator's Office for permitting me to put this volume together, and to Columbia University Press for publishing it. The selections and judgments, and whatever errors there are in concept and text, necessarily are entirely my own and I absolve all others of responsibility.

My thanks in particular go to William J. McGill, president of Columbia University until his retirement in 1980; Osborn Elliott, dean, Columbia Graduate School of Journalism; Joseph Pulitzer, Jr., chairman, Pulitzer Prize Board; John Moore, director and editor, Columbia University Press; William F. Bernhardt, associate executive editor of the Press, and my own highly capable and understanding editor at the Press, David Diefendorf.

I could not, however, have produced this book without the helpfulness and friendship of my Columbia colleague and successor, Professor Richard T. Baker, administrator of the Prizes, and my two long-time associates in the Pulitzer Prize Office, Mrs. Rose

Valenstein and Mrs. Robin Holloway Kuzen, who responded so often and so effectively to my calls for help. Once again, I also acknowledge the assistance of the guardians of the Pulitzer Prize Collection, Wade Doares, the director of the Columbia Journalism Library, and his assistant, Jonathan Beard.

I am sure that my work on this book, coming on top of my other responsibilities at the University of Tennessee, must have complicated the lives of my wife JoAnn Fogarty Hohenberg, and my children, Pamela Jo and Eric Wayne. Yet, regardless of the depth of my involvement, I was always able to count on their support. Surely, an author's family deserves a particular expression of gratitude, which I gladly convey to them.

Finally, for permission to reprint articles, sections of articles, photographs, and cartoons, I want to thank the following and their news organizations, and I take note of the copyrighted nature of all the material involved.

Jack Anderson, columnist, and David Hendlin, vice president and director, United Feature Syndicate; Lee Anderson, editor, the *Chattanooga News-Free Press* and Robin Hood, photographer, Office of the Governor, Nashville, Tn.; George Beveridge, senior assistant managing editor, the *Washington Star*; Barry Bingham, Sr., chairman of the board, the *Courier-Journal* and *Louisville Times*; Louis D. Boccardi, executive editor, the Associated Press; Robert T. Collins, president and publisher, *Valley News Dispatch*, Tarentum, Pa.; Donald E. Doyle, publisher-general manager, the *Daily Gazette*, Xenia, Ohio; Katherine Fanning, editor and publisher, *Anchorage* (Alaska) *Daily News*; William H. Fields, executive editor, the *Atlanta Constitution*; Earl W. Foell, managing editor, the *Christian Science Monitor*, and Kathleen W. Allison, copyright and trademark administrator, the *Christian Science Monitor* (all Monitor articles reprinted by permission of the *Christian Science Monitor* and copyright in year of publication by the *Christian Science Monitor* Publishing Society, all rights reserved); Donald H. Forst, editor, *Boston Herald American*; Herblock and Jean Rickard of Herblock Cartoons, the *Washington Post* (Mr. Block's cartoon © 1978 by Herblock in the *Washington Post*); Seymour M. Hersh, Room 1236 National Press Building, Washington, D.C., and Dispatch News Service; William H.

Hornby, editor, *Denver Post*, and Paul Conrad for Mr. Conrad's 1963 *Denver Post* cartoon, also Johnnie M. Walker of the *Los Angeles Times* Syndicate which circulated the cartoon (Mr. Conrad's cartoon copyright in year of publication, all rights reserved); John H. Johnson, president and editor of Johnson Publishing Company and Moneta Sleet, Jr., for Mr. Sleet's picture, which is reprinted by permission of *Ebony* magazine and copyright 1968 by Johnson Publishing Company; Kenneth P. Johnson, executive vice president and editor, *Dallas Times Herald*; Thomas A. Kelly, editor, the *Palm Beach Post*; Fred Kinne, editor, *San Diego Evening Tribune*; Clayton Kirkpatrick, executive vice president and editor, *Chicago Tribune*, and William Jones, managing editor, news, *Chicago Tribune*; Howard Kleinberg, editor, *Miami News*; John S. Knight, editor emeritus, Knight-Ridder Newspapers Inc.; David Laventhol, publisher, *Newsday*; David Lawrence, Jr., executive editor, *Detroit Free Press*; John E. Leard, vice president and executive editor, *Richmond Times-Dispatch* and *Richmond News Leader*; Warren L. Lerude, publisher, *Nevada State Journal* and *Reno Evening Gazette*; Richard H. Leonard, editor, *Milwaukee Journal*; John McMullan, executive editor, *Miami Herald*; Michael J. O'Neill, editor, and John H. Metcalfe, assistant to the editor, *New York Daily News*; Richard A. Oppel, editor, the *Charlotte Observer*; Ralph Otwell, editor, the *Chicago Sun-Times*; Eugene C. Patterson, president and editor, the *St. Petersburg* (Fla.) *Times*; Warren H. Phillips, chairman of the board and president, the *Wall Street Journal*, and Peter R. Kann, associate publisher; Paul A. Poorman, editor and vice president, *Akron* (Ohio) *Beacon Journal*, and the particular assistance of the former executive editor of the *Beacon Journal*, Robert H. Giles, now the executive editor of the *Rochester* (N.Y.) *Democrat & Chronicle* and the *Times-Union*; John C. Quinn, senior vice president and chief news executive, the Gannett Co., Inc., with particular assistance from Paul Miller, director, the Gannett Co., Inc., and Don O. Noel, Jr., of Hartford, Ct.; Gene Roberts, executive editor, the *Philadelphia Inquirer*; A. M. Rosenthal, executive editor, the *New York Times*; Howard Simons, managing editor, the *Washington Post*; John H. Stauffer, editor and general manager, the *Topeka Capital Journal*; H. L.

Stevenson, vice president and editor-in-chief, United Press International; William F. Thomas, executive vice president and editor, the *Los Angeles Times*, with Cheryl Preston of the *Times's* Permissions Department, Paul Conrad, and Johnnie M. Walker of the *Los Angeles Times* Syndicate (all *Los Angeles Times* articles © in the year of publication and reprinted by permission, Mr. Conrad's *Los Angeles Times* cartoon 1970, and reprinted by permission); Garry Trudeau and Sara Hurley of the Permissions Department of Universal Press Syndicate; Thomas Winship, editor, *Boston Globe*, and S. J. Micciche, associate editor.

THE PULITZER PRIZE STORY II

INTRODUCTION:
THE PULITZER PRIZES
IN A TIME OF TRIAL
AND TESTING FOR AMERICA

The Pulitzer Prizes in Journalism for 1959–1980, the years covered by this book, reflect one of the most difficult and dangerous eras in American history.

It was the period of the nation's most disastrous foreign war, and of a thunderous social upheaval at home. More than that, it was marked by the assassination of one President, the involuntary retirement of a second, the disgrace and resignation of a third, and the unelected accession of a fourth.

It was, in short, a time of trial and testing for America.

Manifestly, in presenting the face of so troubled an age, the press in a very real sense had need of the Constitutional guarantees of its freedom to gather, process, and distribute the news to the people of the United States.

But ironically, this was also the period in which pressures inside and outside government increased enormously to regulate newspapers by one means or another—or force them into unacceptable forms of self-regulation.

That was the salient difference in the circumstances under which numerous Pulitzer Prizes were awarded in 1959–1980, as compared with the period from 1917–1958, which was illustrated in my earlier volume, *The Pulitzer Prize Story*.

The press had not encountered such virulent hostility in this country since the passage of the Alien and Sedition Acts in 1798.

The courts restricted press coverage of criminal trials by closing pretrial proceedings and, in some cases, even ejecting reporters from open court.

The police, under court sanction, exercised an unprecedented authority to raid newsrooms without a search warrant to seek evidence of the commission of crimes.

Reporters were sent to jail for indefinite periods because they remained faithful to the principle of protecting confidential sources and refused to disclose their informants' identities under court order.

At least one newspaper, the *New York Times*, was heavily fined for supporting that principle, and others were threatened by irate judges with similar treatment.

In the Congress, the Senate passed and sent to the House a viciously restrictive bill that would, if it is finally enacted in the Senate-approved form, be the virtual equivalent of Britain's crippling Official Secrets Acts.

As for the executive branch, four separate administrations raised the cry of national security to attempt to justify suppressing—even falsifying—the news or issuing misleading information.

Going into the critical decade of the 1980s, both the Supreme Court and the Congress showed some willingness to ease these pressures. The high court finally ruled that press and public had a right to attend criminal trials and Congress drafted other remedial legislation.

But in the absence of positive assurance that the First Amendment would not be further diluted in one way or another, the softening of such pressures could only be viewed as temporary.

Under these circumstances, many of the larger and stronger newspapers felt obliged to widen the distance between themselves and the government. The position, strained though it was, also became policy for a number of the more courageous medium- and smaller-sized newspapers.

The government thus came under intensive and rigorous scrutiny, regardless of whether it turned out to be Republican or Democratic.

To some, this appeared to signal an excessive hostility to the governmental process on the part of the press as a whole. But that, certainly, was not the intention either of the proprietors or the principal editors, the leaders of the press. It was very far from what any of them considered to be a proper requirement for the press in a self-governing society.

What they *did* require, and what they *did* believe to be necessary, was a continued watchdog role for the press over both governmental and private business and societal activities. No matter how much the political leadership may have longed for a cheerleader press, in the image of American newspapers during World War II, there was a general recognition among journalists that such a function in this unsettled era eventually would have proved fatal both to a free press and to any government it blindly supported.

They believed Joseph Pulitzer when he wrote, soon after the beginning of the 20th century:

"Our Republic and its press will rise or fall together. An able, disinterested, public-spirited press, with trained intelligence to know the right and courage to do it, can preserve the public virtue without which popular government is a sham and a mockery. A cynical, mercenary, demagogic, corrupt press will produce in time a people as base as itself."[1]

The inevitable result was a stiffening of the adversary posture of the press in its relationships with both powerful governmental and nongovernmental forces. It was this attitude, in part at least, that led the *Washington Post* into its Watergate investigation and caused the *New York Times* to publish the Pentagon Papers—the two outstanding journalistic accomplishments of the post-World War II era.

Such feats gave heart, courage, and a renewed sense of purpose to a press that badly needed it. Had the nation not been confronted with such conclusive evidence of the value of an unfettered press, public sentiment might very well have swung strongly behind the gathering pressures on newspapers to yield to the government's attempts to curb its influence.

[1] *North American Review* (May 1904)

In some quarters, notably among aspiring politicians in a Presidential election year, there has been a tendency to react against the press by equating its power over public opinion with the power of government itself.[2] But surely, such a comparison is wide of the mark, for the press has no authority to make or unmake laws, to rule on the administration of justice, to collect taxes and spend public funds, to maintain the armed forces and the police, to hold elections, and to deal with both internal and external threats to the national interest.

The press does have power, to be sure, but it is of an entirely different kind from that of the government. It arises out of the authority that a democratic society gives to the governed to oversee the acts of their governors; and, because so few citizens are able to do this for themselves, it falls to the press to do it for them. This was one of the hallmarks of press performance as reflected in the Pulitzer Prizes between 1959 and 1980.

There are other differences between the newspapers of the current period and their predecessors in the earlier years of the Pulitzer awards. In the 1960s and 1970s, American newspapers were transformed by an electronic revolution that created newer, swifter, and far more efficient methods of production. This, in turn, contributed to a prosperity for the press on this continent that exceeded anything it had known in the three centuries of its existence.

There was also an intensified consolidation of ownership, a trend that virtually eliminated newspaper competition in the first half of the century in all but a handful of American cities. In the latter part of the century this process continued on a vast scale and led to the virtual elimination of the family newspaper as a social force in the land.

It was argued that the coming of a chain to a city where there was an impoverished, struggling newspaper could not help but improve the quality of the product, and, for all save chains with irresponsible ownership, there was a lot of truth in this. Nevertheless, there was also a sense of unease over the process, particularly when large group owners of press and television branched out to

[2] *New York Times* (May 2, 1977), p. 31.

include undertakings that had nothing to do with the field of communications.

In the Congress, there was a movement to give a tax break to the owners of individual newspapers whose heirs faced the steepest kind of inheritance taxes so they would not have to sell out to the chains. But the legislative effort came too late, for the most part, to save many family-owned newspapers.

Finally, there has been decided change in the people who make up the press—the reporters and editors, writers and photographers, cartoonists and commentators, and all the rest of the editorial crew.

In the early years of the century, those with a college education were often an embattled minority in the nation's newsrooms— many becoming victims of the rampant anti-intellectualism that was then so marked a characteristic of the American press. It was a time, moreover, when few working newspeople bothered very much about the ethics of a line of work that was then very far from a profession.

The pay was low. The hours depended on the whim of the boss. There was no job security and precious few fringe benefits. Of the elderly, very few could look forward to pensions; their social security, if they were lucky, was a job on the night copy desk or on rewrite doing handouts and obits. Personnel practices were so chaotic that a journeyman with a drinking problem could drift from one job to another, month after month, with very little trouble. No wonder that newspapermen (there were few women) were held in low esteem except for a few big names.

All that changed for the better in the latter half of the century. University training became the rule rather than the exception among newspaper people; curiously, however, anti-intellectualism lingered on in the form of a general suspicion about the usefulness of journalism schools. Despite that, journalism itself took on more of the trappings of a profession. Mainly through the pressures of changing times, journalists enjoyed an increase in prestige. And through a combination of governmental action, labor organization, and rising prosperity for the press, the pay and working conditions for newspeople showed a dramatic improvement, although journalism as a whole still trailed most other professions.

Inevitably, such changes had an effect on the Pulitzer Prizes in

Journalism. From the five prizes that were available in 1917, only two of which were actually awarded, the list expanded to the round dozen that are now given annually—a gold medal in public service for newspapers, four reporting awards, one award each for editorials, editorial cartooning, criticism, commentary, and feature writing, and two for news photography. (The non-journalism awards also expanded, with poetry, nonfiction, and music being added to the original prizes for fiction, drama, history, and biography.)

The governing body, originally called the Advisory Board on the Pulitzer Prizes, changed its name, shortened the terms of its members, increased in size, and raised more than $1 million to add to Joseph Pulitzer's bequest of $500,000.

As the Pulitzer Prize Board, its new name, it became the real arbiter of the awards following the withdrawal of the Trustees of Columbia University from the prize-giving process. The first woman member, President Hanna Gray of the University of Chicago, and the first two black members, William Raspberry of the *Washington Post* and Roger Wilkins, formerly of the *New York Times*, were added in 1979 to the original 13, consisting of a dozen newspaper executives and the President of Columbia University.[3] Maximum service on this self-perpetuating body was henceforth limited to three terms of three years each. The $1,000 accompanying each prize, except the public service gold medal, remained the same.

The Board also shifted the timing of the prize announcement from the traditional first Monday in May to a flexible date in the middle of April and maintained its authority to change the verdicts of its nominating juries. While the administration of the prizes remained at Columbia University, the Board tightened its control over the process in a number of respects.

With the changing patterns of journalism in the later years of the century, notable differences appeared as well in the substance of the awards. As before, the greatest number of prizes were

---

[3] The Board's membership also included two nonvoting academic figures, the dean of the Columbia Graduate School of Journalism and a faculty member who is the administrator of the prizes and the Board secretary. The President of Columbia inherited the power of the trustees to veto an award, but didn't exercise it. The trustees themselves did it only once—to W.A. Swanberg's *Citizen Hearst*, in 1962.

granted for exposés of graft and corruption at all levels of government, but fewer such exposés were the work of individuals. Many had to be conducted by entire newspaper staffs—a reflection of the complex nature of such undertakings. As for war reporting and foreign correspondence in general, the second largest category of awards, the emphasis in the latter part of the century shifted from Europe to other parts of the world and seemed destined to remain there for some time to come.

The coverage of civil liberties violations in general and the immense social problems arising from racial conflicts became even more intense in the post-World War II era, as the prizes for the 1960s and 1970s demonstrate.

Then, too, different kinds of prizes were awarded as new issues developed, such as the distress over pollution and other environmental issues, a deeper interest in community affairs, a significant increase in the coverage of crime reporting that testified to the public's fear of unsafe streets, and concern over the rising narcotics traffic. Only the moon landings and other space flights remain unrepresented among the awards, chiefly because no newspeople could compete with astronauts and the pictures were primarily a television spectacular.

A revised calculation shows that 446 Pulitzer journalism prizes were issued from 1917 through 1980. Of these, 374 went to individuals, 68 to newspapers or their staffs, two to a newspaper chain and its news service, and two to large groups of journalists. Because some of the 374 awards to individuals were shared by more than one person, the total number of recipients was 392. Of these, 373 were men and 19 were women.

The table shows a revised list of the largest categories of awards divided into two periods, 1917–1958,[4] and the period covered in this volume, 1959–1980. New headings in the latter period are shown in italics. (See page 8.)

The remaining awards were scattered over a wide area including sports, finance, labor, humor, economics, health, education, medicine, and other subjects.

The organization of this volume by subject matter was based

[4] There is a slight numerical difference between the 1917–1958 list shown here and the one included in *The Pulitzer Prize Story* of 1959, primarily because of a shift in classification by categories.

SUBJECT	1917–1958	1959–1980	TOTAL
Exposing government corruption	33	43	76
War reporting	22	31*	53
Civil liberties	12	24	36
U.S. racial conflict	16	16	32
Crime reporting	12	17	29
Human interest	6	10	16
Foreign coverage, general	8	7	15
Reports on Russia (except war)	9	5	14
Washington coverage, general	6	8	14
Storms, accidents, etc.	6	8	14
Environment reporting	1	10	11
Cultural affairs	0	8	8
Science	8	1	9
Community affairs, general	0	5	5

* Sixteen prizes were for Vietnam War reporting and related domestic affairs.

primarily on the categories shown in the table. The works reproduced in the book were selected as worthy examples of the hundreds of distinguished winners in the Pulitzer Prize archives. The editor was solely responsible for making the selections and deeply regrets that many more could not be included. A complete list of all winners for 1959–1980, with citations, will be found in the appendix.

Whatever changes that time and circumstance have wrought in the Pulitzer Prizes, their appeal for journalists has remained constant and their fundamental purpose has not changed. That purpose is identical with the mission of the journalist in a free society, which Walter Lippmann expressed as follows just five years after the awards began:

"It is possible and necessary for journalists to bring home to people the uncertain character of the truth on which their opinions are founded, and by criticism and agitation to prod social science into making more usable formulations of social facts, and to prod statesmen into establishing more visible institutions. The press, in other words, can fight for the extension of reportable truth."[5]

[5] Walter Lippmann, *Public Opinion* (New York: The Free Press of the Macmillan Co., 1922; paperback, 1949), pp. 227–28.

When the fight for truth succeeds, the press fulfills its principal function as well as its responsibilities to the public. It was to reward such efforts, in large part, that the Pulitzer Prizes in Journalism were established. It is also the reason for their enduring strength as journalistic standards that display the best aspects of American journalism. For as long as these prizes stimulate the search for truth, they will be sought after in the United States and will do honor to the profession they represent.

I. ASSIGNMENT—AMERICA: RIDING THE CREST OF THE NEWS

Richard Cooper of the *Rochester* (N.Y.) *Times-Union* worked without sleep and very little food for almost 24 hours during the Attica Prison riot of Sept. 13, 1971.

With other reporters, he heard a supposedly responsible New York state official say that several of the 43 hostages and inmates who were killed in the uprising had been found with their throats slashed.

The reporters who wanted to believe that the convicts were to blame for the senseless killings immediately spread the story of the slashed corpses to the nation. But Cooper had his doubts. He had nothing tangible to go on—just a reporter's hunch that something about the story didn't ring true.

And so next morning, he stopped by the Monroe County Medical Examiner's office, where autopsies on the victims were being performed, and asked casually whether the causes of death had been determined. A supervisor nodded.

"Gunshot wounds," he said abruptly.

Cooper was stunned. He knew the convicts had had no guns, which was what had made the slashed-throat story credible to many other reporters. But if the convicts didn't do the shooting, then certainly the police must have, he concluded.

Cooper demanded to see the medical examiner, Dr. John F. Edland, but the official wouldn't say one word to confirm the real cause of death until all the autopsies were concluded. Somewhat discouraged, Cooper phoned his office and was assigned elsewhere. Another reporter, John Machacek, was sent to the medical examiner's office to wait for the verdict.

Strangely, of all the small army of reporters who had covered the Attica uprising, Machacek was the only one that morning who had been assigned to make certain of the manner in which 43 people had died. When Dr. Edland emerged, he confirmed without a moment's hesitation that all the victims had been shot.

The *Rochester Times-Union*, alone among all the news organizations that had covered the Attica story, broke the medical examiner's findings at about noon on Sept. 14. The Associated Press picked up the report, with credit to the paper, and spread it throughout the nation. As a result, a censorious public attitude toward the convicts underwent a rapid change and the police, instead, had to assume blame for the killings.

Cooper and Machacek were jointly awarded the 1972 Pulitzer prize for General Local Reporting. What they had done, by following basic reportorial practice, had averted the creation of a monstrous injustice.

So often, in reporting, what seems like the barest routine deeply affects the course of the news. One such story began because the weekly Sun Newspapers of Omaha stumbled across a copy of Internal Revenue Service Form 990, a public report that all nonprofit institutions are obliged to file under the Tax Reform Act of 1969.

The form had been filed in 1972 by Boys Town, Nebraska, a famous charitable institution. Looking into the figures, Sun reporters soon showed the organization's net worth was $209 million. Moreover, upon further inquiry, it developed that Boys Town had increased its net worth by $16 to $18 million annually while continuing to send 33 million letters each year to the American public in an appeal for more aid.

That touched off a six-month investigation, resulting in the publication of a special section about Boys Town. While no allegations of wrongdoing were made, Boys Town subsequently revised its fund-raising procedures and pledged $70 million of its idle funds to support new programs for the benefit of children. The

Sun papers won the 1973 Pulitzer Prize for Local Investigative Reporting as a result.

But it doesn't follow that adherence to basic reporting disciplines always pays off quickly. Sometimes reporters have to wait years. This was the case for Nat Caldwell and Gene Graham of the *Nashville Tennessean*, who suspected as early as 1955 that there was undercover cooperation between management interests in the coal industry and the United Mine Workers, the great coal union. The ostensible objective was to revive the deeply depressed coal industry, but the reporters found evidence that indicated some small operators were being forced out of business with consequent job losses by miners.

Graham and Caldwell worked on this story, on and off, for six years without much success. But at last, on May 20, 1961, the UMW was found guilty in federal court in Knoxville of violating federal antitrust laws by conspiring with some coal companies to monopolize the soft coal industry.

While the verdict was still under appeal, the two reporters were awarded the Pulitzer Prize for National Reporting in 1962.

Far more common to most reporters is the coverage of natural disasters—storms, floods, earthquakes, and the like. The category is one of the largest in the Pulitzer Prize records. Now and then, a conscientious reporter provides a threatened community with a great public service by trying to avert a disaster.

This was the mission that was undertaken by Mel Ruder, the 50-year-old publisher of a weekly newspaper at Columbia Falls, Montana, called the *Hungry Horse News*, circulation 4,721. On Monday, June 8, 1964, the U.S. Weather Bureau issued an urgent flood warning for the area, which includes the Flathead Valley. Ruder knew he couldn't get his paper out until Friday at the earliest and he doubted that radio would reach all the inhabitants of the sparsely settled region.

That night he flew over the area of potential disaster in a rented airplane and put out the first warning bulletins over a cooperating radio station. Next day he drove his car as far as he could to warn people; when he came to washouts, he drove along railroad tracks. Now and then, he had to rent boats as well.

He collected his own news meanwhile and took his own pictures.

With the help of his wife, two printers, and some part-time help, he got out his paper on Friday with a full account of the flood danger and a warning to all concerned to move to higher ground. Not satisfied with that, he put out extra editions on Saturday and Sunday as well.

When the flood waters reached their peak, as a result of his efforts not a single life was lost. Robert S. Bennett, manager of radio station KGEZ in Kalispell, credited Ruder with effectively spreading the warning in good time. He was awarded the Pulitzer Prize for General Local Reporting in 1965.

The demise of that prince of journalists, the reporter, has been predicted many times in the three-century history of newspapers in the English-speaking world. But whether reporters do their work with quill pen or lead pencil, typewriter or video display terminal, a radio microphone or videotape, they are a durable breed. When they go into specialties, ranging from politics and finance to the most intensive investigations, they still manage somehow to come up with the big story.

In the following section, their assignment is America and, like their predecessors in the earlier years of the Pulitzer Prizes, they ride the crest of the news.

1. WALTER MEARS OF THE AP CALLS
A TIGHT PRESIDENTIAL ELECTION

The "Human Typing Machine" Picks Carter
Over Ford at the End of a Close Race

Every once in a while in journalism, somebody will come along who writes faster than anybody else. And generally thinks faster, too.

Often, the pack is scornful. "A word slinger," some say. And others scoff, "A human typing machine."

If the newcomer writes well, it's taken for granted. Particularly if he has a Phi Beta Kappa key from a good college. But if he happens to hit a clinker, nobody lets him forget it.

Walter Mears was that kind of reporter. He was Massachusetts-born (in Lynn, Jan. 11, 1935) and earned his Phi Beta Kappa key at Middlebury College, where they aren't handed out as souvenirs. Once he had his

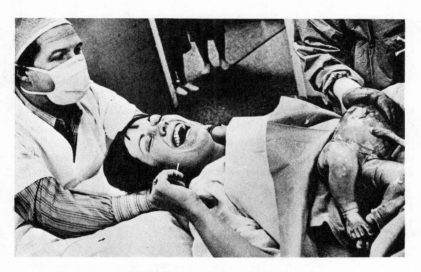

THE MOMENT OF LIFE
Pulitzer Prize for Feature Photography, 1973

BRIAN LANKER'S PHOTO OF LYNDA COBURN, JOYFUL AT THE BIRTH OF HER
DAUGHTER IN A TOPEKA HOSPITAL, PUBLISHED IN
THE TOPEKA CAPITAL-JOURNAL

degree, he headed for the Associated Press office in Boston and broke in during the Presidential election year of 1956.

He didn't get much of a look-in at handling the big news that year. But three years later, he won his way to Washington, worked up through the ranks of the biggest, toughest, and most competitive AP bureau in the country, and became chief of the Senate AP staff.

All the time, his reputation as a speed merchant was his trademark.

But he was a lot better than that, as subsequent Presidential elections proved. Although the general public didn't know who he was, the journalists did. And in Tim Crouse's book about the 1972 election, *The Boys on the Bus*, Mears was portrayed as the reporter who was most consulted by the other reporters on the campaign trail.

That election, for reasons that the Watergate and associated "dirty tricks" inquiries made clear, was a walkaway for President Nixon. No matter how much reporters may have mistrusted and disliked the man, they picked him to win over Senator McGovern. It was no contest.

But 1976 was different and Mears knew it from the outset.

He covered 32 Presidential primaries, reporting the emergence and finally the dominance of Jimmy Carter of Georgia; then, in the campaign against President Ford, there was even more work and even greater responsibility.

At one point, Mears put out 18 leads—beginnings—on a single breaking development just to keep up with the news. And of course, he was criticized for it. Who can handle 18 leads in a single night on a desk without screwing up, his competitors asked?

But at last the campaign wound down to that critical point just before election day when you either pick 'em or you don't. And many a working journalist—and pollster with immensely sophisticated equipment— ducked for the storm cellar, saying it was "too close to call," because the Carter-Ford contest really was that close and everybody knew it.

Mears had another difficulty. Had he been a "special"—a writer for one of the great dailies or a television commentator—he might have assumed without consultation that he had the right to call the election if he had sufficient evidence to document his position. "Specials" nearly always have more freedom than those who have to run for the wire—or the telephone.

As a wire service man, Mears was responsible not only to the editors of the AP, the great American news cooperative, but also to the editors of some 1,200 member newspapers in this country representing all shades of political opinion, plus radio and TV and thousands of foreign clients.

The AP had never been very enthusiastic about letting its people forecast elections on their own; about the most that could be done was to quote the polls and influential opinion. But Mears was different. And he went ahead in the face of an extremely shaky political situation.

A few days before the election, with the certainty that the shift of a few thousand votes here or there might make a very real difference in the outcome, he sat at his video display terminal (an electronic typewriterlike device with a TV screen on which the written words appear), and after a guarded beginning, he wrote in the stillness of the big newsroom:

"The Electoral College arithmetic leans Carter's way, and Ford is confronted with a list of must states—sudden death contests—any one of which could be his undoing."

Mears pointed out the obvious: that a Presidential battle cannot be one contest under the American system. It has to be 51 separate votes in each of 50 states and the District of Columbia to determine who wins the majority in the 538-member Electoral College. And, he concluded, Ford would have to take all the undecided big states to win.

"With his presumed base of Southern support, and as the candidate of the stronger party, Carter could assemble an Electoral College majority without such a sweep," he wrote.

That was it. He had laid it on the line and the AP had gone along with its man. As a result, many a newspaper throughout the land plastered its first page with the story and a qualified headline indicating a Carter victory.

Mears and the AP turned out to be right in one of the closest Presidential elections of modern times. And some of the most scientific polling organizations in the land were wrong.

No wonder editors began saying, once the election was over, that Mears was a prime candidate for a Pulitzer Prize. But he couldn't have won just on the basis of a forecast. It was his work throughout the campaign that had to be judged, and here the opinions of his colleagues became almost as important as those of the jury that was to look over his work.

The best of these was an article in the *Wall Street Journal*, written by a competitor, who had paid him the extraordinary tribute of doing a piece about him that landed on Page 1 two weeks before election day. Here it is, in its essentials:

NO. 1 AMONG THE BOYS ON THE BUS

By Ronald G. Shafer

From the Wall Street Journal, Oct. 21, 1976

EAU CLAIRE, Wisconsin—During a recent campaign stop here, reporters traveling with Jimmy Carter rushed to an auditorium room where phones were set up for their use and found that the door was locked. As they pounded on the door, they didn't notice a pay phone on the wall behind them—or the man who was calmly striding toward it.

At the sound of a phone being dialed, the group turned to see Walter Mears of the Associated Press dictating a news story to his office. Mr. Mears flashed a Jimmy Carter grin, waved to his pals and kept on transmitting the news.

A nose for phones as well as news is essential for a wire service reporter. Walter Mears has combined both qualities with a remarkable talent for speedy writing and has earned a reputation as a top political reporter.

The 41-year-old Mr. Mears isn't as famous as some of the Washington political reporters who work for big newspapers or write columns. But he probably has more readers than any of them.

AP teletype machines clatter in the newsrooms of most of the nation's 1,768 daily newspapers and at most radio and television stations. Each news organization that is a member of AP uses the material as it wishes; a few big newspapers with their own staffs rely on AP hardly at all. But for readers of hundreds of small and medium-size newspapers, Mr. Mears is the man who tells them much of what they know about the political campaign.

"Mears can type 100 words a minute and carry on a conversation at the same time," says James Perry of the *National Observer*.

Mr. Mears is also known for his ability to write good "leads" to news stories. The lead is the first paragraph; it is supposed to give the essence of the story in a concise, snappy fashion, catching the reader's attention. The lead also is usually the part of the story on which the headline is based.

Thus, what goes into the lead paragraph and what doesn't is one of the most important writing decisions a reporter makes. Mr. Mears makes such decisions remarkably fast.

During the recent presidential foreign policy debate from San Francisco, Mr. Mears—seated before a TV set and a high speed computerized typing machine at AP's Washington office—fired off seven leads and the top several paragraphs of stories as the debate unfolded. When it ended at 11 P.M., Eastern time, Mr. Mears, his fingers flying over the keyboard, wrote a six-page summary plus an eighth lead that was completed by midnight—in time to transmit for use in morning papers.

On the campaign trail, Mr. Mears's reputation for spotting the heart of a story can influence other reporters. After Jimmy Carter finished a speech in Chicago the other day, the AP reporter headed for a phone to file a story. He was stopped by an NBC-TV correspondent who discreetly inquired: "Walter, what do you think you're going to write your lead on?"

"Wire services are about the last place where there really is man-to-man competition," says Mr. Mears, who contends that "some of the best writers in the business work for the wires." Mr. Mears himself, after nearly 20 years at the AP, left in late 1974 to become the *Detroit News*'s Washington bureau chief. Less than a year later, he returned to AP as a special correspondent, saying he missed the wire services' "sense of urgency."

Mr. Mears began his wire service career rewriting auto accident reports in Boston, where he joined AP in 1956 right out of Middlebury College in Vermont. His first coverage of presidential politics was in 1960 while he was AP's state house reporter in Vermont. Mr. Mears went to Washington in 1961 and he has covered every Presidential election since the Goldwater campaign in 1964. In 1968 he became AP's top writer for fast-breaking Washington stories because, as his boss explained, "Mears writes faster than most people think and frequently faster than he thinks."

In fact, some of Mr. Mears's detractors say that his reputation is based more on speed than on the substance of his reporting. And the veteran wire service reporter sometimes falters. During the second Presidential debate, those leads he churned out hardly mentioned President Ford's Eastern European gaffe and they overplayed a Ford remark about strategic arms limitation talks.

The easy-going Mr. Mears seems unaffected by either praise or criticism. On the campaign, he is just one of the boys on the bus, where he is known for writing funny campaign song lyrics—which the boys then sing on the bus. During a recent Carter visit to Chicago, Mr. Mears quickly dashed off a verse about the search for ethnic votes. He showed it to the *Washington Post*'s David Broder, who took one look and said, "Mears, you may not be good but you're fast."

No matter how high Mears's standing was among the boys on the bus, he wasn't No. 1 on the wire on the early morning of November 3, 1976, the day after the Presidential election. While he waited helplessly beside his computerized typewriter for AP's field reports to flash a decision in the extremely close race between Jimmy Carter and President Ford, the United Press International made what seemed like a risky call at 2:57 A.M. (Eastern time) on the basis of partial returns from Mississippi:

FLASH: WASHINGTON—CARTER WINS PRESIDENCY

For the better part of an hour, the more cautious AP waited before concurring in the verdict of its great competitor—all of which pushed Mears back into the field with the sit-down television commentators and their checkout counter reporting. But when all the returns were in and the Pulitzer Prize Jury for National Reporting assembled at Columbia University in the spring of 1977, it was Mears who carried off the top award. As the jury wrote:

"Beyond detailing events as they unfolded, he brought to his task an impressive talent for getting to the heart of stories and putting real muscle on the bones of political happenings. His was a most impressive job by a wire service reporter who, in our judgment, amply deserves the honor of a Pulitzer for his superb work under difficult services."

The Pulitzer Board quickly agreed with that verdict.

Today, in the face of the Presidential election contests of the 1980s, the "human typing machine" has taken on different responsibilities. What he now bats out at 100 words a minute on his video display terminal are "rockets"—queries and complaints—to his staff people in the field. For he is the chief of the Associated Press Washington Bureau.

No mere word merchant could handle so taxing a job. But if another one happens to come along, Mears will be the first to understand that, as the old International News Service's highly unofficial slogan had it, you get it first even if you have to get it right.

2. THE SAN DIEGO TRIBUNE COVERS
THE NATION'S WORST AIR TRAGEDY

*An Alert Staff Responds When a Mid-air Crash Kills 144
Only 28 Minutes Before the First Edition Deadline*

Two aircraft collided over San Diego at 9:02 A.M. on Sept. 25, 1978.

This was the first news that came to the *San Diego Evening Tribune.*

"I'll be Jack Kennedy . . . Who do you want to be?"

Pulitzer Prize for Editorial Cartooning, 1977

PAUL SZEP IN THE BOSTON GLOBE

Nothing else. And the first edition deadline for all copy was 9:30 A.M.

How many were dead? Injured? How did it happen? And why?

Over radio and TV, there was a lot of meaningless babble. But no hard information.

In the *Tribune*'s city room, everybody felt instinctively that this was the big story—the one for which a newspaper staff lives. And everybody swung into action at the city desk's direction.

In a frantic few minutes, reporters were out talking to eyewitnesses, people who lived near the site of the crash, hospitals, police, firemen, airline officials—anybody and everybody who could contribute information. They gave their notes by telephone.

Photographers, who were taking pictures of the wreckage where it fell in the city streets, and of damaged houses and fires, rushed the negatives back to the paper.

For the emergency, the copy deadline was extended 40 minutes to get news and pictures into the first edition. But the production staff, forewarned, was so geared up that the paper hit the streets only five minutes late with the first definitive account of what had happened.

Because no survivors could be found either at the scene or in hospitals, the enormity of the tragedy was apparent. The very high death toll, however, could not be confirmed in that edition.

But there were two pages of news, which included a Page 1 aerial picture of the crash site, other pictures inside, a main story, and six side stories. From the time of the crash until the paper was out, only 90 minutes had elapsed.

For the second edition, with a 12:10 P.M. deadline, and the final edition, with a 1:50 P.M. deadline, the coverage was completed. It was established beyond doubt that the death toll was at least 144 and that it was the worst air crash in the nation's history up to that date.

The story was told in the *Tribune* in six full pages, a color picture on Page 1 and black and white pictures in profusion elsewhere. The main story carried no byline but there was a box that credited these staff people: Nick Canepa, Pat Calloway, Bill Callahan, Bob Dorn, John Durham, Patricia Dibsic, John Gilmore, Hugh Grambau, Joe Hughes, Frank Saldana, Rex Salmon, and Gus Stevens. There were many others, including the always unsung copyreaders and editors, who contributed their share, for this was, by all odds, a magnificent staff job.

Here is the main story:

"THE MOST HORRIBLE THING I EVER SAW"

By Jim Nichols

From the San Diego Evening Tribune, Sept. 25, 1978

A Boeing 727 collided with a smaller plane over San Diego today and crashed in flames to the ground, killing at least 144 people—the deadliest tragedy in U.S. aviation history.

A residential neighborhood instantly became a ghastly collage of fire, black smoke, bodies, and debris as burning wreckage slashed through and the big jet vanished in a ball of flame and smoke.

Clarence Montiel, of 3315 Palm, said the Pacific Southwest Airlines jet was approaching Lindbergh Field when it was hit in the right side by the smaller plane.

"The small plane just blew up and the engine on the right side of the PSA jet burst into flames," he said. "It looked for just a second like the PSA pilot was going to be able to straighten the plane out, but then it just exploded in the air and crashed nose-first. It was the most horrible thing I ever saw in may life."

About two hours after the 9 A.M. tragedy, city police and PSA spokesmen said there apparently were no survivors from the 727, which was carrying 129 passengers and a crew of seven.

The student pilot of the small plane and his instructor were also killed.

At least six others died on the ground when the big jet smashed into the 2300 block of Dwight Street in San Diego's North Park area.

The wreckage covered a mile-wide area, starting several fires that gutted at least ten residences. Within an hour, several looters were arrested in the shattered neighborhood.

City police reported finding 25 bodies along Felton Street alone. They were believed to be passengers from the large jet, which was due at Lindbergh Field at 9 A.M. on a flight from Sacramento and Los Angeles.

Three investigators from the National Transportation Safety Board were rushed from Los Angeles to San Diego immediately after the crash. A PSA spokesman said it would be hours before an initial finding could be made as to the cause of the crash.

Firemen hurried to the scene and area hospitals implemented disaster plans, calling in all surgeons and setting up makeshift treatment rooms.

"It's a pretty gruesome sight," one witness said. "A lot of homes are on fire, people are in their back yards with hoses trying to keep the fire from getting to their homes, and the streets are jammed with people trying to get close to the crash. It's a mess."

The small plane—a Cessna 172 with a student from Camp Pendleton at the stick and an instructor beside him—crashed at Polk and 32d Streets. Several witnesses reported seeing the body of one occupant of that plane.

Bill Gibbs, president of the Gibbs Flying Center, said the Cessna, owned by a satellite firm, was on an instrument approach to Lindbergh Field under the student's control when it and the big jet both vanished from the radar screens.

A Federal Aviation Administration spokesman said the Miramar Naval Air Station had just handed control of the jet to Lindbergh Field and was still handling the small plane.

In a terminal approach area such as both aircraft were in, the spokesman added, planes are not required to maintain specific altitudes. Their instructions are "to see and be seen," he explained.

The FAA spokesman declined to speculate on which plane had been responsible for the collision.

A seat and a crumpled bit of fuselage from the smaller craft fell into the street in front of Ruth Perry's home at 3085 Polk.

"It was a small plane and I saw it go over my house in flames," she said. "There was debris flying everywhere and also hundreds of what looked like pieces of mail."

A flaming piece of wing set fire to an apartment at 4127½ Iowa Street, more than 150 yards from the main crash site, said Joseph Glover, who lives nearby.

"I saw the wing hit the house," he said. "It [the 727] exploded in midair and pieces went down like fiery meteors. I was standing in the courtyard and I had to duck."

Around the scene, pieces of furniture and personal belongings were scattered in the ashes. Huge crowds of sightseers gathered, complicating the task of emergency personnel.

Alfred Jacoby, ombudsman for the *Tribune*'s sister morning newspaper, the *San Diego Union*, wrote in a column, "If any special praise should be assigned, it should go the *Union*'s across-the-hall third-floor neighbors, the staff of the *Evening Tribune*." With that verdict, a Pulitzer Prize jury agreed, saying in its report:

"Five hours and 54 minutes after the collision, the *Tribune*'s final edition laid down a well-written, comprehensive package of ten stories. The newspaper's competition had added little new information to its coverage hours later. . . . The jury recommends the *Tribune* without reservation."

Accordingly the *San Diego Evening Tribune* won the Pulitzer Prize for Local General Reporting for 1979.

3. A TORNADO STRIKES XENIA, OHIO, AND THE XENIA GAZETTE TELLS THE STORY

Its Stricken Staff, Despite Personal Hardships,
Reports on 33 Dead, 1,600 Injured, and Huge Losses

In an apologetic note on Page 1 of its issue of April 4, 1974, the *Xenia* (Ohio) *Daily Gazette* informed its readers:

"Your Daily Gazette, a little late today, was being delivered in as near normal a manner as possible. . . ."

There was reason for the slight delay. At 4:40 P.M. on April 3, a devastating tornado roared into the pleasant little city of 27,000, killing 33 persons, injuring 1,600, and causing at least $100 million in property damage.

The *Gazette*, which had not missed a day's publication in 106 years, rallied its family of some 80 employees, 14 of whom had lost their homes and belongings, and put out a complete tornado extra the next day to maintain its record.

With water from the storm pouring into the newsroom, and with the power out, Jack Jordan, the editor and general manager of the paper, stood in the city room where the staff already was at work by candlelight and flashlight and told his people what they instinctively knew: they were going to get the paper out for their 15,000 readers, many of them commuters to nearby Dayton.

Just how the job would be done, nobody was certain. For the paper's main building was unroofed, its plate glass windows were smashed and its production facilities were knocked out beyond immediate repair.

But, as Jordon said, this was something more than a demonstration of journalistic courage, determination, and skill. To tell the story of what had happened to Xenia and to encourage people to rebuild was also an act of community leadership and the ravaged city badly needed it.

The staff of the evening paper responded to the challenge in the classic manner of newspaper people under pressure. The copy and the pictures, the lists of dead and injured, and the detailed account of damaged property were all rushed to a neighboring sister newspaper, *The Middletown Journal*, where the *Gazette* was produced and trucked back to town.

"Efforts are being made," the Gazette noted, "to reach as many carriers as possible to get copies to our customers."

The successful production of the tornade extra was one thing. It was quite another to try to plumb the emotions of the people who did the work under tremendous emotional and physical pressure. Here was one such account, tucked away among all the straight reporting jobs, that told the human story behind the big story:

"WE SHOULD ALL BE DEAD TODAY"

By Rich Heiland

From the Xenia (Ohio) Gazette, April 4, 1974

I will cry a hundred years from now, no matter how many memories come and go, when I think of what this wind did to my city and its people.

Yes, my city, now more than ever, though I have absolutely nothing left to show for my existence here except the most important thing of all—life. My life, the lives of my children, and my wife.

We should all be dead today as, sadly, too many are. But we are alive and we will be back, and we will survive, as will my city, our city, your city.

It was terror, a time when people, myself included, did things that today will make us vomit and tremble when we recall them.

Something funny hit me moments before the tornado struck yesterday, something funny that made me call my wife and tell her to lie down in the only protected part of our Arrowhead home, only 75 yards from the shell that was Warner Junior High School.

Not more than 10 seconds later, we heard a sheriff's deputy scream over his radio, "Twister by the bypass and 42." For some reason (we had just told each other we'd never do something like that) Randy Blackaby and I grabbed a camera and ran down Second Street to his car.

We thought the twister was on the edge of town. My God, how wrong we were! At the Five Points intersection, I got out of the car and looked almost straight up at the funnel, swirling with dead birds and debris as it neared St. Brigid Church, which it ripped and killed like a demon that had waited 2,000 years for a victory.

We got back to the car, the roar around us, and escaped the path of the funnel somehow. Our first thoughts were to be newsmen, find out what happened and fast. I copped out, failed, I guess.

As soon as we got near Cincinnati Avenue, I knew. It had hit my house. There was no way it could have missed. We circled around on the bypass, trying to get to Arrowhead. No luck.

I finally found a boy, the son of Tom McCatherine, our associate editor, to show me a short cut behind Warner Junior High.

When I rounded the corner, I just thought, "No, God, no. Don't go any farther, remember them like they were."

The house was destroyed. A couple of walls were standing, the rest had caved in. No one could have lived through it. But, like a ray of sunshine out of the most terrible sky to ever cover Xenia, came my wife's voice, and I never knew how much I loved her and my six-week-old son and five-year-old daughter, who were untouched.

Our only casualty was the family Doberman Pinscher, a gentle dog named Baron who I think escaped. I pray someone will return him to us.

After I rushed the family down to my parents' home in Wilmington, I came back to begin an all-night grind with hundreds of other people trying to help.

There were moments of beauty in terms of sacrifice:

—Men straining to lift fallen timbers off bodies that might still have life in them.

—Bob Stewart, Xenia's city manager, with only half a city, taking charge of a massive rescue and cleanup operation, and not knowing until early morning if his family was alive or dead.

—Gene's Corner, throwing open its doors and coffeepots to anyone who needed a warm drink and a doughnut.

By the time the sun came up, it was apparent what the wind had done, and I hate it for that. But we are alive, most of us, although many of us are homeless and must now dig through the wreckage of our dreams for bits of furniture, mementos such as a family photo album.

And dig we will. And survive we will, dammit.

With a tremendous task of rebuilding Xenia under way in the spring of 1975, the professionalism of the staff of the *Xenia Daily Gazette* was recognized with the award of the Pulitzer Prize for Local General Reporting. That day, they had a celebration to end all celebrations in Xenia.

But the paper still came out next day on time.

4. TOM FITZPATRICK JOINS 200 RIOTERS DURING CHICAGO'S FOUR DAYS OF RAGE

A Sun-Times Reporter Runs With the Weathermen Mob
in an Anti-war Battle with the City's Police

The demonstration had been carefully planned.

The Weathermen, the extreme radical wing of the Students for a Democratic Society (SDS), were mobilizing in 1969 for nothing less than an attack on American society.

What they sought to do, as later events demonstrated, was to use a violent protest against the Vietnam War in Chicago to begin the radicalization of America's college campuses. Some already were aflame with riots, instigated in part by a few of the leading spirits of the Weathermen. One such, led by Mark Rudd, already had paralyzed Columbia University.

Today the aims of the Weathermen seem ridiculous, their conduct puerile, their cause a shrunken monument of self-deception. But at the height of the antiwar protest movement, anything seemed possible to these sons and daughters of America's substantial middle- and upper-class families.

Only about 300 of them showed up in Chicago for what had been planned as an epic of revolutionary street fighting between October 8 and 12, 1969. They had expected thousands of new recruits.

And yet, such was their misguided zeal and their desperation that they determined to go ahead anyway. They knew full well that they would be outnumbered and outgunned by the Chicago police, that many would be beaten and arrested, and some would be jailed. But they charged the ranks of the police on October 8 and began a fruitless and hysterical battle for a worthless cause.

It was the beginning of what they called the Four Days of Rage.

Later on, after their ranks had been shattered by the police, the Weathermen re-formed in Chicago's Lincoln Park at night and massed for another hopeless engagement. Here, Tom Fitzpatrick of the *Chicago Sun-Times* came across them and decided to run with them to try to find out who they were, what they wanted, and why they were so determined to fight.

This was his story:

A WILD NIGHT'S RIDE IN CHICAGO

By Tom Fitzpatrick

From the Chicago Sun-Times, Oct. 9, 1969

Bad Marvin had been standing in front of the fire he had made of a Lincoln Park bench for about 30 minutes, shouting to everyone in the crowd and warning them how bad he was.

It was 10:25 P.M. . . . and now about 200 kids began racing out of the park, heading toward the Chicago Historical Society. Bad Marvin started running, too, brandishing a long piece of burning board in his right hand.

"Viva Ché," he kept shouting as he ran. "Viva Cuba."

"Bring the war home now," screamed a girl running alongside him.

She was so caught up with running in the dark that she ran right into a large tree outside the Historical Society and collapsed in a lump, the first casualty of the night.

By now the main force of the group had reached North Federal Savings, at the northwest corner of North and Clark. It's a big, impressive building with large plate glass windows and here's where the tide turned.

A tall skinny kid in a white helmet ran a little in front of the crowd and tossed a rock through one of the large windows. The first rock was soon followed by a second and a third, and then cheering.

Now everyone is shouting at the top of his lungs and it's amazing how many of them have come out of the park with rocks in their hands.

"Ho, Ho, Ho Chi Minh!" they're shouting. A blond in the front row is waving the Viet Cong flag.

Once on Clark Street and heading south, the kids have taken over the entire street. The street is narrow enough to create an echo as the windows start exploding on each side.

Three rocks go through the windows of the Red Star Inn and apartment windows on all sides are falling.

The sound of shattering glass hits everyone in the group like an electric shock. You are not alone when you are in a group like this. From now on, it was going to have to be a wild ride. And if you were going to find out what happened, you had to go along with it.

By this time you have already learned one important rule about running with mobs who are tossing rocks. You have to stay up front and stay right on the street with them.

If you get on the sidewalk, you'll never see the rock that hits you instead of an apartment window. There is a risk in this, too, because you must time your moves so that you get away from the whole outfit as soon as you see the line of police forming ahead of you.

The police weren't in sight and the wild march went on all the way to within 50 yards of Division Street. And there the police were waiting.

They were lined up across the street and they weren't saying a word. It was a sight so formidable that you didn't blame the kids when they turned and ran back north on Clark and then turned east on Goethe to escape.

Goethe was where it really got bad. Every car window for a two-block stretch was smashed and so were the lobby windows of a high-rise apartment on the corner of Dearborn and Goethe.

The kids knew it was all over for them but they kept on the attack.

And now, as we're heading into the eye of the storm on Division Street, I see a beautiful thing happen. It's Bad Marvin, the guy with the flaming stock who was bragging to everyone how bad he was going to be. Bad Marvin is running away and his torch has burned out.

It always makes you feel good when the tough-talking guys cave in, but now what does happen is not good. All the kids who have been wound up so tight from listening to the inflammatory speeches in the park are going to take it in the head.

"Charge!" one little kid screams as he runs for the police line. "Charge!" the cry comes back as about a dozen more follow him.

The squad cars are at the intersection and the kids are being thrown into them as quickly as possible. One policeman is leaning over a squad car holding his head. He's been hit by a rock and he's bleeding and he's mad.

But the kids aren't stopped yet. Some of them head east to Lake Shore Drive. Another group turns back and races west along Division.

This is the first confrontation. You will see three more at different intersections before it ends at Crilly Court on North, just west of Wells. There are only about 50 kids left and this is the time it scares you.

Walking in the middle of the street, you're amazed to see cars heading toward you as if they meant to run you over. The cars are filled with policemen, some in plain clothes, some in uniform.

As they leap out, you can see at least three of them have their revolvers drawn. The others are wielding clubs.

The kids run but they don't have a chance. They have been asking all night for a confrontation and now they get one.

Within minutes the street is cleared and Deputy Supt. James Rochford is walking toward Sgt. James Clark to get a final report. But there is no smile of triumph on Rochford's face. He was through this same thing during the Democratic National Convention of 1968 and he didn't take any delight in it then, either.

"All right," Rochford says to Clark. "Get the men to clear the street. Let's all just get out of here."

When the Four Days of Rage ended in Chicago, almost all of the 300 original combatants had been arrested, many had been beaten, and at least three had been shot during sporadic gunfire on and off during the fighting. Among those who escaped without harm, although she was arrested when she charged the police lines with others, was Diana Oughton, the daughter of a wealthy Illinois family, who was to die the following spring in an accidental blast that destroyed a Weathermen bomb factory in New York's Greenwich Village.

It was the last public demonstration by the Weathermen during the tumultuous decade of the 1960s. From then on, they went underground or, like Mark Rudd later, emerged to face the charges that had piled up against them.

Fitzpatrick, an experienced reporter and ex-World War II paratrooper, was then 41 years old and had been on the *Sun-Times* staff only eight months when he went on riot-reporting duty. A Pulitzer Prize jury wrote of his work:

"His vivid I-was-there account of the rock-throwing, window-smashing, and final confrontation with the police is an excellent job of objective reporting and good writing."

The Pulitzer Prize Board awarded him the Pulitzer Prize for Local General Reporting for 1970.

5. TWO UPI REPORTERS PROBE THE LIFE
AND DEATH OF DIANA OUGHTON

Lucinda Franks and Thomas Powers Reconstruct the Conversion of a Rich Girl to a Terrorist Who Died in a Bomb Blast

Patricia Hearst, who was kidnapped by a tiny gang of radicals and later convicted and jailed for participating in one of their crimes, has survived her trying experience.

Diana Oughton, who joined another radical faction of her own free will and was arrested and fined as a rioter in Chicago, died in a bomb blast in New York.

Both came from wealthy homes. Both had everything they ever wanted. But both somehow were drawn into a fringe of American society that was dominated by those who sought to alter or destroy it—Patty Hearst against her own will, Diana Oughton willingly and even joyously at times.

The turns and twists of the Patty Hearst story—from her seizure by the so-called Symbionese Liberation Army on Feb. 4, 1974, to her arrest on bank robbery charges seven months later and her conviction and imprisonment—remained in the forefront of national interest for years. Her captors were wiped out or imprisoned for long terms.

But Diana Oughton, an earlier victim of a radical cause, is all but forgotten and the few survivors of her group went underground—hunted men and women now verging on a hopeless middle age.

Had she not been the subject of a month-long inquiry after her death by two reporters who then worked for United Press International, Lucinda

Franks and Thomas Powers, very little would be known of how and why she was persuaded to turn her back on a family she loved, leave a life of wealth and ease, and plunge into a radical career that could only end in tragedy.

Miss Franks, then 24 and a Vassar graduate, and Powers, then 29, whose AB is from Yale, traveled over much of the eastern part of the country and Diana Oughton's own cherished midwest to reconstruct her story in numerous interviews with her family, her friends, her teachers, and some of her later radical associates.

From this outpouring of words there emerged, dimly at first and later with increasing clarity, a portrait of a young woman possessed of a demonic urge to destroy everything that she had once cherished—her family, her home, her social class, and her country—without having the faintest notion of what she sought to replace them.

There have been many strange stories in the mottled history of American radical movements, but none quite as strange—and as poignant—as the Franks-Powers account: "The Story of Diana: The Making of a Terrorist."

This is an abridgement of their 12,000-word report as it was distributed by UPI, the great American rival of the Associated Press, and reprinted in more than 300 American newspapers plus many others abroad:

THE MAKING OF A TERRORIST

By Lucinda Franks and Thomas Powers

From the United Press International File, Sept. 14–18, 1970

When Diana Oughton, dead at 28, was buried in Dwight, Ill., on Tuesday, March 24, 1970, the family and friends gathered at her grave did not really know who she was.

The minister who led the mourners in prayer explained Diana's death as part of the violent history of the times, but the full truth was not so simple.

The newspapers had provided a skeleton of facts. Diana Oughton and two young men were killed March 6 in a bomb explosion that destroyed a townhouse in New York's Greenwich Village. Two young women, their clothes blown off, had run unharmed from the crumbling house and disappeared after showering at the home of a neighbor. It had taken police four days to find Diana's body at the bottom of the rubble and another week to identify it.

Diana and the others were members of the violent revolutionary

group known as the "Weathermen." They had turned the townhouse into what police described as a "bomb factory." Months
later, they were all to be cited in a grand jury indictment as part
of a conspiracy to bomb police, military, and other civic buildings
in their campaign to destroy American society.

The facts were clear but the townspeople of Dwight (pop. 3,086)
could not relate them to the Diana they remembered. Her family,
too, had their own memories. Diana's father, James Oughton, had
watched her tear away from a closely knit family and a life where
beautiful and fine things were important.

Diana's mother, Jane Oughton, wondered whether her daughter
had been making the bomb that killed her.

Diana had never stopped loving her family but the bomb that
took her life had been designed ultimately to kill them and their
kind. The revolution she died for would have stripped her father of
his vast farmlands, blown his bank to pieces, and destroyed in a
moment the name and position it had taken a century to build.

· · ·

The world that Diana Oughton grew up in was a world of spacious, elegant homes, sweeping lawns, the best schools, and an
ancestry of distinguished and monied men.

She was born Jan. 26, 1942, in a town where her family had been
prominent for decades. The Oughtons had paved the village
streets of Dwight, built the waterworks, furnished the land for the
schools and athletic fields.

Diana grew up as a farm girl, huntress, and horsewoman. She
was close to her three younger sisters—Carol, now 26 and a television writer; Pamela, a 24-year-old housewife; and Deborah, 17, a
senior at Madeira School.

When she walked onto the suburban, spreading campus of Bryn
Mawr outside Philadelphia in the fall of 1959 she was a tall, bony
girl with short blonde hair and long aristocratic hands. A Midwestern Republican, she was against social security, federal banking regulations, and everything else that smacked of "liberalism"
or "big" government.

By the time she had graduated from Bryn Mawr in June 1963,
she had traveled among the poor in the byways of Europe and

worked closely with children in one of Philadelphia's decaying ghettos, but she did not really begin to learn about poverty until she went to Guatemala.

Throughout her two years in Guatemala after her graduation, she struggled with the questions of poverty, social justice, and revolution. As time passed, she began to feel that American economic aid was only consolidating the control of Guatemala's ruling families without ever reaching the broad mass of the people.

By the time she left, she had a totally new view of the problems faced by underdeveloped peoples and of the U.S. role in the struggle to solve those problems. When an Aid for International Development (AID) official, impressed by her fluency in Spanish, offered her a job, she was flattered but refused to take the offer seriously.

The Diana Oughton who returned from Guatemala in the fall of 1965 was not the same young woman who had graduated from Bryn Mawr two years earlier.

Her family was bothered by her seriousness and a new air of melancholy present in everything she did. After living in a single room with a dirt floor and no plumbing and electricity for two years, she found it hard to adjust to the luxury of the Dwight estate. Her family's way of life made her uneasy.

In the spring of 1966, she left Philadelphia for Ann Arbor to enroll in the University of Michigan Graduate School of Education to get her master's degree in teaching. She was adamant about being on her own and at times tried to conceal her family's wealth. When asked what her father did, she often said, "Oh, he's a farmer," and quickly changed the subject.

In Ann Arbor she again lived frugally, ate little, and refused to let her father give her money. She joined the Children's Community School, a project based on the Summerhill method of education and founded by a group of students the year before. It was here that she met Bill Ayers, the son of the chairman of Commonwealth Edison Co. of Chicago and one of the Weathermen later indicted on bomb conspiracy charges.

Ayers probably exercised the single most powerful influence over Diana until her death. Bill and Diana grew closer and eventually began to live together in an attic room near the university. Like most of the men she had been attracted to, he was charming, manipulative, and a bit cruel. She was always at his side and when she went home to Dwight she talked about him frequently.

Members of her family felt her ideas, which were becoming increasingly more progressive, were a reflection of his.

. . .

Despite its early acclaim, the children's school began running into severe problems in the spring of 1968. The American Friends Committee complained that the kids were running wild, marking up the walls, and damaging property in their basement. Two professors withdrew their children, saying that the black students were dominating the school and terrorizing the white children and that, in fact, the school was teaching their children to become racists.

When the school ran into still other problems because of state zoning regulations, Bill and Diana, too disappointed to go on, looked elsewhere for involvement and became more active in the Ann Arbor chapter of Students for a Democratic Society (SDS).

Diana and Bill became convinced that direct action rather than education and peaceful reform were the way to change society.

Diana was deeply affected by the demonstrations at the Democratic National Convention in Chicago in August 1968, which she and the SDS and eventually the Walker Commission believed was actually a "police riot." At the peak of the violence, she called her sister, Carol, in Chicago for $150 to help bail Tom Hayden, one of the founders of SDS in 1962, out of jail. A day or two later she called again and said she and Bill were leaving the city because "it's getting too rough."

They returned to Ann Arbor that fall in an activist mood. At the first meeting of the Ann Arbor SDS on Sept. 24, 1968, a sharp division in the group was apparent. Diana and Bill along with some 40 other radicals banded together against the moderates and formed a faction which they called "The Jesse James Gang."

The gang declared themselves revolutionary gangsters. They held peaceful methods in contempt. They urged direct action instead of talk, individual violent confrontations instead of big peace marches. Contained in their still half-formed ideas about the role of America in the world and of white radicals in America was the germ of the Weathermen analysis which would later call for violence.

Within a few weeks, the Jesse James Gang triumphed within the SDS chapter at Ann Arbor. Early in October 1968, the moderates decided they had had enough and walked out to form their own group. Through psychological warfare and threats of violence, the gang had captured the single most important SDS chapter in Michigan, which automatically gave them a powerful voice in the national organization.

In November 1968, Diana became a regional organizer for the SDS in Michigan. Early in 1969, she organized a "Cuba month" on campus, a series of films and seminars on the Cuban revolution. Gradually she became known less as Bill Ayers's sidekick than as a radical "sister" in her own right.

. . .

The final nine months of Diana Oughton's life were absorbed almost entirely by the disintegration of the SDS and the growth of a new, much smaller organization that turned to terrorism as the Weathermen.

In June 1969, the SDS, long troubled by deep differences on questions of ideology, suddenly burst apart at a chaotic, slogan-shouting convention in Chicago. By the end of the Chicago convention, the Weathermen had captured control of the SDS national headquarters in Chicago's West Side ghetto. The new SDS leadership was committed to action and over the summer of 1969 gradually worked out a plan for turning student radicals into a "Red Army" which would fight the establishment in the streets of America.

The 25,000-word manifesto—named after a line in a Bob Dylan song, "You don't need a Weatherman to tell which way the wind blows"—argued that white radicals in the United States could help bring on a worldwide revolution only by fighting in the streets of the "mother country."

While the SDS was beginning to plan for a four-day series of antiwar demonstrations in October, Diana's relationship with Bill Ayers and with her family both came under increasing strain.

Ayers had been elected one of the three national officers of the Weathermen, along with Mark Rudd and Bernardine Dohrn, and was spending most of his time in the national office.

Friends of Diana and Ayers say he was increasingly fascinated by Bernardine's toughness, intelligence, and hard beauty, so unlike Diana's warm, almost enveloping softness of spirit. Ayers told Diana he would not allow himself to be tied to one woman and she began spending her time with a number of other men.

The passionate intensity with which the Weathermen took their political ideas created a state of mind in Diana which her father later called "a kind of intellectual hysteria." He found her less and less willing to really talk about politics, increasingly heated when she did. She finally refused to discuss the subject altogether.

"I've made my decision, Daddy," she said. "There's no sense talking about it."

Diana's difficulty in talking about politics with her family was only a reflection of the difficulty all Weathermen found in trying to explain why violence was necessary.

The group's opponents argued that the Weathermen were repeating the errors of the "Narodniki" (Russian terrorists) who assassinated the Czar in 1881 and set back the cause of reform in Russia for decades. Like the "Narodniki" the Weathermen were an elite, self-appointed body from the upper classes who wanted the revolution now and, like children, could not force themselves to be patient. The Weathermen themselves joked about their upper-class origins, saying that the first requirement for a prospective member was a father who made at least $30,000 a year.

On the morning of Saturday, Sept. 6, 1969, only a few hours before Diana's sister Pamela was to be married in Chicago, Diana called her family in Dwight and abruptly told them she would not be able to come and be a bridesmaid after all. To a family which had been close, Diana's absence was a painful disappointment. When the family left Dwight for Chicago, with Diana's bridesmaid dress still at home on her bed, a kind of wall had begun to emerge between her and her family.

That weekend Diana attended the Cleveland SDS conference where the Weathermen strategy of total commitment to revolutionary violence finally emerged as a comprehensive position. During the following weeks Weathermen raided a Pittsburgh high school, invaded a community college outside Detroit, took a gun away from a policeman in New York, attacked Harvard University's Center for International Affairs, and provoked fights at drive-in restaurants and on beaches in Chicago, Cleveland, and other Midwestern cities.

When the Four Days of Rage began with a rally in Chicago on Wednesday, Oct. 8, only 300 Weathermen in helmets and denim jackets turned out for the battle. The group went ahead anyway, charging through the Loop and Gold Coast areas, smashing windows and windshields, and even charging directly into the ranks of police. More than 50 were arrested.

The following day Diana joined 70 Weatherwomen who marched to Grant Park for an all-women's action. When they got there they found themselves outnumbered by the police, who threatened to arrest them if they tried to leave the park wearing their helmets and carrying Viet Cong flags at the end of long, heavy poles.

Diana was one of a dozen Weatherwomen who gritted their teeth and plunged into the police lines but were immediately overpowered. She was scared but elated that the Weathermen had overcome their fear and fought in the streets. Despite the arrests (290 in all), the $1 million in bail (her father had posted hers), and the injuries (three Weathermen had been wounded by gunfire the first day, dozens of others had been severely beaten) she felt they had created the core of the Red Army.

She went back to Dwight, where she stayed a few days, resting and eating ravenously. Her mother, distraught at the thought of her daughter fighting with police, tried to talk her into abandoning the Weathermen.

"But Honey," she said, "you're only going to get yourself killed."

Diana refused to argue. "It's the only way, Mummy," she said, stalking back and forth in the hall. "It's the only way."

. . .

Diana saw her family in Dwight for the last time on Christmas Day, 1969. She left immediately after Christmas dinner, as abruptly as she had in the past.

That afternoon she returned to Flint, Mich., to help with final preparations for the Weathermen war council that began on Dec. 27. During the four-day council, Weathermen leaders slipped away to meet secretly in a seminary across the city where they debated the fate of the organization.

The enormous legal difficulties, which sapped their energy and their finances following the Days of Rage, and the hostility of much of the radical movement, made it clear that "wild in the streets" was not a strategy that could be sustained. Before the council ended on Dec. 30, Weathermen leaders decided they should make a final break with American society and go underground.

On Feb. 4, Diana appeared in court in Chicago and was fined $450 for her part in the women's action the previous Oct. 9. On Monday, March 2, just four days before she died, she called her sister Carol in Washington. She asked lots of little questions about the family. Carol felt that perhaps Diana was beginning to move away from the violent politics of the Weathermen. About halfway through the conversation, Diana asked, "Will the family stand by me, no matter what? Will they help me if I need it?"

Carol said of course.

.   .   .

In the end, Diana Oughton relinquished her humanity in hopes of creating a new world where she thought people could be more human. She denied her own nature and everything she loved. She grew more and more distant from her family; she gave up teaching children, the thing she loved to do best; she gave up her relationship with Bill Ayers when he argued that the revolution came first. Willingly she became an instrument of the revolution. She stopped asking questions to make bombs.

She regarded the world she saw around her as the implacable enemy of everything she believed in. Like the rest of the Weathermen, the privileged children of the world, in the end she had only one ambition: to be its executioner.

The bomb, which exploded a few minutes past noon on Friday, March 6, 1970, killing Diana and two other Weathermen in the townhouse at 18 West 11th Street in New York City, was a bomb designed to kill. It was made of dynamite surrounded by heavy metal nails which acted as shrapnel. The doctor who examined the remains of her body said she had been standing within a foot or two of the bomb when it exploded. It may, in fact, have gone off within her hands.

Four days after the explosion, bomb squad detectives found Diana's body near a workbench in the rubble-filled basement of the devastated house. At the end of another week, a detective discovered the tip of the little finger from a right hand. A print taken by a Police Department expert was matched later that day with a set of Diana's prints in the Washington files of the FBI. The prints had been taken in Chicago following her arrest during the Days of Rage.

That evening the New York Police Department called the tiny police force in Dwight. A member of the Dwight force then went to the Oughtons' house on South Street and told Mrs. Oughton her daughter was dead.

Lucinda Franks and Thomas Powers were jointly awarded the Pulitzer Prize for National Reporting in 1971 for their research into the Diana Oughton story. Her friends in what they called the Weather Underground—Bernardine Dohrn and Bill Ayers, Jeff Jones, Kathy Boudin, who escaped the Greenwich Village bomb blast, and Cathy Wilkerson, whose house was destroyed—never mentioned her when they made a clandestine film for TV on May 1, 1975. But when it was shown later that year on a PBS station and repeated in 1979, they were still talking revolution in a desultory kind of way. If they had learned nothing, like the Bourbons whom they despised, they had conveniently forgotten the one whose life and death might have taught them something.

For one of these survivors, the end came ten years after the blast that destroyed Diana Oughton. Cathlyn Platt (Cathy) Wilkerson, whose father had owned the bombed Greenwich Village house, emerged from hiding on July 8, 1980 and gave herself up to the authorities to answer charges of criminally negligent homicide and possession of a dangerous instrument—dynamite. Trembling with emotion, she pleaded not guilty on arraignment and, at 35 years of age, embarked on the painful process of coming to terms with her past before facing up to an uncertain future. [1]

[1] *Washington Post*, July 9, 1980, p. 1.

II. THE ENDLESS BATTLE
FOR HUMAN RIGHTS

The denial of human rights takes many forms.

In Milwaukee, it was cruelty and appalling neglect of the aged. In Santa Barbara, Calif., It was the formation of a secret society founded on hate and intolerance. In Florida, it was the shame and desolation imposed on helpless people in a migrant labor camp. And in South Africa, it was a whole nation that had dedicated itself to the persecution of its minority peoples.

These were just a few of the cases involving human rights into which reporters and editors of American news organizations thrust themselves in the latter part of this century. For every one that was rewarded with a Pulitzer Prize, there were numerous others—no one can say how many—that fought the battle with far less reward.

The cynics will nod wisely and say, "Oh, yes, the papers will do anything for circulation." But how much circulation is there in trying to help the aged, in easing the lot of migrant workers, attacking a secret society involving some of the "best people" in town, or describing the ravages of a policy known as "Apartheid" in far-off South Africa?

There is no profit for the press in such matters. Such assignments are acts of conscience in a hard and embittered world and they are paid for by the skill and devotion and unremitting labor of the journalists who willingly accept many such thankless tasks.

It is, in fact, one of the duties of a good newspaper in an open society to seek out such denials of the American dream and expose them to public view, to prod a less vigilant and more complacent governmental apparatus into action, to see that justice is done for those unable to help themselves.

Almost a century ago, Joseph Pulitzer put the principle into words when he wrote this message for the dedication of the cornerstone of the *New York World*'s new building—the great golden dome that towered above New York's Park Row and now is only a memory:

"God grant that this structure be the enduring home of a newspaper forever unsatisfied with merely printing news—forever fighting every form of Wrong—forever Independent—forever advancing in Enlightenment and Progress—forever wedded to true Democratic ideas—forever aspiring to be a Moral Force—forever rising to a higher plane of perfection as a Public Institution."

For most newspaper people, who prefer plain talk and straight writing, such high-flown language to describe a part of their daily work sounds unreal today. For they don't think that way, nor do they ordinarily pull out all the stops in expressing themselves.

Rather, when they act in defense of human rights, their work speaks for them. And here is how it happens:

Margo Huston, a reporter for the *Milwaukee Journal*, disclosed case after case of neglect of old people, some in their 80s and 90s, in a series called "I'll Never Leave My Home, Would You?" She found that profit-making care agencies were doing little to help these tragic shut-ins, that cold-eyed bureaucrats simply didn't enforce protective laws, that available in-home care aside from nursing homes was scarce and ineffective. A shakeup in the state's home health care system and a move to expand Medicaid services followed, and Miss Huston won the Pulitzer Prize for General Local Reporting in 1977.

In Santa Barbara, an 84-year-old publisher, Thomas More Storke, determined in 1961 that the newly formed John Birch Society was leveling undercover attacks against teachers, churchmen, and government officials in what amounted to a campaign of intolerance and hate. And even though some of the most respected conservatives in the city had become Birchers, Storke editorially attacked the group's professed anti-Communist campaign as a cover for discrediting people it didn't like. His *Santa Barbara*

News-Press was the first in the nation to take on the Birchers and it led in the battle that destroyed the secret society's effectiveness in his city. For his work, Storke won the Pulitzer Prize in Editorial Writing in 1962.

Howard Van Smith had a much less prominent target when he sought to help the thousands of distressed migrant laborers in Florida's neglected camps. But his articles in the *Miami News* brought a statewide crackdown on unsanitary camp conditions and a steady flow of relief supplies and food from private and public sources to the distressed farm workers. It was a campaign that brought him the Pulitzer Prize in National Reporting in 1959.

For Jimmie Lee Hoagland of the *Washington Post*, the issue was a national policy in the Republic of South Africa that was little understood in the United States at the time he was assigned to Africa in 1970.

True, from the time of the publication of Alan Paton's great novel, *Cry, The Beloved Country*, in 1948, there had been world-wide discussion of South Africa's "Apartheid," a system of racial separation and segregation to preserve white dominance. But few extended efforts had been made by American newspapers to explore the issue and make it more relevant to the American public.

What Hoagland accomplished in a series of articles in the *Post* and syndicated newspaper publication over a period of two months was to show how cruel and repressive the system is, what its economic and political pressures are, and the effect it has on people both inside and outside the Republic of South Africa. It won him the Pulitzer Prize for International Reporting in 1971.

Many other instances of the attack of the American press on violations of human rights could be cited, but those that follow are among the most significant in the records of the Pulitzer Prizes.

MIGRATION TO MISERY
Pulitzer Prize for Feature Photography, 1970

**FROM THE PORTFOLIO OF DALLAS KINNEY OF THE PALM BEACH POST, ILLUS-
TRATING THE PLIGHT OF FLORIDA MIGRANT WORKERS
AND THEIR FAMILIES**

6. *TWO MEN ARE FREED FROM DEATH ROW*
BECAUSE GENE MILLER CARED ABOUT THEM

An Eight-and-a-Half-Year Battle by the Miami Herald Reporter
Ends in Vindication for Wrongfully Convicted Prisoners

Gene Miller cares about people. He believes deeply in human rights.

But unlike those who loudly proclaim their devotion to the cause of the underprivileged just before election day, Miller has done something about it.

In the 12 years between 1963 and 1975, he produced the evidence that caused four innocent people to be freed from prison in three separate cases after they had been wrongfully convicted of murder.

Miller is very far from being a glamorous crusader who swings for the headlines, particularly on Monday mornings when the news is dull. Nor is he a high-priced lawyer or powerful politician. For more than 20 years he has been a general assignment reporter for the *Miami Herald*, taking the news as it comes along.

He had no special legal preparation for his battles with the courts, with judges and prosecutors. He was born in Evansville, Indiana, in 1928, and went into newspapering when he was still a boy. Following graduation from the University of Indiana and Army service, he began work as a reporter and joined the *Herald* in 1957.

It was in 1963 that he came across the case of Mary Katherin Hampton, who had been sentenced to prison for life in Louisiana in 1960 following her conviction for two murders. However, when he investigated the case, he found that she had been several hundred miles from the scene of the killings at the time they were committed.

The Louisiana Parole Board was convinced by the new facts in the case. On Nov. 30, 1966, Mary Katherin Hampton's sentence was commuted and she was set free.

But while the inquiry into that case was under way, Miller became convinced that there were fatal flaws in the case of Joseph Shea, an airman who had been convicted of murder in Miami, Fla., in 1959, after which he was imprisoned for life.

Here, too, the reporter produced new evidence that led to a retrial and Shea's acquittal on Feb. 19, 1966, by the unanimous vote of another Miami jury.

For his work in these two case, Miller was awarded the Pulitzer Prize for Special Local Reporting in 1967. Only one other reporter in the annals of the Pulitzer Prizes had been honored for such a reversal of a miscarriage of justice, Ed Mowery of the lamented *New York World-Telegram & Sun*, who had won a prize in 1953 for establishing the innocence of a prisoner on Sing Sing's Death Row.

But Miller's labors had only begun.

At just about the time he had ended work on the Hampton and Shea cases, he learned of two indigent black men, Freddie Pitts and Wilbert Lee, who had been convicted of murder in Florida in 1963 and sentenced to death, although both insisted they were innocent.

This one was tough—much tougher than anything else Miller had ever tackled. But with extraordinary determination, patience, persistence, and skill, he worked on the Pitts-Lee case for eight and a half years because he became convinced that they had been wrongfully convicted. Even more important, he convinced his editors at the *Herald* that he was right and they fully supported his initiative.

And this is what happened, as it was told by a colleague on the *Herald* staff after Pitts and Lee were set free by order of the Governor of Florida in 1975:

THE STORY THAT WOULDN'T GO AWAY

By Rob Elder

From the Miami Herald, Sept. 20, 1975

The freeing of Freddie Pitts and Wilbert Lee is a triumph for *Miami Herald* reporter Gene Miller.

But the victory was a long time coming. For nearly nine years, the Pitts-Lee case was an albatross around Miller's neck.

"It wouldn't go away and it wouldn't go away and it wouldn't go away," Miller would say at one point. "It was still there, and there was nothing to do about it but just keep writing."

For this newspaper, he wrote more than 150 columns of type about the case. That's about 300,000 words.

In the meantime he got slugged in the mouth.

He was publicly accused of writing lies, defaming public officials, and using yellow journalism to stir up ill will.

At one point, one of the public officials he was writing about threatened to launch a grand jury investigation of him.

Gene Miller, at 47, has the physique of an underfed canary and the tenacity of a barnacle. He wears short-sleeved, Kool-Aid colored shirts and Paisley bow ties.

In his trade, he is one of the most respected men in America. He did not need Pitts and Lee to make his reputation.

When he first heard of them late in 1966, he had wrapped up two other investigations which would win him a Pulitzer Prize.

In those cases, Miller had helped free persons who'd been convicted of murders they didn't commit. At best, the Pitts-Lee affair would be more of the same. And besides, it involved people in northwest Florida where the *Herald* doesn't even sell newspapers.

One of Miller's stories, published in the *Herald*'s Sunday magazine, was entitled, "The Unending Trials of Pitts and Lee." There were times when the case seemed to be an unending trial for Gene Miller.

The low point came three and a half years ago. Miller was sitting as a spectator in a courtroom in Marianna, a Panhandle town just under the Alabama-Georgia line. He was absorbing enough hostile stares to make his neck redder than that of any farmer in the county.

At that point, he had been writing about Pitts and Lee for five years. He had uncovered evidence that had been suppressed by the state, and that served as the basis for a new trial.

Now he sat and listened incredulously as a second all-white jury pronounced Pitts and Lee guilty of the murders of two white service station attendants, Jesse Burkett and Grover Floyd.

At 6:03 P.M. on March 15, 1972, despite all that Miller had written and all that the *Herald* had published, a second judge pronounced the death sentence for the second time.

Miller left Marianna within minutes. The Klan had made threats and he feared for his life. He was a crestfallen man, back in Miami, when he talked to Larry Jinks, executive editor of the *Herald*.

"I believe they are innocent men," Jinks told him. "We're in this for the long haul."

When Miller first encountered the case in 1966 through Warren Holmes, a Miami polygraph expert, neither thought it would lead to two black men on death row at Raiford Prison.

Holmes and Miller had never heard of Pitts and Lee. They were unaware that two white service station attendants had been abducted from Skipper's Mo-Jo Station in Port St. Joe in 1963 and that the men had been robbed and killed on a canal bank.

Miller, Holmes, and the *Herald* were interested in what they thought was an entirely separate case. The newspaper had posted a $15,000 reward in connection with a similar but apparently unrelated murder in Broward County, the killing of another service station attendant named Floyd McFarland.

A Raiford inmate, Jesse Pait, wanted the reward. He had heard another prisoner, Curtis Adams, brag about killing McFarland. Pait told the story to a Broward detective.

Adams was questioned about the Broward murder. He said his girl friend, Mary Jean Akins, had done it.

Warren Holmes was called in to run a lie detector test on Mary Jean Akins. She told him Curtis Adams had committed the Broward and the Port St. Joe murders.

That was on Dec. 15, 1966, the day Miller first became aware of the Pitts-Lee case. He would write nothing about it for seven weeks while he investigated.

But within one day Curtis Adams would plead guilty to the Broward killing. And five days later, Adams would confess to Warren Holmes that he had also committed the Port St. Joe murders for which Pitts and Lee were on Death Row.

Immediately Miller and Holmes began running into obstacles. The crime had occurred three and a half years earlier. The trail was cold. The witnesses were scattered.

Pitts and Lee are black men. Curtis Adams is white. The murder victims were white. So far as Panhandle authorities were concerned, the case was closed.

Earl Faircloth, then Florida's attorney general, took the position that "the issue in this particular case is not the guilt or innocence of Pitts and Lee but rather did they receive a fair trial."

Technically there had been no trial but only a so-called "mercy hearing" to decide whether Pitts and Lee would get the electric chair or life imprisonment. And in a stifling courtroom in Wewahitchka on Aug. 28, 1963, as the Rev. Martin Luther King

Jr. was making his "I have a dream" speech in Washington, Pitts and Lee had publicly confessed to the Mo-Jo murders.

Miller's first obstacle was J. Frank Adams, the original prosecutor. With Miller was Maurice Rosen of Miami, who was representing Pitts and Lee for the American Civil Liberties Union. Miller and Rosen took along the tape-recorded confession of Curtis Adams. They asked J. Frank Adams, no relation, to listen to it.

He refused.

Miller went to see Bay County Sheriff M.J. "Doc" Daffin. Miller told him there was reason to believe Pitts and Lee had not killed Burkett and Floyd. "I don't *think* they did it," Daffin bellowed. "I *know* they did it."

Miller confronted Chief Deputy Wayne White. He told him Freddie Pitts claimed he had been beaten into confessing. White denied it. "If anyone says I beat him, I'll resign long enough to settle this face to face and man to man," he said.

In February 1967, the *Herald* published Miller's first two stories about Pitts and Lee.

"There's not a word of truth in the whole mess," said J. Frank Adams, the prosecutor. "Better reading can be found in pocket book pulps."

Miller persisted. While he kept digging, Philip Hubbart, a Miami lawyer, kept Pitts and Lee alive on a legal technicality. Blacks had been systematically excluded from the original 1963 grand jury.

Eventually, there was another hearing in Port St. Joe before a state court. As Miller walked out of the courtroom with a 50-pound file cabinet on his shoulder, a muscular young man, a nephew of one of the murder victims, strode up to him and punched him in the face.

Miller, who weighs 162, was knocked flat.

In time, Robert Shevin replaced Earl Faircloth as Attorney General. Shevin did not immediately or enthusiastically embrace the Pitts-Lee case but he allowed Miller to read through the state's files.

Sitting on a sofa in Shevin's office on Dec. 16, 1971, five years and one day after he began working on the story, Miller made an astounding discovery.

Willie Mae Lee, the main prosecution witness, had recanted her story in 1968. She hadn't been present for the murders, she said. She wasn't a witness to anything.

The state had had the retraction for four years without turning it over to the defense as required by law. Officials had sat on it while talking Willie Mae Lee back to her original version.

It was enough to get a new trial, but a new trial was not enough to free Pitts and Lee.

Within a month after the second conviction for Pitts and Lee, Miller signed a contract to write a book about them. He took a leave of absence and was at home working on it one day in 1974 when something good finally happened.

"I got a telephone call from a young man who identified himself as Don Middlebrooks," Miller said.

Middlebrooks was a legal aide to the governor of Florida, Reuben Askew. "He said that Askew had assigned him to look into the case," Miller recalled.

On June 13, 1974, Middlebrooks went to Raiford with Holmes and Miller to see Curtis Adams. Again, Adams confessed to the Port St. Joe killings.

Without fanfare, Askew had begun his own investigation and it was exhaustive, lasting 18 months. When it was finished, the governor announced,

"There is more than enough evidence for me to seriously question the guilt of Pitts and Lee. The evidence, in fact, points to their innocence."

On Sept. 10, 1974, the governor recommended a full pardon. On Sept. 11, he and Attorney General Shevin signed an executive order that would grant it. Subsequently two other cabinet members, Phil Ashler and Ralph Turlington, signed as well, making the necessary majority of the state's seven-man pardon board.

And so, 12 years and 48 days after they had been jailed, Freddie Pitts and Wilbert Lee were freed.

Miller was with Pitts and Lee at Florida State Prison in the final hour before their release. And this is what he told them:

"Gentlemen, we're going to walk out of here in a minute or two and catch a flight to Miami. I'll go back to the office and write a news story.

And then," here he was quite deliberate, "I will never write another story about you for as long as I live."

This is how he began his story for next morning's *Miami Herald*, dated Sept. 20, 1975:

PITTS-LEE WALK AS FREE MEN

Freddie Pitts and Wilbert Lee walked away from the shadow of death at 37 minutes past noon Friday. They did not look back.

The clamorous din of the men behind bars faded behind them. A wave of men behind cameras receded before them.

Unsmiling, Pitts and Lee acknowledged neither.

After 12 years and 48 days of imprisonment for another man's crime, they walked into the world as free men, a Xerox copy of the governor's pardon folded in their billfolds.

"I've had enough of this hotel," Pitts said mildly. "They have very poor accommodations."

"I've got my prison clothes off and I've got my free world clothes on," Lee said, "and gee, baby, I feel like a Philadelphia lawyer."

They left with immediate plans. They did not announce them. . . .

Quietly and evenly, Miller's account went on for the better part of two columns as he recorded, with painstaking reportorial accuracy, every detail of the story. Not a line, not even a word, would have given the casual reader a hint that this was a case on which Miller and his paper had struggled with the law for so long. From beginning to end, he was the complete professional.

True to his word, he never did write another story about Pitts and Lee for his newspaper. Other reporters did, quite naturally, and the freed men themselves stayed in the news as they pressed their claims against the state. But if they looked back, he did not.

"I guess I am one who prefers not to look back," Miller said some years after he had won his second Pulitzer Prize, this time for General Local Reporting in 1976. At the end of the decade, however, he seemed rather pleased to report that all four of the people whom he had helped in such a spectacular way were, as he put it, "well, independent, employed and, most important, lawful."

Like every general assignment reporter, he went on to a lot of other important stories—the Guyana mass suicides and murders, the Three Mile Island nuclear alarm, and the Florida murder trial of Theodore Bundy, who was convicted on the overwhelming evidence against him.

In the annals of the Pulitzer Prizes, Gene Miller always will stand high among those in American journalism who have demonstrated their devotion to human rights.

7. A REPORTER TURNS AMBULANCE DRIVER, EXPOSES CHICAGO'S "MISERY MERCHANTS"

William Jones of the Chicago Tribune Breaks Up
a Police-Linked Ring That Preyed on the Poor

It all began with a tip, as so many good stories do.

Certain private ambulance companies, an informant told the *Chicago Tribune*, were making a profit out of human misery in the poorest sections of the city.

They were aiding and abetting in the bribery of a number of policemen, the tipster went on, to make sure that sick people in these areas were put in the "right" ambulances, often at exorbitant cost either to the city or themselves, and sometimes both.

It was a difficult story to break. The *Tribune* needed eyewitnesses—and in the ghetto nobody talks because everybody is afraid.

But the editors were determined to break up the "Misery Merchants," as they were called, for here was a violation of basic human rights that was unconscionable—in Chicago or anyplace else.

William Jones, an ex-Marine then 31 years old, had received the original tip and was assigned to break the story. Having been a *Tribune* reporter for six years, he set about his preparations in a businesslike way, first taking case-work training and then obtaining a job as an ambulance driver.

What he witnessed and what he had to do sickened him. He found that poor and helpless people were receiving sadistic treatment from the ambulance men who were supposed to help them. He piled up first-hand evidence of police collusion. And, when he had finished two months of ambulance driving, he returned to his desk at the *Tribune* and began a six-part series as follows:

"I WORKED AS A MISERY MERCHANT"

By William Jones

From the Chicago Tribune, June 7, 1970

They are the misery merchants and they prowl the streets of our city 24 hours a day as profiteers of human suffering.

Waiting in filthy garages scattered throughout the city, they prey on families faced with an urgent need for transportation and medical care for a loved one.

They are the hustlers among the city's private ambulance operators and they are waiting for your call for help.

Their business is big business in Chicago. The multi-million-dollar industry accounts for nearly $1 million of Cook County's welfare fees each year.

At the same time, the misery merchants are exacting a toll in needless suffering and sadistic treatment of the ill that may never be inventoried.

You may have to call the misery merchants this afternoon or tomorrow or next week. When you do, a member of your family may be gasping after a heart attack or screaming in agony after fracturing a hip or a leg. As you frantically leaf through the telephone directory to find an ambulance company, you unwittingly will be playing a game of Russian roulette with the person you are trying to help.

The stakes are high. If you are poor or black or on welfare, they are even higher. I know because I worked as a misery merchant and this is how they operate:

1. A middle-aged man lies gasping from an apparent heart attack in his North Side apartment. His throat makes a rasping sound as he desperately tries to continue breathing. A two-man ambulance crew stands over the body, arguing with a friend of the victim that the $40 fee must be paid before the man is placed on the stretcher. They are told the victim has only $2 in cash. The crew shrugs, then lifts the gasping man onto a kitchen chair where he slumps across the table. As they walk out of the apartment, one of the attendants reaches across the table and pockets the $2.

2. An elderly black man, his body wracked with cancer, pleads with a private ambulance crew to handle him gently because even the slightest pressure causes extreme pain. The attendant in charge ignores his plea and grabs the man under the arms, drags him across the floor to the stretcher, and drops the patient. As the old man's face contorts in agony and breaks into a sweat, the attendant mutters to his fellow worker: "Next time the guy will walk to the stretcher."

3. An epileptic with a fractured hip lies in the rear of a police squadron car for nearly two hours until a private ambulance firm that makes payoffs to policemen is able to respond to the call. Instead of taking the victim to a hospital in the car, the police spend a dime to call a misery merchant. Then they wait until the ambulance—and the $10 payoff—arrive. When the ambulance finally responds, the victim is ordered to crawl from the police car onto the stretcher. Hospital records later will be falsified to show that the victim was picked up at a neighbor's home.

4. An ambulance crew demands that a Northwest Side housewife with a broken back write out a $40 check as she lies in a hospital. When she complains that the pain is making it difficult for her to perform the task, they fill out the check and hand it back to her to sign.

5. An ambulance driver hurls insults at a black woman while her daughter waits for emergency transportation after suffering a miscarriage. The daughter is screaming. "She looks all right," the ambulance driver decides. "She can walk down the stairs." The apartment is on the third floor. It is raining and once outside the victim is ordered to crawl into the ambulance through a side door.

These are a few of the incidents observed during a two-month investigation of the misery merchants by the *Tribune* and the Better Government Association. The probe was prompted by complaints from other ambulance operators who told of payoffs to police and firemen, welfare fraud, and sadistic treatment of the ill and injured.

They feared a scandal that would damage the entire industry and volunteered their cooperation to end the activities.

Working with George Bliss, chief BGA investigator, I obtained a city ambulance attendant's license. My partner in the undercover probe was William Recktenwald, one of Bliss's top investigators. Despite warnings of what we would find as ambulance attendants, neither of us was ready for what we saw in the world of the misery merchants.

"It was the most sickening display of mistreatment of human beings I have ever encountered," Recktenwald reported. "I would go home completely outraged at what I had seen and heard." At one point, Recktenwald walked off the job after 31 hours on duty with only 40 minutes' sleep. "I just couldn't take it any more," he said.

At the same firm, several days earlier, an owner became suspicious of my credentials and threatened me with a beating if the company learned that I was a private investigator. I managed to talk my way through an interrogation by several employees and finished my 24-hour shift with the company. The owner will not know until he reads this story how correct his instincts were. . . .

For the remainder of that first story and the other five articles, Jones documented his charges in meticulous detail.

The series shocked Chicago's civic authorities into action. Two private ambulance companies were barred from carrying welfare patients. Sixteen persons, including 10 police, were prosecuted on charges including bribery and grand theft. And the city adopted a new law tightly regulating private ambulance service.

For his work, Jones won the Pulitzer Prize for Special Local Reporting in 1971. And some years later, he became managing editor of the *Tribune*.

8. A BLACK AND WHITE TEAM SEES FAMINE STALKING ACROSS ASIA AND AFRICA

William Mullen and Ovie Carter of the Chicago Tribune
Find Millions Who Are Threatened with Hunger

Middle-class America is well-fed, comfortable, pleased with its easy life style. And middle-class America, in most cases, does not like to be reminded of unfortunates in the lower reaches of society.

It goes almost without saying, therefore, that hunger is not a popular story in these United States. Nor do self-satisfied people want to be reminded here that there are starving millions in this world.

But in the summer and fall of 1974, the *Chicago Tribune* decided that it was necessary—even imperative—for Americans to face up to what the world was really like.

During that time span, a white *Tribune* reporter, William Mullen, and a black photographer, Ovie Carter, were sent on an appalling journey of 10,000 miles across Africa and Asia to look famine in the face and report on what they saw.

Both were shocked at the terrible sights they witnessed in many an African and Asian village and town—children who were walking skeletons, villages where people were helplessly watching their neighbors die a slow and inexorable death, whole areas where the fields were parched and brown and no food could be found.

When Mullen came back with his story and Carter returned with his portfolio of pictures after almost three months, the *Tribune* printed their team effort over the five-day period of October 13–18.

This was not just the usual account of how people were starving to death in an overpopulated world and how awful it all was. Not at all, for Mullen found that bungling relief agencies had wasted some of the enormous resources placed at their disposal—that red tape and corruption had deprived millions of people of food—that bad weather had created six years of drought across thousands of miles of once-fertile land and little was being done about it.

And for those who could not accept his words as fact, there were Carter's dramatic and compelling pictures that showed what famine was doing to the human race.

In one province of Ethiopia alone, the Wollo, they saw people dying because almost one million tons of American food, paid for with American taxes, had not arrived in time and been fairly distributed.

And in a refugee camp in Upper Volta in Africa, the condition of the people was so distressing that a special airlift of food was ordered as soon as the *Tribune*'s men were able to report what they found.

So it went, from Dakar to the eastern coast of India, from Timbuktu to Cooch Behar. And it wasn't ever easy, for the *Tribune*'s team had to survive storms and pestilence, bad roads and clouds of voracious mosquitos, and—almost as bad as anything else—the interminable battles with alarmed officialls who were afraid to have the story told.

Back in America, a surprising thing happened. Somehow, Mullen's words and Carter's pictures broke through the hard shell of American indifference and touched a responsive nerve.

The generous side of the American character showed itself to far-off peoples who were begging for help. People wrote, called, asked: "What can I do to help?"

All of them were referred to the proper organizations and government authorities. And the *Tribune*, encouraged, reprinted many thousands of copies of the Mullen-Carter series, for they had shown that world hunger, lack of food, and overpopulation were news of the first magnitude which would have an enormous impact everywhere.

Here is the substance of Mullen's first article and some of Carter's illustrations:

SLOW DEATH FOR 500 MILLION PEOPLE

By William Mullen

From the Chicago Tribune, Oct. 13, 1974

It is the same sun that rises each day over Singimarie Pachuniper, a tiny village in eastern India, and Kao, a tiny village in central Niger in the middle of Africa.

Dawn comes first to a refugee camp for farmers in Singimarie where six-year-old Saku Barman rises unsteadily to his feet and totters out of an open lean-to into a listless day of numbirg hunger.

Six hours later dawn comes to the Sahara nomad camp in Kao where a spindly four-year-old girl names Hameda weakly gets to her feet to face the same sort of day.

Once in the sun, Saku and Hameda, although 5,500 miles apart, cast the same shadow.

They are the shadows of ghastly apparitions, of walking child skeletons, doomed by the same natural and man-made forces to a short, unhappy existence on Earth.

"I don't think Hameda will survive much longer," a village official told the *Chicago Tribune*'s photographer, Ovie Carter, and me when we visited him on a chilly desert morning early in August.

"It will only take a cold now, or a case of diarrhea, and she will be gone."

Already too weak to stand on her own for very long, Hameda's emaciated body clung spiderlike to her mother's back most of the day.

Mother and child stayed close to each other and close to their skin tent. A row of tents stretched like a finger from the village into the rolling brown desert dunes.

THE FACES OF HUNGER

FROM OVIE CARTER'S PULITZER-PRIZE-WINNING PORTFOLIO, AN AWARD HE
SHARED WITH WILLIAM MULLEN IN 1975. BOTH WERE
CHICAGO TRIBUNE STAFFERS

THE FACES OF HUNGER (Cont.)

"There just isn't enough food coming in," the village official said. "We are losing two or three people every day now."

When we visited Singimarie several weeks later, the village teacher gave Saku Barman about the same chances for survival.

"Unless he gets some milk within a few days," the teacher said, "he will be dead. Twenty people have died already this week."

Saku and a younger sister spent their days walking like stick figures through the sweltering little town, wandering among a gaunt, ragged populace that was just as hungry as they.

Hameda is black, the child of desert nomads whose cattle and livelihood have been destroyed by a six-year African drought.

Saku is brown, the child of rice farmers killed in a devastating August flood in India.

Until this summer, they were children of different worlds, separated by race, religion, culture, and way of life.

Weakened in the aftermath of flood and drought, starved by the world's inability to get food to them when they needed it most, they faced the same fate.

By the end of the summer, Saku and Hameda looked like brother and sister—dirty, naked, and dying. Their faces were no longer the faces of children but immobile masks, deeply lined with unfilled folds of skin.

The only emotion left was the terror that sometimes silently filled their eyes while they sat quietly through the day, haunted perhaps by their own private child dreams.

By now, it is likely Saku and Hameda are dead.

The thin lifeline of trucks that brought irregular food shipments to Hameda's village was stopped in the middle of August.

When we visited Saku's village, India had no food at all to deliver there. The government was just starting to ask around the world for emergency food donations.

The story of Hameda and Saku is, of course, not a new one. Famine has been a killer every year since history began.

But there is growing concern among world food, agricultural, and weather experts that the world has fallen into a situation much more serious than ever before.

They fear that many thousands of children like Saku and Hameda who died this year have been carried away by the first wave of what may become the greatest disaster in history.

Many experts are predicting that 500 million people will perish in famine by the year 2000.

Sayed A. Marei, secretary general of the World Food Conference, believes current crop failures and poor food distribution have left 460 million people permanently hungry.

"Over the past two years," he said, "the world food shortage has become so serious that it quite literally threatens the survival of hundreds of millions of human beings around the world.

"Such a threat carries with it the gravest implications for the peace and security of the world."

In three months of travel through the African Sahel—the semi-desert area just south of the Sahara—and the flood-stricken northeast region of India, we saw why the experts are worried.

We saw in West Africa thousands upon thousands of acres of once productive pastureland destroyed by the growing Sahara. No amount of aid or work could reclaim it—and so the entire lifestyle of nomadic cattlemen, who for centuries were able to live off the land, has been destroyed.

In India we saw the intense resistance by mothers and fathers to any form of birth control. Their reasoning was simple: they must have at least six or seven children so that one or two would survive to adulthood and take care of them in their old age.

The story was the same in each of the countries we visited— Senegal, Mauritania, Male, Upper Volta, Niger, Chad, Ethiopia, and India. Each country has more people than it has land and resources to feed them.

Mullen, a native of LaCrosse, Wis., was 30 (eight years out of the journalism school at the University of Wisconsin) when he wrote this series. Carter, 29 and Mississippi-born, had attended Forest Park (Ill.) Community College and a photography school before becoming a *Tribune* photographer in 1969.

The Pulitzer Prize Board, always sensitive to journalistic achievements bearing on human rights, voted them the Pulitzer Prize for International Reporting for 1975.

THE KINDLY TIGER
Pulitzer Prize for Editorial Cartooning, 1961

CAREY ORR IN THE CHICAGO TRIBUNE

9. A BLACK WOMAN REPORTER APPEALS
FOR BETTER RACE RELATIONS

Shirley Scott of the Hartford Times Makes a Contribution
to the Gannett Series, "The Road to Integration"

It was a time of troubles for America.

Across the land, there was a seething discontent in the black ghettos of the crumbling inner cities. In the schools, where the Supreme Court had decreed integration in 1954, progress was halting and white resistance was fierce. Jobs were scarce. Money was tight. And seemingly little was being done to create change.

A sense of crisis was developing among 20 million Negroes in America. They had not yet accepted, as a mass, the simple term "black." Nor had it become popular to think of black as beautiful. And those extremists who preached hatred and fear were finding an ever-larger response for themselves and their doctrines.

It was in this difficult situation that the Gannett newspapers, then a relatively small regional chain of 15 newspapers with a total circulation of 750,000, determined to try to find some cause for better feeling.

The notion that newspapers could lift morale in their communities by publicizing some of the positive developments in the integration effort came to Paul Miller, then the president of Gannett, during a speaking engagement in St. Louis. He noticed a piece in one of the St. Louis papers that reported on such progress in the difficult field of race relations and determined to follow it up.

He wrote this memo to his associates from his office in Rochester, N.Y.: "Every city has the same problem. If it has not, it soon will have. Every city is trying to find answers. Have any cities found answers that might be useful in Rochester and elsewhere? If so, what are they?"

Vincent S. Jones, editorial director of the organization at the time, carried on from there, encouraging all Gannett editors to look for some of the good news, no matter how modest, as well as the continual run of calamitous headlines.

It was the beginning of a year-long series under the general title, "The Road to Integration."

Nearly a hundred articles were gathered by some three dozen reporters and editors for publication in most of the Gannett chain. These were not, for the most part, the stories of crisis that grabbed the big headlines;

instead, they told of progress, of job opportunities, the chances for better housing and better education, and of hope for the future.

There were other, bluntly written pieces, too, in which the black point of view was thrust without compromise before white America. One of these was written by Shirley Jackson Scott, then a 31-year-old reporter for the *Hartford Times*.

Mrs. Scott had been born and educated in Painesville, Ohio, and beginning in 1949, she had served in the Women's Army Corps. Following her marriage to Darwin B. Scott, she became the mother of two boys and took an active role in Hartford community affairs.

For a time, Mrs. Scott was the chairman of the Hartford chapter of the Congress of Racial Equality and worked for the *New England Tribune* and *Creed* magazine, both of which were interested in the affairs of the black community. She had been on the reporting staff of the *Hartford Times* for only a few months when the integration series began.

The following article, representative of the sense of black outrage and despair at the time, was published in the *Hartford Times* and then picked up by other Gannett Newspapers. The version below was used in the flagship *Rochester Democrat & Chronicle*. It was something more than a statement of civil rights. It was an appeal for human rights and human understanding.

WHAT IT'S LIKE TO BE BLACK

By Shirley J. Scott

From the Rochester (N.Y.) Democrat & Chronicle, Dec. 5, 1963

Imagine, if you can, your skin not white but black. Imagine your present job, education, and income the same, but your family shades of brown.

The same things bother you. You worry over the possibility of war, you complain about taxes, you pay the rent and grocery bill, and you work for the health and welfare of your family.

Then how are you different from other men? Are you different?

You will soon discover that the most annoying fact of color is the ambiguity of the role you play in life. You don't feel different, yet you are treated differently. You can't justify the treatment accorded you, but you must live and cope with white justification.

For instance:

If you are a man, regardless of your efforts, promotion will come slowly—if at all. Fellow workers are polite, perhaps friendly, but always at arm's length. Association ends at 5 o'clock.

You are stuck at the bottom of the ladder—not because of what you do but because you are a Negro.

If you are a woman, doors open to you that remain closed to your husband or your brother. Your children present a special problem.

In addition to washing, mending, cooking and healing little hurts, sometimes early in their lives, you must explain the taunts of Johnny Whiteboy. Could you explain that there's nothing wrong with being black?

Will they believe you instead of Johnny?

You fight back tears and maybe anger because you know there's no way to protect them. You pray that somehow your strength will be transmitted to them.

You decide between explaining the problems they will meet or letting the problems explain themselves. In either case you wonder whether you chose the right path.

If you are a child, you wish your parents had straight hair and white skin without really understanding why. Your own lips seem too thick, your hair too curly, your skin too dark. You fight if anyone calls you black, especially if the description fits your color.

Black seems ugly to the Negro child. Good things happen only to the white. Television and movies support this childhood notion.

Adult or child, after the first rude awakening, you always will be conscious of what you are and who you are. Mistakes are twice as embarrassing because people identify them with your color.

Your individuality seems always overshadowed by your color. Achievements? Not remarkable in themselves, but remarkable because you are a Negro.

The Negro community puts a high value on Negroes in mediocre jobs usually held by whites.

As an adult Negro, you live in two worlds: the white world where you make your living; the black world where you make your friends.

Poorly dressed or ill-mannered people, if Negro, you feel reflect on you personally.

These are only a few of the many problems faced by the Negro daily. How does he react inwardly? How would you react?

Pulitzer Prize for Editorial Cartooning, 1980

A DRAWING OPPOSING THE DEATH PENALTY, BY DON WRIGHT
OF THE MIAMI NEWS

At times he hates himself, his family, and the world around him. He wants to strike back at the invisible standard that sets him apart. And at the same time he wants to bury his head and pretend that that standard doesn't exist.

The very word Negro seems to identify not his race but his social status.

The everyday problems of every man are special problems to him.

Finding an apartment means steeling himself against the first expression that greets his ring of a doorbell.

Job hunting means preparing to answer questions remote from the position, or getting a quick answer: "Sorry, it's filled."

He is tired of being cast in a stereotype mold. He is weary of people talking about slums and segregation and of white liberals constantly picking his brain. He wants more action and less talk even while he realizes that little action will be taken without talk.

Demonstrations embarrass him, yet he's glad to see them come.

He is confused by the confusion created by his existence and resentful that the white world resents him. The paternalistic attitude of well-meaning whites distorts his own concept of his worth.

More than anything else he wants to live just as others live; to make honest mistakes and receive honest objections.

The psychological distance between the American Negro and the idea of democracy fuels his continued resentment of his status in American society.

He is taught the value of freedom and asked to settle for less.

Little wonder the delinquency, the resentment, the demonstrations, and the revolt.

Despite all this, somehow, he must find understanding and purpose in his life. He must protect his family as best he can from the psychological damage of extremes. On one side, the pitfall of self-hatred; on the other, hatred of the white.

The Negro walks on eggshells. The miracle of it all is his endurance.

The Gannett series won a Pulitzer Prize Special Award in 1964 and Shirley Jackson Scott's article was among those that had a prominent place in the exhibit that went before the Pulitzer Board.

In the many disasters that broke over America in the ensuing years—the fatal riots in Newark and Watts and Detroit and lesser ones in cities like Rochester and others—there were few signs of hope that better times and better understanding of racial problems were possible in America. But the Gannett series remained one of them.

Today the Gannett chain, under the leadership of 56-year-old Allen H. Neuharth, is the largest in the land with 82 daily newspapers having a total circulation of 3,580,000, more than a billion dollars in annual revenue, and earnings of $134 million in 1979 (up 19 percent over the previous year). But it still strives for excellence and in 1980 its enormously expanded Gannett News Service won the Pulitzer Prize gold medal for public service. Its prize-winning feat was to expose the gross mismanagement of a fund-raising drive by the Pauline Fathers, a Catholic order in Pennsylvania, which was climaxed by a papal inquiry. The award brought honor to three Gannett reporters, John Hanchette, William F. Schmick, and Carlton Sherwood, all of whom—like Mrs. Scott—worked selflessly on a project for which they knew they would receive little comfort and much criticism. [1]

Mrs. Scott remained with the *Hartford Times* for several years. One of her editors, Don O. Noel, Jr., remembers her as a "good and aggressive reporter." However, politics attracted her more than journalism and she went on to work with an antipoverty agency in New Haven, ran unsuccessfully for mayor of New Haven on the Republican ticket, and served as a delegate to the Republican National Convention in Kansas City in 1976. In the following year, she died of an embolism, a tragic loss to her community as well as to the many in journalism who gratefully remember her.

10. A. M. ROSENTHAL VISITS AUSCHWITZ
AND WRITES A MEMORABLE STORY

The New York Times's Correspondent in Poland Recalls
the Horror of Four Million, Mostly Jews, Who Died There

When A. M. Rosenthal became the *New York Times's* correspondent in Poland in June 1958, one of his earliest trips outside Warsaw was to Auschwitz.

The Nazi murder camp where four million people were put to death during World War II, most of them Jews, made such a deep impression on him that he could not help writing an article about it.

[1] *Time*, April 28, 1980, p. 93.

WHEN THE PARADE PASSES BY
Pulitzer Prize for Feature Photography, 1977

ROBIN HOOD'S PHOTO OF A DISABLED VETERAN AND HIS CHILD AT CHAT-
TANOOGA'S ARMED FORCES DAY PARADE IN 1976, PUBLISHED IN THE
CHATTANOOGA NEWS-FREE PRESS

The piece was short, only about 700 words, but it led the *New York Times Magazine* when it was published and has since become an enduring classic of American journalism.

"THERE IS NO NEWS FROM AUSCHWITZ"

By A. M. Rosenthal

From the New York Times, August 31, 1958

BRZEZINKA, Poland—The most terrible thing of all, somehow, was that at Brzezinka the sun was bright and warm, the rows of graceful poplars were lovely to look upon, and on the grass near the gates children played.

It all seemed frighteningly wrong, as in a nightmare, that at Brzezinka the sun should ever shine or that there should be light and greenness and the sound of young laughter. It would be fitting if at Brzezinka the sun never shone and the grass withered, because this is a place of unutterable terror.

And yet, every day, from all over the world, people come to Brzezinka, quite possibly the most grisly tourist center on earth. They come for a variety of reasons—to see if it could really have been true, to remind themselves not to forget, to pay homage to the dead by the simple act of looking upon their place of suffering.

Brzezinka is a couple of miles from the better-known southern town of Oswiecim. Oswiecim has about 12,000 inhabitants, is situated about 171 miles from Warsaw, and lies in a damp, marshy area at the eastern end of the pass called the Moravian Gate.

Brzezinka and Oswiecim together formed part of that minutely organized factory of torture and death that the Nazis called Konzentrationslager Auschwitz.

By now, 14 years after the last batch of prisoners was herded naked into the gas chamber by dogs and guards, the story of Auschwitz has been told a great many times. Some of the inmates have written of those memories of which sane men cannot conceive. Rudolf Franz Ferdinand Hoss, the superintendent of the camp, before he was executed wrote his detailed memoirs of mass exterminations and the experiments on living bodies. Four million people died here, the Poles say.

And so there is no news to report about Auschwitz. There is merely the compulsion to write something about it, a compulsion that grows out of a restless feeling that to have visited Auschwitz and then turned away without having said or written anything would somehow be a most grievous act of discourtesy to those who died here.

Brzezinka and Oswiecim are very quiet places now; the screams can no longer be heard. The tourist walks silently, quickly at first to get it over with and then, as his mind peoples the barracks and the chambers and the dungeons and the flogging posts, he walks draggingly. The guide does not say much either, because there is nothing much for him to say after he has pointed.

For every visitor, there is one particular bit of horror that he knows he will never forget. For some it is seeing the rebuilt gas chamber at Oswiecim and being told that this is the "small one." For others it is the fact that at Brzezinka, in the ruins of the gas chambers, and the crematoria the Germans blew up as they retreated, there are daisies growing.

There are visitors who gaze blankly at the gas chambers and the furnaces because their minds simply cannot encompass them, but stand shivering before the great mounds of human hair behind the plate glass window or the piles of babies' shoes or the brick cells where men sentenced to death by suffocation were walled up.

One visitor opened his mouth in a silent scream simply at the sight of boxes—great stretches of three-tiered wooden boxes in the women's barracks. They were about six feet wide, about three feet high, and into them from five to ten prisoners were shoved for the night. The guide walks quickly through the barracks. Nothing more to see here.

A brick building where sterilization experiments were carried out on women prisoners. The guide tries the door—it's locked. The visitor is grateful that he does not have to go in, and then flushes with shame.

A long corridor where rows of faces stare from the walls. Thousands of pictures, the photographs of prisoners. They are all dead now, the men and women who stood before the cameras, and they all knew they were to die.

They all stare blank-faced, but one picture, in the middle of a row, seizes the eye and wrenches the mind. A girl, 22 years old, plumply pretty, blonde. She is smiling gently, as at a sweet, treasured thought. What was the thought that passed through her young mind and is now her memorial on the wall of the dead at Auschwitz?

Into the suffocation dungeons the visitor is taken for a moment and feels himself strangling. Another visitor goes in, stumbles out, and crosses herself. There is no place to pray at Auschwitz.

The visitors look pleadingly at each other and say to the guide, "Enough."

There is nothing new to report about Auschwitz. It was a sunny day and the trees were green and at the gates the children played.

Rosenthal, now the executive editor of the *Times*, was 36 when he wrote this piece. He had been well established as a newspaperman for more than a decade, having served the *Times* at the United Nations from 1946 to 1954 and thereafter as its correspondent in India.

During his 17 months in Poland, he won a reputation among news-starved Poles for reliability, tact, and unfailing accuracy. But his reporting of the problems of the Polish government and the difficulties of the Communist Party caused him to be expelled in November 1959.

"The question of falseness or otherwise does not enter," a spokesman for the Polish government told him. "You have written very deeply and in detail about the internal situation, party matters, and leadership matters, and the Polish government cannot tolerate such probing reporting."

The Pulitzer Prize Board voted him the Pulitzer Prize for International Reporting in 1960 for his coverage from Poland, which was termed "perceptive and authoritative." And although the piece from Auschwitz was not a part of the record that was submitted, it was his best—and that is why it is included here.

III. DEMOCRACY'S WATCHDOGS: INVESTIGATIVE REPORTERS

Bob Woodward and Carl Bernstein of the Washington Post are enshrined in American journalism as investigative reporters because they were fortunate enough to break the Watergate scandal.

Few others in that most critical and difficult area of American journalism have been as well rewarded for their work—or as lucky.

Don Bolles, one of the best of the breed, was the victim of a bomb planted in his car on June 2, 1976, while he was investigating crime and graft in Arizona. He died 11 days later.

But with his dying breath he implicated John Harvey Adamson, a small-time racketeer whom he had gone to meet at a parking lot in downtown Phoenix before he was fatally injured. Adamson, after pleading guilty, caused the arrest of two others in a gangland plot on Bolles's life. They in turn were convicted, but in 1980 these convictions were reversed on appeal.

J. Edward Murray, Bolles's former managing editor at the *Arizona Republic* and now publisher of the *Boulder* (Colo.) *Daily Camera*, had this to say about him:

"In 14 years of trying, Don Bolles was not able to make a sufficient dent on the Arizona criminal scene to prevent his own murder.

"For the most part, he fought too single-handedly, unable to attract the necessary support from either public officials or private citizens to make any substantial headway. Increasingly, the state became known as a place where crime paid.

"In the face of these impossible odds, Don Bolles, during his last months as a reporter, tried to curb his own investigative idealism. But he couldn't. So he was blown up—a martyr. . . ." [1]

There was an unexpected reaction to the Bolles murder among investigative reporters themselves. With the cooperation of a number of newspapers, a team of investigative reporters and editors came to Arizona to finish the job for which Bolles had given his life. The result was a 23-part series: "Legacy of a Murder: The Arizona Story," in which the links of crime to officialdom were exhaustively explored.

It was the beginning of a determined assault on organized crime in the state, in which all law enforcement agencies participated, and for which the *Arizona Republic* continued to enlist its services. If Bolles never won a Pultizer Prize, he nevertheless inspired some of those who came to avenge him and received the accolade for achievement.

In the earlier years of this century, the investigative reporter— with few exceptions—was mainly an undercover man working in the field of crime or against municipal graft and corruption. Today there are so many men and women in the field, and they are active in so many different areas, that one of the most ancient truisms in journalism has taken on new meaning: "Every reporter is an investigative reporter."

There is a cum laude graduate of Harvard at the *Boston Globe*, Timothy Leland, a small and inoffensive-looking fellow who seems for all the world like a mild and prosperous suburban householder. And yet, when Timmy Leland came back to his paper from a year in London in 1970, he was so full of enthusiasm for the *London Sunday Times*'s Insight Investigative Team that he persuaded the *Globe* to let him form its own Spotlight Team of investigators. And in the following year, he and his teammates, Gerald O'Neill, Stephen Kurkjian, and Ann DeSantis, broke a corruption scandal in Somerville, Mass., that won them the Pulitzer Prize for investigative reporting in 1972. Kurkjian and four teammates also won the 1980 Pulitzer investigative reporting award for their inquiry into the Boston transit system.

[1] J. Edward Murray, "The Real Villains in the Don Bolles Case," *ASNE Bulletin* (March 1977), p. 13.

There is still another fine investigative team—Donald L. Barlett and James B. Steele of the *Philadelphia Inquirer*—that has had enormous success in pursuing specialized inquiries through the sifting of thousands of official records and computer analyses. They won a Pulitzer Prize for National Reporting in 1975 for their series, "Auditing the Internal Revenue Service," which exposed the unequal application of federal tax laws. In their own quiet and unassuming way, they have also exposed the ills of the courts, the shortcomings of foreign aid, and the ugly side of politics in their city and state.

Nor is crime reporting confined today to the old-time police reporters, who were so active in the field earlier in the century. Two rather quiet and studious financial reporters for the *Wall Street Journal*, Monroe Karmin and Stanley Penn, won a Pulitzer Prize in National Reporting in 1967 for disclosing how American criminal interests had become involved in gambling in the Bahamas.

Out of the hundreds of instances of investigative reporting in the annals of the Pulitzer Prizes, the following illustrate the extent of the work today and the kinds of reporters who do it.

They include reporters and editors who work for large papers and small ones, youngsters and veterans, people from widely separated sections of the land and cases that would scarcely have created a ripple of interest among reporters 50 to 60 years ago. By their efforts, these are the investigators who—with so many others—have earned their right to be called the "Watchdogs of Democracy."

11. A NEW YORK NEWS REPORTER UNCOVERS

A $1 MILLION MEDICAID FRAUD

William Sherman, Posing as a Medical Recipient, Finds
Widespread Abuses Among Doctors in New York City

There was once a doctor in New York City who said he had treated 300 patients in a single day. Even if he had put in a 16-hour working day, and only heroic physicians do, that would have meant almost 19 patients in an hour—about one every three minutes.

There were also some psychiatrists who billed New York City for more hours than there are in a day. And a dentist who rolled up $800,000 in bills against the city over a two-year period.

These and other palpable frauds were uncovered by William Sherman, a 27-year-old reporter for the *New York Daily News*, when he posed as a down-and-out Medicaid recipeint who needed treatment for a cold.

To its credit the city's Health Department supported his inquiry, gave him a Medicaid card, and monitored the prescriptions he was given and the places where he went with a photographer (posing as a friend) to seek treatment.

Sherman is a native New Yorker, born in the city on Dec. 9, 1946, and educated at the Bronx High School of Science, Bard College (A.B.) and Boston University, from which he received his M.S.

Here is the way his Medicaid series began:

A COLD? TAKE 3 DOCTORS EVERY HOUR

By William Sherman

From the New York Daily News, Jan. 23, 1973

Disguised as a welfare client complaining of a cold, a reporter with a medicaid card wandered into a group medical office in Ozone Park, Queens, one day last week and asked to see a doctor.

The patient was first sent to a foot doctor, then twice to an internist with instructions to come back a third time, and then to a psychiatrist who arranged for weekly visits. On his second visit, the patient was given an electrocardiogram, three blood tests, two urine tests, and an X-ray.

He was handed six prescriptions in one day and doctors directed him to a pharmacy on the second floor of the center to have them filled. He walked out that day with a mixture of foot powders, a mild foot cream, a vial of sleeping pills, a bottle of powerful tranquilizers, penicillin tablets and a bottle of cough medicine—all in response to his initial complaint of a cold—a feigned cold, at that.

The visit to the medical offices in Queens was part of an intensive investigation by the *News* into medicaid and its abuses. The inquiry was conducted with the close cooperation of the city's Human Resources Administration and of the Department of Health, which monitored the probe every step of the way.

These agencies agreed to issue the temporary medical card to the reporter, who was in sound health when he visited several group practices in Manhattan, the Bronx, and Queens. The Health Department then audited his treatment at the various centers and analyzed the drugs he received during the investigation.

Accompanied by a *News* photographer, who posed as the patient's cousin, the reporter strolled into the Park Community Medical Building at 131-12 Rockaway Blvd., where he joined 25 other patients nervously waiting to receive medical care. At that moment the reporter was, in effect if not in fact, just another ailing welfare client with a cold. He tried to act and talk like those around him.

At the reception area, a women in white Xeroxed his medicaid card several times and asked, "Your first name, please, your date of birth and do you have a phone?"

She entered the information on a medicaid invoice, which would follow the patient, along with additional bills, throughout the center. Then she asked, "Why are you here?"

"I have a cold, I think, and I'd like to see a doctor."

"Well, the medical doctor is busy right now; first you should see the podiatrist to have your feet checked. He's not busy."

"Why? I just have a cold."

"You should have your feet checked."

"Okay," said the patient, and with his "cousin" in tow he was ushered into the office of podiatrist S. David Geller, a mild-looking man who directed the cold victim to lie down on a couch and "relax."

Socks and shoes were removed and the podiatrist squeezed both feet, looked up and asked, "Ever have any trouble with these feet?"

"Nope. I have this cold. How come I'm seeing a foot doctor?"

"Well, here we examine everybody from the ground up and we're starting with your feet. We'll get to the rest of you later."

A light rash on the patient's left foot was noted and Geller asked, "How long have you had that?"

"A couple of days," said the patient.

"I'll write you out some prescriptions; you get them filled upstairs. Rub the cream on and it will be all better."

"Why should I get them filled upstairs? I have a drugstore in my neighborhood."

"The pharmacist here knows what the doctors write for and they stock accordingly," said the foot specialist.

Medicaid regulations specifically require that doctors give patients complete freedom of choice in choosing a pharmacy to fill prescriptions.

Geller wrote out the prescriptions for a combination of foot powders and the cream and told the patient his rash was a fungus growth. (A Health Department podiatrist said later that for such a reading a culture should have been taken. This was not done.)

The Park Community podiatrist completed his examination in five minutes, reminded the patient "not to worry" and beckoned for the receptionist. She promptly whisked the patient into another office, this time a 4-by-8-foot examination room manned by an internist. . . .

There was a lot more of this. The internist gave him a shot of penicillin for what was diagnosed as "London flu," a psychiatrist asked him if he had a girlfriend, and a pharmacist loaded him up with a variety of prescribed drugs.

Sherman was given a lot of this kind of "treatment" as his investigation continued. All his bills were forwarded to the Health Department to be checked and then the *News* paid them.

But afterward, prosecutions began and the city opened suit for restitution against those who had defrauded the city. In all, his 14-article exposé resulted in the repayment to the city of more than $1 million in excessive charges for Medicaid cases.

A Pulitzer Prize jury, reviewing more than 100 exhibits of local investigative reporting, called Sherman's investigation "a remarkable example of individual initiative" and praised his writing and his resourcefulness. He was awarded the Pulitzer Prize for Special Local Reporting for 1974.

12. THE RENO NEWSPAPERS ATTACK
A BROTHEL KEEPER IN NEVADA

Three Editorial Writers Combine Forces to Contain
a Clandestine Political Force in the City

A letter came to the Pulitzer Prize Office at Columbia University early in 1977 that read like something out of the free-wheeling, damn-your-eyes journalism of the Old West.

It was written by Warren Lerude, executive editor of the *Reno Evening Gazette* and *Nevada State Journal*, and this was how it began:

"Joe Conforte runs what may be the most celebrated whorehouse in the United States. (His operation has been written up in everything from *Rolling Stone* to the *Los Angeles Times*.) Through a curious set of circumstances, he managed to become a power in the communities of Reno and its next-door neighbor, Sparks. His influence reached into the county government and the state as well. . . ."

Lerude didn't like what Conforte stood for, nor did he appreciate the brothel-keeper's developing influence. But the man had violated no law, so far as anybody knew, and in Nevada anybody can run a brothel outside Reno and Las Vegas, where it has been declared illegal.

However, Conforte's place of business was across the county line in Reno and he was quite comfortable. After all, prostitution hadn't been a crime in the Old West, where men were men and there were very few women around. And nobody was about to challenge Conforte's right to run a whorehouse as long as he paid his taxes and complied with the prevailing health rules.

What upset Lerude was Conforte's growing influence in Nevada and local politics. For he was a colorful character, flashing a roll of bills now and then just to prove he had money, and contributing generously to various charities and causes—and eventually supporting various political movements and people.

And so, as Lerude put it, "The Reno newspapers began to stand against Conforte, exposing him for what he was coming to be, a clandestine political force whose money was spread widely among public officials.

"During this last year, our editorials have pressed the point, unpopular though it proved to be in many quarters, that the community must accept the responsibility for creating the Conforte condition and now clean it up."

There is no law on the statute books or any canon of journalism that makes reporters alone responsible for investigative reporting. On the contrary, in the days of such fighting journalists as Greeley, Dana, and Pulitzer, the editorial page banged the drums and clashed the cymbals for righteousness and the news columns murmured an obbligato. And that was the way it turned out in Reno.

Lerude and two of his editorial writers, Foster Church, editorial page editor of the *Nevada State Journal*, and Norman Cardoza, editorial page editor of the *Reno Evening Gazette*, combined forces to take on Conforte.

While the situation turned ugly at times, and threats were made against the newspapers and the three crusaders, it really turned out to be no contest. Here, in a major editorial written by Lerude, is why:

THE WHOREHOUSE PROBLEM IN NEVADA

By Warren LeRude

From the Reno Evening Gazette and Nevada State Journal, May 25, 1976

For decades, Reno was known as the divorce capital of the world.

That's a reputation the citizenry at large, businessmen in particular, and appreciators of the Truckee Meadows as a good place to live, have tried to live down.

In recent times, divorce has gotten to be legally acceptable in many other states and Reno has matured as a pleasant family tourism center and sprouting business environment, through the likes of warehousing, light manufacturing.

Now, however, Reno faces a new reputation problem, created by the frequently national and sometimes international brothel promotion of Joe Conforte, coupled with the links some public officials have with him.

At the same time the community is trying to attract tourism and business by showing Reno to be a city of good values, Reno is becoming known as a whorehouse town, the kind of city that thinks it's great to have Joe's place called home.

Not long ago a foreign film crew was in Reno. Were they excited about filming the beauty of Lake Tahoe, the cosmopolitan and free lifestyles of Reno, the excitement of the state's legal gambling?

What really excited this film crew from Japan was Joe Conforte's whorehouse. That's what they wished to film for the multitudes of tourists back in Japan who one day might visit Reno—the whorehouse town.

Over the weekend, a tragic shooting occurred at Mustang. A world-famous boxer lay dead in a pool of blood a few feet from the fortresslike structure and its big fence and guarded towers.

Around the world the story sped on high-speed news teletypes. It's news when a world-famous person dies in gunfire. And it's news where that takes place—the whorehouse, the one Joe Conforte runs, the one so many people around Reno have tolerated for so long as "just another business."

"Just another business?" Conforte? He who Washoe County sheriff's deputies say called them "dogs" and who was quoted by lawmen as pointing to the dead boxer's corpse and saying, "It's just a dead man . . . so what?"

If Reno wishes to continue to build the reputation it is getting as being home base for Joe Conforte and his brothel, a reputation the city deserves when some of its highest officials connect themselves with Conforte, the present course of action will continue.

Reno charities, organizations, politicians, businesses will continue to cater to Conforte.

But if Reno is to move forward now into a constructive and wholesome tourism future, it should cast aside the relationships with Joe Conforte.

As this newspaper has stated before, if Conforte wishes to run a whorehouse, let him do it just as others do it in Nevada—without all the fanfare that is beginning to stigmatize Reno. The madams of the brothels are not the most widely known citizens of Elko, Winnemucca, and Ely. It's about time Reno put Joe Conforte's ambitions in the same Nevada perspective.

It is time he got the message from a city too silent so far that Reno does not want him to ride in its parades, finance its bus lines, influence its politicians, be front-row-center as the gamblers celebrate him with the best showroom tables.

As before, the question is: Who has guts enough in this city to declare Conforte persona non grata?

Harrah's?

Harold's?

John Ascuaga and his Sparks Nugget?

Charlie Mapes?

Public officials who don't have connections with Conforte?

The YMCA?

The Reno Rotary Club?

The United Way?

Service clubs?

The YWCA?

The Reno Service League?

St. Mary's Guild?

Any clergy person who might feel it inappropriate for his or her city to be known as a whorehouse town?

The Greater Reno Chamber of Commerce board of directors—by

name—has had the courage to stand against Conforte's arrogance. The chamber was backed up by the Washoe County Grand Jury, which was critical of Conforte's power.

Who, now, cares enough about Reno to stand with these business men and women?

The means are simple—a resolution declaring that Conforte's influence in local government is bad for this city. Get the resolution to this newspaper. We will report the news.

The word will begin to get around the country, just as has Conforte's promotion of prostitution, just as has the bad name public officials have brought the city because of relations with Conforte.

And maybe Reno can start living down the whorehouse reputation our silent citizens have allowed Conforte to build.

Conforte had to pipe down, for public sentiment clearly turned against him after a year of this kind of vigorous protest. His rising power as a political force was curbed, his influence vastly reduced.

While he continued his business, he kept a low profile. "To use a Nevada mining camp term," Lerude said at the climax of the papers' campaign, "Conforte has broken his pick as a power in political life."

The Pulitzer Editorial Writing Jury, which included two appreciative Texans, wrote of the three-man Nevada task force, "They waded into a tough issue, named names, didn't stop, and were effective."

For those reasons, Lerude, Church, and Cardoza were jointly awarded the Pulitzer Prize in Editorial Writing for 1977.

13. THE ANCHORAGE NEWS EXAMINES
A UNION'S RISING POWER IN ALASKA

Local 959 of the Teamsters' Union Is Shown to Be Creating
An Empire With Major Political and Economic Interests

Katherine Woodruff Fanning went to Alaska in the mid-1960s and, with her husband, Lawrence S. Fanning, took over a struggling little paper, the *Anchorage Daily News*.

Mrs. Fanning had been a fixture in Chicago's social life, having been born there as a member of a prominent family and having been the former wife of Marshall Field, Jr. But Alaska was a new land to her and running a newspaper was not something for which she had been trained at Smith College, where she received her A.B. in 1949.

Fortunately, her husband had been a life-long newspaperman and the executive editor of the *Chicago Daily News*, so the new publishing venture got off to a fair, if somewhat wobbly, start in 1965. But after less than seven years, he died and Katherine Fanning found herself the editor and publisher of the *Anchorage News* in 1972.

It was not easy for her. The way the newspaper finally was kept alive was through a joint operating agreement with the larger and more powerful *Anchorage Times* which, with a circulation of about 50,000 and most of the advertising in town, ran the advertising, circulation, accounting, and mechanical departments for both papers. The *News*, with a total news staff of only 21 persons and a circulation of 16,500, ran its own news and editorial operation.

Under these circumstances, a less determined and venturesome publisher would have played it safe and hoped for the best—which inevitably would have ended in disaster. Instead, Mrs. Fanning looked for a challenge—and very quickly found it. But it was a lot larger and much more dangerous than she had expected.

For in 1975, the great pipeline boom had hit Alaska and had a terrific impact on the state's economy. Vast new influences were being shaped that would play a decisive part in the future of this last American frontier—and one of the most prominent was Alaska Teamsters Union Local 959.

Everybody knew the basic story—how in 15 years the Teamsters had grown from 1,500 to 23,000 members, how it had put together a $100 million pension fund that was heavily invested in the state, how it now owned an enormous amount of property and was accumulating still more.

But there was a lot more that was discussed mainly in whispers or behind closed doors. And in consequence, rumors were circulating about what the Teamsters were doing to exercise their influence in Alaska.

Mrs. Fanning knew that she was taking a risk. But when her editorial people proposed to go into the Teamsters' story, she approved the project without hesitation. And two reporters were detached from the staff for three months of full-time work, together with a third reporter who was on the investigation part-time.

A large newspaper from the "lower 48" meanwhile had taken on the same inuqiry and came up with a series of articles based on what was termed an Alaskan crime wave and a conclusion that the Teamsters were interfering with Alaska's development. However, the *News*'s conclusions were not that sensational. The local investigation uncovered no organized crime network that was cooperating with the Teamsters, and no evidence of rumors of organized theft from the pipeline project.

What the *News* team did was put together, in laborious detail, a chart of the union's personnel and its massive financial interests plus examples of the use of Teamster power for personal gain and of the recruiting of key former public officials who landed on the Teamster payroll. The use of the Teamster Trust Fund was painstakingly examined and the employment of a number of ex-convicts at the Teamster pipeline warehouse was documented.

The *News*'s reporters traveled more than 3,000 miles in Alaska to do their work, interviewed more than 100 persons, listed and cross-indexed more than 250 corporations and 300 individual incorporators in an effort to trace Teamster connections, examined 900 deeds, mortgages and land records and 300 election campaign contribution reports. It was, altogether, an inquiry that would have done credit to the staff of a major paper.

This was the salient part of the first article:

A TEAMSTER EMPIRE IN ALASKA

By Howard Weaver and Bob Porterfield

From the Anchorage Daily News, Dec. 4, 1975

Teamster Union Local 959 is fashioning an empire in Alaska, stretching across an ever-widening slice of life from the infant oil frontier to the heart of the state's major city.

Secure under the unquestioned leadership of Secretary-Treasurer Jesse L. Carr, the empire has evolved in just 18 years into a complex maze of political, economic, and social power which towers over the rest of Alaska's labor movement—and challenges at times both mighty industry and state government itself.

In recent weeks the union has come under increasing observation in Alaska and Outside, but basic, key questions have been left unanswered. How has the union amassed its power? Where does its structure reach? Who are its primary architects? What lies ahead?

To answer these and other questions, the *Daily News* made a lengthy study of the empire. These are the basic facts.

Local 959 has amassed its power in a number of ways:

—With 23,000 registered members, the union is by far the most influential and successful special interest group in the state.

—No other group, including the Republican Party which elected the governor, even approaches the concentration of power which Teamsters have vested in Carr, the secretary-treasurer and moving force of the union.

—By means of a pension fund rapidly approaching the $100 million level and an investment policy which gives it considerable influence over the state's major financial institutions, 959 represents the most potent financial force of any Alaska-directed organization. Measured in terms of Alaska interest, this appears true even in comparison with the oil giants and emerging native corporations now operating in the state.

—Despite an occasional upset, no other group has displayed such consistent political power here as the Alaska Teamsters. Spanning as it does both party and ideological boundaries, the union outstrips either political party in this respect.

The web of Teamster power stretches across the face and beneath the surface of Alaska society, manifesting itself in a wide variety of forms. Local 959 and its related enterprises own property in Juneau, Anchorage, Fairbanks, Valdez, and Palmer. It is developing multimillion-dollar headquarters, office, commercial, and recreational facilities here and in Fairbanks, and plans development in other areas when justified by the rapidly growing membership.

The union has also invested more than $80 million drawn from four trust funds to which employers contribute money.

By channeling that money through the National Bank of Alaska (NBA)—where Carr sits on the board of directors—and investing it almost entirely in Alaska, the union has achieved considerable influence in the Alaska financial community and has become one of the area's biggest landlords.

In past years the investments were divided between mortgages, real estate bonds, and the stock market, but lately have been solely directed toward Alaska housing and development.

The trans-Alaska pipeline, disputed though its ultimate impact on Alaska may be, has unquestionably been good to Local 959. The swelling employment rolls and spiraling salaries generated by construction of the oil line have pushed the fortunes of the union to all-time highs—and likely will have an impact greater than their dollars.

Since many of the union workers employed on the pipeline project—some 8,000 to 9.000—are unlikely to remain in Alaska long enough to collect from retirement funds taken in on their behalf, the pipeline dollars are a double bonanza for the union.

Not only do the pipeline funds mount up quickly. Since some of the workers will never claim their retirement, a lot of that money will stay put. In addition, the union and its building corporation have direct property holdings—some $33 million in planned assets at last count.

That total includes more than $25 million for the planned mall-hospital-professional office complex which will sit on a controversial state land lease at Airport Heights Road and 15th Avenue. Now under challenge from the state—which has declared the contract invalid—the lease first was called to question in November 1974, when the *Daily News* reported the contract had been negotiated with former state officials to allow the union to pay less than $350 monthly to lease the 20 acres of public land.

Also in the Teamster portfolio is a 44.14-acre site in Fairbanks—now valued at about $3 million—on which the union is constructing another massive office-headquarters complex. Advance publicity has put the eventual price tag there at $6.5 million.

The former Anchorage union hall, located at 1833 E. Fifth Avenue, pales in comparison but is itself assessed at about $661,350. The empire also owns a lot and building at Valdez worth $154,000; the 14.2-acre site of a planned recreational complex near the intersection of Boniface Parkway and Tudor Road valued at $355,000; a large lot near Lake Otis Parkway and DeBarr Road pegged at $354,600; three downtown Fairbanks lots worth about $317,525; and a lot and building at 306 Willoughby Avenue in Juneau valued at $35,100.

The Medical Dental Building Corporation, associated with the union through investments with Anchorage Community Hospital, controls another $1.5 million in property.

Teamsters also have access to their own credit union, a federally chartered institution which began in 1964. Now managed by Emmitt Wilson, who served a commissioner of commerce under

Governor William A. Egan, the facility automatically enrolls Teamsters through a seven-cents-per-hour payroll deduction plan and claims more than $2 million in assets. More than 8,000 members earn seven per cent interest on deposits with the Alaska Teamsters Federal Credit Union, which has in its 11-year history handled more than $10 million in loans.

The union also commands three leased aircraft and employs two pilots to fly the sleek Lear jet and two Merlin turbo-props. The aircraft are on standby as emergency medical evacuation ambulances for Teamsters, a chore they handle on the average of seven times monthly, but are also used to ferry Carr and others to meetings in Alaska and Outside.

Local 959 has built its empire on a number of foundations, but the most important clearly is its ability to win hefty contracts from employers in Alaska.

Representing nearly 80 crafts and trades ranging from surveyors to long distance telephone operators, the impact of Teamster-won wages and fringe benefits spreads pervasively throughout the state. The fact that Teamsters earn such hefty incomes and have services from medical care to recreation, some employers say, means that Alaskans must pay more to live in the 49th state.

The Pulitzer Public Service Jury called the series "a remarkable performance by a small but vigorous newspaper." And it won the Pulitzer Prize Gold Medal for Public Service in 1976.

When the news was telephoned to Mrs. Fanning's office, she and her little staff were overwhelmed. All of a sudden every phone in the place began ringing and bottles of champagne appeared as if by magic. For the rest of that day, the newsroom was thronged with well-wishers and even the next day the paper was put out with difficulty.

Very soon the euphoria vanished, for the *News*, to use Mrs. Fanning's own analysis, "hit the financial doldrums." On Page 1, she ran a candid announcement that without major financial support from the community, the paper would have to close.

She cut her little staff nearly in half, to a total of 14 editorial employees, and only 5 of them remained as reporters. For more than two years, a committee of volunteers actively solicited subscriptions and advertising to keep the *News* afloat.

"In my view," Mrs. Fanning wrote afterward, "it was the awarding of the Pulitzer Prize more than any other single factor that kept the *Daily*

News alive. Because of the publicity received from the Pulitzer and the national reputation that resulted, a number of individuals in the Midwest and on the East coast came forward with over a half million dollars of low interest loans simply to keep the newspaper going."

But better times were coming. A long antitrust lawsuit by the *News* against the *Anchorage Times*, charging monopoly and a breach of contract, was settled out of court in 1978 with the *Times*'s payment to the *News* of $750,000 and other benefits. However, the joint operating agreement ended and the paper was thrown entirely on its own resources.

Here again its reputation as an effective, crusading newspaper helped to save it, for in 1979 the McClatchy Newspapers of California bought an 80 percent interest in the *News*. Mrs. Fanning and her family retained 20 percent and she remained as editor, publisher, and chief operating officer.

Today the *News* is in a million-dollar building with a computer type-setting system and a 7-unit Goss press, and a staff of 110 people. The size of the paper itself has been doubled, with more news services, features, and columns. And best of all the circulation, which had fallen to a calamitous 12,500, has surged past 30,000 and is still building.

As for the Teamsters Union, it remains powerful but—like so many other organizations in Alaska—it is in a period of transition. To newcomers, it does not present the facade of an awesome force any longer. Jesse Carr's influence has diminished and a grand jury has looked over some of the union's records.

The Pulitzer gold medal is still Mrs. Fanning's cherished possession, a symbol of all that has happened to her since she began her Alaskan venture. "For the first time," she writes, "the *Daily News* has a very good chance to become financially successful and possibly even the dominant newspaper in Alaska."[1]

14. TWO PHILADELPHIA REPORTERS ASSAIL MISTREATMENT OF THE MENTALLY ILL

Acel Moore and Wendell Rawls, Jr., of the Inquirer Expose a Pattern of Crime and Neglect at Farview Hospital

A patient at Farview State Hospital in Pennsylvania got into a fistfight at the institution in 1938 and spent the next 32 years there without a chance of being released.

[1] Letters from Katherine Fanning dated Aug. 9, 1979, and March 25, 1980; *Newsweek*, March 31, 1980, p. 72.

Another patient punched a guard and for seven years was kept naked in a small cell.

For the pleasure of some of the guards at the hospital, patients had to take part in bloody human "cockfights."

These were some of the horrors that a former inmate at Farview related to Acel Moore and Wendell Rawls, Jr., of the *Philadelphia Inquirer* toward the outset of their investigation of the institution.

Moore, who was 36 and Philadelphia-born, had then been on the paper for nine years as a reporter and was a founding member and president of the Black Journalists of Philadelphia.

Rawls, who was 35, born in Tennessee and a graduate of Vanderbilt, had worked on the *Nashville Tennessean* and had been an *Inquirer* reporter for four years.

Their inquiry in the spring of 1976 took three months and uncovered appalling abuses at the overcrowded, unsanitary institution. This was the substance of the first article of their series:

TERROR AT FARVIEW HOSPITAL

By Acel Moore and Wendell Rawls, Jr.

From the Philadelphia Inquirer, June 27, 1976

WAYMART, Pa.—Farview State Hospital, in the rolling wooded countryside north of the Poconos, looks almost like what it was once intended to be—a benign circle of three-story brick buildings where the mentally ill who have committed crimes are treated and, if possible, cured.

A passerby, driving through this anthracite region, could almost mistake it for a small college or a resort hotel or a monastery.

It is none of those things. Over and over, those who have been patients at Farview and who have been lucky enough to get out describe it as a living hell on earth.

And there is a wealth of evidence from others—guards, administrators, scholars, and even government investigators whose findings have been suppressed—that the description is chillingly accurate.

A three-month investigation by the *Inquirer* has revealed that:

Farview State Hospital is a place where men have died during or after beatings by guards and by patients egged on by guards.

It is a place where men who have died in this way have been certified as victims of heart attacks.

It is a place where men have been pummeled bloody and sense-less—for sport.

It is a place where an unwritten code requires all the guards present to hit a patient if one guard hits him.

It is a place where patients have been forced to commit sodomy with guards and other patients.

It is a place where men have been forced to live naked for years on end, sometimes handcuffed on icy floors.

It is a place where guards have sponsored patients in human cockfights and bet on the outcome.

It is a place where there is virtually no treatment aside from the use of mood-altering drugs, some of which other institutions abandoned a decade ago.

It is a psychiatric hospital without a board-certified psychiatrist.

It is a place where a man under a 30-day sentence for disorderly conduct can wait 30 years for his freedom.

It is a place where decades—26 years in one case—can elapse between the time a patient is admitted and the time he gets a psychiatric evaluation.

It is a place where men have been denied such basic amenities as toilet paper.

It is a place where staff members and patients alike must live in a system based on hustles, extortion, and theft.

These are some of the findings of the *Inquirer*'s investigation—an investigation prompted by the complaint of an embittered former patient and based on scores of interviews and on the study of numerous documents previously not made public. Those interviewed include present and former guards, administrators and state officials, as well as patients who have been freed or transferred to prison.

The main findings—homicide, coverup, neglect, corruption, brutality, sodomy—form a pattern that spans the last three decades and possibly longer.

The current administration at Farview, interviewed last week, says it is trying and succeeding in stamping out many past abuses.

But the pattern of crime and neglect at Farview has easily survived all past attempts at reform, and two high-level staff members interviewed in recent days say that any new attempts at reform have yet to penetrate the guard structure that runs the hospital.

State law enforcement authorities have long known about the abuses at Farview. Their files include strong evidence of crimes, including murder, and yet nothing has been done.

The files also include admissions from investigators that their work was superficial in crucial ways.

In November 1974, State Attorney General Israel Packel ordered an investigation of "alleged threats, beatings, illegal contraband, and deaths at the institution" at the request of Helene Wohlgemuth, then secretary of the Department of Public Welfare. Most of the investigating was done by the Bureau of Investigations, but the State Police also conducted inquiries about deaths at Farview.

By the time the results came in, Packel was no longer attorney general. On April 16, 1975, his successor, Robert P. Kane, wrote his conclusions in the matter to Frank S. Beal, then secretary of Public Welfare. He said, ". . . There have been a multitude of occasions where staff has used force against patients," but he concluded that such force had not been "excessive or unlawful."

"There is no evidence supporting allegations of criminal violations at the hospital," Kane said, but he did conclude that "there are serious problems caused by patients' possession of money and other contraband . . . and there has been a lack of administrative resolution of these problems. . . ."

How was that conclusion reached?

By listening to guards and ignoring patients, according to an accompanying letter by Cecil H. Yates, director of the Bureau of Investigations.

Yates cited two predicaments that he said made his department's investigation superficial. One problem, he went on, was that the credibility of patients certified as both criminal and insane "must be viewed as questionable."

However, Robert Hammel, current acting superintendent at Farview, says that fully 30 percent of the 453 patients at the hospital have never been convicted of a crime. And the records at Farview are filled with accounts of patients who were admitted, not because they were insane, but because they were trouble-

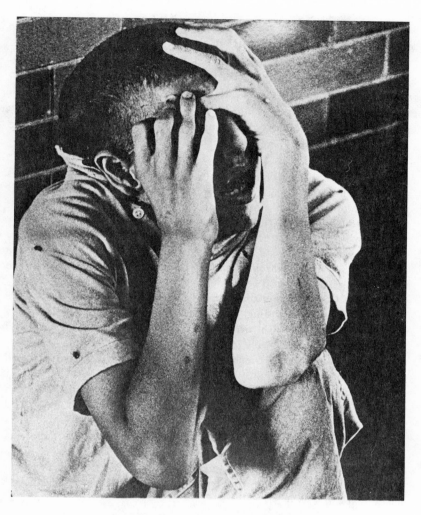

CHILDREN IN PURGATORY
Pulitzer Prize for Feature Photography, 1971

FROM THE PORTFOLIO OF JACK DYKINGA, ILLUSTRATING OVERCROWDING
AND OTHER DEPLORABLE CONDITIONS AFFECTING RETARDED CHILDREN IN
ILLINOIS STATE INSTITUTIONS, PUBLISHED IN THE CHICAGO SUN-TIMES

makers elsewhere or, in some instances, because a court somewhere simply made a bureaucratic error.

Yates also noted that his investigators had perused the medical
records of guards injured by patients but not those of patients who
claimed to have been injured by guards. To do the latter, he said,
would be "legally questionable." Thus it was, he said, that "no
attempt was made . . . to thoroughly analyze the problem" or to
recommend corrective action.

As a result of the *Inquirer*'s investigation, every patient at Farview was
given a psychiatric test and 58 were transferred. Eventually, at the recommendation of state investigators, half the remaining patients were shifted
to five medium security state hospitals elsewhere.

Farview's highest ranking physician resigned.

A statewide bill of rights for mental patients was adopted. Whenever a
patient died at Farview from then on, the coroner's office was notified so
that an investigation could be conducted if necessary.

A Wayne County grand jury, after sitting for 19 months, indicted 36
persons in 20 cases, including four murders that were alleged to have been
committed at Farview. But even when overwhelming proof was provided
in some cases, Farview trial juries refused to convict people who were
neighbors in some cases, friends in others, except for one former guard
who was convicted of assault.

As one juror put it, "Why put somebody in jail for doing something to a
crazy?" And another said, "I have to live here. If I'd said guilty, I'd
probably be dead the next day."

Moore and Rawls shared the Pulitzer Prize for Special Local Reporting
in 1977. Their work was a part of the *Inquirer*'s impressive record of six
straight Pulitzer Prizes annually since 1975, climaxed by a staff award in
1980 in General Local Reporting for the paper's coverage of the nuclear
accident at Three Mile Island.

IV. A CRUSADE TO SAVE
OUR NATIONAL HERITAGE

During the last months of a brittle peace in America, just before the nation was plunged into World War II, the *St. Louis Post-Dispatch* won a public service gold medal for its successful campaign against the city's "smoke nuisance."

It was the first time in a quarter century of Pulitzer Prizes that the struggle to preserve our environment had been recognized as news worthy of special distinction. Even so, the "smoke nuisance" as described in that 1941 citation showed how little the nature of air pollution and its dangers were then understood.

Moreover, the prize itself was greeted with magnificent indifference on the part of the public and an outraged cry from critics that it had been bestowed on the *Post-Dispatch* merely because it was "Pulitzer's paper."

It was another two decades before the pollution of air and water and the desecration of the earth itself were recognized by journalists in general as matters of vital concern to the public—and not just a "nuisance." For as late as the 1960s, many a reporter in the nation's city rooms didn't have the faintest idea of what was meant by plant and animal ecology. I remember one otherwise well-informed journalist who thought "ecology" was some kind of misprint.

The truth is that the public was far ahead of the press, with few exceptions, in recognizing that the quality of life in this country—and, indeed, on this planet—was endangered by the carelessness of factories in disposing of their waste, the continual pumping of noxious gases from millions of automobile exhaust pipes into the atmosphere, and the dumping of many millions of tons of human excrement into rivers, lakes, and oceans.

Many in the press, in fact, were inclined to accept the argument of industry that the black smoke from factory chimneys and the rape of the earth through surface coal mining (strip mining) were necessary to maintain full employment and efficient production. But with the development of such problems as the disposal of atomic waste from the nation's nuclear plants, even the most permissive editors realized that there was a limit to public tolerance of pollution.

By that time, the demonstrators against waste and pollution had taken to the highways, the waters, and the brown and mottled countryside to shake complacency out of the indolent and make a major political issue out of the environment.

The press has long since made up for lost opportunities. Beginning in the mid-1960s, pollution became a national story and most of the newspapers that aspired to national and regional prominence recognized it.

The Pulitzer Prizes have since become a barometer for achievements in the field. In place of the single award for one newspaper that was concerned over the environment between 1917 and 1958, a respectable number of prizes were given in the 20 years between 1959 and 1980 for distinguished efforts in public service, local and national reporting, editorial writing, and commentary. These are some of the outstanding examples of environmental journalism:

15. THE LOUISVILLE COURIER-JOURNAL
COMBATS KENTUCKY STRIP MINING

The Newspaper Forces the Enactment of Strict Laws
to Save the Beauty of the State's Hill Country

There is an explosive charge of human indignation stored up somewhere inside Norman E. Isaacs' small and wiry frame.

Early in the 1960s, while he was the executive editor of the *Louisville Times and Courier-Journal*, the desecration of Kentucky's beautiful hill country by strip miners set him off on a major campaign.

DEATH ON A FIRE ESCAPE
Pulitzer Prize for News Photography, 1976

FROM STANLEY FORMAN'S PORTFOLIO FROM THE BOSTON HERALD
AMERICAN, SHOWING A 19-YEAR-OLD GIRL FALLING FROM A COLLAPSED
FIRE ESCAPE WITH A THREE-YEAR-OLD CHILD. THE GIRL, A BABY SITTER,
DIED; THE CHILD SURVIVED

With the support of Barry Bingham, Sr., then the publisher of the newspapers, Isaacs sought nothing more nor less than the strict regulation of the state's powerful coal operators. This was the position, as he put it in an editorial outcry that was addressed to the nation:

"The stinking mess that exists in parts of eastern and western Kentucky is the direct heritage of politically excused commercial plunder. It is the result of strip mining turned loose, of loggers free to overcut the great forests at will, of oil and gas speculators permitted to let the runoffs pollute the watersheds.

"Gone are the natural protections of the mountain towns; each year, water gushing down the slopes of the strip mine spoilbanks tears through these towns with mounting violence. Once all of it was beautiful and unspoiled, the 'great meadow' and the 'happy hunting ground' of Indian lore. Now thousands of acres are taken out of production yearly by the giant mining machines.

"What Kentucky needs is a state law that would prohibit strip and augur mining in the eastern mountains and require open pit miners in the west to restore stripped land so it could be used for farming and timber growing." [1]

This was all very well when it was addressed to fellow-environmentalists who understood what was at stake. But to arouse an apathetic, heedless, and—in some cases—even a hostile public opinion required the most forceful kind of journalistic approach. Therefore, Bingham, Isaacs, and their colleagues decided to put out a special section in the *Courier-Journal*'s Sunday edition, which was beautifully printed in color, as the key to their campaign.

It was published early in 1964. The story under the title, "The Ravaged Land," was spread through the entire section. As illustrations, there were hideously effective pictures in color of the damage that strip mining already had caused in the state. This was how the long crusade began:

THE RAVAGED LAND

From the Louisville Courier-Journal, Jan. 5, 1964

The first visit to a strip mine is a chilling voyage into a grotesque twilight zone that combines Dante's Inferno, the wastelands of the Far West, and a horror movie.

Man shrinks into insignificance alongside giant mining machines, mammoth coal trucks, towering highwalls of broken, jagged rock, and sprawling spoilbanks of lifeless soil.

[1] *Saturday Review* (May 22, 1965).

Chaos is everywhere. In Eastern Kentucky the spoil from strip or augur mining creeps down the mountainsides like cancers. In Western Kentucky it looms in monstrous dunes of mud and rock. The sight is hideous. Streams are poisonous mustard, gray, and copper.

This is the strip miners' legacy. Farms and woodlands have been destroyed in East and West Kentucky. Mountain homes and villages have been flooded with the mud, rock, and debris thrown down the mountain slopes. Strip mine debris, dislodged from its unstable perch on steep hills by rain, freezing and thawing, has oozed and thundered down to cover fertile valleys, to clog rivers and creeks.

A recent U.S. Department of Agriculture study proves that strip mining has caused incredible erosion, destruction of fish life and game cover, the conversion of farmland into swamps, and in many instances a shocking waste of coal reserves. Evidence indicates that stripping contributes to the floods which ravage the state.

Equipped with an ineffective law, the State Department of Conservation wages a hopeless battle. Some operators, doing far more than the law requires, have worked out conscientious reclamation projects, but they are by no means typical.

And strip mining is but one form of the land destruction in Kentucky. The most casual observer could compile a depressing list:

1. In both Eastern and Western Kentucky, coal and clay mining are taking many thousands of acres yearly out of production, polluting and clogging streams with debris and acid, ruining farm, timber, and grazing lands.

2. The beach and water at Cumberland Falls State Park, one of Kentucky's busiest tourist playgrounds, are awash with coal and silt, apparently from strip mines along the Cumberland tributaries.

3. Black Mountain in Harlan County, the state's highest peak (at 4,150 feet) and a mecca for hunters, is being ripped to pieces.

4. The waters of once-sparkling Leatherwood Creek are black and slimy with coal silt.

5. The state stopped an oil well owner from polluting the swimming area at Natural Bridge State Park. In other counties, refuse from gas and oil wells leaves streams unfit for men or cattle to use.

Farmers believe it is also rendering underground water supplies useless.

6. Buckhorn Reservoir (where the state is building a new park) and Lake Cumberland (where it has three) for half the past tourist season were muddied by silt carried down from stripped hillsides.

7. Except for a few tracts, Kentucky's forests, which once provided jobs for thousands and were considered among the world's finest, now grow mangy trees ravaged by fire and disease. Last year, one of the worst on record, forest fires burned 289,000 acres of Kentucky woodland.

8. Kentucky's rivers are still polluted by sewage and clogged by garbage, rotting tires, old cars, and abandoned furniture.

9. Studies made by the Soil Conservation Commission indicate that erosion, which it labeled the No. 1 problem of Kentucky's agriculture, has destroyed more than three-quarters of the topsoil on almost half the farmlands of the state.

10. An entire valley near Kingdom Come State Park is being filled with sludge from a nearby deep mine. Smoldering, stinking slag piles blacken the countryside throughout the coal regions.

State, federal, and interstate agencies are counterattacking some of these evils. Disposal plants and modern water systems are easing the problem of pollution. Kentucky's small watershed program for controlling farm erosion and flooding is regarded as among the nation's best. But other forms of destruction, especially strip and augur mining and improper logging, go almost untouched.

Some violence against nature cannot practically be avoided while strip and augur mining are in progress. But it can be controlled. Once the mining operation is completed, the damage can and should be corrected through sensible reclamation.

After that beginning, the story took up the damage in specific detail with graphic color illustrations. No fair-minded person, putting the special section down, could have doubted that Kentucky was up against a major problem.

From then on, day after day, the *Courier-Journal* ran news articles, editorials, columns, interpretive pieces, cartoons, and pictures to maintain public interest in the issue. There seemed to be very little movement at first, but gradually the conservation of natural resources became a political issue in Kentucky.

Despite pressures that powerful mining interests put on the publisher and his editors to cease and desist, and they were very great, the campaign continued through 1964 and 1965 without let-up. As the state's legislature began to debate methods of regulating the coal industry early in 1966, the *Courier-Journal* published another special section, "Outlook for 1966," which included conservation as a principal issue.

The tough Kentucky Strip-Mine Control Act was approved by the State Senate on Jan. 27, 1966, completing legislative action on the issue, and Governor Edward Breathitt signed it. The governor publicly expressed his gratitude to the *Courier-Journal* and the Bingham family for their leadership. And the *Courier-Journal* commented editorially:

"Generations from now, Kentucky land will be green and lovely instead of scarred and ugly because this act was passed. Hundreds of thousands of acres will yield wealth and recreation and respite from urban living instead of problems and expense. And even those who had opposed these strict controls will soon, we predict, have cause to approve.

"For what is good for the land is good for Kentucky." [2]

Without a dissenting vote, the Pulitzer Prize Board awarded the *Louisville Courier-Journal* one of two gold medals for public service that were given out in 1967.

16. THE MILWAUKEE JOURNAL FIGHTS
WISCONSIN'S WATER POLLUTION

A Series, "Pollution: The Spreading Menace,"
Spurs the Passage of Stronger Laws for Cleaner Water

The *Milwaukee Journal* examined Wisconsin's lakes and rivers in the mid-1960s and was alarmed by its findings.

Pollution had become so great in the northern lakes that ruin was forecast for all of them within 25 years unless drastic action could be taken.

"What happens then to a billion-dollar resort creation industry whose chief assets are swimming and fresh water for fishing?" the *Journal* asked.

The cities were no better off. An old sewage treatment plant in South

[2] *Louisville Courier-Journal* (Jan. 28, 1966).

Milwaukee could handle only 35 percent of decomposable organic matter and the rest flowed directly into Lake Michigan.

Within the central city itself, a rush of water from storms could flush the raw wastes of a quarter of a million people over restraining sections into the Milwaukee River and Lake Michigan through 150 overflow outlets.

One result was that pollution had so damaged Lake Michigan that, to quote Senator Gaylord Nelson of Wisconsin, some scientists warned it could not be reclaimed. And yet, 27 Wisconsin communities were still taking their drinking water from the lake.

If there was any doubt that strong and determined action was necessary, the *Journal*'s survey of Wisconsin settled the matter. In the fall of 1965, its management and its editors determined to use their rotogravure section to try to persuade the state's legislature to tighten what had been thought to be a fairly good water control law.

The *Journal* had been one of the few daily newspapers in America that had recognized the importance of conservation reporting earlier in this century. It claimed to be the first paper in the land to make water conservation and natural resources a full-time reporting assignment.

At any rate, in its campaign against water pollution, the *Journal* was able to take advantage of the background and talent of its resources specialist, Richard C. Kienitz, and a photographer, George P. Koshollek. Together they were assigned to tour the state's lakes and rivers and report what they saw in detail in stories and pictures.

The plan was to run a three-part series entitled "Pollution: The Spreading Menace," in the *Picture Journal* at a time when the state's legislature was about to meet in 1966.

The assignment was carried out brilliantly. The impact of Kienitz's story and Koshollek's photographs in the *Picture Journal* was enormous.

The public finally began to understand that Wisconsin's varied business activities for decades had been endangering its water. Lumber, mining, tanning, canning, and cheese and butter-making had been pouring millions of tons of waste into streams, rivers, and lakes with little or no attempt at regulation. The state's hydroelectric development, in addition, was forcing a change in many drainage systems, thus intensifying the water problem.

What the *Journal* demanded was a drastically tightened and strongly enforced new water control act—a statute that, by most conservative estimates, would cost the state $300 million.

"A century ago," Kienitz wrote, "Increase Lapham said the state's natural resources could be frittered away because of the failure to recognize what he called 'the right of usufruct.'

"This is a legal term having to do with the right to use another person's property without impairing its substance. Lapham was referring to Wisconsin's vast and valuable pineries which vanished because of neglect. Our lakes and streams have proved more durable, but at the rate they're being polluted it's plain that the right of usufruct is still being violated."

Here is the way he began his first story of the long and effective campaign:

IN WISCONSIN: SAVING THE WATER

By Richard C. Kienitz

From the Milwaukee Picture Journal, April 24, 1966

Parts of the hard-working Wisconsin River stink; its fish have a sulphurous odor. Sludges pouring down the spoiled Fox River have kept Green Bay beaches closed for 25 years.

A cataract of South Milwaukee sewage, hardly more than one-third treated, tumbles several hundred feet down a tangled gully and gushes across a strip of sand into Lake Michigan.

On a summer day Wisconsin Dells, the state's best recreation area, tries to launder 870,000 gallons of its wastes in a treatment plant built to digest 350,000 gallons in 1939.

Dusts of grain and coal sprinkle an obnoxious film across Superior harbor, the busiest in the Midwest. Ships of the world, plying the Great Lakes, spew out oily ballast and bilgewater by the hundreds of gallons.

The awesome Mississippi River sweeps out of Minnesota at Ellsworth gorged with assorted bacteria. The pollutional load is three times the level that might make a bathing beach unhealthy.

Bitter seepage from a vine stack at a Cambria canning factory killed 27,000 fish in Columbia County's Tarrant Creek last summer.

Discharges from overloaded septic tanks bubble out of soil unable to absorb them. A single septic tank can damage a half mile in a small stream.

Wisconsin is ruining its inherited water resources. Its citizens are polluting water used for farming, drinking, industry, and recreation. Mud Creek near Appleton is murky with effluent from suburban septic tanks. A small boy, tossing a chip of wood into the stream, explained why he couldn't go wading: "It's polluted."

He was only eight. Yet even at that age he realizes what is happening to many of our streams.

A man out for a stroll along the historic Portage Canal shook his head over a blanket of green scum washed against a locked gate. "People just use the river to toss things in," he sighed. "They throw their garbage into it."

What, then, is the condition of Wisconsin waters? To find out, this writer took an extensive tour about the state late last autumn and again this year. Everywhere I went I found our streams polluted and getting worse. The spreading menace spares no river or lake.

My findings on pollution coincide with those of the State Board of Health and the Committee on Water Pollution, whose undermanned staffs manage to complete surveys of Wisconsin's 28 drainage basins only once every seven years.

Sometimes our waters are badly polluted. Grossly polluted, a fisherman will declare when bass and perch give way to the hardier carp and suckers that thrive in soured water.

Filthy, a boater concludes when Milwaukee River grime cakes the bottom of his boat in a few days.

"The sum of small pollutions will be a sour, black water with low recreational value," a water quality expert warns. And recreation is a billion-dollar business in the Badger state.

The Wisconsin River burns up its dissolved oxygen in all but a few of its 170 miles between Rhinelander and Castle Rock Dam in a vain effort to absorb paper mill and sewage wastes.

Without oxygen, fish cannot live; wood fiber, dead algae, and sewage scum smother the river bottom. Appleton wants to tap Lake Winnebago for its drinking water. Even though the lake is thick with filaments of algae, it is five times cleaner than the Fox River the city now laboriously cleans for its taps.

How do you determine pollution of a waterway? The best gauge is the number of pounds of materials making a biochemical demand on a stream's dissolved oxygen.

In 1960, the pulp and paper industry created raw waste containing 1,200,000 pounds of biochemical demand. Treatment removed 329,000, leaving 871,000 pounds of pollutional material.

This gigantic load plagues the biggest rivers—the Wisconsin,

Fox, Flambeau, Chippewa, and Menominee. On the Fox, the state's dirtiest waterway, 90 percent of the pollutional load comes from industry.

But over all, industry is only half the problem. In 1961, treatment of wastes reduced the total biochemical demand of all cities and industries only 53 percent—from 2,400,000 to 1,132,710 pounds.

Of some 480 sewage systems that flow into 420 Wisconsin treatment plants, one-third provide only primary processing, which filters out about 35 percent of the solids and adds chlorine to kill germs. The total reduction by all plants in 1961—when they handled 1,531,000 pounds—was 76 percent. But 90 percent plus efficiency at Madison and Milwaukee—where most of the people live—boosts the average.

Tumbling over rocks and riffles, rivers can purge themselves of some of this pollution. Yet, with a growing population demanding more paper and cheese and canned vegetables while it continues to develop a "septic tank suburbia," dilution really is no longer an adequate solution to pollution. Even a kitchen garbage disposal unit doubles the amount of household wastes going into a sewer.

Little wonder, then, that conservationists call some rivers "open sewers."

Kienitz went into horrifying detail, illustrated by Koshollek's pictures, to demonstrate that these conditions applied to every part of the state and not just a few big cities or popular resorts in the countryside. It was a convincing statement.

In follow-up articles, with still more pictures, the *Journal* presented its case not only to the public but also to the state's lawmakers, who were then debating what they thought were more urgent matters. It is true that, as was the case in Kentucky and other states that were tightening conservation laws, industrial interests tried to soften proposed legislation and also attempted to influence the *Journal*'s campaign.

But all such pressures failed.

In 1966, Wisconsin's legislature approved one of the toughest antipollution laws in the United States—a statute that was stronger even than the one that Wisconsin's governor had proposed. Stewart L. Udall of Arizona, then Secretary of the Interior, called it the best that had ever been enacted in the cause of cleaner water and a better life.

In the same year that the *Louisville Courier-Journal* won its gold medal
for its campaign against strip mining, the *Milwaukee Journal* also was
voted a gold medal for its water preservation battle. They shared the
Pulitzer Prize for Public Service for 1967. For the press as a whole, and
not only for a few progressive newspapers, conservation had become a
major issue.

17. THE CHRISTIAN SCIENCE MONITOR
EXAMINES THE NATIONAL PARKS

The "Crown Jewels" of Our Land Face New Pressures
and Difficult Decisions in the Next Generation

Not too many years ago, the National Park Service proclaimed that
"Parks are for People," and actively promoted enlarged attendance.

A conservation critic, Peter Farb, writing in the Christian Science
Monitor, gloomily forecast that overuse of the parks, if continued, "will
see the destruction of the national parks in our time."

Long before the gasoline crunch of the 1970s, as a result of these and
other warnings, the Park Service quietly abandoned its hype policy to
boost attendance. But the crowds continued to grow, nevertheless.

Even the 1973 gas crisis, and its brief reprise in the summer of 1979,
failed to put an appreciable dent in the vast outpouring of millions of
Americans who each year visit the great woodlands that have been called
the nation's natural "crown jewels."

What, then, can be done to save the parks from the ills of overuse in the
years ahead? In 1968, the *Christian Science Monitor* dispatached one of
its Washington staff, Robert Cahn, on a 20,000-mile journey to study the
parks and return with findings and recommendations.

This exploration, together with a questionnaire in which 2,000 *Monitor*
readers participated, made it the largest survey that had ever been
made—up to that time at least—of national parks policy.

Courtney R. Sheldon, managing editor of the *Monitor* at the time,
wrote of Cahn's study:

"In 1872, with the opening of Yellowstone National Park, this country
pioneered in the world with its policy of setting aside as national parks
large natural areas for the benefit and enjoyment of all peoples. The
original idea was to have just enough development to permit the public to
view the parks' natural wonders, gain some inspiration and pleasure, and

go on their way. But the pressures of increased use have in some areas endangered preservation of natural resources. Unless vital policy decisions are made soon, much of the value of park experience could be lost for future generations."

And so Cahn journeyed from Everglades National Park in Florida to Olympic National Park in the State of Washington, from Great Smokies National Park in Tennessee to California's Yosemite, and everywhere he asked the question that became the title of his series: "Will Success Spoil the National Parks?"

Cahn, then 52 years old and a graduate of the University of Washington in Seattle, was a veteran journalist and well qualified for his task. The answers he brought back were neither clearly affirmative nor negative, but they gave strong warnings of dangers ahead. Here is an excerpt from the conclusion of his series:

SAVING THE NATIONAL PARKS

By Robert Cahn

From the Christian Science Monitor, May 8, 1968

In 20,000 miles of travel through many parts of the national park system, I discovered that every park has problems in varying degrees of seriousness.

Overcrowding does exist in the developed areas of such older national parks as Yosemite, Yellowstone, Grand Canyon, Everglades, Mesa Verde, and Mount Rainier—but only during the peak periods of use.

Crime, while still insignificant in total amount, is growing in the national parks at double the rate of crime in American cities. Several parks are undergoing water shortages either from man's interference with the source or from too many people using the normal supply.

Park rangers are so busy with management, safety, maintenance, and traffic during peak periods that they have too little time for helping the public to understand the parks.

Many visitors add to the difficulties by trying to do too much, too fast; seeking and demanding the creature comforts of home in pristine areas of nature; failing to respect the land and the wildlife or refusing to see it on its own terms.

Despite all this and more, it is only fair to say that, on the basis of my observations, the national park system appears to be in relatively good physical condition. No disaster situation is evident.

But looking ahead 10, 20, or 30 years, the story could be different, indeed. The mounting pressures of use . . . point to a crisis of decision-making.

If the right decisions are not made, or if they are made too late, the national parks could be spoiled for both present and future generations of visitors.

The crisis of decisions involves not only old-line popular parks like Yellowstone, or those like Yosemite, near urban areas. Even in new and remote areas of the national park system, the pressures of use already are forcing some difficult decisions.

Consider Virgin Islands National Park, for instance. Four years ago, on the second day of a Caribbean vacation, my wife and I "discovered" this national park and its delightful campground at Cinnamon Bay on St. John Island. We instantly fell in love with its quiet beauty. Finding that the concessionaire had housekeeping accommodations available, we stayed there our entire two weeks.

Park Service Guide Noble Samuel, a native of St. John, taught us how to snorkel and also interpreted the fantastic display of underwater life we encountered around coral reefs. Evenings we sat by a beach campfire and listened as park service naturalists unlocked the secrets of St. John's marine, animal, and plant life. We explored the island and lounged on its white sand beaches, some of the best in the world.

The open-hearted concessionaires, John and "Dib" Woodside, managed to create a homey atmosphere for the 70 of us who were occupying the tent sites and screened-in one-room beach cottages. There was no organized entertainment and everyone went his own way.

If you didn't mind the *no-see-ums* (minuscule sand flies with a maxipowered bite), cooking on a barbecue grill or Coleman stove, using a kerosene lamp, and having no running hot water, it was an idyllic vacation spot.

When we returned to Cinnamon Bay last fall, everything looked unchanged. But it wasn't. At Christmas, Easter, and other popular vacation periods, accommodations were booked solid a year in advance; visitors arrived without reservations, forcing overflow camping. Too much foot traffic along the beach had caused severe erosion; the limited water supply was running dangerously low. A proposed airport for nearby St. Thomas threatened the tranquility of the park. . . .

Cinnamon Bay illustrates the problem as a whole. On a system-wide basis, a number of decisions basic to many national parks also are demanding attention.

How many more public campgrounds or lodges should be built within the parks? Are there other solutions to the vast "housing" needs?

How much of each park should be set aside as wilderness? How much, if any, should be given over to roads, restaurants, stores, lodging, and other services for the public?

The questions may be different now from what they were when the National Park Service was founded in 1916. Yet the one underlying issue remains: preservation vs. use.

Much of what Cahn wrote more than a decade ago has been borne out by the passage of time and his warnings are just as pertinent today, despite the gasoline crunch, as they were in 1968. Most conservationists now agree that the heritage of our national parks is one that we can destroy through sheer carelessness.

A Pulitzer jury studying entries in the national reporting category wrote of Cahn's series: "This [the series] represents a thoughtful, thorough job of reporting on an unspectacular issue that is of deep and lasting importance to all Americans. The *Christian Science Monitor* is to be commended for investing the resources necessary to explore a significant subjec: not in the spotlight of public concern—but which deserves to be."

Cahn was awarded the Pulitzer Prize for National Reporting in 1969.

18. A LOS ANGELES TIMES REPORTER WARNS THAT SOME OF OUR DAMS ARE IN DANGER

Gaylord Shaw Shows That Many Aging Dams Threaten the Lives and Property of Thousands of People

Gaylord Shaw of the *Los Angeles Times* began an 18-month campaign against the nation's unsafe dams on June 7, 1976.

It was the morning after the collapse of the great Teton Dam in south-

SNOWBOUND
Pulitzer Prize for Feature Photography, 1979

FROM THE PORTFOLIO OF SNOW PICTURES TAKEN BY THE BOSTON HERALD
AMERICAN STAFF TO ILLUSTRATE THE WORST WINTER STORMS IN NEW
ENGLAND'S HISTORY. THIS PHOTO WAS BY CHIEF PHOTOGRAPHER
KEVIN COLE ALONG ROUTE 28 IN 1978

eastern Idaho, which caused 11 deaths and $400 million in property damage.

For the Teton failure demonstrated to the nation that even the newest and most sophisticated dams can be unsafe.

Shaw, born in Oklahoma in 1942 and educated at the University of Oklahoma, had served as White House correspondent of the Associated Press for four years before joining the *Los Angeles Times* in 1975 and he knew the ins and outs of Washington coverage. For many months he studied thousands of pages of government reports on the nation's 50,000 privately owned and publicly owned dams and conducted scores of interviews to pinpoint the unsafe structures.

Here are some of his original findings in a *Times* series about the dams that began on March 13, 1977:

Of the nearly 300 dams supervised by the Interior Department's Bureau of Reclamation, at least 20 would be unable to cope with floods while five other of the Bureau's dams had severe leakage or seepage problems.

Bureau inspectors in 1976 made 54 recommendations for emergency remedial work on dams, adding to 1,333 other recommendations that apparently had not been acted on at the time.

The Corps of Engineers, after the Teton collapse, found that some of its 64 dams had cracks and other signs of distress and that 64 others might not "perform well" under the stress of floods.

The National Forest Service had warned in 1975 that more than 1,000 dams on national forest lands had "structural deficiencies."

"The story is the same throughout the federal government's multi-million-dollar, 50,000-employee dam-building bureaucracy," Shaw wrote. "Repair or modification of existing structures to make them safe often receives much lower priority than building new dams."

But the bureaucracy was unmoved by Shaw's disclosures. Nor was there much public reaction.

The reporter, with the support of his newspaper, continued at work. He was able to disclose that despite Congressional passage of a dam inspection law in 1972, not a single dam had been reviewed among the many deficient ones under private ownership.

Then on the night of July 19–20, 1977, the Laurel Run Dam at Johnstown, Pa., burst with disastrous consequences, realizing Shaw's worst fears. He hurried to the scene of the devastation and wrote an eyewitness account, the main part of which follows:

THE VALLEY OF DEATH

By Gaylord Shaw

From the Los Angeles Times, July 23, 1977

JOHNSTOWN, Pa.—The helicopter swooped low through the ugly gap in Laurel Run Dam, then hovered over an expanse of mud and rock where two days earlier a reservoir had contained 100 million gallons of water.

Joseph Ellam, Pennsylvania state dam safety engineer, surveyed the scene and said with frustration: "For 19 years I've been trying to tell people they had time bombs up every one of these hollows. They didn't believe me."

By "time bombs," Ellam was referring to scores of aging dams that dot the narrow valleys of southwestern Pennsylvania, some of them clearly inadequate to cope with torrential rainstorms that periodically strike the region.

One of those storms dumped a dozen inches of rain during last Wednesday's early morning darkness and caused about one-third of the 400-foot-wide dam to collapse, releasing a wall of water that fed a flood now blamed for at least 55 deaths and $250 million in damage.

Laurel Run Dam, built 60 years ago to supply water to Johnstown, suddenly became an instrument of disaster. And it became the latest tragic symbol of an international problem disclosed earlier this year in a month-long *Los Angeles Times* investigation: hundreds of aging, defective dams pose the potential for catastrophe because they are unable to hold back severe floods.

Engineers like Ellam have known for years that hazards lurk in some of the nation's 50,000 large dams, but their warnings and pleas have usually fallen on the deaf ears of politicians and other officials who must pass the laws and appropriate the money to deal with the problem.

Thus, frustration seemed to surround Ellam as he made a helicopter inspection Friday of Laurel Run Dam and a smaller dam several miles away that also collapsed in Wednesday's storm.

Ironically, this second dam, which had held about eight million gallons of water, is just a short distance upstream from the remnants of a 70-foot-high dam that failed in 1889 and killed 2,200

THE TEXAS COWBOY
Pulitzer Prize for Feature Photography, 1980

ONE OF A SERIES OF 23 PICTURES DEPICTING THE TEXAS COWBOY, BY ERWIN H. "SKEETER" HAGLER OF THE DALLAS TIMES HERALD

people—the nation's worst dam disaster. "I stop there every year," he said of the 1889 disaster scene. "It's a sobering reminder."

The valley downstream from Laurel Run Dam offers a new sobering reminder of the destructive force held in check by America's dams.

Once it was the community of Tanneryville, the tranquil home of middle-class steelworkers, carpenters, and truck drivers, of families named Dragovich, Felix, Peskorich, and Thomas.

Now it is a valley of death, destruction, and despair.

The shattered remnants of houses are piled atop one another. Cars and trucks are submerged in mountains of mud. Telephone poles and other debris are strewn about like toothpicks. And the people, some with tears, some with stoic silence, are searching for friends and relatives.

Charles Kramer, 39, a home remodeler, found the body of a fishing companion partly buried in the mud beneath three uprooted trees. "His trailer washed away when the dam went down," Kramer said. "Nobody knows what happened to his wife and children. . . . I know of at least 30 persons who are missing."

William Rayha and his wife said eight of their neighbors were missing. They scrambled to safety themselves, but their home, two cars, and all their clothing and furniture were swept away. All that's left is the red concrete floor of their garage. "This is it . . . all we have left in the world," Mrs. Rayha said. "Twenty years of work and struggle. . . ."

Further downstream, in the community of Seward, Gary Henderson, 26, has spent the last two days poking in the mud for bodies. He found one, "a little boy, 9 years old," Henderson said. "I was sick."

Henderson, the manager of an aviation company, said many of the bodies in Seward has been found in cars. "It seemed like they were trying to get away but something must have happened real fast," he said. "It was the dam, I guess."

Some bodies were believed to have been carried for miles downstream and authorities feared that some would never be found. The force of the water was so intense, witnesses said, that massive boulders were bouncing like pebbles.

"Rumble—rumble—rumble—you could hear the rumble, and

then you could hear the houses cracking," said one witness, Harry Ashcroft.

John Beltz, a township supervisor who carried a list of 42 persons he said had died in the valley, maintained that residents should have been given some warning about a possible dam collapse.

His neighbors agreed—and were angered by initial official comments that the dam had not caused the damage—that it simply had been the immense amount of rain that fell within a short time and set off the flooding.

"What do they think—that a little creek did all this?" asked Sammy Felix, a 30-year-old housewife, as she motioned toward the wrecked houses. "Somebody fell down on the job. Why didn't they blow the sirens and get the people out when the dam was filling up?"

The dam tender, Timothy Lentz, told reporters the collapse occurred suddenly when the dam's spillway could not cope with the rapidly rising reservoir. The water surged over the top of the 42-foot-high earthen structure and soon it was breached. There was, Lentz said, "a gigantic roar louder than thunder. . . . I thought the side of the mountain was coming down."

Ellam cited "grossly inadequate spillway capacity" as the probable cause of the overtopping and subsequent failure of the dam and said the same problem plagued many of the state's 900 other large dams.

"These dams were built 50, 60, 70 years ago," he said. "The state of the art is much different today but what do you do about all the old dams?"

The *Times* reported earlier this year that only half of the states had dam safety programs and that 36,000 large dams in the country had never been inspected by state or federal engineers.

Pennsylvania's dam safety program, although limited in funds and manpower, is ranked by experts as one of the top ten in the nation. Ellam said Laurel Run Dam had been inspected by his office a year ago and found to be well maintained and in apparently good condition.

In addition to examining the two failed dams Friday, Ellam completed an emergency inspection of ten other "problem dams" near Johnstown, accompanied by a Corps of Engineers expert, Stuart Long. "They look a lot better than they did yesterday—they're all OK," Ellam said of the ten dams. "I'm relieved. Thank God it didn't rain again."

Even after Johnstown, Shaw soon learned that the government's bureaucracy still was not pushing inspections of unsafe dams on a priority basis. He had written, in a note to his editors:

"We are flirting with disaster as far as dams are concerned. One of these days a catastrophe far greater than Teton will rivet attention on the problem. It may not happen tomorrow and it may not happen for 20 years. But it will happen."

Johnstown already had suffered. Where would the next dam burst, and when? How many more lives would be lost? How much more property would be damaged or swept away by raging flood waters?

It happened on Nov. 6, 1977 when the Toccoa Falls Dam was swept out in Georgia and killed 39 people. And next day, Shaw reported that the dam had been leaking for years.

That did it. President Carter freed federal funds for the immediate inspection of private dams and numerous investigations at last prodded the federal bureaucracy into action.

Gaylord Shaw was awarded the Pulitzer Prize for National Reporting in 1978.

V. FOREIGN REPORTING:
THE EMPHASIS SHIFTS

At the high point in the history of American foreign correspondence at the end of World War II, there were 2,500 accredited practitioners of the art abroad. But these melted away in less than two years.

In two subsequent wars in which Americans fought, there were temporary increases: in Korea, about 450 reporters covered for the American news media; in Vietnam, at the high point, about 600 were accredited in Saigon. These, taken with the remainder of global coverage for American news organizations, probably boosted the total temporarily to about 1,000 correspondents.

The sharp decline following the Vietnam War, despite other conflicts in the Middle East and the Indian subcontinent, and smaller outbursts elsewhere, was attributed to a steep rise in the costs of keeping staff people abroad due to worldwide inflation and the disinterest of a very large section of the American public in foreign news.

Of course it was impossible for the few hundred remaining reporters, no matter how devoted and talented, to cover world news without assistance.

True, many of them rushed from one crisis to another in a heroic attempt to report on all the big news for the home front, particularly in the Iran and Afghanistan crises. But often, people had to be sent on temporary assignment from New York and Washington or the large West Coast news centers. Or foreign nationals had to be employed (at local rates that were much lower than the going pay for Americans) in greater numbers than usual on a different basis than staff people.

But at the bottom of the foreign news pyramid, there remained a ragtag army of temporary employees called "stringers" who were ill paid and often not very reliable. In theory, if a "stringer" broke a major story somewhere, a staff person could be sent at once to take over. But in practice, it often didn't work out.

In consequence, all but a comparatively few American news organizations had to depend on an undermanned and overworked system for their foreign intelligence until the seizure of American hostages in Iran at the end of 1979. In 1980, spurred by revived public interest in foreign news, there was a turnaround that caused the *Wall Street Journal* to field a foreign staff of importance. Moreover, the Knight-Ridder Newspapers combined forces with the *Chicago Tribune* and the *New York Daily News* to put 20 correspondents abroad. In Asia, the *International Herald Tribune* and the *Wall Street Journal* both began publishing Far Eastern editions in Hong Kong. The Associated Press, with more than 85 correspondents, and United Press International, with about 65, beefed up their services.

Then came the *New York Times*, with about 30 full-time foreign correspondents, and a major syndicate operation that served around 300 newspapers. The *Los Angeles Times*, with a group of 20 foreign correspondents, and the *Washington Post*, with about 12, were the *New York Times*'s closest competitors and combined 16, were the *New York Times*'s closest competitors and combined to run a news syndicate with around 200 clients. The *Baltimore Sun*, *Christian Science Monitor*, and *Chicago Sun-Times* rounded out the foreign service of the daily press. *Time, Newsweek, U.S. News and World Report, Fairchild Publications*, and *Business Week* probably mustered around 80 correspondents between them. The three television networks, at any given time, appeared to have between 40 to 50 staff people abroad but not all were permanently assigned.

On the basis of my own researches and other comparable surveys, the realistic estimates of what it cost to keep a correspondent abroad for a year ranged between $100,000 and $150,000—depending on the conditions at the various posts—at the outset of the 1980s. And costs were not likely to go down.

As for the assignment of correspondents, until the Iran crisis, most were in relatively few cities: London, Paris, Bonn, Rome, and Moscow in the west; Beirut, Jerusalem or Tel Aviv, and Cairo in the mideast, and Tokyo, Hong Kong, and Peking in east Asia. While that soon changed, more than half the nations on earth had no correspondents for American news organizations and either were covered by "locals," as in South Korea, or on what was called a parachute run—hordes of correspondents who descended from their bases in a motley group if big news broke far afield.

It was not really a system that could inspire much confidence among the public at large, for the "locals" were under the thumb of their respective governments, few of the parachute journalists had the slightest background on what they were assigned to cover, and some developing countries had seldom even seen a representative of an American news organization. On a trip to New Delhi in the 1970s, I counted exactly nine resident correspondents for American news organizations, who also were supposed to cover Pakistan, Bangladesh, Sri Lanka, Nepal, and Bhutan—and keep an eye on troubled Afghanistan and hermitlike Burma as well. This, of course, was before the Soviet invasion of Afghanistan.

The coverage of sub-Sahara Africa was even more skimpy, except for crises in South Africa, Zimbabwe (Rhodesia), and a flap over an occasional freak dictator. And for some reason that is difficult to understand, the reporting in the United States of events in neighboring lands of North and South America was also minimal unless the news was tied in some way to Fidel Castro, the separatists of Quebec, or natural disasters.

Even the greatest of newspapers could be embarrassed under such circumstances. When a Panamanian dicator was assassinated some years after World War II, a world-famous American newspaper did not hear from its local "stringer" at all and had to fill in with brief wire service dispatches until a staff correspondent arrived. The correspondent looked up the stringer, an elderly woman, who apologized for her failure to file but explained that she had misplaced her eyeglasses.

Mort Rosenblum, editor of the *International Herald Tribune* in Paris, tells the story of a more recent encounter by a wire service correspondent, who was covering Queen Elizabeth's visit to an island republic-to-be, with the principal minister of the land.

The minister, it turned out, was also the news agency's local "stringer," a most convenient arrangement for him.

"Whatever audiences might really want," Rosenblum writes, "news organizations have put increasingly diminished emphasis on foreign coverage over the past decade. The number of correspondents abroad has been dropping sharply and steadily. Editors are relying more and more on substitute means of coverage which adds new forms of distortion to the system." [1]

While the nations of Western Europe remained the center of American foreign correspondence, the larger news organizations could come up with a knowledgeable correspondent or even a small staff, when necessary, to cope with the flow of the news. The old-time resident correspondents, from London to Moscow, had been in place for so long that they sometimes were consulted by many a newly arrived ambassador.

But with the gradual shifting of the news affecting America to Asian lands, from the oil-rich Arabs and the embattled Israelis in the west to Japan, Korea, Indochina, and China itself in the east, expert correspondents were hard to find. And in Africa and Latin America, there were fewer still.

It was a small triumph when a news organization could engage a competent American correspondent who happened to know Japanese or Chinese or Russian, Hindi or Urdu, Arabic or Swahili. For Asian and African languages, to 99 percent of American correspondents, remained a great wall that separated them effectively from the people of the lands to which they were assigned.

What saved the American news media from the consequences of their casual initial neglect of much of the foreign news that shaped the destinies of the nation was the presence, the skill and the dedication of a relatively few distinguished correspondents at the scene of great events. Sometimes, as in the early days of the Vietnam War, the repeated warnings of a handful of knowledgeable correspondents were disregarded; and in Iran, just before the rebellion that forced the Shah out of office, the last representative

[1] Mort Rosenblum, *Coups and Earthquakes: Reporting the World for America* (New York: Harper & Row, 1979), p. 22.

of a major American newspaper was told to close his office and come home. Similarly, the Soviet invasion of Afghanistan thoroughly surprised the news media.

But the annals of the Pulitzer Prizes, between 1959 and 1980, contain numerous instances of distinguished correspondents who *did* get through and serve a significant purpose. Because so many of them dealt with Vietnam and Cambodia, the following section in its entirety illustrates the work of the prize-winners who covered that conflict. This section is devoted to those who made important contributions to public knowledge, always so necessary to the functioning of a self-governing society, and they came out of everwhere.

In addition to those whose work is represented here, there were others of distinction, among them Joseph Martin and Philip Santora of the *New York Daily News*, who forecast Castro's coming to power in Cuba in 1959; Lynn Heinzerling, who covered the African war in which the nation of Zaire was born in 1960; Walter Lippmann of the *New York Herald Tribune* in 1961 and Hedrick Smith of the *New York Times* in 1974, who reported from the Soviet Union; J. A. Livingston of the *Philadelphia Bulletin*, with an economic survey of the client states of the Soviet Union in Eastern Europe in 1964; John Hughes of the *Christian Science Monitor* with its report of the crushing of a Communist coup attempt in Indonesia in 1965–66, and Jim Hoagland of the *Washington Post* for his coverage of the struggle against apartheid in South Africa in 1970.

The international reporting that follows illustrates how American foreign correspondents and others dealing with foreign news operated under pressure in the Middle East, in the Indian subcontinent, and in China. These were representative of the journalists who kept hope alive for the future of foreign correspondence.

19. A WALL STREET JOURNAL MAN WITNESSES INDIA'S CONQUEST OF PAKISTAN

Peter Kann Records the Collapse of the Pakistani Army in His Diary During the Eastern War of 1971

A single person, cut off from both sources and communications, can have only a limited perception of the unfolding of great events. And yet, there is an enduring fascination in reliving the past through the eyes of one who was present at the making of history.

Tolstoy realized it in taking the frightened Pierre Bezukhov through the terror of the burning of Moscow around Napoleon's conquering army in *War and Peace*. And Stendhal, in *La Chartreuse de Parme*, recaptured the clash of arms at Waterloo and Napoleon's downfall through the wanderings of Fabrizio del Dongo on the sodden battlefield.

Peter Kann of the *Wall Street Journal* did not deliberately plan to relate the dramatic end of the 15-day war between India and Pakistan in 1971 in terms that would emulate the great masters of the novel. This 29-year-old New York-born graduate of Harvard was covering a real war, after all, and he could scarcely reflect on it as history or create fictional scenes and fictional characters to interest his hard-headed audience.

But circumstances had conspired against him. He was penned up in the beleaguered city of Dacca by the oncoming Indian armies. The shattered Pakistani army was on the verge of collapse. The new state of Bangladesh was struggling to be born as the successor to the dismembered skeleton of East Pakistan.

And all communications for correspondents in Dacca were sealed off.

As the *Wall Street Journal*'s Far Eastern correspondent, Kann had begun to cover the troubled affairs of the Indian subcontinent in March 1971, when West Pakistan began its fateful attempt to put down the eastern rebellion. He had forecast the eventual independence of East Pakistan.

The American State Department, in another of its diplomatic gaffes, had been saying to the world that there would be no war between India and Pakistan, that all would be well in the east and that there was no danger. But there was—a lot of it. And when war came, Kann was right in the center of it—at Dacca.

In a dozen dispatches, he had been pointing unerringly to this climactic result of the eastern revolt—a better assessment than that of the State

Department. But now that he was actually in a dangerous situation, he did have the option of leaving as his paper suggested. He chose to stay.

But without communications and no place to file his reports, what was he to do? Earlier in the war, he had filed a part of his diary to the *Journal* and it had been published on Page 1 on Dec. 14.

For want of anything better to do as the victorious Indian army and its local allies swept into Dacca, the correspondent noted what he saw, heard, and felt in his diary. And when the war was over, he filed it and the *Journal* published it on Page 1 again in a second installment. Here is an excerpt from that final installment:

"WE ARE BEATEN EVERYWHERE"

By Peter R. Kann

From the Wall Street Journal, Dec. 21, 1971

DACCA—Throughout the short and bloody war here, it was all but impossible to get news out of the country. Thus, I began keeping a diary when war broke out Dec. 3. It is not meant to be a history of the war—if only because from here one could see only a very small slice of the conflict that engulfed the subcontinent.

Some of my notes are editorial and even somewhat personal, for which I can only offer the excuse that facts were scarce during the war and the situation encouraged reflection.

Sunday, Dec. 12—Father Timm of Holy Cross College arrives at the Intercontinental Hotel to say mass about 9:15 but word has just arrived that evacuation flights are on the way. Foreigners are rushing to get to airport. "Now I know what it feels like to be a bride left standing at the altar," the priest says.

Ride out to airport with elderly American couple booked on evacuation flight. Man is wearing aluminum hard hat, lady is clutching at cage with two squawking mynah birds. "I had to leave my dog," she said. "It was terrible."

Scenes like Pakistani army major approaching American official to ask if his wife could please be evacuated. Answer is no, and the Pakistani says thankyou and turns away. Soviet cousul general is in good spirits. "I am happy my fair lady is aboard plane," he says.

Monday, Dec. 13—A morning paper announces with bold

headline, "Enemy Advance Halted," but longest article in paper is "Specter of Famine Haunts Upper Volta." From breakfast room, one can watch hotel employee pulling bits of ack-ack shrapnel out of swimming pool with a magnet tied to the end of a rope.

Drive to city center during six-hour period when curfew was lifted. Much of Bengali population has deserted city, but many Biharis (non-Bengali minority) visible on streets and, of course, the rickshaw peddlers. I see fewer Pakistani flags flying today. "Every sewing machine in Dacca is busy working on Bangladesh flags," a diplomat says.

Tuesday, Dec. 14—By early afternoon, it appears the battle of Dacca is about to begin. Indian MIGs rocket "Government House"—governor's office—in central city. Two reporters return from several-hour drive southeast of city. They report Indian troops seven miles from city and advancing with only one river to cross. Considerable fighting. Indian planes drop leaflets on city calling for all military and paramilitary forces to surrender to nearest Indian unit with guarantees of protection for lives and property.

Red Cross official says food situation in Dacca has become desperate. All foodstuffs in short supply, many shops closed, curfew prevents people reaching open shops, and prices now so high that poor cannot afford to buy remaining food anyway.

News of resignation of A. M. Malik, governor of East Pakistan, and rest of civilian government. One UN official who was in the governor's office about 1 P.M. says Malik wrote out his resignation longhand between the first and second Indian air strikes on Government House. Then Malik washed his feet, knelt, and prayed.

Wednesday, Dec. 15—Indian air strike during breakfast. Dining room empties in about ten seconds. Whole roomful of half-eaten instant scrambled eggs.

Gen. Farman [a Pakistani commander] arrives about 9 A.M. Will the Pakistani army surrender? "Why should we surrender? The question of surrender does not arise." Farman is riding around in a Mercedes camouflaged with mud, two general stars on its license plate. No armed escort.

A few minutes after 10, a British journalist runs by, yelling that

Farman is coming to hotel to surrender within the hour. Great excitement. TV types pleading with one another to get organized, form a line. "For once," they say, "let's not have to photograph each other."

Farman enters gate on schedule but turns corner and gives TV cameras nothing but long shots. Rumor is that President Yahya gave approval to surrender plan last night but Gen. Niazi (Pakistani top commander) may be balking.

Pak army doctor arrives at hotel. Sad conversation. "What is honor?" he asks. "How much sacrifice must be made for honor's sake? In the old days we fought duels for our honor. Now a million men must die to satisfy honor." He says Pak army has taken terrible casualties.

Gen. Farman leaves hotel. Many surrender rumors still floating. Too many.

Thursday, Dec. 16—At 10:10 A.M., a hotel official walks up: "It's definite, it's definite. It's surrender." Five minutes later, UN aides in the hotel make it official: "The ultimatum to surrender has been accepted."

Rush out to airport with other reporters. At 12:45, a Pak army staff car with two stars on the plate rolls up. Figure it's a Pak general coming to meet Indian helicopter. But a general in purple turban and another in cavalry hat get out; that isn't Pak military headgear. "Hello, I am Gen. Nagra, Indian army," cavalry hat says, "and this is Brigadier Kler," he adds, introducing turban. They had led Indian column that pushed into Dacca suburbs from north early this morning.

We hear of mob trouble at Intercontinental Hotel and return. A hysterical Mukti is carried through hotel gate with a light leg wound. Mukti finally is laid out on three hotel chairs. Hotel official arrives, dapper as ever in glen plaid suit. "He's bleeding all over my damned best chairs and all the bastard did was to stub his damned toe," hotel man says.

This city is full of panicky men with guns; excited young Muktis, confused Indians, and frightened Pak troops who are trying to surrender but who don't know how or where to do so.

This afternoon Gen. Nagra and Pak Gen. Farman come to hotel gate in jeep. Mob begins shouting at Farman: "Butcher, killer, bastard." Farman walks toward mob and says soft-spoken, "But don't you know what I did for you?" He means the surrender, which saved lives. Maybe the mob knows but it doesn't care.

It's 5 P.M. and reporters rush to golf course for formal surrender ceremony. Surrender papers are signed in quadruplicate. Takes awhile because Gen. Niazi reads the documents as if for the first time.

Scene after signing is complete chaos. Mob trying to carry Indian generals on shoulders, Pak generals being jostled by crowds. Gen. Farman is wandering alone, dazed, through milling mob. "You see, we are beaten everywhere," he mumbles as two running Bengalis bump into him.

Farman continues walking slowly, one hand in sweater pocket. "How do I get out of this place?" he asks no one in particular before I lose him in the crowd.

Friday, Dec. 17—At 5:55 P.M., two Soviet correspondents arrive. "We are Tass and Pravda. We have just arrived. What is the news?"

Two hours later, sipping Scotch in a hotel room, a reporter says, "Hey, the lights are on." And so they are. It's the first night in nearly two weeks that's not spend by candlelight.

Later, three Indians arrive to report, "The city is all quiet now. A curfew has been imposed. We have stopped all this bloody shooting business and. . . ." The rest is drowned out by automatic weapons fire.

But today *was* quieter than yesterday.

Saturday, Dec. 18—Considerable shooting and some killings, especially of Biharis, still continuing. A Bangladesh victory celebration turns into a bloody spectacle; four West Pakistani sympathizers are tortured and killed. Earlier today Muktis uncovered mass graves of prominent Bengali intellectuals who had been taken hostage by local militiaman and butchered night before last. This is a traditionally bloody society that has just gone through a nine-month bloodbath. Why should the bloodletting suddenly stop?

Dacca appears to be calming down gradually.

A Pulitzer jury in international reporting was impressed with Kann's diary and other war correspondence and appraised them in these terms:

DEATH IN DACCA
Pulitzer Prize for News Photography, 1972

ONE OF MANY SCENES OF TERROR IN DACCA AT THE END OF THE INDIA-
PAKISTAN WAR OF 1971, TAKEN FROM THE PORTFOLIO OF HORST FAAS AND
MICHEL LAURENT OF THE ASSOCIATED PRESS

"Better than anyone else he [Kann] told what it all meant. He displayed initiative in getting into the story early, and in depth, and the quality of his writing in every dispatch vividly told the reader what was going on and why."

Early in May 1972, Kann was rudely awakened by a phone call from his editor in New York who told him that he had won the Pulitzer Prize for International Reporting for 1972. When he looked at the clock, it was 5 A.M. and he found nothing in his room with which to celebrate except the burnt-out stub of an evil-smelling cigar.

He lit it and smoked it in bed.

In later years he became the first editor and publisher of the *Asian Wall Street Journal*, published by the parent Dow Jones firm in Hong Kong (1976), and eventually the assistant to the chairman and chief executive officer of Dow Jones, Warren Phillips (1979).

20. JACK ANDERSON DISCLOSES SECRET PAPERS REVEALING U.S. 'TILT' TOWARD PAKISTAN

The Columnist Quotes Kissinger: "I'm Getting Hell . . . from the President for Not Being Tough Enough on India"

American foreign policy, in the view of its critics, was a disaster for much of the period after World War II.

They pointed out, with varying degrees of sarcasm and bitterness, that the United States, for all its vast wealth and power, had been on the losing side in China, Cuba, and Vietnam among other international trouble centers and that Korea could scarcely have been called a glorious victory.

Not even the recollection of the success of the Berlin airlift in 1949 and the confrontation with the Soviet Union in the Cuban missile crisis of 1962 could silence the outcry. For with the opening of the Indo-Pakistan War of 1971 on Dec. 3, there was a spreading suspicion throughout the land that the United States once more was backing a loser—Pakistan.

The sensible thing, opponents of the Nixon administration argued, was to maintain absolute neutrality in order not to force India into a closer alliance with the Soviet Union. Under Prime Minister Indira Gandhi, the rapprochement between New Delhi and Moscow already was too well developed for comfort in Washington.

But every clue available to the press indicated that the American position was anything but neutral. However, there was no proof and nobody in a responsible policy-making position was talking in anything but the usual well-worn State Department charades.

But on Dec. 14, 1971, in the midst of the war, Jack Anderson managed to procure a file of top secret papers about the secret meetings that had been going on in the White House's closely guarded Situation Room and he broke the story in his Washington Merry-Go-Round column for his audience of millions of readers in 750 American newspapers. He quoted Henry Kissinger, then President Nixon's top international security adviser, who had been presiding over the policy conferences:

"I'm getting hell every half hour from the President that we're not being tough enough on India. He's just called me again. He doesn't believe we're carrying out his wishes. He wants to tilt in favor of Pakistan. He feels everything we do comes out otherwise."

The column went on to report that the conferees had discussed a speech that had been prepared for delivery by Ambassador George Bush at the United Nations that afternoon, but Kissinger thought it wasn't tough enough on India. Assistant Secretary of State Joe Sisco, another participant, was quoted as suggesting that economic moves could be made against India, and Pakistan could be threatened with similar steps just to maintain a diplomatic balance.

Kissinger again was quoted: "It's hard to tilt toward Pakistan if we have to match every Indian step with a Pakistan step."

Anderson also quoted from a top secret cable sent to the State Department by Ambassador Kenneth Keating in New Delhi, which sharply disputed the White House's view favoring Pakistan. "I do not believe those elements of the (White House) story either add to our position or, perhaps more importantly, to our credibility," the Keating message was reported to have said.

In later Anderson columns, more Keating messages were broken to show that the 71-year-old ambassador was waging a most vigorous campaign to keep the United States from totally alienating India, the prospective victor of the war. The British, too, got into the act with a cabled top secret warning, forwarded by the American embassy in London, that the American government had "made a tactical error in taking a public stance critical of the Indians."

But President Nixon was calling the shots in favor of Pakistan, Anderson reported, and the President was insisting on action against India. A column on Dec. 19 quoted Kissinger again:

"The President does not want to be even-handed. The President believes that India is the attacker. We are trying to get across the idea that India has jeopardized relations with the United States."

So that was it. No one who could read while running, or even walking at a brisk pace, could doubt that American policy was being shaped in favor of another loser and that the Indian-Soviet alliance under the Gandhi government would be strengthened thereby. And that is how it turned out.

Anderson virtually defied the government to prosecute him for breaking top secret dispatches, arguing that it was in the public interest for people to know what was being done to the country's foreign policy in the secrecy of White House meetings. Particularly when the outcome was bad.

But the policymakers who stormed at lesser journalists and the judges who bravely tossed little-known reporters in jail for refusing to divulge sources didn't have the guts to take on Jack Anderson. Not then, at any rate.

He was too tough and he was too likely to go for the jugular.

This was the kind of exposé that had made him the No. 1 investigative reporter in Washington, a fit successor to his mentor, Drew Pearson, and to the lawyer-journalist, Clark Mollenhoff of the *Des Moines Register-Tribune*, who for so many years had gone raging around the capital against erring politicians.

Anderson had come up the hard way—born in California on Oct. 19, 1922, a reporter for the *Salt Lake Tribune* in 1939, a student briefly at Utah University until World War II knocked him off course into the Merchant Marine and the Army. But one day in 1947, he showed up in Drew Pearson's office and—after some discussion—was hired as an investigative reporter by the then proprietor of the Washington Merry-Go-Round column. Upon Pearson's death, Anderson succeeded him.

Here is the substance of his summary column on his disclosures about American policy in the Indo-Pakistan War:

"THE U.S. POSTURE IS IN A SHAMBLES"

By Jack Anderson

From The Bell-McClure Syndicate, Dec. 30, 1971

WASHINGTON—Publication of the secret Pentagon Papers exposed, all too late, the miscalculations and misrepresentations that entangled the U.S. in a jungle war in faraway Vietnam.

Without waiting for history to overtake the Indian-Pakistani War, therefore, we have decided to publish highlights from the secret White House Papers dealing with the crisis.

These papers bear a variety of stamps: "Secret Sensitive,"

"Eyes Only," "Specat (special category) Exclusive," "Noform" (no foreign dissemination), and other classifications even more exotic.

Yet astonishingly, the documents contain almost no information that could possibly jeopardize national security. On the contrary, the security labels are used to hide the activities—and often the blunders—of our leaders.

We believe the public is entitled to know about these blunders. For the U.S. posture is in shambles on the Indian subcontinent, which is enormously more important than Vietnam. Every year, the births alone exceed the entire population of Vietnam.

Here are our conclusions from studying the White House Papers:

1. President Nixon, apparently because he liked Pakistan's strong man Yahya Khan and disliked India's Prime Minister Indira Gandhi, placed the U.S. on the side of a minor military dictatorship against the world's largest democracy. Thereby, he aligned the U.S. against the Bengalis, whose freedom Yahya brutally repressed. He overturned their free election, jailed their elected leader and sent troops to terrorize the populace.

2. The President gruffly overrode the advice of the State Department's professionals who urged him to use his special influence with Yahya to stop the Pakistani persecution and to grant the Bengalis a measure of autonomy. When the Indian Army finally came to the aid of the Bengalis, the pros pleaded with Nixon to remain neutral if for no other reason than Pakistan looked like a sure loser. Instead, he supported the repressor and associated the U.S. with Pakistan's eventual humiliation.

3. In a fit of petulance, the President sent a naval task force to the Bay of Bengal and risked a military confrontation with Soviet warships. Russia's Ambassador to India Nikolai M. Pegov, according to "reliable" intelligence, immediately assured Indian officials that "the Soviet Union will not allow the Seventh Fleet to intervene." Nixon's derring-do served merely to increase India's dependence upon Russia.

4. As a reward, the Russians are expected to seek military bases on the subcontinent. "The Soviet military ambition in this exercise is to obtain permanent usage of the port of Visakha-

patnam," suggested Admiral Elmo Zumwalt, the Navy chief, at a secret strategy meeting. An intelligence report also declares that Bangladesh, the new Bengali state, has "already offered military bases in Chittagong to the Soviet Union in exchange for economic aid."

5. At the height of the two-week war, the White House scrabbled around for some way to rush arms shipments to Pakistan. This would have been a violation of our own 1965 arms embargo against both India and Pakistan. Since 1965, the U.S. has delivered only "nonlethal" supplies, chiefly spare parts, to the two antagonists. To get around the ban, Nixon's chief foreign policy maker, Henry Kissinger, explored the possibility of sneaking arms to Pakistan through third countries.

Here are excerpts from the "Secret Sensitive" minutes of Kissinger's White House strategy sessions:

"Dr. Kissinger asked whether we have the right to authorize Jordan or Saudi Arabia to transfer military equipment to Pakistan," declare the December 6 minutes. "Mr. Vam Hollen (Asian expert, State Department) stated the United States cannot permit a third country to transfer arms which we have provided when we, ourselves, do not authorize sale direct to the ultimate recipient.

"Mr. Sisco (Assistant Secretary in charge of Asian affairs) went on to say that as the Paks increasingly feel the heat, we will be getting emergency requests from them. Dr. Kissinger said that the President may want to honor those requests. . . .

"Mr. Packard (Deputy Defense Secretary) then said we should look at what could be done. Mr. Sisco agreed but said it should be done very quietly."

The December 8 minutes pick up the subject again: "Dr. Kissinger referred to an expression of interest by King Hussein relative to the provision of F-104s to Pakistan. . . .

"Ambassador Johnson (Ambassador-at-Large) said that we must examine the possible effects that additional supplies for Pakistan might have. It could be that eight F-104s might not make any difference once the real war (in West Pakistan) starts. They could be considered only a token. . . .

"Mr. Packard stated that the overriding consideration is the practical problem of either doing something effective or doing nothing. If you don't win, don't get involved. . . ."

The following day, a secret message was flashed to Ambassador Jordan L. Dean Brown: "You should tell King Hussein we fully appreciate heavy pressure he feels himself under by virtue of request from Pakistan. We are nevertheless not yet in a position to give him definite response. Whole subject remains under intensive review at very high level of USG."

In New Delhi, Ambassador to India Kenneth Keating received a copy of the secret orders to Brown. Keating sent an anguished message to Washington pleading: "Any action other than rejection (of the plan to ship planes to Pakistan by way of Jordan) would pose enormous further difficulties in Indo-U.S. relations."

Why didn't the American policy-makers listen to Keating? First of all, President Nixon stubbornly refused to recognize that Pakistan was about to be dismembered. And, almost as important, Henry Kissinger kept downplaying the importance of the Indian-Soviet rapprochement. Quoted in an Anderson column (of Dec. 19), he said:

"The lady (Mrs. Gandhi) is cold-blooded and tough and will not turn India into a Soviet satellite merely because of pique."

Kissinger, it turned out, was only partly right. India could scarcely have become anybody's satellite (with 600 million people, some satellite!) but Prime Minister Gandhi, for all her days in office, remained bitterly and convincingly anti-American, as her celebrated father, Jawaharlal Nehru, had been before her. More than anything else, it was a part of her heritage and the American position in the Indo-Pakistan War merely fortified her prejudices.

A Pulitzer jury in national reporting, looking over Anderson's work, wrote:

"The jury unanimously agrees that the Anderson Papers represent an excellent example of investigative reporting into the manner in which foreign policy decisions are made by the government. The Anderson Papers brought to light facts that would not have been available through any other public channels. It is this kind of exposure to the sunlight of public opinion that contributes to the integrity and ultimate success of the democratic process."

Anderson was voted the Pulitzer Prize for National Reporting in 1972.

21. RICHARD BEN CRAMER TAKES A WALK
THROUGH A MIDEAST NO MAN'S LAND

A Young Correspondent of the Philadelphia Inquirer
Finds an Eery Stillness in Occupied Lebanon

Although the world's leaders loftily proclaimed peace year after year in the strife-torn Middle East, there was no peace.

When the Arab states weren't fighting Israel or warring among themselves in a more discreet but nonetheless deadly fashion, Israel and the Palestine Liberation Organization were grappling in a desperate guerrilla war.

From their bases in Southern Lebanon, the Arab terrorists were able to slip by a small United Nations peacekeeping force with impunity and try to bomb or shoot up Israeli border villages or blow up the centers of Israeli cities. And Israel entered upon a policy of preemptive strikes across the Lebanese border, sometimes by air but almost as often by raiding land forces.

In any event, the border populations of both countries were the principal sufferers in this undercover warfare. Through their powerful platform in the United Nations, the Arabs could and did proclaim their outrage over Israel's attacks, as did the United States and the Soviet Union and almost everybody else beholden to the oil-rich Arabs. But nobody did anything to stop the Arab terrorists, who were being proclaimed as national heroes by their admirers.

This was the kind of war that put any correspondent in extreme personal danger, for—as in Vietnam—there were no front lines and no neat patterns of attack and defense. A bomb or a bullet could come out of anywhere—and frequently did. It was this type of situation that had claimed the lives of 60-some American correspondents and photographers during the 30 years of guerrilla war in Indochina. And everybody who tried to tell the story knew it.

In the Middle East, there was still another drawback. Both sides—the Israelis and Arabs alike—mistrusted the changeable Americans, whether they were diplomats, soldiers, or correspondents. Any one of them could be a part of the CIA apparatus, in the view of the combatants, and any one of them could therefore be a target.

This was the position in which Richard Ben Cramer found himself when he was sent to the Middle East in 1977 by the *Philadelphia Inquirer*. He was only 27 (born in Rochester, N.Y., in 1950) and had degrees from Johns Hopkins and the Columbia Graduate School of Journalism (M.S., 1972). Following four years with the *Baltimore Sun* after leaving Columbia, he had joined the *Inquirer* staff in 1976.

He left the bulletin news, and the filing of statements about military and diplomatic developments, to the wire services that served the *Inquirer* and concentrated, instead, on describing how the continual warfare in the Middle East had affected the lives of ordinary people. When Israel invaded Southern Lebanon in 1978 to wipe out the PLO bases, Cramer hired a taxi in Tel Aviv to take him northward as far as he could go. But the Israeli command blocked him.

Instead of being forced back to Tel Aviv to report what the Israeli government put out, Cramer told his driver to go to Tel Aviv airport, caught the first available plane for Athens, then flew on to Beirut and hired a Lebanese taxi to take him southward as far as possible. At the last Arab checkpoint, he was warned against pushing ahead but, in rumpled suit and tie and very much in the spirit of Richard Harding Davis, he walked on into the silence of a No Man's Land. Here is an excerpt from his long and distinguished report:

A WALK IN NO MAN'S LAND

By Richard Ben Cramer

From the Philadelphia Inquirer, March 17, 1978

RAS EL BAYADA, Occupied Lebanon—It is eerily still in no man's land, a two-mile testament to the lesson that people are as much a part of the landscape as houses and fences and fields.

Here, eight miles from Lebanon's southern border, between the last Fatah commando checkpoint and the spearhead of the advancing Israelis, the chickens come out to meet you on the road. It has been 48 hours since grain was scattered for them in their yards.

Here, everything is frozen in time, like a Pompeii without the lava. Crates of oranges are stacked, unattended, next to empty houses. Telephone wires dangle broken and useless from their poles. An open spigot pours an endless stream of water onto a swamp that was once a garden.

Here, the mere whoosh of a breeze through the leaves can make you sprint for cover, scanning the sky for warplanes until you dive into the orange groves . . . only to emerge a moment later feeling foolish and shaky from the rush of adrenalin.

To be sure, there is noise and plenty of it. There are real planes and antiaircraft guns nearby. Artillery blasts thudding on the hillsides make the sheep bleat as they scatter and the frogs wail in the ditches.

But it takes man's noise to break the stillness—a child's cry, an engine, or a laugh. And without man, the eeriness is unrelieved in this world between two worlds.

Behind the last Fatah checkpoint, the teenagers bearing Kalashnikov submachine guns and wearing jaunty red berets talk quietly among themselves for long, nervous hours.

The fear of the Israelis is palpable. The sky is constantly watched. For 48 hours, on the streets and in the fields, the little bands have shifted.

They move constantly—occasionally fighting, more often just moving, farther and farther back.

This is Fatahland, as the Israelis call it, where everyone might be a commando and children of 10 know how to handle the Kalashnikov. Fatahland has been shoved north from the border, helter-skelter, so that it now is near the ancient Mediterranean port of Tyre. Still, the welter of movement and talk is quite organized.

For two days, in the face of Israel's massive asault, the Palestinian forces have had to shoot and run away.

"There is no way for us to face such heavy weapons," said a commando officer in Tyre. "It would be useless. It would be foolish."

Still, on the village streets and in the camps along the coast, the spirit among the commandos is broodingly vengeful. "With every step they will pay," the officer said. "They will pay a price such as Israel has never had to pay."

Close to the last Fatah checkpoint, the fear shows on every face. No one knows whether the Israelis will push forward again.

The civilians have begun to disappear. Cars and trucks full of refugees have been leaving for the last two days. One Mercedes heading north last night was filled with 16—three in front, four

FIRING SQUAD IN IRAN
Pulitzer Prize for Spot News Photography, 1980

THIS PICTURE OF A GOVERNMENT FIRING SQUAD EXECUTING NINE KURDISH
REBELS AND TWO FORMER POLICE OFFICERS OF THE DEPOSED SHAH IN
SANANDA, IRAN, WAS MADE BY AN UNIDENTIFIED PHOTOGRAPHER AND
DISTRIBUTED BY UNITED PRESS INTERNATIONAL. HIS IDENTITY
WAS KEPT SECRET TO PROTECT HIM.

children between the seats, five on the back seat and four sitting in the open trunk.

In the streets and fields, there is constant movement.

The commandos at the last barrier are startled by footsteps. "It is impossible, don't go," they say. "The Israelis are very near. They kill for nothing."

And then, all is past, and the stillness sets in. On the lone walk, there are monuments to the violence of the last 48 hours.

A BMW sedan with a flat tire is pulled to one side of the road. Except for the tire, the car is intact. There is no explanation for its presence until a door is opened to reveal upholstery spattered with blood.

Farther along, five cars are burning. Their stink testifies to the accuracy of the Israei aerial assault. The blistered hulks sit on bare wheels, tires burned off in the explosions that halted the cars.

There are daisies in the bushes, and the air holds the scent of honeysuckle. Birds sing in the intervals between explosions on a hillside to the east.

Suddenly, around a bend, a shortwave radio cuts through the air. Ahead, two giant Israeli tanks stand on either side of the road, their snouts pointed toward Fatahland.

The tanks form a gate of sorts to a new world, one of pure geometry and punctilious organization. To the left and right, fields have been cleared of their crops and American-built personnel carriers scuttle over the raw earth on rubber treads. The Israelis are settling in, bringing a new order.

A visitor causes some consternation. There is nothing in the manual. "Go there," says a private atop one of the tanks. He points to a spot on the road, cutting off further questions. "They don't let us talk," he says.

The Israeli equipment almost gleams. It is huge and new, as American as a baseball bat. Communication here is by radio. There is no shouting, only the machinery's roar on the earth.

About 50 soldiers surround the machines. They pass without words. A couple of them gawk. One smiles. In the middle of a field, a group on foot is listening to rock music on Israeli radio.

But there is worry on their faces, matching the fear on the Palestinian faces up the road. "They are all around us here," a freckled private says. He looks west to an orange grove and the Mediterranean, only 150 yards away.

"I cannot tell you that there are not terrorists behind those trees right now."

Another complains that the personnel carriers are not armored. "They are only aluminum," he says. "Even a regular bullet passes right through them."

A third soldier cuts him off. "Don't talk," he says.

A major pulls up in a jeep. He has a printed itinerary taped to a band on his arm. There is a discussion about whether the visitor should be forced to leave. No one can seem to imagine walking through the orange groves in Fatahland.

The major says the Israeli forces are going nowhere this day. "If you ask me, I'm not the prime minister," he says, "but I'd say this is it."

Hebrew barks over the radio of his jeep. He answers with a monosyllable and climbs back in.

"You will go back?" he asks, incredulous, with a look up the road. "You are crazy."

It was to be expected that Cramer's recognition of Arab suffering, as well as the trials of the Israelis, would not sit well with the Jewish community in Philadelphia. Almost as soon as he began writing sympathetically about the Arabs, the attack began in the weekly *Jewish Exponent* which remarked editorially: "War is hell. Cramer has chosen to zero in on a small, highly charged corner of hell. . . ."

But within the profession, there was admiration for the kind of unfettered journalism that Cramer practiced and his effort to seek out the human side of this complex conflict. Peter Binzen, metropolitan editor of the opposition *Philadelphia Bulletin*, sent a note to the *Inquirer* calling the no-man-land story "the best piece on Israel and the PLO that I've read anywhere."

A Pulitzer Prize jury in international reporting thoroughly agreed, unanimously recommending an award for Cramer in these terms: "His reporting from the Mideast during 1978 was perceptive and distinguished. He coupled that with writing that was clear and graceful."

Accordingly, he was awarded the Pulitzer Prize for International Reporting for 1979.

22. MAX FRANKEL COVERS NIXON'S OPENING
TO CHINA FOR 8 WORK-FILLED DAYS

The New York Times's Correspondent Leaves with a Feeling
of the Excitement of a Marco Polo and Disturbed Memories

Toward the end of his long and definitive account of President Nixon's historic 1972 visit to China in the *New York Times*, Max Frankel observed:

"The Chinese allowed hundreds of technicians and newsmen to run through their cities in every direction to manage this technical extravaganza, with the help of two ground stations that fed the television signals to a satellite over the Pacific for relay to New York."

Frankel, who had come up through the ranks after graduating from Columbia and serving as a local reporter and foreign correspondent, then was 42 and the chief of the *New York Times's* Washington bureau. But for eight work-filled days in China, while recording the renewal of Sino-American relations, he was alone and in competition with those other hundreds from the news media.

In the thousands of words of news dispatches and colorful observations in his "Reporter's Notebook," he did not attempt cosmic journalism; nor, for that matter, did he try to predict the future course of Chinese-American relations. Occasionally, what he did do was to venture a modest observation either on the concern everybody seemed to feel about the advancing age of China's leaders, Mao Tse-tung and Chou En-lai in particular, or the significance of China's willingness to tolerate an unparalleled degree of press freedom for the visiting American journalists.

These were what he referred to when he began one "Reporter's Notebook" article:

"They are probably insignificant on any seismic political scale, but they certainly belong in the accounts of this strange visitation."

Beyond that he would not go for he realized, quite early in the Nixon visit, that it would be a long time before Sino-American relations could be considered "normal," whatever that much-overused word can be taken to mean. Merely dumping Taiwan as unnecessary diplomatic baggage for the United States did not then meet Peking's strict conditions for mutual recognition; nor, for that matter, did the cautious pledges for an increase in Chinese-American trade mean very much unless they were implemented with some degree of confidence.

The straight news reporting, among the best in Frankel's long career, was therefore both accurate in detail and distinguished in composition.

But it was in the occasional pieces in his "Reporter's Notebook" that he caught the spirit of the "strange visitation." Here is the final one, as excerpted from his general coverage:

NOTES ON 8 DAYS IN CHINA

By Max Frankel

From the New York Times, Feb. 28, 1972

SHANGHAI, Monday, Feb. 28—The last glimpse of China for the American voyagers is through weary eyes. They felt the excitement of Marco Polo but they had only days where he had years. To be precise, they had eight days to fill a hunger of decades—one day for every 100 million Chinese, most of whom were babies when Americans last strolled these streets.

The streets leave a drab memory—clean drabness, to be sure, and blue drabness when the people are milling in the streets in their ultramarine suits, which is almost always. But how can you call anything drab that has so much life and so many lives and so many unknown ambitions and misfortunes and adventures and dreams?

The census bureau in Washington has now put the number of people in China at 850 million, give or take 50 million, and the life expectancy at 55 or 60, give or take five years.

Chairman Mao Tse-tung is defying all the figures, living now in his 79th year and insisting that the dream shall be only one: self-sufficiency or self-respect or constant revolution and equality, a pure and innocent collective spirit triumphant over ego, individualism, and all the recorded experience of societies.

The people leave a disturbing memory, repeating the slogans of Chairman Mao and retreating behind the mask of political conformity. But the same mask makes them inordinately civil and hospitable and self-assured. They seem to believe that everything except political power and individual liberty is indeed their business and they express themselves vigorously and cheerfully across the lines of rank whether the issue is how best to wrap up a package or how to carve a peacock-shaped radish for a banquet.

"What do the Chinese people laugh at, what jokes do they tell?" a visitor asks.

"You would not ask that question if we had not lost contact for 22 years."

"Perhaps. But humor can be different in different societies. We eat with forks, you with sticks. It does not make one better than the other."

"All right, what do you want to know about jokes?"

"Do men make jokes about women?"

"Yes," nods a man.

"No, never," says a woman.

"Do you make jokes about Chairman Mao?"

"No. He is a figure of respect and esteem for everyone."

"Do reporters make jokes about their editors?"

"Yes, of course."

"Do soldiers joke about their officers?"

"Yes, when it is not a time of serious work, or challenging the work of the collective."

"Then where do you draw the line between officers and editors and the Chairman and the Premier? Against whom can you joke?"

A table of gracious hosts maintained for the next ten minutes that it could not understand such a silly question.

.   .   .

At a dinner in Hangchow, President Nixon closed his toast to friendship with a tribute to an interpreter, Tang Wen-sheng. At the first mention of praise for her, the English interpreter for Premier Chou En-lai, Chang Fan-chih, jumped from her seat and hastened to the microphone. She was ready for the translation when the President finished, sparing her colleague the embarrassment of speaking well of herself on behalf of President Nixon.

.   .   .

"That's very dangerous," Mrs. Patricia Nixon said to Chang Hong, her fifth-grade student guide in an orange jumper, as she was being shown an exhibition of old-style swordplay at the Shanghai Children's Palace.

"Oh, that's not a real sword," said the assured 12-year-old.

As they moved on . . . Mrs. Nixon encountered a large poster stressing that recreation also has a purpose in China. "Strive for progress, all boys and girls of China," one of them read.

"We study very hard in this place," said Chang Hong. "We learn everything we can and then go back to our schools and teach the others, as Chairman Mao told us."

Mrs. Nixon and the little girl moved on to hear a beginners' orchestra playing "Can She Bake a Cherry Pie, Billy Boy?"—just as the People's Liberation Army band had played it for the Nixons in the Great Hall of the People in Peking. But an officious adult led the group on into a dead end of the building corridor.

"The children knew the way but the others got lost," said Chang Hong to Mrs. Nixon, who kissed the girl.

And there was the merry puppet show, in which hidden children manipulated the dolls with great skill. As they were about to leave, Chang Hong took Mrs. Nixon by the hand and led her behind the stage. "See?" she said. "They're real people!"

. . .

China is very exhausting.

Times have changed in both China and the United States since that historic visit.

Chairman Mao and Premier Chou are dead, Chairman Mao's wife is held under arrest with the "Gang of Four," a successor government operates under the nominal direction of Premier Hua Kuo-feng and the actual rule of Teng Hsiao-ping, his first deputy, and even the transliteration of their names into English is done under a new system.

As for the United States, Richard M. Nixon, after his fall from the Presidency over the Watergate scandal, must plan on a visit to China without official encouragement except in Peking.

But the tenuous opening to China, made with such fanfare in 1972, continues to widen slowly—sometimes almost painfully—because neither side has a great deal of confidence in the other despite all the stagecraft that surrounded plans for a visit to Peking by President Carter in 1980.

The correspondent who won the Pulitzer Prize for International Reporting for his illuminating dispatches from China, Max Frankel, also has changed roles. He now broods upon the woes and the triumphs of mankind from an aloof perch above Broadway as the *New York Times* editorial page editor.

VI. HEROISM AND DISCLOSURE: THE PRESS IN VIETNAM

The United States suffered more than defeat in the Vietnam War. In the manner in which it was conducted, no less than in its outcome, this was a conflict that drove a poisonous wedge of mistrust between the American government and a very large section of the American public.

It sapped the strength of American leadership. And it arrayed a substantial part of the American press against the aggressive policies of the American government in Indochina as a whole.

This could only be dimly foreseen at the outset of what was, at first, called "a dirty little war." For in 1961, when American intervention began by stealth, most people in the United States had never even heard of Vietnam and comparatively few knew where it was.

Among the elite in Washington, not many in authority had any doubt that the might and power of the United States, applied through a client regime in South Vietnam, would put down a rebellion by a few thousand ragged guerrillas known as the Vietcong whose sole support at the time came from Ho Chi Minh, the veteran Communist ideologue who had created a personal fiefdom in North Vietnam.

Almost the first lesson that any reporter learns when he sets out to cover a war is that truth invariably becomes the first casualty on the battlefield. The position was best expressed, perhaps, by General William Tecumseh Sherman during the Civil War when he roared at a correspondent who had asked for the truth about a battle:

"We don't want the truth told about things here—that's what

we *don't* want! Truth, eh? No, sir! We don't want the enemy better informed than he is!"[1]

This was in effect the way the grandees of the American government resident in Saigon in the 1960s wanted the war reported. I well remember talking with General William Westmoreland a few days after he came to South Vietnam as the American commander and hearing him complain bitterly about the suspicions and antagonism of most of the few American reporters who then were in Saigon. That was in the summer of 1964.

The military people simply couldn't understand that the press in a democratic society had an obligation to examine the credibility of the grandiose claims that then were being put out by both Washington and the Saigon government for victory after victory over the Viet Cong. After a small engagement at Ap Bac, for example, Admiral Harry D. Felt called Malcolm W. Browne of the Associated Press to account for doing a piece describing it as something less than the glorious victory the Saigon regime had proclaimed.

"Look here, boy!" the admiral snapped. "You'd better get on the team!"[2]

The better reporters, although lamentably few in number, remained both skeptical and unregenerate. At one point, David Halberstam of the *New York Times* crumpled up a press statement issued in the name of the American embassy in Saigon, called it a lie and refused to transmit it to his newspaper. As might have been expected, the loyalist section of the press—then by far in the majority—began complaining about what some called "disloyal" reporters.

Joseph Alsop, a columnist for the *New York Herald Tribune*, charged that there existed among the correspondents in Saigon a "high-minded crusade" against President Ngo Dinh Diem of South Vietnam. Marguerite Higgins, who had won a Pulitzer Prize in the Korean War as a reporter for the *New York Herald Tribune*, objected vigorously to stories that the war—even at that early stage—was being lost and that American claims of victory were hollow at best and lies at worst.

[1] Louis M. Starr, *Bohemian Brigade* (New York: Knopf, 1964), p. 170.
[2] Malcolm Browne told me the story in Saigon in 1964.

FLIGHT TO SAFETY
Pultizer Prize for Photography, 1966

KYOICHI SAWADA'S PHOTO FOR UNITED PRESS INTERNATIONAL, SHOWING A
VIETNAMESE FAMILY CROSSING A RIVER TO ESCAPE
AN ATTACK ON THEIR VILLAGE

"Reporters here," she wrote from Saigon, "would like to see us lose the war to prove they are right."

Time magazine, which was then represented in Saigon by a distinguished correspondent, Charles Mohr, attacked the entire press corps in these scathing terms: "The news men have themselves become a part of South Vietnam's confusion; they have covered a complex situation from only one angle, as if their own conclusions offered all the necessary illumination."

Halberstam fired back angrily, "What's been exaggerated? The intrigues? The hostility? It's all been proven. We've been accused of being a bunch of liberals but even that's not true." [3]

It is worth noting that the Pulitzer Prizes gave at least a partial answer to the questions that had been raised against the correspondents' veracity and good faith. For in 1964, Malcolm Browne and David Halberstam shared the award for international reporting for their coverage of the overthrow of the Diem regime. And a third of the chief defendants, the redoubtable Neil Sheehan of United Press International, lost out only because he happened to be on a brief vacation in Japan at the time. Mohr, who had not been eligible for prize consideration, parted company with his critics on *Time* magazine and joined the *New York Times*.

There was a brief epilogue to the editorial campaign to downgrade the more aggressive reporters in Saigon. It became widely known that on October 22, 1963, President Kennedy asked Arthur Ochs Sulzberger, the publisher of the *New York Times*, if he had been thinking of transferring Halberstam from Saigon—that Halberstam, in brief, was "too involved." Sulzberger responded that the *Times* was satisfied with Halberstam's work, which ended the incident. [4]

There was reason to criticize the American press at that juncture, but it was not because of prejudice or bad reporting among the correspondents. The fact is that throughout the early and most critical years of the Vietnam War, when correspondents by the hundreds should have been examining the extent of the American war effort, fewer than a score of relatively young reporters were

[3] *Time*, Sept. 20, 1963, p. 44 and Oct. 11, 1965, p. 65; *Newsweek*, Oct. 7, 1963, pp. 44–45.

[4] Letter to author from Arthur Ochs Sulzberger dated Jan. 19, 1965.

actually assigned to South Vietnam by American news organizations and television was represented mainly by Peter Kalischer, the tough Columbia Broadcasting System veteran, and one or two occasional stringers for the rival networks. The trouble was not with what the correspondents reported; it was simply that there were too few of them to oversee an incredibly diffuse and difficult conflict. [5]

As the Pentagon Papers made clear when the *New York Times* began publishing them in 1971, the Johnson administration and those it sent to Saigon as its representatives embarked on a policy of deceit, misrepresentation, and intrigue (even before the Tonkin Gulf incident in 1964) that sometimes made it virtually impossible for the press to get at the truth of what was being done.

Once President Nguyen Van Thieu and his fellow generals came to power in Saigon in 1965 and President Johnson boldly escalated the war, it was inevitable that the homefront would react strongly. And with the coming of the antiwar demonstrations, the Vietnam War at last became big news.

As American troop strength reached 550,000 and the conflict turned into the longest, most costly, and most divisive in American history, some 600 accredited correspondents came to Saigon and spread over the countryside. But the nucleus still consisted of the first ones who had come to South Vietnam, some of whom remained on the job, plus a relatively few dedicated and talented newcomers who were not afraid to attack the specious claims of victory that persisted until the Vietcong's Tet offensive of 1968.

Even after President Johnson's decision not to seek reelection and the increasing turmoil on American campuses that was climaxed when four students were shot and killed at Kent State University in 1971, American officialdom persisted in hopefully seeing "light at the end of the tunnel."

When they did, the light was cast by the burning city of Saigon on a lovely spring day in 1975 as victorious North Vietnamese and Vietcong troops toppled an independent South Vietnam and celebrated the defeat of American arms.

[5] Personal observation of the author in various parts of Indochina in 1963–1964.

This was not the kind of story the American press had wanted to tell. For in the tradition of Richard Harding Davis, our war correspondents gloried in reporting the great deeds of heroes, such as Theodore Roosevelt leading his Rough Riders in a charge up San Juan Hill during the Spanish-American War. And in the tradition of Ernie Pyle, they deified the humble GI as the architect of American victories in World War II.

In Vietnam, there were no victories. And there were no heroes.

But in the record of the Pulitzer Prizes, there is proof positive that the sorry tale of immense duplicity, discouragement, and defeat was told—and told truthfully. For in addition to Malcolm Browne and David Halberstam, the Pulitzer archives contain the matchless war correspondence of Peter Arnett of the Associated Press, the shock of the disclosure of the My Lai massacre by Seymour Hersh as a freelancer, and the investigative reporting of William Tuohy of the *Los Angeles Times*. And in Cambodia, there was the gallantry and devotion of Sydney Schanberg of the *New York Times*, who risked his life to stay with the enemy when Phnom Penh fell and who revealed the enormity of the genocide that later took place in that beautiful but unhappy city and the surrounding countryside.

Nor was there any hesitation to attack the conduct of the war on the home front, as was demonstrated by the editorial writing prizes for John S. Knight of the Knight Newspapers and Robert Lasch of the *St. Louis Post-Dispatch*. Both were early and determined critics of the Vietnam adventure and both gave warning, years before the end, of what the outcome was likely to be.

The editorial cartoonists, too, displayed courage, particularly Don Wright of the *Miami News* and Patrick Oliphant of the *Denver Post*, who won prizes in 1966 and 1967 respectively, mainly on the strength of their views of the Vietnam War. It goes almost without saying that such great veterans as Herblock of the *Washington Post*, Paul Conrad of the *Los Angeles Times*, and Bill Mauldin of the *Chicago Sun-Times*, prize-winners all in other years, were not found wanting in this crisis, either.

Among the most remarkable group of Pulitzer Prize winners were the photographers, who took such long chances in the paddy fields and the jungles to bring the enormity of the war home to the

American people. It is no accident that all the prize-winning
photographers were wire service people and that in their ranks
were two Japanese, a German, and a Vietnamese in addition to
three Americans: Horst Faas, Edward T. Adams, Slava Veder,
and Huynh Cong Ut of the Associated Press; Toshio Sakai,
Kyoichi Sawada, and Dave Kennerly of United Press International.

In addition, at Kent State in Ohio, the *Akron Beacon Journal*'s
staff won a Pulitzer Prize in Local Reporting for its coverage of the
student massacre by trigger-happy troops. One of the youngest of
all prize-winners, 21-year-old John Paul Filo, received another
award for his unforgettable picture of a distraught little girl kneeling over one of the student victims in a agony of tears. The photo
went up almost at once on the walls near college campuses all over
the country and became as much an emblem of the Vietnam War
as was the Marines' flag-raising at Mount Suribachi in World
War II.

But of all the Vietnam War correspondence, the most significant
in terms of the history of that desolate period was the disclosure of
the Pentagon Papers by the *New York Times*, for which the newspaper received a public service gold medal. To understand what
went wrong with American policy and why it went wrong, Americans of generations yet unborn will have to read these documents
and ponder their meaning; if they do not, then they may one day
have to relive the history they have forgotten.

The story of the Pentagon Papers leads off this section of distinguished correspondence and photography about the Vietnam War,
an arbitrary selection that can only serve to illuminate a small
part of the best work ever done for the American press; to do justice to all of it would require a shelf of volumes. For if the government failed in this conflict, the journalists did not.

23. *THE NEW YORK TIMES MAKES HISTORY*
BY PUBLISHING THE PENTAGON PAPERS

The Newspaper Defeats a Government Effort in Supreme Court
to Suppress the Secret Origins of the Vietnam War

Robert S. McNamara, Secretary of Defense in the Johnson administration, was deeply disillusioned over the course of the Vietnam War in the summer of 1967.

At that time, the United States had been waging war in Indochina, openly and covertly, for the better part of two decades with staggering consequences in casualties and treasure. But the enemy appeared to be stronger than ever.

On October 14, 1966, Secretary McNamara had written an "evaluation of the situation" for President Johnson, saying bluntly, ". . . I see no reasonable way to bring the war to an end soon. Enemy morale has not broken—he apparently has adjusted to our stopping his drive for military victory and has adopted a strategy of keeping us busy and waiting us out (a strategy of attriting our national will). He knows that we have not been, and he believes we probably will not be, able to translate our military successes into the 'end products'—broken enemy morale and political achievements by the GVN."[1]

After that memorandum, in which a stabilized U.S. armed force and a negotiated settlement were recommended, McNamara on May 19, 1967, proposed what amounted to a compromise end to the war. He fought against a demand by General Westmoreland for 200,000 more American troops in Vietnam for a total of 670,000 and sought to curb the air war as well. But President Johnson, while not going all the way with Westmoreland, swung away from McNamara's break with established policy and toward the all-out war philosophy of the Joint Chiefs of Staff.[2]

It was against this background that the disenchanted McNamara ordered the preparation of the Pentagon Papers on June 17, 1967.

What he asked for, and what he received after a year and a half of work by the Pentagon's office of International Security Affairs, was a top-secret study directed by Leslie H. Gelb that consisted of 47 volumes—about 2.5

[1] Memo #118, dated Oct. 14, 1966, as published in *The Pentagon Papers* (New York: Bantam Books paperback, 1971), pp. 542–51.
[2] Memo #129, dated May 19, 1967, Ibid., pp. 577–85.

'Good news, we've turned the corner in Vietnam!'

Pulitzer Prize for Editorial Cartooning, 1970

A REPORT OF PROGRESS IN THE VIETNAM WAR, AS SEEN BY
THOMAS F. DARCY OF NEWSDAY

million words of narrative and documents—covering the United States involvement in Indochina from World War II to May 1968.

The *New York Times* itself has never revealed how it obtained all but the four volumes of the study that covered the secret diplomacy of the Johnson administration. What the newspaper has done consistently is to credit the disclosure to the efforts of its Pentagon correspondent at the time, Neil Sheehan, who also had had long experience as a Vietnam War correspondent.

No one at the *Times*, to my knowledge at least, has ever commented publicly on the assertions of Daniel Ellsberg, a member of the Pentagon's study group, that he provided the *Times* and other newspapers with the documents. Nor has Gelb, the study director who later became a member of the *Times* staff and is now in foundation work, given any public statement about the manner in which the Pentagon Papers came to the *Times*.

Whatever the origin of the Pentagon Papers, the *Times* began publishing them on June 13, 1971, despite their top secret nature. Actually, they did not create much of a stir the first two days because they dealt with so much history of years past. But when the Justice Department on the third day of publication obtained a temporary restraining order from Federal Court in the Southern District of New York, the case became an immediate sensation in this country and abroad.

It was the first time in the history of the United States that the government had attempted, without a declaration of war, to apply prior restraint on publication, which is generally regarded by most journalists as a breach of the First Amendment.

Upon the insistence of Attorney General John N. Mitchell, and with the tacit support of President Nixon, the Justice Department contended that if the *Times* continued to publish the Papers "the national defense interests of the United States and the nation's security will suffer immediate and irreparable harm."

Once the *Times* halted publication, the *Washington Post* obtained some of the material and also began using it in print, later becoming a second defendant in the government's unparalleled attack on the press. Still other newspapers had bits and pieces of the controversial history but the *Times* and the *Post* were the chief targets. Both were restrained for 15 days from publication while the case was tried in the courts.

The legal battle ended on June 30, 1971, with the U.S. Supreme Court's 6–3 decision that the government had proved its case and that the press had a right to disseminate the history despite the top secret stamp. In his concurring opinion for the majority, Justice Hugo L. Black wrote:

"Only a free and unrestrained press can effectively expose deception in government. And paramount among the responsibilities of a free press is the duty to prevent any part of the government from deceiving the people and sending them off to distant lands to die of foreign fevers and foreign shot and shell. In my view, far from deserving condemnation for their courageous reporting, the *New York Times* and the *Washington Post* and other newspapers should be commended for serving the purpose that the Founding Fathers saw so clearly. In revealing the workings of government that led to the Vietnam War, the newspapers nobly did precisely that which the founders hoped and trusted they would do."[3]

There was, however, an implicit warning in the court's decision that prior restraint of publication might be upheld in a future case if the government could show that national security would be endangered by such an act. It was not, therefore, by any means a complete victory for the press, even though the *Times*, the *Post* and other newspapers affected by the case were vindicated.

Why did the *Times* take so grave a risk, knowing what the consequences of failure would be? Long after the Supreme Court's decision, A. M. Rosenthal, the executive editor of the *Times*, wrote in a reflective mood:

"The Pentagon Papers was probably the most formative single journalistic experience in my life and I believe that is true for most of us who had a part in it.

"All of us knew that we were doing something that had never been done before and that was potentially quite dangerous to us as individuals and to the paper we loved so much.

"We had no fear that it would be dangerous to the country. We had spent months examinig the Papers and we were convinced that they were not a security threat. We believed with all our professional intellect that it was essential to print them to give the reader for the first time a clear picture of what had been taking place in Vietnam and of the involvement of the United States.

"It was as if history were a covered box. With the Pentagon Papers we were open to lift the lid and look down.

"In that box we saw a number of compartments—the Eisenhower compartment, the Kennedy compartment, the Johnson compartment, and the Nixon compartment.

"The actors within those boxes did not know how their decisions might affect the actions and decisions in a later box.

"But, with the Pentagon Papers *we* did. We were able to see how one

[3] Ibid., pp. 662–65.

decision in one Presidency, or one failure to make a decision, or one falsehood, affected another compartment.

"To my recollection, never in history has there been available such documentation of a war or a national trauma still in progress. Usually it is not until long after the event that this kind of documentation becomes available.

"So, knowing by careful examination that there was really very little if any security information involved, the question was not how could we print such information but how could we not. What right did we have to withhold it?

"And yet we knew that it would create an enormous explosion. Never before had this kind of documentation been published during the course of a war. We knew that we would probably be denounced as endangering the national security. We even had to face the possibility that, though we considered ourselves right, not only the government, but the public also would consider the *Times* irresponsible and dangerously wrong.

"We had to face that and it was not an easy thing for a paper like the *Times* to do. Everything was wrapped up in that one decision to publish. It was a decision all the editors supported but eventually it had to be made by the publisher.

"Placed before us was almost everything that counts—the questions of national security and national danger, the meaning of journalism and its boundaries, career self-interest. Some of us felt that there was a good chance that we might not be able to survive, professionally, the decision we had to make. Even more important, really, was the knowledge that we might be endangering the existence or reputation of a paper that was at the center of our lives. We knew the decision had to be made but it was without precedent and therefore we could not really foretell the consequences in terms of our own careers and the reputation of the paper.

"Once a decision was made, all of us found ourselves on an emotional roller coaster. On my wall is a plaque. It has two engraved front pages. One is the paper reporting in an 8-column head that the Supreme Court had upheld us. That is the paper of July 1, 1971. The other, the paper of June 15, carries the head, 'Mitchell Seeks to Halt Series on Vietnam But *Times* Refuses.'

"Every time I look at that plaque I realize that if it had said, 'The *Times* Agrees,' the history of this paper and I believe of American journalism, would have been radically different. If we had surrendered to Mitchell, and had allowed the government, without a court battle, to dictate to us, I really believe that the heart would have gone out of the paper and American newspapering.

"For the next two weeks, we were on that roller coaster, up and down as different courts gave their decision. There were days when the tension seemed to be unbearable. And what really held us together was a sense of collegiality and shared professional purpose.

"I'm often asked whether, given the fact that the victory was not a complete one, and that the courts have become harsher than ever as far as the First Amendment is concerned, we would do it again. The answer is still the same as it was then; how could we not." [4]

This first test of strength between the American government and the American press in modern times had an enormous effect on the judging of the Pulitzer Prizes of 1972. Athough several newspapers had published parts of the Pentagon Papers, the *Times*—as the original source—alone entered exhibits in the competition. One was a massive public service entry consisting of the more than 50 full-size pages of the entire series. The other formed the basis for consideration of Neil Sheehan for a separate prize in either the national or international reporting categories. [5] The Pulitzer Journalism Juries, meeting at Columbia University on March 7–9, 1972, consolidated the two entries in a single unit, after which the Public Service Jury unanimously recommended a joint award for the *Times* and for Sheehan.

"It is fortuitous," the jury reported, "that the Pulitzer Prizes can recognize the accomplishments of both the newspaper and of a persistent, courageous reporter, and thus reaffirm to the American people that the press continues its devotion to their right to know, a basic bulwark in our democratic society."

But the Pulitzer Board, meeting on April 13, had serious doubts about the general proposition that top secret government material should be published by newspapers. While the debate was relatively brief, it was intense and the Board was narrowly divided. Joseph Pulitzer, Jr., editor and publisher of the *St. Louis Post-Dispatch* and chairman of the Pulitzer Board, led the fight for a gold medal for the newspaper, and Vermont Connecticut Royster, then the editor of the *Wall Street Journal*, was most concerned about the propriety of such an award. James Reston, the *New*

---

[4] A. M. Rosenthal, letter to author dated Sept. 11, 1979.

[5] The *Times* ran the following credit (issue of June 13, 1971, p. 38) for the Pentagon Papers: "The accompanying article, as well as the the the rest of the series on the Pentagon's study of the Vietnam War, was a result of investigative reporting by Neil Sheehan of the *New York Times* Washington Bureau. The series has been written by Mr. Sheehan, Hedrick Smith, E. W. Kenworthy, and Fox Butterfield. The articles and documents were edited by Gerald Gold, Allan M. Siegal, and Samuel Abt."

York Times columnist and a Board member, was not in the room, for under the Board's rules no one involved in an award can participate in such a debate or vote.

Almost the first thing that happened was that the proposed prize for Sheehan was set aside as a complicating factor and the Board concentrated on the main issue. As the debate flagged, one of the Board's members finally asked Royster with elaborate casualness, "Vermont, if the *Wall Street Journal* had had the Pentagon Papers, would you have published them?"

Without a moment's hesitation, Royster answered, "Yes."

Accordingly, it was the decision to publish the documents that the Board unanimously supported and that was the way the citation for the gold medal of the 1972 Public Service award was drafted:

"The *New York Times*, for the publication of the Pentagon Papers."

The Columbia University 22-member Board of Trustees, which up to that time had always asserted its right to approve or disapprove the decisions of the Pulitzer Board and actually make the awards, debated the issues involved for even a longer period. In addition to the *Times* prize, the Pulitzer Board also had voted its National Reporting Prize to Jack Anderson for his disclosure of the secret State Department papers on the American government's "tilt" toward Pakistan in the Indo-Pakistan War of 1971. Both disturbed the Trustees.

It was a rather strained period for Arthur Ochs Sulzberger, the publisher of the *New York Times* and also a member of the Columbia Trustees. He did not, of course, participate in a marathon private session of the Trustees on Sunday, April 30, at which the issues were thrashed out.

Twice at that meeting at the Columbia University Club, the Trustees informally voted down both awards and twice President William J. McGill prevailed on them to reconsider. They finally agreed to approve the prizes but they issued a dissenting statement, saying that "a majority (of the Trustees) had reservations about the timeliness and suitability of certain of the journalism awards."

"Had the selections been those of the Trustees alone," the statement concluded, "certain of the recipients would not have been chosen. The decision to accept all of the Advisory Board's recommendations this year was arrived at, in large part, in consideration of the prescribed and historic role of the [Pulitzer] Advisory Board."[6]

[6] *The Pulitzer Prizes*, a history by John Hohenberg (New York: Columbia University Press, 1974), pp. 307–13, 346–47, and the personal and unpublished diaries of the author.

Three years later, again perturbed over the 1974 National Reporting award to Jack White of the *Providence* (R.I.) *Journal-Bulletin* for disclosing President Nixon's meager income tax returns of 1970-71, the Columbia Trustees withdrew from the Pulitzer Prizes entirely and delegated their authority to the President of Columbia University.[7] It didn't matter to the elated Sulzberger, however. In accepting the Public Service gold medal for 1972, he said,

"All of us on the *Times* are deeply proud of this award for the Pentagon Papers. It is important to us today and it will be important to us always."[8]

The following excerpt from the *New York Times*'s publication of the Pentagon Papers is taken from the first article, with a slight but necessary stylistic revision of the opening paragraphs:

THE SECRET WAR IN VIETNAM

By Neil Sheehan

From the New York Times, June 13, 1971

The Pentagon Papers disclose that in the six months before the Tonkin Gulf incident in August 1964 the United States had been mounting clandestine military attacks against North Vietnam and planning to obtain a Congressional resolution that the Johnson administration regarded as the equivalent of a declaration of war.

The Papers make it clear that these far-reaching measures were not improvised in the heat of the Tonkin crisis.

When the Tonkin incident occurred (the attack by North Vietnamese PT boats on two American destroyers), the Johnson administration did not reveal these clandestine attacks, and pushed the previously prepared resolution through both houses of Congress on August 7.

Within 72 hours, the Administration, drawing on a prepared plan, then secretly sent a Canadian emissary to Hanoi. He warned Premier Pham Van Dong that the resolution meant North Vietnam must halt the Communist-led insurgencies in South Vietnam and Laos or "suffer the consequences." This threat,

[7] Announcement of the Pulitzer Prizes by the Columbia University Department of Public Information, May 5, 1975.

[8] *The Pulitzer Prizes*, p. 311.

COMRADES-IN-ARMS
Pulitzer Prize for Photography, 1965

FROM THE VIETNAM WAR PORTFOLIO OF HORST FAAS
OF THE ASSOCIATED PRESS

however, and the administration's plan to enter into open warfare if the overture was rejected, were kept secret.

The section of the Pentagon Papers dealing with the internal debate, planning, and action in the Johnson administration from the beginning of 1964 to the August clashes between North Vietnamese PT boats and American destroyers—portrayed as a critical period when the groundwork was laid for the wider war that followed—also reveals that the covert military operations had become so extensive by August that Thai pilots, flying American T-28 fighter planes, apparently bombed and strafed North Vietnamese villages near the Laotian border on August 1 and 2.

Moreover, it reports that the administration was able to order retaliatory air strikes on less than six hours' notice during the Tonkin incident because planning had progressed so far that a list of targets was available for immediate choice. The target list had been drawn up in May, the study revealed, along with a draft of the Congressinal resolution—all as part of a proposed "scenario" that was to build toward openly acknowledged air attacks on North Vietnam.

Simultaneously, the papers disclose, Secretary McNamara and the Joint Chiefs of Staff also arranged for the deployment of air strike forces to Southeast Asia for the opening phases of the bombing campaign. Within hours of the retaliatory strikes by air on August 4 and three days before the passage of the Congressional resolution, the squadrons began their planned moves.

What the Pentagon Papers call "an elaborate program of covert military operations against the state of North Vietnam" began on February 1, 1964, under the code name Operation Plan 34A. President Johnson ordered the program on the recommendation of Secretary McNamara in the hope, held very faint by the intelligence community, that "progressively escalating pressure" from the clandestine attacks might eventually force Hanoi to order the Vietcong guerrillas in Vietnam and the Pathet Lao in Laos to halt their insurrections.

In a memorandum to the President on December 21, 1963, after a two-day trip to Vietnam, Mr. McNamara remarked that the plans, drawn up by the Central Intelligence Agency and the military command in Saigon, were "an excellent job."

"They present a wide variety of sabotage and psychological operations against North Vietnam from which I believe we should aim to select those that provide maximum pressure with minimum risk," Mr. McNamara wrote.

President Johnson, in this period, showed a preference for steps that would remain "noncommitting to combat," the study found. But weakness in South Vietnam and Communist advances kept driving the planning process. This, in turn, caused the Saigon government and American officials in Saigon to demand more action.

Through 1964, the 34A operations ranged from flights over North Vietnam by U-2 spy planes and kidnappings of North Vietnamese citizens for intelligence information to parachuting sabotage and psychological warfare teams into the North, commando raids from the sea to blow up rail and highway bridges, and the bombardment of North Vietnamese coastal installations by PT boats.

These "destructive undertakings," as they were described in a report to the President on January 2, 1964, from Maj. Gen. Victor H. Krulak of the Marine Corps, were designed "to result in substantial destruction, economic loss, and harassment." The tempo and magnitude of the strikes were designed to rise in three phases through 1964 to "targets identified with North Vietnam's economic and industrial well-being."

The clandestine operations were directed for the President by Mr. McNamara through a section of the Joint Chiefs' organization called the Office of the Special Assistant for Counterinsurgency and Special Activities. The study says that Mr. McNamara was kept regularly informed of planned and conducted raids by memorandums from Gen. Krulak, who first held the position of special assistant, and then from Maj. Gen. Rollen H. Anthis of the Air Force, who succeeded him in February 1964. The Joint Chiefs themselves periodically evaluated the operation for Mr. McNamara.

Secretary of State Dean Rusk was also informed, if in less detail.

The attacks were given "interagency clearance" in Washington, the study says, by coordinating them with the State Department and the Central Intelligence Agency, including advance monthly schedules of the raids from Gen. Anthis.

The Pentagon account and the documents show that William P. Bundy the Assistant Secretary of State for Far Eastern Affairs, and John T. McNaughton, head of the Pentagon's politico-military operations as the Assistant Secretary of Defense for International Security Affairs, were the senior civilian officials who supervised the distribution of the schedules and other aspects of interagency coordination for Mr. McNamara and Mr. Rusk.

The analyst notes that the 34A program differed in a significant respect from the relatively low-level and unsuccessful intelligence and sabotage operations that the CIA had earlier been carrying out in North Vietnam.

The 34A attacks were a military effort under the control in Saigon of Gen. Paul D. Harkins, chief of the United States Military Assistance Command there. He ran them through a special branch of his command called the Studies and Observation Group. It drew up the advance monthly schedules for approval in Washington. Planning was done jointly with the South Vietnamese and it was they or "hired personnel," apparently Asian mercenaries, who performed the raids, but Gen. Harkins was in charge.

The second major segment of the administration's covert war against North Vietnam consisted of air operations in Laos. A force of propeller-driven T-28 fighter-bombers, varying from about 25 to 40 aircraft, had been organized there. The planes bore Laotian Air Force markings but only some belonged to that air force. The rest were manned by pilots of Air America (a pseudo-private air line run by the CIA) and by Thai pilots under the control of Ambassador Leonard Unger.

Reconnaissance flights by regular U.S. Air Force and Navy jets, code-named Yankee Team, gathered photographic intelligence for bombing raids by the T-28's against North Vietnamese and Pathet Lao troops in Laos.

The Johnson administration gradually stepped up these air operations in Laos through the spring and summer of 1964 in what became a kind of preview of the bombing of the North. The escalation occurred both because of ground advances by the North

Vietnamese and the Pathet Lao and because of the administration's desire to bring more military pressure against North Vietnam.

As the intensity of the T-28 strikes rose, they crept closer to the North Vietnamese border. The U.S. Yankee Team jets moved from high altitude reconnaissance at the beginning of the year to low altitude reconnaissance in May. In June, armed escort jets were added to the reconnaissance missions. The escort jets began to bomb and strafe North Vietnamese and Pathet Lao troops and installations whenever the reconnaissance planes were fired upon.

The destroyer patrols in the Gulf of Tonkin, code-named DeSoto patrols, were the third element in the covert military pressures against North Vietnam. While the purpose of the patrols was mainly psychological, as a show of force, the destroyers collected the kind of intelligence on North Vietnamese warning radars and coastal defenses that would be useful to 34A raiding parties or, in the event of a bombing campaign, to pilots. The first patrol was conducted by the destroyer Craig without incident in February and March, in the early days of the 34A operations.

The analyst states that before the August Tonkin incident there was no attempt to involve the destroyers with the 34A attacks or to use the ships as bait for North Vietnamese retaliation. The patrols were run through a separate chain of command.

Although the highest levels of the administration sent the destroyers into the gulf while the 34A raids were taking place, the Pentagon study—as a part of its argument that a deliberate provocation was not intended—in effect says that the administration did not believe that the North Vietnamese would dare to attack the ships.

But the study makes it clear that the physical presence of the destroyers provided the elements for the Tonkin Gulf clash. And immediately after the reprisal air strikes, the Joint Chiefs of Staff and Assistant Secretary of Defense McNaughton put forward a "provocation strategy" proposing to repeat the clash as a pretext for bombing the North.

Of the three elements in the covert war, the analyst cites the 34A raids as the most important. The "unequivocal" American responsibility for them "carried with it an implicit symbolic and

DESOLATION IN VIETNAM
Pulitzer Prize for Feature Photography, 1972

FROM DAVE KENNERLY'S PORTFOLIO FOR UNITED PRESS INTERNATIONAL

psychological intensification of the U.S. commitment," he writes. "A firebreak had been crossed."

The fact that the intelligence community and even the Joint Chiefs of Staff gave the program little chance of compelling Hanoi to stop the Vietcong and the Pathet Lao, he asserts, meant that "a demand for more was stimulated and an expectation of more was aroused."

On January 22, 1964, a week before the 34A raids started, the Joint Chiefs warned Mr. McNamara in a memorandum signed by the Chairman, Gen. Maxwell D. Taylor, that while "we are wholly in favor of executing the covert actions against North Vietnam . . . it would be idle to conclude that these efforts will have a decisive effect" on Hanoi's will to support the Vietcong.

The Joint Chiefs said the administration "must make ready to conduct increasingly bolder actions," including "aerial bombing of key North Vietnam targets, using United States resources under Vietnamese cover," sending American ground troops to South Vietnam and employing "United States forces as necessary in direct actions against North Vietnam."

And after a White House strategy meeting on February 20, President Johnson ordered that "contingency planning for pressures against North Vietnam should be speeded up."

"Particular attention should be given to shaping such pressures so as to produce the maximum credible deterrent effect on Hanoi," the order said.

The impelling force behind the administration's desire to step up the action during this period was its recognition of the steady deterioration in the positions of the pro-American governments in Laos and South Vietnam, and the corresponding weakening of the United States hold on both countries. North Vietnamese and Pathet Lao advances in Laos were seen as having a direct impact on the morale of the anti-Communist forces in South Vietnam, the primary American concern.

This deterioration was also concealed from Congress and the public as much as possible to provide the administration with maximum flexibility to determine its moves as it chose from behind the scenes.

It didn't work.

All the double-dealing and deception that was practiced at the highest level of government to keep the war going did not change the eventual outcome. The enemy's Tet offensive of January 30, 1968—a blinding thrust by a tiny army against the greatest military power on earth—showed how hopeless the American military postion really was.

From then on, it was all downhill. From the peak of 543,000 U.S. ground troops in South Vietnam, the pullout reduced the American military commitment by slow degrees until the last combat troops left Vietnam on Aug. 11, 1972. By that time, the protest movement in the United States had become so powerful that North Vietnam could afford to play for time at the bargaining table of the Paris peace conference.

With President Nixon's assumption of power, there had been intermittent attempts to delay the inevitable by air attacks on North Vietnam, the mining of Haiphong harbor, and forays into Laos and Cambodia. But all these desperation blows produced such a terrible reaction at home that they proved counterproductive. At last, after five years of negotiation in Paris, the peace agreements were initialed in Paris on January 23, 1973, between the U.S. and South Vietnam, on. one side, and the North Vietnamese and the Provisional Revolutionary Government of South Vietnam on the other. But except for the return of most American prisoners of war, they settled nothing.

After 30 years of war, the revolutionaries of Hanoi were not going to settle for anything less than all of Vietnam and, many suspected, all of Indochina as well. The end came for South Vietnam on April 30, 1975, when Saigon fell to the victorious North Vietnamese and the Vietcong.

George Esper of the AP—who had stayed behind—dispatched this terse bulletin:

SAIGON (AP)—South Vietnam has declared unconditional surrender to the Vietcong, ending 30 years of warfare."

And Keyes Beech of the *Chicago Daily News*, after a headlong flight with the last Americans from the embassy in Saigon, radioed his paper from the U.S.S. Hancock offshore that same day:

"My last view of Saigon was through the tail door of the helicopter. Tan Son Nhut (air field) was burning. So was Bien Hoa. Then the door closed—closed on the most humiliating chapter in American history."

The deceptive and wrong-headed policies recorded in the Pentagon Papers had cost the nation more than 50,000 dead, 150,000 wounded and at least $150 billion. Thus, the Papers are far more than history. They are an indictment of a whole generation of American policy-makers, Republican and Democratic alike.

There is little argument today over the *New York Times*'s decision to publish the Pentagon Papers. Most newspapers at the time generally agreed with the view of the *Washington Post*: "Those of us who believe that the reader . . . always gains from the maximum possible comprehension of what the government is doing and how it works . . . can only applaud the *Times*'s enterprise."[9] And this is the feeling that has prevailed.

Like the *Times*, Neil Sheehan has no regrets, even though he twice lost out on Pulitzer Prizes connected with the Vietnam War that his colleagues, in large part, believed that he should have won. He took a leave of absence from the *Times* in August 1972 to write a biography of one of the most dramatic personalities of the Vietnam War, the late John Vann. As a result of complications that developed from his injuries in an automobile accident and various legal matters arising from his work, Sheehan's leave was extended to 1976 when he resigned from the *Times* amid mutual regrets and expressions of good will.

Following the completion of the Vann biography, on which he continued work through 1979 as a Fellow at the Woodrow Wilson International Center for Scholars, Smithsonian Institution, Washington, D.C., Sheehan planned to return to daily newspaper work. Of all the participants in the Pentagon Papers operation, he was the most important; without him, there might never have been such a major disclosure of a secret government war plan. And this, finally, was how he felt about it when he received the first Drew Pearson Prize in 1972 at the National Press Club in Washington:

"We are told that in writing the First Amendment that 'Congress shall make no law abridging the freedom of speech, or of the press,' the Founding Fathers meant to give us a mere privilege to report and publish, a license that can be revoked or restricted when those who govern us see fit to revoke or restrict it for what they believe to be the greater good of the nation.

"Those who hold this view will learn that journalists who take their work seriously will reject it, regardless of the personal consequences. The Founding Fathers did not give us a privilege, a license that is held at the convenience of the government. Rather, in writing the First Amendment, they imposed upon us a duty, a responsibility to assert the right of the

[9] *Washington Post* editorial, June 17, 1971.

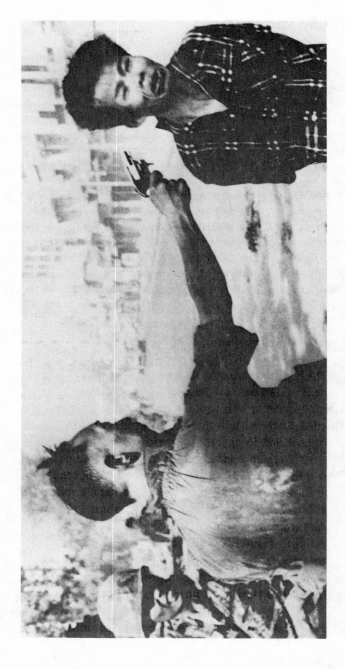

SAIGON EXECUTION

Pulitzer Prize for News Photography, 1969

EDWARD T. ADAMS'S PHOTO FOR THE ASSOCIATED PRESS OF THE EXECUTION OF A VIETCONG SUSPECT

American people to know the truth and to hold those who govern them to account.

"In the pursuit of this responsibility, some of our colleagues, a number of them my friends, have given their lives in Vietnam. No one intimidated them and no one is coming to intimidate us. When the *New York Times* printed the Pentagon Papers, my publisher and my editors also sought to do that duty, to fulfill that responsibility." [10]

Seven years later, Sheehan was even more convinced of the ultimate responsibility of the press to make such disclosures as the Pentagon Papers whenever they serve the public interest. "I shall feel just as strongly about the First Amendment until the day I die," he wrote. "This country would not have come through 200 years with our liberties intact had the Founding Fathers not had the wisdom to write it." [11]

24. PETER ARNETT FLIES TO BATTLE
AND SEES A U.S. FORCE DESTROYED

The Associated Press's War Correspondent Risks His Life
in Vietcong Territory to Join Americans Under Fire

Peter Arnett, a doughtly little New Zealander with the face of a cherub and the heart of a lion, covered the Vietnam War for the Associated Press for eight and a half years. More often than not, he risked his life under fire to get the news.

The pitiless accuracy of his stores about American defeats, when Washington was claiming glorious victories, earned him the enmity of the American Establishment in Saigon. He was spied upon, attacked in the most scurrilous terms by the Embassy's men and treated as if he had been an enemy agent.

The wonder of it all is that he emerged from the cauldron of war unscathed and unmarred, invariably cheerful and plain-spoken, and unchanged either by the vicious criticism he had undergone or the many honors that had been heaped upon him.

He won the Pulitzer Prize for International Correspondence for his Vietnam War reporting in 1966, the 50-year anniversary of the awards,

---

[10] Quoted in the preface to the *New York Times*'s Pulitzer Prize entry in the Pentagon Papers.

[11] Letter of Sept. 2, 1979, to the author.

and he was recommended for another prize by at least one additional jury in a subsequent year.

Actually, as one juror remarked after reviewing his work, he would have qualified for a prize in any of the years in which he worked in Vietnam.

Arnett came out of an older tradition of war correspondence—inner-directed, self-trained, schooled on the battlefield. With a battle helmet drooping down over his ears, a battle jacket flapping about his thin and wiry body and big combat boots encasing his short legs, he looked like a little scarecrow thrust out in the middle of a wheat field. But if he was no Richard Harding Davis in a well-pressed Bond Street uniform, he proved himself the equal as a war correspondent of William Howard Russell and Archibald Forbes, Will Irwin and Philip Gibbs, Herbert Bayard Swope and and Floyd Gibbons, Homer Bigart, Keyes Beech, Pat Morin, and—perhaps the greatest of all—Ernie Pyle.

Arnett came up without benefit of a Harvard or an Oxford education or anything faintly like it. He was born in 1933 in Riverton, New Zealand, and at 17 went into newspaper work on the *Southland Times* at Invergill. Three years later, he moved on to the *Standard* at Wellington. But he was restless, anxious to see the world, and after 18 months he made his way to Australia, where he put in a year as a reporter for the *Sydney Sun*.

Next, he set out for London on a Dutch freighter in 1955 but, like many another young adventurer footloose in Asia, his money quickly ran out and he was stranded in Bangkok. Fortunately for him, there was an English language newspaper in the Thai capital, the *Bangkok World*, one of the strangest publications in the English language, for which he worked until he joined the Associated Press in 1958.

He roamed Southeast Asia as a correspondent for the AP, acquiring a growing reputation as a dependable reporter and gifted writer; eventually, in the early 1960s, he wound up in Vietnam as a member of a talented AP bureau of which Malcolm W. Browne was the chief and the great Horst Faas was the principal photographer. All became Pulitzer laureates.

Many a time, in the early days of the war, the three of them would set out, together or individually, in a hulking pickup truck to race to some tiny outpost where the American embassy had proclaimed victory over the Vietcong, only to find from the survivors that the guerrillas again had sprung a successful ambush. From these experiences, Arnett learned early on never to trust official announcements of any kind but to go directly to the scene and talk with participants. It was difficult. It was risky. Often he came back from days and nights in the jungles and rice paddies with nothing to show for his efforts. But he had courage, enormous will power and the patience of a stone-faced Buddha.

During 1965, the year that marked the beginning of massive United States commitment to the war, he went on patrol repeatedly with American troops into Vietcong territory and wrote of the valor of these green and inexperienced soldiers. He and Horst Faas broke the first story on the American use of nonlethal tear gas against the enemy, and he also did a remarkable piece on the way surgeons were able to remove a live grenade that somehow had become lodged between the ribs of a Vietnamese farmer.

In his assessment of the American war effort, he was devastatingly correct. At the end of 1965, he showed convincingly that the American bombing campaign against North Vietnam had been a failure, that the Communists had been able to keep pace with the American troop buildup, and that the Americans and South Vietnamese did not have enough troops at the time to hold the territory they then occupied.

One of his best stories was one in which he landed by accident in the midst of a firefight between a Marine supply column and the Vietcong in the Ia Drang Valley. Here it is, as he wrote it that hot summer afternoon with the smoke of battle still lingering about him:

THE AGONY AND DEATH OF SUPPLY COLUMN 21

By Peter Arnett

From the Associated Press in the Louisville Times, August 19, 1965

VAN TUONG, Vietnam (AP)—The mission of U.S. Marine Supply Column 21 yesterday was simple: Get to the beachhead, resupply a line company and return to the 7th Fleet mother ship anchored a mile out in the bay.

It never found the line company. And it never returned.

Supply Column 21 was a formidable force made up of five steel-shod amtraks—35-ton amphibious vehicles—to carry food and ammunition—and two M48 tanks to escort them once ashore.

The column packed a total of 287 tons of steel. It was made up of 30 men.

The paths that led to its destruction were paved with confusion.

Failing to locate the designated line company immediately, Column 21 set out to look for it.

But the huge amtraks, once out of the water, were unwieddy. They flopped from one rice paddy to another, with their crews calling at one battalion and then the next. No one seemed to pay much attention.

At 11 A.M., Supply Column 21 was about 400 yards ahead of the nearest Marine riflemen. The vehicles were deep in Vietcong territory and, suddenly, were deep in trouble.

Survivors said the Vietcong rose out of hedge rows and swamps.

Lance Corporal Richard Pass of Homewood, Ill., said his amtrak veered aside as explosions erupted around them. The leading tank was hit with an armor-piercing shell. Two men inside were wounded.

The terraced paddies made maneuvering difficult and the supply men were not trained for it. Attempting to get into good firing positions, three of the five amtraks backed into a deep paddy and bogged down.

The other two edged toward the tanks for shelter. One didn't make it. A Vietcong knocked it out by dropping a grenade down its hatch, killing two Americans inside and wounding others.

Mortar fire bounced off the vehicles and cannon put three holes in one tank. The wounded driver squeezed himself through the 18-inch wide escape hatch under his vehicle only to be riddled by bullets.

Corporal Pass saw Vietcong with ammunition bandoliers, black pajama uniforms, and camouflaged steel helmets move right up to an amtrak 30 yards to his left.

He said the doors of the vehicle clanged open as the two drivers tried to make a break to Pass's vehicle. One of the Americans was killed as he leaped out.

The other was plunging through the paddyfield swinging his Marine knife when he went down. When pulled out dead today, he still had the knife clutched in his hand.

Soon after noon, as the hot sun beat down on the scurrying figures and the steel vehicles, the Vietcong knocked out a third amtrak. Survivors massed in the other two.

Corporal Frank Guilford of Philadelphia said machine guns sliced into the guerrillas, but they kept coming.

The men took turns as sharpshooters at peepholes on top of the vehicles. All were wounded in some degree.

"I couldn't maneuver up there," said Pfc. James Reeff of Seattle, who escaped with a slight injury.

A young corporal shouted, "Okay, men, we're marines. Let's do the job."

He started to climb out of the vehicle but never got his rifle to his shoulder. A bullet hit him between the eyes.

Among those sweltering in the other amtrak was Staff Sgt. Jack Merino of Limita, Calif. He said he almost passed out from heat exhaustion. The men took turns splashing water over each other from resupply cans within the vehicle.

Merino said that in midafternoon he heard a man outside whispering, "Amtrak, amtrak." He proved to be a wounded tank crewman. Merino and others pulled him inside.

"It was a hair-raising moment but we managed it," Merino said.

The Marines continued with the nerve-wracking task of keeping off the attackers. The enemy bodies began piling up.

In late afternoon, air strikes eased the pressure.

By this time, a lieutenant had been killed and another wounded.

Another tank joined the beleaguered group.

At daybreak, a solitary helicopter landed at the scene. It had mistaken the landing zone.

At the drone of the helicopter, the Americans surged from their amtraks like moths to a flame.

Crouched, and with weapons at the ready, the Americans slipped past the bodies of their own and the enemy. They carried the wounded to the helicopter and left the dead.

The helicopter came back once for more wounded.

Ground forces arrived to relieve the others. In the interval they had scoured the nearby paddyfields and brush for Vietcong bodies. They found 18.

Corporal Earle Eberly of Sycamore, Ill., said:

"We don't like being here and killing people and being killed. But this is a job we've been told to do, we have to do it, and we're going to do it."

The fate of Supply Column 21 was sealed at noon.

The men thought the disabled vehicles might be carted off and repaired. But an officer of the relief force told them:

"Take your personal belongings out of the vehicles. We're going to blow them up."

The remains of the amtraks at Van Tuong will be a reminder of Supply Column 31.

Arnett rode to battle in the supply helicopter that landed by mistake in the midst of the dying column while it was still under heavy fire from the Vietcong.

He had managed to talk his way on the helicopter at Da Nang at 5 A.M. after having landed from Saigon in an emergency flight with only two hours' sleep. He was the only reporter to see action that bloody day.

When he was plumped into the thick of the fighting, he found a U.S. tank and three amtraks had been destroyed, seven Americans dead, 28 others wounded, and many survivors in shock from the intensity of the ferocious Vietcong attack.

Arnett remained on the job with Supply Column 21, sharing the Marines' agony and their danger, until the relief column arrived six hours later. And when he emerged, dirty and tired but intact, he found outraged American information officers loudly denying that the enemy had knocked out any U.S. armor.

But Arnett had pictures to prove his story and, once again, the lying was demonstrated to be a sorry part of the American military command character in Vietnam. There was never any doubt in his war reporting, during the eight and a half years he spent in Vietnam, about who was telling the truth.

25. *JOHN S. KNIGHT ATTACKS VIETNAM WAR*
AND WARNS OF AN AMERICAN DEFEAT

The Editor Writes That Asians Will Seek Their Own Destiny
Despite the United States Military Intervention

Long before the United States became involved in the Vietnam War, John Shively Knight was warning against it. He used the considerable resources of his great newspaper chain to put his views before the public, hoping all the while to persuade the government to avoid what he believed was the road to unmitigated disaster.

What Knight wrote and what he did were unpopular then. Such large and prestigious news organizations as Time, Inc., were impugning both the motives and the patriotism of reporters in Vietnam who were challenging the government's claims of victory over the Vietcong. The outraged conservatives in the United States were attacking anybody who dared question the policy of making war on Communism wherever it challenged any established order. And the campuses of the land were seething with revolt.

It was at this stage that Knight recalled, in his Editor's Notebook in the *Akron Beacon Journal* and other Knight newspapers, that he had warned in 1954 against American involvement in Indochina.

On Feb. 21, 1954, he wrote:

"It is almost certain that at some stage France will pull out of Indochina. Are we prepared to cope with such a contingency? The plain answer seems to be no.

"Our government lacks a coherent policy. It does not know the answer to a problem as large as Indochina."

Later that same year, on April 4, he commented:

"Haven't we learned from Korea that 'united action' in Asia would be little more than a phrase; that we could expect only token assistance from other nations?

"Can't we recognize the dangers of gradual involvement? That they inevitably lead to war? Members of Congress . . . must be made to see the folly of engaging our land forces in the jungles of Indochina."

Knight went on to write, in a column on February 5, 1967:

"At that time, some 13 years ago, these warnings went unheeded. They were dismissed by the Secretary of Defense, Charles E. Wilson, who said he saw no possibility that American troops would be involved and that 'no such plan is under study.'

"Mr. Wilson, as has been the case with our present Secretary of Defense, proved to be a poor prophet."

Knight then quoted advice from Edwin O. Reischauer, former U.S. ambassador to Japan, who appealed against "new commitments" to make war in Vietnam. The editor commented disconsolately: "Good advice, indeed, but is anybody listening?"

Nobody in authority in Washington was listening. The troop buildup in Vietnam continued. The war widened. And on March 12, 1967, the U.S. command in Saigon announced the heaviest casualties of the war, 232 dead, 1,381 wounded and four missing. Knight wrote that day in his Editor's Notebook:

"This 'dirty little war' is now assuming the proportions of a major conflict. General William C. Westmoreland reminds us that American forces in Vietnam total 417,400 and will continue to increase. The end of the war and its outcome defy prediction.

"To those of us who have long opposed U.S. intervention in Vietnam, there is no solace to be found in our past warnings that 'little wars' have a way of erupting into big ones.

"The blood, the tears, the sacrifices of our gallant men in the field leave us sick at heart. We are saddened by this cruel slaughter, depressed over our inability to make the slightest contribution to our young men who are but the instruments of what we believe to be irrational foreign policy."

And yet, the proclamations of victory continued to flow from Washington and Saigon, though they had a hollow ring to them. The protests increased in fury, leading to insistent demands by the prowar forces that something should be done to stifle dissent. Not once, but a dozen times in the same year, Knight defended the right of dissent and warned against the efforts that then were being made to crack down on dissenters.

The climactic Tet offensive, which forced President Johnson to step aside at the end of his term instead of seeking reelection, was still months away when Knight wrote a prophetic column about the future. Here it is, taken from the exhibit that won him the Pulitzer Prize for Editorial Writing in 1968:

THE NATION FACES A MOMENT OF TRUTH

From the Akron Beacon Journal, August 6, 1967

A Miami business man writes as follows: "My friends and I are greatly disturbed by your criticism of President Johnson's handling of the Vietnam War problem. None of us has any idea of a good solution.

"We would like to suggest a 'Notebook' column of your thoughts as to the solution of this tragic situation."

In reply, I must be brutally frank in saying there can be no "good solution." If there were, I feel sure President Johnson would have thought of it a long time ago.

The war as presently conducted could drag on for years. We are not winning despite President Johnson's statement on July 13 of this year that he was "generally pleased with the progress that we have made militarily."

On the other hand, if we go all out to win by bombing Hanoi and Haiphong into rubble—as many people have suggested—the risk of bringing Red China or Russia or both into the war is indeed very real.

The civilized world could not survive a third world war fought with nuclear weapons.

As an opponent of our involvement in Vietnam since 1954, I have neither enjoyed criticizing three Presidents nor accurately predicting the tragic consequences of their policies.

Since 1963, the American people have been deluded by our government with such nonsense as the following:

—"The momentum of the Communist drive has been stopped. The South Vietnamese themselves are fighting their own battle, fighting well."—Secretary of State Dean Rusk, Feb. 13, 1963.

—"Secretary McNamara and General Maxwell Taylor reported their judgment that the major part of the U.S. military task can be completed by the end of 1965, although there may be a continuing requirement for a limited number of U.S. training personnel."—White House statement, Oct. 2, 1963.

—"I am hopeful we can bring back additional numbers of men. I say this because I personally believe this is a war the Vietnamese must fight. . . . I don't believe we can take on the combat task for them."—Secretary of Defense Robert McNamara, Feb. 3, 1964.

Other examples of similar misjudgments run to pages and are available upon request. Let it merely be said the Presidents Kennedy and Johnson were not well advised as to true conditions in Vietnam.

It is the commonly accepted theme that we are fighting to repel Communist aggression; that it constitutes a threat to Southeast Asia and to the free world.

If this be so, then our reputed allies should join in the effort. The Southeast Asia Treaty organization, formed in 1954, includes Australia, France, New Zealand, Pakistan, the Philippines, Thailand, the United Kingdom, and the United States.

Of these nations, France and Pakistan are disenchanted, the British lion is toothless, Australia and New Zealand have supplied less than 6,000 men, Thailand is a staunch ally and token support has come from the Philippines.

Japan, the mightiest pro-Western power in Asia, wants no part of the Vietnam War. Premier Sato has said the U.S. should stop the bombing of North Vietnam. World opinion is almost universally opposed to what we are doing.

Since it is evident that our military tactics are not about to bring the North Vietnamese to the conference table, President

Johnson might summon a conference of those nations that profess to be on our side and say quite plainly,

"Gentlemen, we have been carrying the brunt of this war—almost quite alone. If you are convinced that the Communists must be defeated, we shall need your help. We are not prepared to do it alone forever. What is your answer?"

In the likely event that no strong support is forthcoming, the President must then consider the alternatives of total war, continuing to fight a holding action without victory, or pull out.

We cannot conquer the North Vietnamese or the Vietcong. Even if North Vietnam is totally bombed and a victory of sorts is achieved, the U.S. would have to garrison the country for a long period of years.

So there is no solution in a permanent sense. Unless, of course, a new Vietnamese government in Saigon to be elected should decide the Americans should go home.

This is not beyond the realm of possibility. In the long run the Asians will shape their own destiny and the white man's military presence will no longer be tolerated.

That, unhappily, is the way things turned out in Vietnam, except that American troops were not invited to leave; instead, they were thrown out, which was a consummation that not even John S. Knight in 1967 wanted to consider for the long view. For in 1917, he went to war with the American Expeditionary Forces in France to fight the war to end all wars, to make the world safe for democracy, and he later wrote that he believed in all those pious phrases. It was what led him to write, on April 9, 1967, this comparison with a more rebellious younger generation:

"If the young people of today are different from those of us who accepted the gauntlet without question, it is because they dare investigate the causes of war and examine its immorality. . . . So let our patriots on the home front—who have been called upon for no visible sacrifice—try to understand the feelings and emotions of our youth when they are less than enthusiastic over our professed goals. For theirs is a new generation which rightly challenges what their elders have done in the past."

Knight was 74 years old when he won his prize. In retirement at the age of 85 in Florida, and facing the new tests of the 1980s, he still maintained his hatred of war and his trust in youth.

THAT'S HIS BABY
Pulitzer Prize for Editorial Cartooning, 1968

A COMMENT ON PRESIDENT JOHNSON AND THE VIETNAM WAR BY
EUGENE GRAY PAYNE IN THE CHARLOTTE (N.C.) OBSERVER

THE TERROR OF WAR
Pulitzer Prize for News Photography, 1973

HUYNH CONG "NICK" UT, ASSOCIATED PRESS PHOTOGRAPHER, TOOK THIS
PICTURE OF A 9-YEAR-OLD GIRL FLEEING, WITH OTHER CHILDREN, WHEN
THE SOUTH VIETNAMESE AIR FORCE DROPPED NAPALM BOMBS
ON ITS OWN PEOPLE

26. SEYMOUR HERSH UNCOVERS THE TRAGEDY OF THE ARMY'S MASSACRE AT MY LAI

A Free Lancer, Acting on a Tip, Tracks Down
Eyewitnesses to the Slaying of 109 Civilians

Seymour Hersh was at loose ends. After graduating from the University of Chicago, he had gone into journalism and had served briefly as a Pentagon correspondent for the Associated Press in 1966–67. In the following year, he had been a press agent for Senator Eugene McCarthy's Presidential primary campaign in New Hampshire but had quit. As he himself explained, the work "was driving me crazy."

Now the Chicago-born Hersh at 32 years of age wasn't quite sure what to do next. It was early in 1969. The Tet offensive by the Vietcong had sickened the nation on the way the Vietnam War was being fought. The campuses were erupting. And in the midst of all the turmoil, Hersh received a tip on a shocking story from a source he had known at the Pentagon.

It was well-nigh unbelievable that the rumored incident could have happened—that well-disciplined, well-trained American troops should have run amok and pitilessly slaughtered Vietnamese civilians in a village in Vietcong territory. But that was the substance of Hersh's tip.

Like many another reporter with a big story beckoning in the distance, he wasn't quite sure what to do next. But of one thing he was certain: He trusted his source and he was bound to investigate.

But how? He had no funds. He belonged to no news organization. He had no credentials as a reporter beyond the narrow circle of his own acquaintances. Somewhere, he heard that a small foundation, the Philip Stern Family Fund in Washington, D.C., was willing to back investigative journalists with modest sums. And, miracle of miracles, he so impressed the people at the Stern Fund that he was given a grant of $2,000.

In these days when a single newspaper spends as much as $300,000 on an investigative story (which was what *Newsday* expended in its "Heroin Trail" campaign), a couple of thousand dollars doesn't go very far. But Hersh didn't need much. What he did was to track down and interview members of the Army unit that was allegedly involved—a platoon of the Eleventh Brigade of the Americal Division.

From them he learned what actually had happened in a hamlet called "Pinkville" by the American military, which was the village of My Lai,

some six miles northeast of Quang Ngai. And he heard for the first time of
the involvement of the platoon leader, a respected Vietnam combat
veteran named Lt. William L. Calley, Jr., in the shooting deaths of more
than a hundred Vietnamese civilians on March 16, 1968.

This by itself was certainly worth pursuing, but who would be likely to
print it on the word of a little-known free-lancer? Hersh kept on digging
and found out, after a time, that the Army itself had been conducting an
undercover inquiry in the incident, that Calley was under detention at
Fort Benning, Ga., and that a court martial was almost certain to result.

Now he had enough. Through a neighbor, 24-year-old David Obst,
Hersh arranged to circulate his story in a series of articles in a hastily
formed news syndicate that Obst headed, the *Dispatch News Service*. Its
"office" was in Obst's bedroom. Its only reporter was Seymour Hersh.

But the series of articles went out, nonetheless, and 36 newspapers
including the *St. Louis Post-Dispatch* ran the story beginning late in
1969. This is a digest of the first article as it was published at the time:

AT MY LAI: "WE CAME IN HOT . . . "

By Seymour M. Hersh

Copyright 1969 by Dispatch News Service and Published in the St. Louis
Post-Dispatch, Nov. 13, 1969

FORT BENNING, Ga., Nov. 13—Lt. William L. Calley Jr., 26 years
old, is a mild-mannered, boyish-looking Vietnam combat veteran
with the nickname "Rusty." The Army is completing an investigation of charges that he deliberately murdered at least 109
Vietnamese civilians in a search-and-destroy mission in March
1968, in a Vietcong stronghold known as "Pinkville." (Its real
name: My Lai.)

Calley has formally been charged with six specifications of mass
murder. Each specification cites a number of dead, adding up to
the 109 total, and charges that Calley did "with premeditation
murder . . . Oriental human beings, whose names and sex are
unknown, by shooting them with a rifle."

The Army calls it murder; Calley, his counsel and others
associated with the incident describe it as a case of carrying out
orders.

"Pinkville" has become a widely known code word among the
military in a case that many officers and some Congressmen

believe will become far more controversial than the recent murder charges against eight Green Berets.

Army investigation teams spent nearly one year studying the incident before filing charges against Calley, a platoon leader of the Eleventh Brigade of the American Division at the time of the killings.

Calley was formally charged on or about September 6, 1969 in the multiple deaths, just a few days before he was due to be released from active service.

Calley has since hired a prominent civilian attorney, former Judge George W. Latimer of the U.S. Court of Military Appeals, and is now awaiting a military determination of whether the evidence justifies a general court martial. Pentagon officials describe the present stage of the case as the equivalent of a civilian grand jury proceeding.

Calley, meanwhile, is being detained at Fort Benning, where his movements are sharply restricted. Even his exact location on the base is a secret; neither the provost marshal nor the Army's Criminal Investigation Division knows where he is being held.

The Army has refused to comment on the case "in order not to prejudice the continuing investigation and the rights of the accused." Similarly, Calley—although agreeing to an interview—refused to discuss in detail what happened on March 16, 1968.

However, many other officers and civilian officials, some angered by Calley's action and others angry that charges of murder were filed in the case, talked freely at Fort Benning and Washington.

These factors are not in dispute:

The Pinkville area, about six miles northeast of Quang Ngai, had been a Vietcong fortress since the Vietnam War began. In early February 1968, a company of the Eleventh Brigade, as part of Task Force Barker, pushed through the area and was severely shot up.

Calley's platoon suffered casualties. After the Communist Tet offensive in February 1968, a larger assault was mounted, again with high casualties and little success. A third attack was mounted and it was successful.

The Army claimed 128 Vietcong were killed. Many civilians also were killed in the operation. The area was a free fire zone from which all non-Vietcong residents had been urged, by leaflet, to flee. Such zones are common throughout Vietnam.

One man who took part in the mission with Calley said that in two earlier attacks, "We were really shot up."

"Every time we got hit it was from the rear," he said. "So the third time in there the order came down to go in and make sure no one was behind.

"We were told to just clear the area. It was a typical combat assault formation. We came in hot, with a cover of artillery in front of us, came down the line and destroyed the village.

"There are always some civilian casualties in a combat operation. He isn't guilty of murder."

The order to clear the area was relayed from the battalion commander to the company commander to Calley, the source said.

Calley's attorney said in an interview: "This is one case that should never have been brought. Whatever killing there was was in a firefight in connection with the operation.

"You can't afford to guess whether a civilian is a Vietcong or not. Either they shoot you or you shoot them.

"This case is going to be important—to what standard do you hold a combat officer in carrying out a mission?

"There are two instances where murder is acceptable to anybody; where it is excusable and where it is justified. If Calley did not shoot anybody because of the tactical situation or while in a firefight, it was either excusable or justifiable."

Adding to the complexity of the case is the fact that Army investigators from the Army inspector general's office, which conducted the bulk of the inquiry, considered filing charges against six other men involved in the action on March 16.

A Fort Benning infantry officer has found that the facts of the case justify Calley's trial by general court martial on charges of premeditated murder.

Pentagon officials said the next steps are for the case to go to Calley's brigade commander and finally to the Fort Benning post commander for findings on whether there should be a court martial. If they so hold, final charges and specifications will be drawn up and made public at that time, the officials said.

Calley's friends in the officer corps at Fort Benning, many of them West Point graduates, were indignant. However, knowing the high stakes of the case, they expressed their outrage in private.

"They're using this as a god-damned example," one officer complained. "He is a good soldier. He followed orders.

"There weren't any friendlies in the village. The orders were to shoot anything that moved."

Another officer said, "It could happen to any of us. He had killed and seen a lot of killing. . . . Killing becomes nothing in Vietnam. He knew that there were civilians there, but he also knew that there were VC among them."

A third officer, also familiar with the case, said: "There's this question—I think anyone who goes to Nam asks it. What's a civilian? Someone who works for us by day and puts on Vietcong pajamas at night?"

There is another side of the Calley case—one that the Army cannot yet disclose. Interviews have brought out the fact that the investigation into the Pinkville affair was initiated six months after the incident, only after some of the men who served under Calley complained.

The Army has photographs purported to be of the incident, although these have not been introduced in evidence in the case and may not be.

"They simply shot up this village and [Calley] was the leader of it," said one Washington source. "When one guy refused to do it, Calley took the rifle away and did the shooting himself."

Asked about this, Calley refused to comment.

One Pentagon officer discussing the case tapped his knee with his hand and remarked, "Some of those kids he shot were this high. I don't think they were Vietcong. Do you?"

A source of amazement among all those interviewed was that the story has yet to reach the press. "Pinkville has been a word among GIs for a year," one official said. "I'll never cease to be amazed that it hasn't been written about before."

That was just the beginning. In a succeeding article, he quoted some of the participants in the My Lai action with telling effect. One of them, Sgt. Michael Bernhardt of Franklin Square, N.Y., who then was completing his Army duty at Fort Dix, N.J., said, "The whole thing was so deliberate. It was point-blank murder and I was standing there watching it."

Bernahrdt was in another platoon and he gave this account of the massacre: "They [Calley's men] were doing a whole lot of shooting up there. . . . I walked up and saw those guys doing strange things. One: They were setting fire to the hootches and huts and waiting for people to come out and then shooting them. Two: They were going into the hootches and shooting them up. Three: They were gathering people in groups and shooting them. . . ."

Another witness quoted by Hersh, Michael Terry of Urem, Utah, said, "They just marched through shooting everybody. Seems like nobody said anything. . . . They just started pulling people out and shooting them."

One of the most horrifying scenes Terry described was when 20 villagers were lined up and shot in front of a ditch—"just like a Nazi-type thing. . . . One officer ordered a kid to machine-gun everybody down but the kid just couldn't do it. He threw the machine gun down and the officer picked it up. . . ."

A third eyewitness, unnamed, was quoted by Hersh as corroborating the stories of Bernhardt and Terry, saying, "I was shooting pigs and a chicken while others were shooting people. It isn't just a nightmare. I'm completely aware of how real it was."

The three eyewitnesses did even more to substantiate the details of what happened at My Lai. They corroborated a three-page letter that had been sent to the Army and a number of government officials by Ronald Ridenhour, an ex-GI who then was a student at Claremont College in California.

When Hersh's series was brought to the attention of the Pulitzer Prize Jury in International Reporting early in 1970, nobody in the room had any doubt of what the result would be. In the jury's report, it "unanimously and enthusiastically" recommended Hersh for the award and wrote:

"In the face of disbelief and disinterest on the part of many newspapers, and operating with limited resources, Hersh showed initiative, enterprise, and perseverance to break the My Lai story—a story that shook the nation and had vast international repercussions.

"In pursuing his story to the point that the topmost officials in the United States, South Vietnam, Great Britain, and other countries became publicly and directly involved, Hersh's performance met the highest journalistic standards for which Pulitzer recognition is traditionally granted."

The Pulitzer Board approved the award unanimously and without debate at its 1970 meeting.

Calley was convicted by an Army court martial in the slaying of 22 Vietnamese civilians after a lengthy trial. His sentence, though overturned when he carried the case to court, was reinstated by a U.S. appeals court in New Orleans on Sept. 10, 1975.

By that time Hersh had joined the staff of the *New York Times* and become firmly established as an outstanding investigative reporter. Among his other feats were the disclosure of the American secret bombing of Cambodia before 1970 and the secret files kept on at least 10,000 American citizens by the CIA. In March of 1979, he left the *Times* to research and write a book about Henry A. Kissinger and his years at the National Security Council and as Secretary of State.

27. THE AKRON BEACON JOURNAL'S STAFF COVERS KENT STATE KILLINGS

The Tragedy Climaxes Four Days of Rioting on the Campus After Nixon Orders a U.S. Invasion of Cambodia

It was a perfect May Day—bright and sunny with the soft breath of spring rustling through the budding trees. On the campus of Kent State University in Ohio, however, the mood of many in the student body was troubled with uncertainty. The night before, April 30, 1970, President Nixon had announced to the nation that he was sending American troops into Cambodia to wipe out the sanctuaries of enemy North Vietnamese.

There were two rallies at Kent State that noon, in which some 850 students joined in a peaceful protest and dispersed. What happened there was not unusual. It was also happening on campuses all over the country.

But just before midnight on a downtown street a mile from the campus, somebody lit a bonfire, students blocked traffic, signs denouncing President Nixon sprouted everywhere and, suddenly, the peaceful crowd turned into a mob.

Windows were smashed at 15 business places in the ensuing riot before police sent tear gas swirling over the demonstrators, who by this time had grown to 500. Fourteen students were arrested for disorderly conduct. The rest fled and the town officials imposed an 8 P.M. to dawn curfew for the rest of the week.

Next night, a Saturday, Mayor LeRoy Satrum called for National Guard troops when he heard reports that there would be more trouble and units of the 145th Infantry responded. But before the Guard showed up a student mob estimated at 300 persons had overwhelmed the security guard at the ROTC building on campus, set it afire, and stoned firemen when they tried to control the flames.

Now it was clear that an ugly situation was building at Kent State. Governor James A. Rhodes came to the university next day, a Sunday, and heard County Prosecutor Robert Kane demand the closing of the institution immediately. The Governor and the university authorities decided against it after a tour of the town and the campus.

There was more rioting Sunday night by more than 1,000 demonstrators. At the height of the turmoil, 200 demonstrators sat down at the campus entrance and were driven off by Guardsmen who used tear gas, and 62 of them were arrested. Everybody in authority was blaming the small radical group of Students for a Democratic Society on campus, but this was no mere staged SDS riot. Too many others were participating.

By this time, the National Guard strength on campus had reached 1,300 with the arrival of a unit of the 107th Armored Cavalry. And all well remembered their rule of engagement: that if somebody shot at them, they were to shoot back.

On Sunday night, however, all they did was to break up crowds and keep the peace.

On Monday, May 4, the sun rose on a deceptively peaceful campus but there was a chill in the air. At noon, a bell tolled and students assembled on campus for another demonstration against the new war in Cambodia. Almost 100 troops of the Ohio National Guard faced them with loaded rifles.

After three nights of rioting, everybody on both sides of that deadly confrontation knew that anything could happen. Certainly, in the newsroom of the *Akron Beacon Journal* 12 miles away, there was preparation for the very worst and, on the scene, two staff reporters and two photographers were watching tensely.

The Guard began to move against the students with the mournful tolling of the campus bell.

Jeff Sallot, a reporter who was on an open phone to the *Beacon Journal* newsroom, told how the first tear gas canister burst among the students. At once, State Editor Pat Englehart dispatched four more reporters and two photographers to Kent State.

They had barely started when Sallot told how students were hurling rocks at the advancing Guardsmen and how the students were fleeing behind Taylor Hall once the troops closed in. Within ten minutes, the Guardsmen turned and began another sweep toward the Commons.

The rocks again filled the air. And the firing began. . . .

Robert H. Giles, then the *Beacon Journal*'s executive editor, recalled: "At the instant of the shooting, we were coming up on the deadline to start the presses for our main afternoon run. The first report was that four persons had been shot. Then UPI moved a bulletin that four were dead, two of them guardsmen. We ordered the presses held. . . ."

Bob Page, a reporter at Robinson Memorial Hospital in nearby Ravenna, phoned just then to say that he had seen the victims wheeled into the emergency room, that a doctor had confirmed all four were dead—two men, two women, but that none were Guardsmen.

The *Beacon Journal* went with that and put out the following story:

"ALL THE GUARDSMEN TURNED AND FIRED"

From the Akron Beacon Journal, Mary 4, 1970

KENT—Four persons were killed and at least 11 others shot as National Guardsmen fired into a group of rock-throwing protesters at Kent State university today.

Three of the dead were tentatively identified as William Schneider, Jeffrey Miller, and Allison Krause. The fourth was an unidentified girl.

Injured were: Dean Mahler, Thomas Grace, Joe Lewis, John Cleary, Alan Canford, Robert Stamp, Dennis Brackenridge, Doug Wrentmore, and Bill Hersler. Two of the nine are National Guardsmen.

Six of those taken to Robinson Memorial Hospital suffered gunshot wounds. Three were in critical condition. Two of those taken to the hospital were identified as Guardsmen suffering from shock. One of the Guardsmen was released this afternoon.

Gunshots rang out about 12:30 P.M., half an hour after Guardsmen fired tear gas into a crowd of 500 on the Commons behind the university administration offices. Demonstrators hurled rocks and tear gas grenades back as they scattered.

Police are holding a man who said he used a gun he was carrying when he was attacked by demonstrators. The man reportedly had press credentials and carried a camera.

A newspaperman, an eyewitness to the shooting, said the gunshots were fired after one student hurled a rock as Guardsmen were turning away after clearing the Commons.

"One section of the Guard turned around and fired and then all the Guardsmen turned and fired," he said.

According to the witness, some of the Guardsmen were firing in the air while others were firing straight ahead.

Guardsmen and police immediately cordoned off all buildings on the campus, permitting no one to enter or leave.

One National Guardsman collapsed during the melee, complaining of chest pains.

The shooting broke out after students had rallied on the Commons in defiance of an order not to assemble.

An officer in a jeep ordered them over a loud speaker to disperse. He begged them to break up "for your own good." The protesters laughed and jeered. The troops, wearing gas masks, then began to launch canisters of tear gas.

The troops were en route back to their original positions when about 20 students, both boys and girls, ran toward them from behind Taylor Hall.

Stones and sticks fell on the troops and obscenities filled the air.

Apparently without orders, the guardsmen turned and aimed their M-1 rifles at the charging students and began firing.

Students in the emergency ward at Robinson Memorial Hospital said they wanted to get on the Commons to discuss demands. They said that as they started gathering the Guardsmen began throwing "pepper" gas at them and the students started throwing rocks.

Then, they said, the firing started.

One student with a guru moustache and long hair said, "They'll pay for it. It's not the radicals, it's the most conservative groups on campus who will bring the university down now."

With National Guardsmen patrolling all of Kent, schools were dismissed, stores were closed, and traffic was blocked from either entering or leaving Kent.

More than 1,000 anti-war demonstrators, many of them students, clashed with Guardsman and police Sunday night before they were driven back with bayonets and tear gas.

Nine persons were reported injured in the rioting, including three Guardsmen. More than 100 were arrested, the majority for violations of an 8 P.M.-to-dawn curfew imposed by Kent city officials.

Militants in three nights have burned the University's ROTC Building, smashed 56 downtown store windows and threatened Kent businessmen.

National Guard Brig. Gen. Robert Canterbury said the Guard will remain as long as necessary.

The rioting Friday night came a day after President Nixon told the nation he was sending troops into Cambodia.

Very soon, the *Beacon Journal* staff came up with an accurate and complete list of the dead and the circumstances under which each of the victims was fatally shot. This was the full report:

"Sandra Scheuer, 20, a sophomore from Youngstown, Ohio. She was walking to class that Monday afternoon when a bullet went through her windpipe.

"Allison Krause, 19 a freshman from Pittsburgh, Pa. The day before, she had placed a flower in the barrel of a National Guardsman's rifle. She was running across a parking lot with her boyfriend when the Guard began to fire.

"Jeffery Miller, 20, a sophomore from Plainview, N.J. Moments before he was shot, he was among a group of students who were taunting the Guard. A bullet hit him in the face.

"William Schroeder, Jr., 19, a freshman from Lorain, Ohio. He was attending Kent State on an ROTC scholarship and was watching the demonstration when he was shot."

In the nearby *Valley Daily News* and *Daily Dispatch* of Tarentum and New Kensington, Pa., 21-year-old John Paul Filo's historic picture was published of a 14-year-old runaway from Florida, Mary Vecchio, kneeling in tears with despairing arms outstretched over the body of Jeffery Miller.

Most of the story itself was told in the *Beacon Journal* on that and subsequent days. On the day of the Guard assault, Bob Giles recalls, the newspaper had 27 reporters and four photographers in action. The *Beacon Journal* also took the lead in the investigation.

The first break in the Guardsmen's story that they had been fired on by a sniper came on May 5 when a reporter, Jim Herzog, was told by one guardsman that he never fired his rifle because he had not felt threatened. Three days later, another reporter, Abe Zaidan, disclosed that Ohio Governor James Rhodes had refused to close Kent State before the shootings occurred and had issued orders to the Guard to break up all campus rallies.

The most controversial break in the newspaper's inquiry came on May 23 when a reporter, Ray Redmond, quoted from a confidential FBI report

TRAGEDY AT KENT STATE
Pulitzer Prize for News Photography, 1971

JOHN PAUL FILO, 21, TOOK THIS PICTURE FOR THE VALLEY DAILY NEWS OF
TARENTUM, PA., AND THE DAILY DISPATCH OF NEARBY NEW KENSINGTON,
JUST AFTER JEFFERY MILLER, 20, WAS KILLED WITH THREE OTHER
STUDENTS AT KENT STATE MAY 4, 1970, WHEN THE OHIO NATIONAL
GUARD OPENED FIRE ON WAR PROTESTORS. KNEELING OVER HIS BODY IS A
14-YEAR-OLD RUNAWAY FROM FLORIDA, MARY VECCHIO, WHO HAPPENED
TO BE ON CAMPUS THAT DAY

that said the Guard's shootings at Kent State had not been necessary. That, basically, was also the contention of the students.

The *Beacon Journal* took a lot of heat for its findings, for public opinion was sharply divided over the tragedy. As Bob Giles wrote long afterward: "There were those who felt that the student demonstrators had received exactly what they deserved and those who were quite ready to charge the National Guardsmen involved with murder. We believed it was vital for the *Beacon Journal* to be deeply involved in the quest for truth." [1]

The *Beacon Journal*'s staff was awarded the Pulitzer Prize in General Local reporting for 1971 and John Paul Filo won the Spot News Photography award.

28. SYDNEY SCHANBERG SEES GENOCIDE AS THE COMMUNISTS SEIZE CAMBODIA

The New York Times's Correspondent Stays Behind to Record the Fall of Phnom Penh and Is Threatened with Execution

The defenses of Phnom Penh were crumbling in the spring of 1975. On every side, Communist forces were advancing toward what was to be final victory in their five-year war to overwhelm Cambodia. All Americans were being evacuated, including correspondents for American news organizations.

All except one—Sydney H. Schanberg of the *New York Times.*

The *Times* had ordered Schanberg to leave along with the rest of the Americans. But he decided on his own responsibility to stay and take his chances on getting out alive.

Syd Schanberg was no wild-eyed young trenchcoat type, but a seasoned, 41-year-old correspondent, married eight years and the father of two small daughters. He was 20 years out of Harvard and had worked his way through the *Times*'s ranks beginning as a copy boy in 1959 and a first-year reporter in 1960. From 1969 on he had been reporting from Asia, first as bureau chief in New Delhi and later in Vietnam. He was well aware of the risks he was taking and the displeasure of the *Times*'s foreign desk was the least of these.

Outside the business, Schanberg still had to make a name for himself.

[1] Letter from Robert H. Giles, now the executive editor of the *Rochester* (N.Y.) *Democrat and Chronicle* and the *Times-Union,* dated Oct. 3, 1979.

But on the inside, present and former correspondents liked to read him because he had a way of putting things in intensely personal terms.

There was, for example, this vignette of a soldier taking his fatally wounded child from a bomb-shattered refugee enclosure: "He picks up his daughter in his shaking arms: his face, bathed in cold sweat, contorts as he tries to hold back the tears that come anyway. 'I love all my children,' is all that he says as he walks away with the dying child."

And this, in the last days of Phnom Penh as a symbol of the old regime:

"Today, with Phnom Penh largely encircled by the Communist-led insurgents, the United States Embassy is burning some of its files in order to 'thin itself down,' to prepare for the possibility of evacuation—and the ashes drift slowly to the embassy courtyard."

And so, soon after sunrise on April 17, he drove to the northern edge of the capital, saw soldiers and refugees pouring in, and knew that the last defense line had collapsed. He returned to his room at the Hotel Le Phnom, heard small-arms fire in the distance and clearly saw that the retreat of the last defense forces had begun.

In his notebook he wrote: "The city is falling."

"White flags sprouted from housetops," he continued. "Some soldiers were taking the clips out of their rifles; others were changing into civilian clothes."

Then in came the conquerors around 9 A.M., to be greeted by some with cheers and embraces and by many others with sheer panic. Very soon, the correspondent noted that a forced exodus of citizens was under way from the city. He reported that some Western observers believed they were seeing genocide being committed on a vast scale.

But Schanberg could do very little about it other than to take notes. He couldn't file. Moreover, his personal safety was at stake, for he had been snatched up with others by the conquerors and was being threatened with immediate execution.

After a time, he and the few non-Americans who had remained to tell the story were released and permitted to go to the Information Ministry where they saw about 50 prisoners, among them the principal leaders of the fallen government, who were soon joined by the premier, Long Boret. The premier's eyes were puffy and red, very possibly from weeping, the correspondent noted; after all, he had been among those marked for execution. He had difficulty speaking coherently.

Schanberg wrote of the premier that day of surrender: "He could mumble only yes, no, and thank you, so conversation was impossible."

The day dragged on and the tension grew ever greater for those like Schanberg who had stayed behind and for the Cambodians who were captives of the conquerors. But as always, the correspondent put down everything he saw and everything he heard.

By one of those strange but fortunate circumstances that sometimes seem to safeguard correspondents and protect them from their own rashness, he found refuge in the French Embassy. And from then until May 8, when he was safely evacuated with others by truck to Bangkok in Thailand, he devoted as much time as he could to gathering information about the countryside and watching at first hand one of the worst instances of human repression of modern times.

For the May 9 issue of the *Times*, he produced an epic account of 8,000 words that told for the first time what was actually happening in Cambodia. His story began:

BANGKOK, Thailand, May 8—The victorious Cambodian Communists, who marched into Phnom Penh on April 17 and ended five years of war in Cambodia, are carrying out a peasant revolution that has thrown the entire country into upheaval.

Perhaps as many as three or four million people, most of them on foot, have been forced out of the cities and sent on a mammoth and grueling exodus into areas deep in the countryside where, the Communists say, they will have to become peasants and till the soil.

No one has been excluded—even the very old, the very young, the sick, and the wounded have been forced out onto the roads—and some will clearly not be strong enough to survive.

The old economy of the cities has been abandoned, and for the moment money means nothing and cannot be spent. Barter has replaced it.

All shops have either been looted by Communist soldiers for such things as watches and transistor radios or their goods have been taken away in an organized manner to be stored as communal property.

Even the roads that radiate out of the capital and that carried the nation's commerce have been virtually abandoned, and the population living along the roads, as well as that in all cities and towns that remained under the control of the American-backed government, have been pushed into the interior. Apparently the areas into which the evacuees are being herded are at least 65 miles from Phnom Penh.

"The operation was a complete success . . . as the autopsy will show!"

Pulitzer Prize for Editorial Cartooning, 1971

PAUL CONRAD OF THE LOS ANGELES TIMES OBSERVES THE OUTCOME OF
THE SECRET U.S. INVASION OF CAMBODIA

In sum the new rulers—before their overwhelming victory they were known as the Khmer Rouge—appear to be remaking Cambodian society in the peasant image, casting aside everything that belonged to the old system, which was generally dominated by the cities and towns and by the elite and merchants who lived there. . . .

The full horror of this mass movement toward tragedy—the removal of two million people who covered the roads "like a human carpet"—became clear in the correspondent's story as he developed his eyewitness account. He wrote at one point:

"A once-throbbing city became an echo chamber of silent streets lined with abandoned cars and gaping, empty shops. Street lights burned eerily for a population that was no longer there."

And he asked:

"Was this just cold brutality, a cruel and sadistic imposition of the law of the jungle, in which only the fittest will survive? Or is it possible that, seen through the eyes of the peasant soldiers and revolutionaries, the forced evacuation of the cities is a harsh necessity? . . . Or was the policy both cruel and ideological?"

These were questions he could not answer. But what he was able to describe in the most painful detail, and with a vivid personal touch, was the last hours before Phnom Penh went down before the Communist wave. He took up the somber tale at the point at which he and the few other foreigners who had stayed behind left Premier Long Boret and the other prisoners to try somehow to find a safe refuge for themselves, and here is what happened to him:

THE FALL OF PHNOM PENH

By Sydney H. Schanberg

From the New York Times, May 9, 1975

After leaving the prisoners and the military commander at the [Information] Ministry, we headed for the Hotel Le Phnom, where another surprise was waiting. The day before, the Red Cross had turned the hotel into a protected international zone and draped it with huge Red Cross flags. But the Communists were not interested.

At 4:55 P.M., troops waving guns and rockets had forced their way into the grounds and ordered the hotel emptied within 30 minutes. By the time we arrived, 25 minutes had elapsed. The fastest packing job in history ensued. I even had time to "liberate" a typewriter someone had abandoned since the troops had "liberated" mine earlier.

We were the last ones out, running. The Red Cross had abandoned several vehicles in the yard after removing the keys, so several of us threw our gear on the back of a Red Cross Honda pickup truck and started pushing it up the boulevard toward the French Embassy.

Several days before, word was passed to those foreigners who stayed behind when the Americans pulled out on April 12 that, as a last resort, one could take refuge at the embassy. France had recognized the new government, and it was thought that the new Cambodian leaders would respect the embassy compound as a sanctuary.

As we plodded up the road, big fires were burning on the city's outskirts, sending smoke clouds into the evening sky like a giant funeral wreath encircling the capital.

The embassy was only several hundred yards away, but what was happening on the road made it seem much farther. All around us people were fleeing, for there was no refuge for them. And coming into the city from the other direction was a fresh battalion marching single file. They looked curiously at us; we looked nervously at them.

In the 13 days of confinement that followed, until our evacuation by military truck to the Thai border, we had only a peephole into what was going on outside, but there were still many things that could be seen and many clues to the revolution that was going on.

We could hear shooting, sometimes nearby but mostly in other parts of the city. Often it sounded like shooting in the air, but at other times it seemed like small battles. As on the day of the city's fall, we were never able to piece together a satisfactory explanation of the shooting, which died down after about a week.

We could see smoke from huge fires from time to time, and there were reports from foreigners who trickled into the embassy that certain quarters were badly burned and that the water purification plant was heavily damaged.

The foreigners who for various reasons came in later carried stories, some of them eyewitness accounts, of such things as civilian bodies along the roads leading out of the city—people who had apparently died of illness or exhaustion on the march. But each witness got only a glimpse and no reliable estimate of the toll was possible.

Reports from roads to the south and southeast of Phnom Penh said the Communists were breaking up families by dividing the refugees by sex and age. Such practices were not reported from other roads on which the refugees flooded out of the capital.

Reports also told of executions, but none were eyewitness accounts. One such report said high military officers were executed at a rubber plantation a couple of miles north of the city.

In the French Embassy compound foreign doctors and relief agency officials were pessimistic about the survival chances of many of the refugees. "There's no food in the countryside at this time of year," an international official said. "What will they eat from now until the rice harvest in November?"

The new Communist officials, in conversations with United Nations and other foreign representatives during our confinement and in statements since, have rejected the idea of foreign aid "whether it is military, political or economic, social, diplomatic, or whether it takes on a so-called humanitarian form." Some foreigners wondered whether this included China, for they speculated that the Communists would at least need seed to plant for the next harvest.

Whether the looting we observed before we entered the French compound continued is difficult to say. In any case, it is essential to understand who the Communist soldiers are to understand the behavior of some of them in disciplinary matters, particularly looting.

They are peasant boys, pure and simple—darker skinned than their city brethren, with gold in their front teeth. To them the city is a curiosity, an oddity, a carnival, where you visit but do not live. The city means next to nothing in their scheme of things.

When they looted jewelry shops, they kept only one watch for themselves and gave the rest to their colleagues or passersby. Transistor radios, cameras, and cars held the same toylike fascination—something to play with, as children might, but not essential.

From my airline bag on the day I was seized and threatened

with execution they took only some cigarettes, a pair of boxer underwear shorts, and a handkerchief. They passed up a blue shirt and $9,000 in cash in a money belt.

The looting did not really contradict the Communist image of rigid discipline, for commanders apparently gave no orders against the sacking of shops, feeling perhaps that this was at least due their men after five years of jungle fighting.

Often they would climb into abandoned cars and find that they would not run, so they would bang on them with their rifles like frustrated children, or they would simply toot the horns for hours on end or keep turning the headlights on and off until the batteries died.

One night at the French Embassy I chose to sleep on the grass outside; I was suddenly awakened by what sounded like a platoon trying to smash down the front gates with a battering ram that had bright lights and a loud claxon. It was only a bunch of soldiers playing with and smashing up the cars that had been left outside the gates.

Though these country soldiers broke into villas all over the city and took the curious things they wanted—one walked past the embassy beaming proudly in a crimson-colored wool overcoat that hung down to his Ho Chi Minh sandals—they never stayed in the villas. With big, soft beds empty, they slept in the courtyards or the streets.

Almost without exception foot soldiers I talked with, when asked what they wanted to do, replied that they only wanted to go home.

The jury that surveyed the field of international reporting, during the deliberations for the Pulitzer Prizes for 1976, had to make a most difficult choice.

For in addition to Schanberg's account of the fall of Cambodia and his exclusive disclosure of how two million people had been moved out of Phnom Penh in a massive peasant revolution, there were dramatic accounts of the capture of Saigon by George Esper of the Associated Press, who also had stayed behind for the sake of the story, and by Keyes Beech and Robert Tamarkin of the *Chicago Daily News*, who had barely escaped with their lives. This was how it came out:

"The jury feels that Mr. Schanberg's excellent and sensitive professional performance and his personal courage in covering this story make him the most distinguished candidate for a Pulitzer Prize in this category this year."

With that judgment, the Pulitzer Prize Board agreed and Schanberg thus received the Pulitzer Prize for International Reporting for 1976.

But that wasn't all of the Cambodia story. The new regime, which had been supported by Communist China, soon was overwhelmed by a North Vietnamese invasion backed by Russia. But the change of rulers did not stop the senseless killing through violence and starvation. Twice more in the next four years, the plight of Indochinese refugees attracted massive coverage and resulted in Pulitzer Prize awards—to Henry Kamm of the *New York Times* in 1978, and in 1980 to a reporter-photographer team from the *Louisville Courier-Journal*, Joel Brinkley and Jay Mather. But despite worldwide protests, there was no end to the horror of Cambodia, for in June 1980, a Vietnamese invasion force attacked the Cambodian refugee camps in Thailand.

VII. PRESIDENCY AND PRESS: A CLASH OF POWER

Most of the Presidents of the United States in the 1960s and 1970s have attempted on occasion to use the press, radio, and television to advance their own image and their policies, but with indifferent and sometimes appalling results. The American press, in particular, does not take kindly to government management.

In consequence, some of the masters of the White House have come to fear the press as the dominant leader of the news media. Others have mistrusted all but the most favored newspapers and columnists and have fought the rest, openly or covertly. Only one, Dwight David Eisenhower, remained unimpressed by the newspapers throughout his eight years in office, sometimes to the point of indifference.

Out of the tensions that inevitably were generated by this uneasy relationship, a clash of power and purpose has developed between the Presidency and a substantial part of the press that is perceived with concern and indeed alarm by influential segments of the American public.

If the newspapers persist in uncovering the frailties of government as a part of what they deeply believe to be their function in a democratic society, and if the government fights back by curtailing their privileges under the First Amendment, many thoughtful citizens fear that all our institutions will be weakened as a result.

Walter B. Wriston, chairman of the First National City Bank of New York: has written: "The freedom of all of us rides with the freedom of the press. Nevertheless, its continued freedom and ours will ultimately depend upon the media not exploiting to the fullest their unlimited power. They can and must criticize the government but they cannot replace constitutional authority by assuming that no secrets are valid. . . . In a world in which one government after another abandons democracy, we must all justify our freedom by the use we make of it every day. When freedom is abused until it becomes license, all liberty is put in jeopardy." [1]

Most journalists find it difficult to accept such a limited role for the press. More than forty years ago, Walter Lippmann wrote: "It is only human for officials to feel that unfavorable news and critical comment are biased, incompetent, and misleading. There is no denying the sincerity of their complaints and there is no use pretending that any newspaperman can regularly give the whole objective truth about all complicated and controversial questions. The theory of a free press is that the truth will emerge from free reporting and free discussion, not that it will be presented perfectly and instantly in any one account. But officials find it hard to remember that." [2]

Franklin Delano Roosevelt was one of the few Presidents of this century who recognized that unpalatable truth and was able to turn it to his own advantage. Despite the enmity of 80 percent of the newspaper publishers of the land, who pounded at him almost daily in their editorial pages, Roosevelt held nearly 1,000 press conferences during his four terms—more than other other occupant of the White House before or since. [3] While he had to withstand the harshest of attacks by his newspaper critics on his policies, his family, and even his dog, he had the sympathy and often the adulation of a very large section of the reporters with whom he dealt almost every day in Washington.

With his superb self-confidence, Roosevelt liked to tell both his friends and various White House correspondents that he wasn't

---

[1] *The Bulletin of the American Society of Newspaper Editors* (September 1976), pp. 9–13.

[2] Clinton Rossiter and James Lare, eds., *The Essential Lippmann* (New York: Random House, 1963), p. 410.

[3] FDR held 337 press conferences in his first term, 374 in his second, 379 in his third, and 8 in his fourth partial term. Total: 998.

unduly concerned about what publishers had editorial writers say about him on their editorial pages as long as he could control the headlines and the news accounts on Page 1.[4] And in this he was phenomenally successful.

None of our first citizens has ever matched Roosevelt's ability to communicate with the American public. He not only was the first President to use the press conference as a major factor in shaping public opinion; he also became the first President to take to the radio with speeches and "fireside chats" in an organized campaign to circumvent both editorial and political opposition.

As Eleanor Roosevelt once said: "There was a real dialogue between Franklin and the people. That dialogue seems to have disappeared from the government since he died."[5]

It is possible, of course, to overestimate the power of the press in working out the terms of this fundamental equation in a democratic society. Many journalists, and even a few bemused scholars, have done so. In a sense, this is in part a compensation for the many years in which the press was virtually disregarded as a factor in governance and thought of by many officials as an annoyance. But, to an even greater extent, it is a recognition of the manifold influences that the press exerts today on the political, economic, and social climate of this nation.

There is no other country in the world in which the press occupies such a special position. It was ordained by the Founding Fathers in forming our system of government and in writing a specific protection for the rights of a free press into the First Amendment. Unlike a parliamentary regime, in which the government is answerable to the elected representatives of the people in regularly scheduled question periods, Americans seem to have tolerated, almost by default, the press's assumption of the role of governmental watchdog.

This aspect of the press's activity was not recognized at the White House, however, until Theodore Roosevelt's administration at the beginning of the century. While he did talk to a few reporters now and then (there were only a handful around the White House at

[4] As a reporter, I heard FDR say this on two occasions.
[5] *W. E. Leuchtenberg, Franklin D. Roosevelt, and the Coming of the New Deal* (Chicago: University of Chicago Press, 1963) pp. 330–31.

the time), he told them little and consigned those who displeased him with their reports to the "Ananias Club."

It remained for Woodrow Wilson to initiate formal press conferences, but he had few of them despite his professed devotion to "open covenants openly arrived at." For that matter Warren Gamaliel Harding was as wary of the press as his predecessors, although he had been a small-town newspaper publisher (in Marion, Ohio).

As for Calvin Coolidge, that amiable cipher, he loftily ignored what the press and its people said about him by conveying, in the words of Walter Lippmann, the impression "that he had never heard of the newspaper with which his guest was connected and had never had anything printed in it called to his attention."[6] The embittered Herbert Hoover, however, gave battle when he was saddled with blame for the great depression, but he lost both his reputation and his high office to Franklin Roosevelt in the 1932 election.

On the surface, Harry S Truman followed Roosevelt's lead in holding numerous press conferences, but there was a difference in the way he regarded the news media—the dawn of the atomic age and the coming of television both wrought changes in the way a President communicated with the public.

And while the press still had things pretty much its own way in the infancy of television, that remarkable medium soon demonstrated that it was to have a profound influence all its own both on American politics and the American way of life. At the same time, the Presidency for the first time was swathed in a mantle of secrecy that spread from the necessity for protecting atomic secrets to such ridiculous details as protecting the amount of coffee beans the Army ordered for its troops.[7]

The passage of the Atomic Energy Act of 1946 and derivative legislation in later years put the press on notice that the government had a new and very powerful weapon for the protection of national secrets, including punishment up to and including life imprisonment and the death penalty for violating the law. It was

[6] Rossiter and Lare, *The Essential Lippmann*, pp. 410–11.
[7] One of my earliest experiences as a Pentagon consultant in 1953.

at this time that many in government began to say openly that the public's "right to know" was less important than peoples' "need to know."

Both Presidents Truman and Eisenhower were deeply concerned over the preservation of a greater security over all kinds of military information. But the regularity of leaks from rival military services at budget-making time, with each trying to undercut the other for some fancied budgetary advantage, led to a continued release of classified data.

And President Eisenhower's classic "cover story" following the Russians' destruction of a U-2 over the Urals and the capture of its pilot made a mockery of the entire secrecy campaign. Nikita S. Khrushchev, the head of the Soviet regime, took a savage delight in showing that the President of the United States had been caught in a colossal lie in denying any such event had ever taken place.

It remained for a Pentagon official, Assistant Secretary of Defense Arthur Sylvester, to put into words the kind of policies the American government had been following. After the two Cuban missile crises, he said, "I think the inherent right of the government to lie to save itself when faced with a nuclear crisis is basic." [8] Even through he retracted the statement in part following a public uproar over his frankness, this was really what many officials believed and it was what Presidents Kennedy and Johnson actually practiced when they thrust the United States into the Vietnam War. The deceit and subterfuge that marked White House policies in that unhappy era, once they were exposed in the Pentagon Papers, did much to increase mistrust of all branches of government among both the public and the press.

The news media, with their large economic stake at issue, were put in a difficult position by the mounting evidence of double dealing on the part of the White House in successive administrations. It didn't seem to matter whether the Presidents in office were Republican or Democratic. Their credibility was questioned at almost every turn, creating a state of mind among many in Washington that led directly to the Watergate exposé and the forced

[8] *Editor & Publisher* (Dec. 16, 1962). p. 14.

resignation of President Nixon for his lamentable attempt to cover up a "third-rate burglary" at Democratic National Headquarters.

What caused the slow shifting of position among the bulk of the news media from virtually all-out support of the government during and immediately after World War II to a position of questioner, critic, and sometime opponent of the government in the 1970s?

Some in journalism proclaim that it was done out of the loftiest of motives, a continual search for the truth, and perhaps this might be so for a few of the more high-minded in the profession. But most of the news media followed public opinion in changing from mild support of the Vietnam War to outright opposition.

And in the Watergate era, after initial doubts for months about the leadership of the *Washington Post* in attacking Nixon, even the most conservative newspapers and the most timid television managers finally followed the *Post*'s lead.

Jimmy Carter was well aware of the delicacy of his own situation at the White House following his election, for he had assured press and public during his campaign against President Ford: "I'll never lie to you." Charles Seib, the *Washington Post's* columnist on the news business, put him on notice bluntly as follows: "After the inauguration, I think we'll go lie-hunting. I think any politician who says, 'I'll never lie to you,' has a real problem or a short career."[9]

It wasn't long before William Safire of the *New York Times* was writing, "Jimmy Carter is trying to sell the Senate a dubious bill of goods about his long-time friend, Office of Management and Budget Director Bert Lance."[10] And following Lance's resignation under fire and his indictment in connection with his banking practices, Carter found himself thrown on the defensive in areas of public policy ranging from inflation to the quality of American representation in the United Nations.

While his character and moral purpose were never questioned, his credibility was—and in this he shared the fate of most of his predecessors in the latter part of the 20th century.

[9] *The Quill* (December 1976), p. 12.
[10] *New York Times*, July 21, 1977, op-ed page.

These patterns of the 1970s are likely to become even more strongly defined in the 1980s as the United States faces a tightened energy crisis and more shocks to its economy. For an embattled Presidency has a thousand critics for every lonely defender. And the press, as past experience has shown, is often more enthusiastic as a critic of government than it is as a friend.

In the following section on relationships between the Presidents and the Press during the 1960s and 1970s, some of the major correspondence, commentary, and editorial pronouncements of the press are presented—prime examples of the very large volume of material on the subject in the Pulitzer Prizes files.

29. WASHINGTON POST EXPOSES WATERGATE AND HELPS TOPPLE A PRESIDENT

Bob Woodward and Carl Bernstein Disclose "Cover-up"
by Nixon White House of a "Third-Rate Burglary"

For Bob Woodward, looking back over the Watergate scandal that he helped uncover, it was a case of dealing with events that were balanced on the knife-edge of history. "The outcome," he said, "might have gone either way."

For Carl Bernstein, Woodward's colleague in the investigation, there weren't as many doubts, for he saw proof positive in Watergate of the power of the American press. But, he added, "We were lucky, I guess."

For Howard Simons, the managing editor of the *Washington Post*, the pursuit of the inquiry and the subsequent resignation of President Richard Milhous Nixon still constituted something of a miracle. "At the beginning," he said reflectively, "we didn't know where the investigation would take us."

For Ben Bradlee, the *Post*'s executive editor, the impact of Watergate continues to affect the Presidency. It is, in his view, "a benchmark against which the performances of Presidents and the performances of journalists" are being measured today.

For Katharine Graham, then the *Post*'s publisher, who took the greatest risk of all, the outcome of Watergate represented vindication—the triumph of a newspaper that had stood alone for many weeks in what seemed to many like an unequal contest against the power of the Presidency. "Are we never going to know about all of this?" she once asked in despair. Eventually, she did, and so did a whole great nation.

Years have passed since the turgid drama of Watergate began to unfold that quiet Saturday morning of June 17, 1972, but the events that developed in a stunning succession of scenes on the great stage that is Washington will never be forgotten by those who were so directly involved.

Nobody is very cocky at the *Washington Post* today, although those who did the investigative work and those who directed it might well be excused if they did put on a few airs. The mood at the *Post*, in the troubled era at the opening of the 1980s, is philosophical rather than boastful, contemplative rather than self-serving.

As Howard Simons put it late one summer afternoon more than eight years after the first arrests were made in the case, "It would be great to say that we knew from the outset where we were going and what we were looking for, but it would not be true. We didn't know. We didn't even suspect at first.

"The whole thing was bizarre. It was a bizarre break-in at Democratic National Committee headquarters in Watergate. The White House's reaction was bizarre—a 'third-rate burglary,' they called it. And we went with an investigation by two kids, one of whom we'd nearly fired (Bernstein) and the other with less than a year's experience as a reporter.

"It's no wonder the White House didn't take us seriously. Even people on our own staff were concerned about what we were doing and why we were doing it. It was risky business. . . the 'left-leaning' *Washington Post* going after a powerful President.

"It must have seemed mighty bizarre to people in Iowa, for example. People kept asking, 'What's happened to that journalistic herd instinct? Why aren't other papers going into the Watergate investigation?' I don't know why they didn't. Maybe some were scared off because Woodward and Bernstein were our principal investigators, and not some big names. Maybe a lot of people in Washington believed all the White House denials.

"But soon, we began seeing that every denial of our stories was turning into a nondenial. Our investigation was standing up. The kids began looking very, very good. We became more confident and, even if we were alone on the story for many weeks, eventually the others had to come along. By that time, thanks to Woodward and Bernstein, we were far out in front.

Surely, we were lucky. But we also were the first paper to get into an investigation that turned out to be a very large piece of the history of our time." [1]

With this assessment, Ben Bradlee largely agrees. "No one really knew the depth of the impact that the Watergate story would have on American journalism and American history," he wrote. And, in a reference to the Pulitzer Prize Board's reversal of a Public Service Jury that refused to recommend a Pulitzer Prize for the *Post* in 1973, he added, "Least of all, the Pulitzer judges, who did not even rank it first, as I recall. Years later, Watergate's impact was still staggering." [2]

Except for that Pulitzer award in public service, however, the benefits the *Post* derived from Watergate were mainly intangible, as both Bradlee and Simons agreed. There was no overall gain in circulation that could have been attributed directly to Watergate except for a few hundred copies that were sold out of town—and at a loss. Nor was advertising affected one way or the other. What did matter very much was that the *Post* demonstrated, through its enterprise and its aggressiveness, that it was a national newspaper leader with such prestige that it could challenge the dominance of the *New York Times*—and do it successfully.

Of all the principals, Woodward remains the most bemused by the manner in which Watergate developed from a relatively small news story into a thundering national event. Reviewing the tangled skein of events in which he was involved, he reflected years later that the whole case might have gone the other way entirely. "And instead of being on the winning side," he said, "we could very well have wound up in the dock ourselves. It was that close."

Woodward, who has since become the chief of the metropolitan staff of the *Post* with the title of assistant managing editor, mused on the events of June 17, 1972—the door at the Watergate complex that was kept open in the hours before dawn with a piece of surgical tape across the lock, the curious watchman who noticed it and called police, the burglars who were caught flat-footed with their scientific break-in and copying equipment.

"It was a colossal accident," he said. "Suppose the watchman hadn't noticed? Suppose the police hadn't arrived in time? Suppose the lookouts had given the alarm in time for the burglars to escape? There would have been no Watergate."

Then, too, there was the circumstance of accidental assignment that

---

[1] Interview at the *Washington Post*, Sept. 11, 1979.
[2] Letter to author, Aug. 2, 1979, and interview, Sept. 11, 1979.

brought Woodward and Bernstein together. At first, they had worked either independently or with other members of the *Post* staff. It wasn't until August 1972 that they came together—the most effective investigative pair in the history of modern journalism.

"But what would have happened if there had been no 'Deep Throat' as our prime source?" Woodward asked, and shrugged. "Maybe we could have done it without him. Maybe not. I just don't know." Like all the others on the *Post*, he declined once again to discuss all the guessing about the identity of 'Deep Throat' except to say, somewhat hesitantly, in response to a question, "Yes, he's still alive, and well."

Woodward ticked off all the other circumstances in the long inquiry—and there were many—in which the scales could have been tipped against *Post* and its two young investigators. One that particularly impressed him was a challenge to the *Post* in a libel suit brought by the Democratic National Committee as a result of the break-in. The defendant Republicans on the Committee to Re-elect the President wanted the Federal District Court in the District of Columbis to direct Woodward and Bernstein to name their sources, but Judge Charles R. Richie refused the request.

"Suppose the judge had ordered us to reveal our Watergate sources and we had refused?" Woodward asked. "A contempt of court citation could have followed and we would have been in the dock, along with the *Post*."

It was this incident that caused Bernstein, in a discussion of Watergate at the Council on Foreign Relations in New York City, to concede that good fortune as well as good work and prime sources had been important in the Watergate inquiry. Woodward, however, did not share his erstwhile partner's rather glorified views of the power of the press as a determining factor in the case.

"Nobody helped us at first," he pointed out. "Nearly everybody but our own editors and our publisher doubted us. It was a scary situation and it didn't seem to reflect much credit on anybody's power at that stage. Because, as you can see, it might have gone either way."

As for the still undetermined factor in the case—the reason the Republican high command ordered the break-in—Woodward was inclined to take the simplest explanation as the most reasonable. "I don't think they had any idea what they were after," he remarked with a small smile. "It was just a fishing expedition. If you go through all the transcripts of trials and Congressional hearings, as I have, this is the only conclusion that stands up. All the other theories have had great big holes poked in them. I think that the people in the White House just decided to try to get some 'inside stuff' on the Democrats—and their people got caught. Then came the cover-up and the rest is history."[3]

That history, however, followed a tortuous course. There is little excuse to be found for the Washington press corps's dilatory conduct in the Watergate case. It is a virtual certainty, had such familiar names as David Broder, James Reston, or Richard L. Strout been signed to the initial disclosures, that the pack would have been in full cry. But Woodward and Bernstein? Who in hell were they? And why should they have been believed in 1972 at the outset of a Presidential campaign when Attorney General John N. Mitchell was saying, with such pompous self-righteousness, that the Watergate burglars "were not operating in our behalf or with our consent"?

Deny it though they will today, many of the Washington correspondents took the easy way out and chose to believe the White House press secretary, Ronald L. Ziegler, when he refused to comment on "a third-rate burglary attempt" and warned that "certain elements may try to stretch this beyond what it is."

Scant wonder that, as one illustrious and completely wrong-headed Washington correspondent of the time remarked to me, "The *Washington Post* is crazy to go with a couple of kids. Nixon is going to take the presses away from them before this is over."

As late as the beginning of 1973, when Bradlee and Simons conferred on the submission of the *Post*'s Watergate exhibit in the Pulitzer Prize competition, all they had to show for seven months of the most arduous work was a lot of unsubstantiated allegations by Woodward and Berstein.

True, the five Watergate burglars had pleaded guilty and a Senate committee was about to open an investigation of its own. At the White House, however, Nixon and his confident wrecking crew were still unshaken in their denials. And while some reporters were beginning to suspect grudgingly that Woodward and Bernstein might have something on the White House, the invariable response was, "So what? They can't hang anything on Nixon. He's too smart. And besides, he's going to be in the White House for another four years."

But Bradlee and Simons gamely ordered the preparation of two large blue cardboard folders containing the *Post*'s principal dislcosures during 1972 in the Watergate case and began a letter over Simon's signature, as follows, for submission to the Pulitzer Prize organization at Columbia University:

[3] Interview with Woodward Sept. 12, 1979, in Washington, D.C. The conversation with Bernstein at the Council on Foreign Relations took place in the spring of 1975 after a discussion there of Watergate and its results.

"The bugging of Watergate began as a caper; a seemingly classical break-in involving some bumbling second-story men. It now is a political embarrassment to the Administration. It is a nagging factor in American ethics. It is a criminal trial, where five defendants pleaded guilty. It is a promising Senate investigation. It is a challenge to democratic values. And it is not yet ended. . . ."

Following a reference to the Nixon White House's attacks on the credibility of the *Post*, the letter concluded: "What started as a caper has become an ever-spreading tumor on the body politic reaching from just outside the Oval Office into the very mechanisms by which Americans conduct their public affairs. 'Watergate' as a euphemism is now more than just wire-tapping and breaking and entering. It is political espionage and sabotage, reaching into the highest echelons of government."[4]

At that stage, not even the *Post* dared name President Nixon himself as the chief conspirator in a monumental cover-up of political bribery, chicanery, and worse.

Here are some of the principal disclosures at the very outset of the Watergate inquiry, as they were reported by the *Post* and summarized in the Pulitzer Prize exhibits (limited under the rules to 20 articles in the Public Service category and ten in National Reporting, for which a separate folder was prepared):

5 HELD IN WATERGATE BREAK-IN

By Alfred E. Lewis

From the Washington Post, June 18, 1972

Five men, one of whom said he was a former employee of the Central Intelligence Agency, were arrested at 2:30 A.M. yesterday in what authorities described as an elaborate plot to bug the offices of the Democratic National Committee here.

Three of the men were native-born Cubans and another was said to have trained Cuban exiles for guerrilla activity after the 1961 Bay of Pigs invasion.

They were surprised at gunpoint by three plainclothes officers of the Metropolitan Police Department in a sixth-floor office at the plush Watergate, 2600 Virginia Ave. NW, where the Democratic National Committee occupies the entire floor.

[4] From the *Washington Post*'s prize-winning 1972 exhibit in the Pulitzer Prize competition on file at the Columbia Journalism Library.

Police said two ceiling panels in the office of Dorothy V. Bush, secretary of the Democratic Party, had been removed.

Her office is adjacent to that of Democratic National Chairman Lawrence O'Brien. Presumably, it would have been possible to slide a bugging device through the panels in that office to a place above the ceiling panels in O'Brien's office.

All wearing rubber surgical gloves, the five suspects were captured inside a small office within the committee's headquarters suite.

Police said the men had with them at least two sophisticated devices capable of picking up and transmitting all talk, including telephone conversations. In addition, police found lock picks and door jimmies, and almost $2,000 in cash, most of it in $100 bills with the serial numbers in sequence.

The men also had with them one walkie-talkie, a short wave receiver that could pick up police calls, 40 rolls of unexposed film, two 35-millimeter cameras, and three pen-sized tear gas guns.

Near where they were captured were two open file drawers, and one national committee source conjectured that the men were preparing to photograph its contents. . . .

There followed an identification of the five prisoners and their pedigrees, but no linkage to the Republican Party or the White House in any manner, nor even an intimation that they had been hired for the work. The first story throughout was strictly deadpan.

Then, on June 18, a Sunday, Woodward and Bernstein went to work on the story by assignment from their immediate superior, Barry Sussman, and the metropolitan editor, Harry Rosenfeld. But they were far from the keen and well-integrated investigating team they later became; at the time, they knew each other only casually and one didn't really trust the other's judgment very much. On Monday, June 19, they broke the first big Watergate exclusive as follows:

GOP SECURITY AIDE AMONG 5 ARRESTED IN BUGGING AFFAIR

By Bob Woodward and Carl Bernstein

One of the five men arrested early Saturday in the attempt to bug the Democratic National Committee headquarters here is the salaried security coordinator for President Nixon's re-election committee.

The suspect, former CIA employee James W. McCord, Jr., 53, also holds a separate contract to provide security services to the Republican National Committee, GOP National Chairman Bob Dole said yesterday.

Former Attorney General John N. Mitchell, head of the Committee for the Re-Election of the President, said yesterday McCord was employed to help install that committee's own security system.

In a statement issued in Los Angeles, Mitchell said McCord and the other four men arrested at Democratic headquarters on Saturday "were not operating either in our half or with our consent" in the alleged bugging attempt.

Dole issued a similar statement adding that "we deplore action of this kind in or out of politics." An aide to Dole said he was unsure at this time exactly what security services McCord was hired to perform by the National Committee.

Police sources said last night they were seeking a sixth man in connection with the attempted bugging.

Other sources said yesterday there was still no explanation why the five suspects might have attempted to bug Democratic headquarters in the Watergate at 2600 Virginia Ave. NW, or if they were working for other individuals or organizations. . . .

Neither in the rest of that first Woodward-Bernstein story nor in any other that they or their rivals dug up was there any detailed and credible explanation of what the burglars expected to find and photograph or what they expected to overhear.

Everything from an exploration of the affairs of the Democratic Natioal Chairman, Lawrence F. O'Brien, to the possibility that the Democrats were accepting money from Fidel Castro has been mentioned as theory, but probably only President Nixon himself could speak with authority on the subject. He has never done so and his blanket pardon by President Ford will prevent him from making any further revelations, even in the unlikely event he chose to clear up that remaining mystery.

Regardless of the motive for Watergate, Woodward and Bernstein plunged ahead separately with the inquiry. On Tuesday, June 20, Woodward and another reporter came up with a story that tied two more suspects to the Watergate conspiracy—but they didn't have the goods on one of them. here was how the story began:

WHITE HOUSE CONSULTANT
TIED TO 'BUGGING' FIGURE

By Bob Woodward and E. J. Bachinski

A consultant to White House Special Counsel Charles W. Colson is listed in the address books of two of the five men arrested in an attempt to bug the Democratic National Headquarters here early Saturday.

Federal sources close to the investigation said the address books contain the name and home telephone number of Howard E. Hunt with the notation, "W. House" and W. H."

In addition, a stamped, unmailed envelope containing Hunt's personal check for $6 made out to the Lakewood Country Club in Rockville and a bill for the same amount were also found in the suspects' belongings, sources said.

Hunt worked for the Central Intelligence Agency from 1949 to 1970. At least two of the five suspects in what Democratic Party Chairman Lawrence F. O'Brien has called "an incredible act of political expionage" have worked for the CIA. The other three are either active in the anti-Castro movement in Florida or are known by leaders of that movement. . . ."

The story went on to report that Colson had brought Hunt into the White House and that Hunt had said, "Good God!" and hung up after being told that two of the Watergate suspects had his telephone number. The White House, of course, denied that either Colson or anybody else there had any knowledge of "this deplorable incident." It was notable that the affair no longer was referred to as a "third rate burglary attempt."

And with good reason. That day the White House log showed the President had met with his domestic policy adviser, John Ehrlichman, from 10:25 A.M. to 11:20 A.M., and with his chief of staff, H. R. Haldeman, from 10:30 A.M. to noon. Subsequently, the White House tape of the conversation with Haldeman showed a gap, attributed to an erasure, of 18 and a half minutes and some participants in the conspiracy blamed the

President himself for it, not his secretary, Rose Mary Woods, who said she had done it accidentally.

Then, on June 23, 1972, there had been an even more devastating tape recording of a Nixon-Haldeman conversation in the White House—the one in which the President had told his Chief of Staff to give instructions for the Watergate coverup to CIA Director Richard N. Helms and his deputy, Lieutenant General Vernon Walters:

". . . Say, 'Look, the problem is that this will open the whole, the whole Bay of Pigs thing, and the President just feels that'—ah, without going into the details. Don't, don't lie to them to the extent to say there is no involvement. Just say, 'This is a comedy of errors,' without getting into it, 'The President believes that is going to open the whole Bay of Pigs thing up again.' And, ah, 'Because these people are plugging for keeps,' and that they should call the FBI in and say that we wish for the country, 'Don't go any further into this case, period:'"

This was the famous "smoking pistol" quotation that clinched Nixon's involvement in Watergate, that was to blast his own contention that he knew nothing of the coverup until John Dean, his counsel, told him about it on March 21, 1973, and that was eventually to be the last blow which severed his hold on the Presidency. Here, Nixon clearly showed that he had not only known of the cover-up but had directed it, and that his statement of May 22, 1973, to the contrary was a fabrication.

But in June of 1972, directly after the burglary, all this could only be the wildest conjecture at the *Washington Post* and Woodward and Bernstein and their prize source, "Deep Throat," could only have the vaguest suspicions, no proof. At this stage, their only interest as reporters was to pursue the story wherever their leads sent them. And pursue it they did.

By Spetember 1, 1972, when they had been an investigative team for a month, they were able to report another major development:

LIDDY AND HUNT REPORTEDLY
FLED DURING BUGGING RAID

By Bob Woodward and Carl Bernstein

Two former White House aides were actually inside the Watergate and narrowly escaped arrest at the time of the June 17 break-in and alleged bugging of the Democratic headquarters there, according to a source close to the federal investigaton.

The two, G. Gordon Liddy and E. Howard Hunt, Jr., carrying at least one walkie-talkie, were warned that police had arrived by a

person or group acting as a lookout at the Howard Johnson Motel
across the street, according to the source. . . .

On the night of the bugging arrests, the five men found inside
Democratic headquarters also were warned but were unable to
elude the police, it was reported.

Hunt and Liddy, who had been in a stairwell or corridor in the
Watergate, may have gone directly to the motel across the street,
the source said. Earlier reports had placed them in the motel at
the time of the incident.

Liddy, a former FBI agent, was finance counsel to President
Nixon's re-election committee at the time of the incident. He was
later fired because he refused to answer FBI questions about the
Watergate incident.

High Republican officials, including President Nixon's campaign manager, Clark MacGregor, have singled out Liddy as the
party's primary connection with the incident.

A General Accounting Office report last week stated that
$114,000 in Nixon campaign funds were in Liddy's hands before
being deposited in the bank account of one of the five men
arrested in the Watergate.

Hunt is a former CIA agent, a prolific writer of spy novels,
former White House counsultant and friend of Charles W. Colson,
the special counsel to President Nixon who specializes in behind-
the-scenes political operations.

Liddy and Hunt have repeatedly declined to discuss the
Watergate incident or any other matter with reporters. A federal
grand jury is still investigating the matter and Republican
officials, such as MacGregor, have said they expected indict-
ments—but not against "key names. . . ."

On September 15, 1972, a little more than two weeks after the publication of this story, Liddy and Hunt were indicted with the five alleged
Watergate burglars on federal charges.

Then followed in rapid succession a series of reports from Woodward
and Bernstein on illegal compaign contributions which by implication
were connected to the cover-up, hints of hush money that was being paid
to some of the arrested men to buy their silence, and a whole series of
exclusive reports of the Nixon "dirty tricks" part of the 1972 Presidential
campaign.

Here was one of the key stories, published on Sept. 29:

MITCHELL CONTROLLED
SECRET G.O.P. FUND

By Carl Bernstein and Bob Woodward

John N. Mitchell, while serving as U.S. Attorney General, personally controlled a secret Republican fund that was used to gather information about the Democrats, according to sources involved in the Watergate investigation.

Beginning in the spring of 1971, almost a year before he left the Justice Department to become President Nixon's campaign manager on March 1, Mitchell personally approved withdrawals from the fund, several reliable sources have told the *Washington Post*.

Those sources provided almost identical, detailed accounts of Mitchell's role as comptroller of the secret intelligence fund and its fluctuating $350,000–$700,000 balance. . . .

The sources of the *Post*'s information on the secret fund and its relationship to Mitchell and other campaign officials include law enforcement officers and persons on the staff of the Committee for the Re-Election of the President.

Last night, Mitchell was reached by telephone in New York and read the beginning of the *Post*'s story. He said: "All that crap, you're putting it in the paper? It's all been denied. Katie Graham (Katharine Graham, publisher of the *Washington Post*) is gonna get —— caught in a big fat wringer if that's published. Good Christ, that's the most sickening thing I've ever heard. . . ."

It was one of the few times that the *Post* edited the raw language of some of the principals in Watergate, including President Nixon's earthy comments. The actual Mitchell quote, as Woodward and Bernstein later conceded, was that Mrs. Graham, if the *Post* published the Mitchell story, ". . . is gonna get her tit caught in a big fat wringer. . . ." The attempt at intimidation, however, did not work. The piece was published.

In calling for an investigation by the House Banking and Currency Committee, the *Post* editorially attacked Mitchell's activities, saying "The public . . . has a right to know how Mr. Mitchell reconciled his public responsibility to exercise prudent restraint in the collection of secret government information about private citizens with his alleged activity in controlling the funds to finance political intelligence operations.

"The public also has a right to know whether Mr. Mitchell and others who held government responsibilities thought that such acitivity was an appropriate use of the time and trust that the people had a right to assume was devoted to the public's business.

"The voters also have a right to know how deeply involved White House aides and other Cabinet and former Cabinet officers were and to what extent this kind of activity is representative of the character and tone of the Nixon administration . . . ."

With the stepping up of the Presidential campaign, a few newspapers and broadcasters began to pay attention to the *Post*'s Watergate investigation, among them the *New York Times*, *Los Angeles Times*, *Miami Herald* and CBS News. But the Post was so far ahead, and Woodward and Bernstein had acquired so many sources, that their newspaper continued to publish exclusive disclosures in the Watergate case. And, as was later learned, the Nixon White House became increasingly concerned privately while vigorously "stonewalling" publicly.

On October 6, Woodward and Bernstein published a story that a $100,000 campaign gift from a Texas corporation had been in large part "laundered" by being passed through a Mexican bank and then $89,000 of it had been deposited to the account of Bernard L. Barker, one of the five men indicted after being caught during the Watergate break-in.

Four days later, on October 10, the two reporters linked the bugging incident to a massive campaign to sabotage the Democratic Presidential campaign and named Donald H. Segretti, a former Treasury Department lawyer, as one of the main figures in the "dirty tricks" drive against the Democratic nominee, Senator George McGovern of South Dakota.

The blowoff came on October 25 when the *Post* revealed, a little more than a week before election day, that the President's Chief of Staff, H. R. Haldeman, was deeply involved in the secret fund and, by implication, in the Watergate coverup which it was allegedly being used to finance. Here was how that story began:

TESTIMONY TIES TOP NIXON AIDE TO SECRET FUND

By Carl Bernstein and Bob Woodward

H. R. Haldeman, President Nixon's White House Chief of Staff, was one of five high-ranking Presidential associates authorized to

"I've decided not to tell you about the alleged shipwreck"
July 11, 1973

Pulitzer Prize for Editorial Cartooning, 1974

PAUL SZEP'S VIEW IN THE BOSTON GLOBE OF THE WATERGATE COVERUP
BY PRESIDENT NIXON AND FORMER ATTORNEY GENERAL JOHN MITCHELL

approve payments from a secret Nixon campaign cash fund, according to federal investigators and accounts of sworn testimony before the Watergate grand jury.

The secret fund, which at times totaled $700,000, was uncovered during the FBI's Watergate investigation of the Watergate bugging incident. It financed an apparently unprecedented spying and sabotage campaign against the Democratic Presidential candidate that—as a basic element of Nixon re-election strategy—was conceived by high Presidential aides, according to investigators.

Haldeman, 47, is generally considered the man closest to President Nixon in the White House and the primary architect of his re-election campaign. He began his political association with the President in 1956 as an advance man for Mr. Nixon's Vice-Presidential campaign.

Informed yesterday of the information obtained by the *Washington Post*, Haldeman issued the following statement through the White House press officer:

"Your inquiry is based on misinformation because the reference to Bob Haldeman is untrue. . . ."

The *Post* would not be silenced by the administration's constant denials. Right up to election day, the disclosures continued to hit Page 1 and the editorial page thundered with denunciations. At one point, shortly before the voters went to the polls, the paper declared: ". . . . If we can learn more and verify more about this whole sordid mess, it is not simply our prerogative to print it—it is our job and our responsibility."

But on November 7, President Nixon and his Vice President, Spiro Agnew, were re-elected by a terrific landslide, winning more than 60 percent of the popular vote and 97 percent of the electoral vote. The only state McGovern carried was Massachusetts.

Despite that overwhelming victory, however, Nixon was in greater danger than ever, for the *Post* kept hammering away at the crimes associated with Watergate. Moreover, following a trial that lasted from Jan. 8 to 30, 1973, all seven of the men indicted for the Watergate burglary wound up in jail, with Liddy and McCord being convicted by a jury and all the rest pleading guilty. This spurred the Senate on February 7 to establish a Select Committee to Investigate Watergate.

That was the situation when the Pulitzer Prize Journalism jurors came to Columbia on March 8–9, 1973, to study the exhibits that had been submitted for the previous year. There was no question that the Watergate case was showing signs of cracking wide open; by this time, all except the most hard-line Republican newspapers had joined the *Post* on the firing line and the White House was under siege. However, some of the jurors didn't see it that way.

When the Public Service report was handed in, the blue-covered *Washington Post* exhibits—one for the entire newspaper in Public Service, with which a separate reporting exhibit for Woodward and Bernstein had been consolidated—finished third. The jury recommended that the *Chicago Tribune* should be given the gold medal for its vote fraud inquiry in Chicago and placed the *New York Times* second for its exposé of municipal corruption. Here was the way the report described the third-place position for the *Washington Post* and Watergate:

"The Washington Post, despite obstacles placed in its path by politicians and use of intimidation tactics, continued on a determined course to reveal the close ties of the Watergate bugging incident and White House personalities.

"This entry was the third choice of three of the five jurors and the second choice of another. However, a fifth juror gave it a substantially lower rating on the ground that the *Post* had overindulged professional restraints on unattributed information in order to make its point."

A somewhat puzzled Columbia official connected with the prizes asked a juror, in view of all that had happened to substantiate the *Post*'s expose, why the newspaper had not been recommended for the gold medal. The reply was incredible: "Watergate is only a pimple on the elephant's ass."

However, when the Pulitzer Prize Board met at Columbia on April 12, it was in an entirely different atmosphere.

On March 23, 1973, in response to Federal Judge John J. Sirica's determined probing, McCord caved in. In open, court, Sirica read McCord's now celebrated letter that charged political pressure had been applied to him and the other six in the Watergate burglary to plead guilty and stay silent, that there had been perjury at their trial, and that higher-ups—presumably in the White House—had approved the break-in. So the cover-up was exposed and some of the most serious allegations by the *Washington Post* were confirmed.

The Pulitzer Board without hesitation unanimously approved the gold medal for Public Service in 1972 for the *Washington Post* but, despite the most earnest plea by James Reston of the *New York Times*, denied a share in it to Woodward and Bernstein. It was, the Board insisted, a gold medal for the newspaper alone, a ruling similar to the one adopted in the Pentagon Papers case.

There was one more hurdle to be taken in the Pulitzer Prize process as it then existed. The Trustees of Columbia University would have to approve, and they did not meet until May 7 that year. Before that date, the President had had ample warning that his counsel, John Dean, would soon go before the Senate Select Committee on Watergate and spill the entire story of the payment of "hush money" in the case, the way the coverup was managed, and the role that had been played by the President and his immediate White House aides.

In consequence, on April 30, 1973, President Nixon tried to stave off the ultimate disaster to himself by making public the resignations of Haldeman and Ehrlichman, Dean's dismissal, and the resignation of Attorney General Richard Kleindienst. Now, there could no longer be any doubt that the Nixon White House was tottering. And on May 7, the Columbia Trustees approved the gold medal for the *Washington Post* for its Watergate investigation but appended this note to cover all their awards:

"The Trustees have acted on the recommendations of the Advisory Board on the Pulitzer Prizes. Under the terms of the Pulitzer bequest the Trustees of the University do not have the authority to substitute their judgment for the judgment of the Advisory Board. They can act to accept or reject the recommendations of the Advisory Board on the Pulitzer Prizes. In this instance all recommendations have been accepted."

It was not a thrust at the *Washington Post*, as it was later explained, for Mrs. Graham received an honorary Columbia degree by vote of the Trustees and the journalism school gave her its own annual award. What the Trustees evidently wanted to do was to remind everybody in general and the Pulitzer Board in particular that they were putting some distance between themselves and the award-giving machinery. In 1975, the Trustees disassociated themselves from the prizes completely, giving their powers to the President of Columbia University.

What the Pulitzer gold medal did was to confirm, through the presentation of journalism's highest honor, the dominant role of the *Washington Post* in uncovering the crimes behind the Watergate affair. It also affirmed the major roles that were played by Woodward and Bernstein, now linked together in journalistic history as Woodstein, and credited the editorial campaign that was waged in large part by Roger Wilkins.

But the Pulitzer, far from slowing the momentum of the inquiry, actually served to speed it up because anything the *Post* now published on Watergate was eagerly picked up, broadcast, and widely reprinted. It was no longer necessary to ask who the hell Bernstein and Woodward were; with one tremendous performance, they had leaped to the very top of their profession and were now acclaimed as heroes who were much sought after.

In a desperate effort to head off further criticism, President Nixon named Professor Archibald Cox of Harvard as Special Prosecutor on May 18, 1973, and four days later once again repeated all his denials. But the jig was up, for in four days of testimony before the Senate Committee beginning June 25, John Dean lodged his now familiar accusations against the President.

Moreover, on July 25, a hitherto unimportant official, Alexander Butterfield, casually testified to the existence of the White House's secret taping system. When Judge Sirica demanded the tapes on August 29, it marked the beginning of the end.

By a striking coincidence, the President's long-time running mate, Vice President Spiro Agnew, was forced to resign on October 10 after admitting to fraud in his income tax returns and pleading no contest. Two days later, the President picked Gerald R. Ford, who had served long and honorably as a Congressman from Michigan, as the new Vice President because confirmation would be certain.

But attention was diverted almost at once from Ford by the "Saturday Night Massacre," in which Professor Cox was summarily fired by the President, and two new Nixon appointees, Elliot L. Richardson as Attorney General and William D. Ruckelshaus as his deputy, as quickly resigned. Soon afterward, the first calls for the resignation of the President echoed throughout the land.

Many of those who had been accused by Woodward and Bernstein in their earliest reports now came to justice, among them Mitchell, Haldeman, Ehrlichman, and Colson. Richard Kleindienst, who had succeeded Mitchell as Attorney General, pleaded guilty to a misdeameanor in a case that was not connected with Watergate, an added blow to the faltering President.

By the time the House Judiciary Committee voted articles of impeachment in televised harings that lasted from July 24 to 30, the calls for Nixon's resignation and reached a ferocious intensity. Even his warmest former supporters, including the *Chicago Tribune*, now turned against him because the "smoking gun" in the White House tapes had left no doubt of his complicity in the conspiracy.

On August 2, 1974, the chief accuser in the President's own official family, John Dean, pleaded guilty to conspiracy and went to prison. And a week later, the *Washington Post* banner-headlined the end:

NIXON RESIGNS AS PRESIDENT

By Carroll Kilpatrick

From the Washington Post, August 9, 1974

Richard Milhous Nixon announced last night that he will resign as the 37th President of the United States at noon today.

Vice President Gerald R. Ford of Michigan will take the oath of office as President at noon to complete the remaining two and one-half years of Mr. Nixon's term.

After two years of bitter public debate over the Watergate scandals, President Nixon bowed to pressures from the public and leaders of his own party to become the first President in American history to resign.

"By taking this action," he said in a subdued yet dramatic television address from the Oval Office, "I hope that I will have hastened the start of the process of healing that is so desperately needed in America"

Vice President Ford, who spoke a short time later in front of his Alexandria home, announced that Secretary of State Henry Kissinger will remain in his cabinet.

The President-to-be praised Mr. Nixon's sacrifice for the country and called it "one of the saddest incidents I have ever witnessed."

Mr. Nixon said he decided he must resign when he concluded that he no longer had "a strong enough political base in Congress" to make it possible for him to complete his term in office.

Declaring that he has never been a quitter, Mr. Nixon said that to leave office before the end of his term "is abhorrent to every instinct in my body."

But "as President I must put the interests of America first," he said.

While the President acknowledged that some of his judgments "were wrong," he made no confession of the "high crimes and misdeameanors" with with the House Judiciary Committee had charged him in its bill of impeachment.

Specifically, he did not refer to the Judiciary Committee

charges that in the cover-up of Watergate crimes he misused government agencies such as the FBI, CIA, and Internal Revenue Service. . . .

It was a cool, calm, dispassionate account—entirely professional from start to finish—in which there was not a word of credit-claiming for the downfall of the Nixon White House. But many who heard Nixon's resignation speech on television could not help but wonder how it all would have turned out if the *Washington Post* had run with the pack and cold-shouldered the eager efforts of Woodward and Berstein.

The epilogue to the Presidential tragedy came on September 8, 1974 when President Ford issued his unconditional pardon to Nixon encompassing all federal crimes he had "committed or may have committed" while he was President. Thereby, the new President may well have created the issue that many believed deprived him of victory in the 1976 Presidential election and, by a very close margin, presented the nation with Jimmy Carter as its 39th President.

By that time, the irascible Mitchell, the conspiratorial Haldeman and Ehrlichman, along with Dean, Colson, and their miserable entourage were in prison along with the original seven culprits in the Watergate breakin. And ex-President Nixon, swathed in righteousness but carefully admitting nothing, was writing his memoirs at San Clemente with the assurance that he would be well paid for his trouble. Somewhere, in his tinseled circus Valhalla, Phineas T. Barnum must have smiled gently at the spectacle.

While the telling and the retelling of the Watergate story in print, on film, and on videotape made millionaires out of Woodward and Bernstein, it also brought solace in the form of book royalties and TV appearances to Dean, Haldeman, and Ehrlichman—and even Judge Sirica.

But in the end, Ben Bradlee was well satisfied with the way everything had turned out. He wrote:

"Unlike the Presidential cast of characters, most of whom went to their disgrace in or out of jail, the journalists did better. Woodward is . . . an assistant managing editor in charge of the metropolitan staff [at the *Post*], just having completed a new book called *The Brethren*.

"Bernstein is on leave from the *Post*, busy on *his* book.

"Harry Rosenfeld, the metropolitan editor in charge of Woodward and Bernstein, is now editor of the Hearst newspapers in Albany. Barry Sussman, Woodstein's immediate editor, has become an expert in polling and runs the *Washington Post*'s polling operation. Simons and Bradlee are still on the same old station.

"'Deep Throat' has not yet been identified, and will not be here."[5]

In the Pulitzer Prize collection, the two slender blue folders that contain the enduring Woodward and Bernstein investigative pieces for 1972—the basis for all that followed—are somewhat battered and the worse for wear at the hands of several generations of journalism students. The clippings are beginning to blur and become unstuck, but all have been microfilmed for posterity.

They are a frail, but enduring, monument to the best in American journalism.[6]

30. MARY MCGRORY REFLECTS ON WATERGATE, HISTORY, AND THE ENGLISH LANGUAGE

The Washington Star's Columnist Sees the Nation
Famished for Civility and Truth After the Ordeal

Among the journalistic community in Washington, where gentlemanly conduct is generally viewed with the deepest suspicion, Mary McGrory is nearly everybody's favorite columnist.

The admiration that has come to her professionally has nothing to do with her womanhood, for there is a kind of unisex about the processes of journalism in Washington. Her particular public—her colleagues—seldom admit privately, whatever they may say in public, that a woman journalist can be as good as a man.

Mary McGrory has had to be better than the best to make her way in Washington and she has done so with grace and kindness and a cheerful camaraderie that is as genuine as it is beguiling. If she has kissed the Blarney Stone, it is a well-kept secret; in any event, she never had to do so.

She was born with the gift of language. That alone would account for

[5] Letter to author, Aug. 2, 1979.

[6] Much of the Watergate narrative in this section is based on printed versions of tapes, documents, and testimony published in the *Washington Post* and the *New York Times* during the Watergate inquiry and the subsequent Congressional investigations and trials. I also gratefully acknowledge the assistance of Messrs. Bradlee, Simons, Woodward, and Bernstein and the summations that were included in the two Woodward-Bernstein books about Watergate, *All the President's Men* (New York: Simon & Schuster, 1974) and *The Final Days* (New York: Simon & Schuster, 1976). Without the privilege of having been at the center of the Pulitzer Prize deliberations, however, I could not have supplied any of the details of the *Washington Post*'s award as recorded here. These are, in the main, from my memory and my diaries.

such phrases as these in the lovely flow of her prose in the *Washington Star*:

Of the Watergate trial: "The defendants came on like Chinese wrestlers bellowing and making hideous faces as if to frighten the prosecutors to death."

Of H. R. Haldeman at his trial: "His eyes were like two burnt holes in a blanket."

Of Gerald R. Ford as he ascended to the Presidency: "A blind date who has been proposed to."

Of Judge John J. Sirica: "A medieval poet with the white headbands favored by Dante."

Nobody else writes like that in Washington. Nobody else even tries, for Mary McGrory comes on with the delicacy of Edna St. Vincent Millay and the authority of Anne O'Hare McCormick.

There was nothing very remarkable about her early life. It was, more than anything else, a study in career confusion. Consider the facts, such as they are:

Born in Boston, 1918 . . . B.A. in English, Emmanuel College, 1939 . . . first job, cropping pictures for Houghton Mifflin, the book publishers, at $16.50 a week . . . secretary, *Boston Herald* . . . occasional book reviewer for the *Herald* . . . *Washington Star*, book reviewer, 1947 . . .

Few in Washington would have given her much chance to emerge from the pack with that record. But in 1954, when the Army-McCarthy hearings began, Newbold Noyes, Jr., editor of the *Washington Star*, called her to his office and told her he wanted her to do some special pieces on the fire-breathing dragon from Wisconsin who was threatening to devour the American military as he had the Department of State.

The journalist recruit from Boston was shaky. How was she to do such a job? What was she to look for? How was she to operate? Noyes gave her the formula: "Write it like a letter to your favorite aunt."

Whether she did or not, her pieces about Senator McCarthy attracted wide attention in Washington and won her a permanent spot on the *Star's* staff. Throughout the Watergate drama, her commentary was sharp and perceptive. And when it was over, she wrote this reflective piece:

RHETORIC AND WATERGATE

By Mary McGrory

From the Washington Star, August 18, 1974

The English language, which underwent severe trials in the last five years, is recovering, revived, like so much else, by the strong remedy of impeachment.

Thanks to the House Judiciary Committee, we have learned that words can say something, that they can lead, instead of mislead, that they can reveal, not just conceal.

The Constitution, we find, not only prescribes government. It affords a kind of pageantry. Many Americans long for the ceremony of the Old World, the changing of the guard, the trooping of the colors, the flash of the sabres of Italian policemen, the swish of the cape of the gendarme. Well, we now know we don't need that. We have the Constitution instead, and because of six days when it paraded across the nation's television screens, it has become a living, breathing document again, cited by cabdrivers as they gave their opinion of the great federal drama recently unfolded.

Enough has been said about the White House transcripts as the Thermopylae of language. That was a war in which words were almost wiped out. Through systematic abuse, they lost their meaning. "Protective reaction raid," one of the baser coinages, meant creating an alibi to bomb the enemy. When our former first citizen said, "I am not a crook," what he meant was, "You can't prove it." When he said, "One year of Watergate is enough," he meant the fire was getting hot. When he said he was "trying to get to the bottom of it," he meant he was trying to get out of it.

It may be a while before the country stops reading "down" for "up" and "white" for "black."

But a noble beginning was made in the House Judiciary Committee. Impeachment, like execution, wonderfully focuses the mind, and the men and women of that group tried with a care almost unknown hereabouts to match their feelings to the Constitution, and to say what they really thought and felt.

The language gradually came to life again during those six incredible days, when people sought to express anguish, dismay, resolution, and anger.

The results were historic both for the country and declamation. The use of the simple declarative sentence was rediscovered.

Said James Mann of South Carolina: "The next time, there may be no watchman in the night."

Said Walter Flowers of Alabama: "To my friends, I say I have pain enough for them and me."

Said Caldwell Butler of Virginia, in the single most fiery and liberating sentence spoken: "Watergate is our shame." He was the first Republican to slash the comforting myth that somebody else, of unknown party origin, was to blame.

The country has not heard language used like that in five and one-half years.

And overlaying all was the language of the impeachment counts, sentences that marched like armies and tolled like bells.

"In his conduct of the office of President of the United States," each began portentously, "in violation of his Constitutional oath faithfully to execute the office of President of the United States, and to the best of his ability to preserve, protect, and defend the Constitution to take care that the laws be faithfully executed. . . ."

And each ended heavily, majestically: "Wherefore, Richard M. Nixon, by such conduct, warrants impeachment, and trial and removal from office."

It was powerful stuff. And the country watched transfixed, as those phrases sounded through the ritual civilities: The chairman addressing Barbara Jordan as "the gentle lady from Texas"; each speaker, no matter how wroth, on receiving recognition, saying politely, "Thank you, Mr. Chairman." The country has been famished for civility, it seems, along with truth.

Thanks partly to those men and women and their words, we now have a new President. On being sworn in, he promised "just a little straight talk among friends."

It is long overdue. The country will survive. So may the English language.

Along with nine others by Mary McGrory, this piece was submitted for consideration for a Pulitzer Prize in 1975 by the *Star*. The McGrory exhibit was selected from almost 100 others by the Commentary Jury, which reported: "The jury found Miss McGrory's work rich in insights and forceful in analysis. Her writing is perceptive, her reporting vigorous. Her wit and cogency lead the reader to fresh perspectives and a sharpened understanding of national events."

Thus she was awarded the Pulitzer Prize in Commentary for 1975.

31. MEG GREENFIELD APPRAISES FORD:
"HE DID A HELL OF A JOB."

The Washington Post's Editorialist Hails Him
for Restoring Civility to the Presidency

For most of the three centuries in which newspapers have been published on the North American continent, the rather sooty ivory tower of journalism—the domain of editorial writers—has been very largely an old men's club.

Here, the crochety elders of journalism have been wont to do their pointing with pride, their viewing with alarm, and their dutiful endorsements of the publisher's political preferences and the publisher's wife's pet charities. The atmosphere in most such sanctums, for scores of years, was so soporific that able people fled from them in despair and readers scanned the editorial page only as a last, pitiful resort.

This may be a harsh judgment, but it is valid, for it is attested to by the relatively few able and talented editors who have risen to eminence in their profession despite the parameters of futility that defined the limits of most editorial pages.

It is not too long ago, for example, that A. H. Raskin wrote while assistant editorial page editor of the *New York Times*: "Most editorial pages are so predictable in position and so pedestrian in style that they seem to have become completely automated." And Vermont Connecticut Royster, while editor of the *Wall Street Journal*, demanded: "If we aren't persuading our readers, why bother? . . . Well . . . a good many newspapers might as well not bother; their editorial columns are sheer boredom." [1]

Creed C. Black, then the editorial page editor of the *Philadelphia Inquirer*, stated the position as follows: "Too many pages still seek the safe middle ground, using the same fuzzy clichés that were in vogue 20 years ago." To prove it he assembled a composite editorial made up entirely of well-worn lines culled from a roundup of editorials, the conclusion of which was as follows:

"It is delusive to pretend that success will come easily. Disrespect for constituted authority is widespread. But something must be done. The

[1] *The New York Times Magazine*, June 11, 1967, p. 5.

only question is how to go about it. Not to do so deliberately is to flout the public interest. The time for action is now."[2]

Into this never-never land of counterfeit solemnity and triteness, few young men ever ventured and women appeared to be even more unwelcome than they were in the city rooms. All of which caused men of strength and talent and decision to protest, as Ralph McGill did on one occasion: "A newspaper . . . must make its news and, equally, its editorials, a part of the tangible issues of the daily lives of its readers. It may thereby make some angry. It may lose some circulation. But even those who are made angry will know what they read touched their lives."[3]

Under such pressures as these, added to the rising scale of public indifference to newspaper opinion, some editorial pages have changed in the latter part of the 20th century. But in all save the news organizations that have tolerated talent and wit and a diversity of opinion—and there still are precious few of these—change has come with the majestic deliberation of a Supreme Court decision.

For a woman to lay siege to this forbidding fastness would have been unheard of at the turn of the century. And even at mid-century, the relatively few women who wrote editorials for daily newspapers were received with the same kind of reserve displayed by an old-time bartender who carefully ushers a lady into the back room of a saloon. But a small, cheerful woman named Meg Greenfield was not intimidated. Against all the signs and portents, she chose to be a newspaper editorialist and became one of the best of her time.

With all her talent and her superior educational preparation, Meg Greenfield could have been a success in almost any profession she chose to enter. She came out of the Pacific Northwest, having been born in Seattle, and at 22 was graduated summa cum laude from Smith College in 1952. Thereafter, for a year, she was a Fulbright Scholar at Cambridge University. In 1957, she became a researcher for *Reporter* magazine and advanced to Washington editor during her 11 years there. Then she joined the *Washington Post* as an editorial writer, again making striking progress, first to deputy editorial page editor and eventually as the editor of the page.

In 1977, while still the deputy editor, the vigor of her ideas and the grace of her phrasing won her the admiration of her colleagues. She had something more than a way with words. She could sum up a difficult position in a single well-turned phrase.

[2] *Editor & Publisher* (Oct. 21, 1961), p. 14.
[3] *Nieman Reports* (January 1961), p. 6.

Thus, she wrote of the "preposterous mirror-image play with the Russians" over various civil defense programs, rebuked the "cheering section polemics" over the Bakke reverse discrimination case before the Supreme Court, and brooded over the wrongs that had been done by the press in general and the *Washington Post* in particular to Gerald Rudolph Ford, 38th President of the United States, saying simply, "We were wrong."

Not many in the topsy-turvy world of Washington journalism had the intestinal fortitude to admit error then—or at any other time for that matter. But the Ford case was one that displayed all the faults of the Washington press corps and very few of its virtues. For most of the reporters in the nation's capital treated the unelected President with the irritated condescension of motorists passing a slow but safe tow car as it pulls a battered wreck off a busy highway.

True, Ford's swift pardon of Richard Milhous Nixon for whatever crimes he may have committed while in the Presidency alienated millions of people. True, also, Ford's implacable conservatism did not sit well with the more liberal-minded adherents of both major parties and the independents.

But that was scarcely an excuse for the continued circulation of weary gibes at the Ford style and demeanor, the hoots that emanated from the press corps whenever he stumbled or bumped his head, the gleeful repetition of Lyndon Baines Johnson's baseless remark that Ford was what he was because he had played center without a helmet for the University of Michigan football team.

To his credit, Ford took it all with a public display of stolid good humor and never let his private feelings intrude on his attitude toward either reporters or editors. While neither the *Washington Post* nor Meg Greenfield had been guilty of such excesses, there came a time at the end of Ford's term when both decided that amends would have to be made. And this is what she wrote on the editorial page about a political opponent:

"DECENCY IN THE WHITE HOUSE"

By Meg Greenfield

From the Washington Post, January 16, 1977

"At no point has he shown a keen or impressive grasp of the complexities of hard questions. Pedestrian, partisan, dogged—he has been the very model of a second-level party man. It is no accident that over his quarter-century of unremarkable service in the House, he has never been put forward for the Presidency."

So we spoke in this space a little over three years ago upon learning that Gerald Ford was about to ascend to the office of Vice President. We do not cite our respondent appraisal because we think it was on the money, but rather because we think it was not. Having been forced to replace his Vice President, and being in not-so-secure condition in office himself, Richard Nixon had just informed a waiting world that Gerald Ford was the one. Frankly, it did not occur to us that Gerald Ford was also the right one.

But we were wrong; he was. The President who will leave office this week brought precisely the needed temperament, character and virtues to the high offices he has temporarily held. These qualities are regularly subsumed under the familiar general heading of "decency," a word that does indeed fit the man. What is so revealing about the times in which we live—and the horrendous political circumstances surrounding Mr. Ford's accession to office—is the vaguely condescending way in which this particular tribute is paid to him: *Well, you have to admit he is a decent human being . . .* or *. . . Don't get me wrong: Of course I think he's a decent person . . .* and so on.

Decency, in this context, becomes as an attribute something roughly comparable to a good posture or punctuality. How odd that so few of us have been willing to acknowledge that decency in the White House can be regarded as a luxury or a bonus or a fringe benefit only at our peril.

It is central. And its absence was central to the sorrows this country endured in the years preceding Mr. Ford's Presidency. In his first days and months, it was as if he had liberated Washington—from its personal fears and hostilities and suspicions, from the dark and squalid assumptions that people had come reflexively to make about one another and the way things "really" worked. God knows who was (and is) still listening in on whose line and who is plotting what gruesome revenge against what political foe. Our point is merely that Gerald Ford brought to the White House an open, unsinister and—yes—decent style of doing things that altered the life of the city and ultimately of the country.

We have found many of the President's programs and positions (and lack of both in some cases) dismal news indeed. But that is yesterday's laundry list. Our summing up of the Ford Presidency draws us only to the overriding legacy he leaves.

Will this city under the Carter Democrats be able to preserve that political and personal civility that Gerald Ford did so much, so unexpectedly, to revive? The Carter administration, more activist and energetic, we would guess, than its predecessor, faster-paced, more intellectually self-certain and combative, is almost by nature destined to put some of these homely but hard-won virtues at risk. We can only hope the new administration will understand their indispensability. Mr. Ford has left it an incomparable gift in the detoxified political atmosphere of the capital and the institutions it is about temporarily to inherit.

The outgoing President has also done a great deal for the honor of his party, although you wouldn't necessarily know it to listen to the samurai-like grunts and howls coming out of the struggle for party control. But Gerald Ford did indeed redeem the Nixon moral disaster. His two and a half years gave point and purpose and respectability to those innumerable straight-arrow Republicans who had come to work in Washington and who had been let down, in fact betrayed, by their own White House. And the exceptional quality of most of Mr. Ford's own high-level appointments—John Paul Stevens, Edward Levi, William Coleman, to name just a few—went a long way to erase the memory of earlier indictment and disgrace.

We will leave it to others to tote up the pluses and minuses of the Ford administration in strict program and/or policy terms. We can frankly do without reviewing it ourselves. We think it is enough to point out that Gerald Ford had an all but impossible assignment—and that he did a hell of a job.

The first woman in the history of the Pulitzer Prizes in Journalism to win an award was Hazel Brannon Smith of the *Lexington* (Miss.) *Advertiser* in 1964. The second was Meg Greenfield of the *Washington Post* in 1978. Both were properly gracious but properly reserved over their admission to what had been, with only two exceptions, a male preserve for more than 60 years.

Pulitzer Prize for Editorial Cartooning, 1975

GARRY TRUDEAU CELEBRATES GERALD FORD'S ACCESSION TO THE PRESI-
DENCY IN HIS CARTOON STRIP, "DOONESBURY," DISTRIBUTED BY
UNIVERSAL PRESS SYNDICATE

32. WILLIAM SAFIRE HELPS TOSS LANCE
FROM CARTER'S WHITE HOUSE

The New York Times's Conservative Columnist Attacks
the Georgian's Free-Wheeling Banking Routine

To *Time* magazine, he is "the fastest gun in Op-Ed Land."

To Ben Bradlee, executive editor of the *Washington Post*, "He's mean—a master of the cheap shot."

To Joe Alsop, no petunia himself when he was in the columning business, he's the Cosell of newspapering: "Everybody reads him—always—even if they hate him."

He's William Safire, a Brooklyn-born college dropout, a flak who once worked for Tex McCrary, an ex-speechwriter for Richard M. Nixon, and since then the *New York Times*'s conservative columnist on its Op-Ed Page—the page opposite editorial. He is one of the very few people in the land who have risen to eminence from the gutter of journalism—political press agentry. And he did it even though many of the old hands in the *Times* newsroom were against him at the beginning.

Arthur Ochs Sulzberger, the *Times*'s publisher, cheerfully concedes now that there was "consternation and outrage" among the *Times*'s noble liberal minds when he brought Safire to the paper in 1973 after Nixon's enormous re-election victory. There were dark rumors on the *Times* and elsewhere, when Watergate began to unravel, that the new acquisition might be involved—but he never was. The closest he came to notoriety was to be identified as the author of one of the most quoted phrases used by the erstwhile Vice President Spiro Agnew—"nattering nabobs of negativism."[1]

Very soon, Safire was making his ability as a polemicist and political undercover operator felt both in Washington and in New York. He did a series of columns on "Koreagate," as he called it, the influence-peddling of Korean businessman Tongsun Park and his largesse to politicians in the nation's capital. Safire also plunged headlong into any promising investigation he could find—or stir up—that involved Democratic politicians. And he was completely unabashed by his admitted partisanship for conservative figures and their causes.

What made him a devotee of thunder on the right is uncertain. As one

[1] *Time*, April 23, 1979, p. 87.

of the children of a Brooklyn widow who didn't have an easy time raising her family, he had the pedigree of a Democratic liberal.

He was a child of the Great Depression, having been born Dec. 17, 1929, a little less than two months after the bottom dropped out of the New York stock market, but there is no record that the New Deal had any effect on him as he grew up.

In fact, instead of doggedly slugging his way through college and achieving a degree of one kind or another in the tradition of Jewish youngsters from New York, he dropped out of Syracuse University in 1949. And while he began as a small-time syndicate reporter, he soon found more fun and more money in working for Tex McCrary, his teacher in press agentry.

Once he became a columnist after his White House experience, his conservative streak broadened. But it didn't make him any more careful. He made errors and had to publish retractions, but none of his mistakes turned out to be irretrievable. In the tough business of political scalphunting, he always managed to save his own.

The *Times* syndicate obtained a modest number of newspapers for his column, mainly on his reputation as a conservative, but he did not come into his own until Jimmy Carter's election as President and the swift ascent of Carter's close friend and sometime banker, Bert Lance, as the director of the Office of Management and Budget in the White House.

Lance was an affable, gregarious, small-town Georgia banker who had risen from teller in a bank at Calhoun, Ga., to president of the respected National Bank of Georgia in Atlanta. Even before the Carter inauguration, the Senate Governmental Affairs Committee recommended his confirmation as director of OMB on Jan. 18, 1977. And on Inauguration Day, Jan. 20, the Senate with great speed but scanty judgment voted the big Georgian into high office as a courtesy to the new President.

There were a few muffled grumbles from the press. The Associated Press carried a piece about Lance's alleged election law violations in 1974 when he ran for Governor of Georgia (and was soundly trounced in the primary). The *New York Times* had a short report that an inquiry into Lance's banking practices had been closed down the day before his nomination to the OMB. Nothing happened, however. Subsequently, the respected financial magazine, *Forbes*, called attention to questionable practices at the National Bank of Georgia, Lance's bank. And *Time* magazine on May 23, 1977, explored his rather chaotic financial dealings.

As summer began, Lance was becoming a story but the Senate Governmental Affairs Committee wasn't at all interested. On July 13, President Carter was so confident of Lance's probity that he asked the Senate committee to extend the Dec. 31 deadline for Lance's divestiture of $3.2 million worth of stock of the National Bank of Georgia. Lance's stock had so declined in value, the President pleaded, that his friend stood to lose more than $1 million through its forced sale.[2]

It was then that Safire weighed in with a column that blew the top off the Lance case. Here it is:

CARTER'S BROKEN LANCE

By William Safire

From the New York Times, July 21, 1977

WASHINGTON, July 20—Jimmy Carter is trying to sell the Senate a dubious bill of goods about his long-time friend, Office of Management and Budget Director Bert Lance.

The Georgia banker should be excused from conflict-of-interest divestiture promises, the President has asserted, because his promise to sell his stock has depressed its market value.

That is a deception. The reason that National Bank of Georgia stock has slid from 16 to 11 this year has little to do with the "overhang." The stock has dropped because of the revelation that Mr. Lance tolerated bad loans on his books. The man who inherited the mess has had to write off the bad loans and suspend dividend payments.

The truth is that Mr. Lance's departure for Washington did not cause his financial embarrassment. On the contrary, we now see how his willingness to carry questionable loans as assets may have artificially maintained the price of his stock.

Mr. Carter is intimately familiar with Mr. Lance's affairs. On June 19, 1975, only a few weeks after borrowing $2.7 million to finance the purchase of his stock, Bert Lance brought Jimmy Carter to the Manufacturers Hanover Bank in New York to meet Lew Jenkins, the bank officer responsible with Bruce Brougham for making the Lance loan.

Purely a social call, insists Mr. Lance, nothing to do with using the former Georgia Governor to shore up his reputation as a bor-

---

[2] The Lance case summary is largely derived from the New York Times and the Washington Post from mid-June to Sept. 22, 1977, Time and Newsweek from Sept. 5 through Oct. 3, and the AP report from mid-June through Sept. 22, 1977.

rower. But Mr. Jenkins was the only banker to whom Mr. Lance took the new presidential candidate that day.

Banktician Lance, who was Governor Carter's highway commissioner, also claims to have had nothing to do with the infusion of the Teamsters Central States pension fund money into his bank in early 1976, as Mr. Carter's star began to rise. At the time, the Lance bank's three-person trust department had no account over $2 million to manage; for no apparent reason, the politically sensitive Teamsters fund put into the Lance bank $18 million that has since grown to $23 million.

Not my doing, says the modest Mr. Lance today. Bank officials want us to believe that Atlantans John Spickerman, Teamster employer trustee, and Robert Pollar, Teamster fund lawyer, initiated the deal with King Cleveland, Mr. Lance's colleague, now retired.

But after Mr. Carter's election on the very morning Mr. Lance's picture was front-paged as the first Carter cabinet likelihood—Nov. 24, 1976—Mr. Lance met in his bank with Teamster pension fund executive director Dan Shannon, John Spickerman, and Teamster lawyer William Nellis of Chicago. Mr. Lance sees no impropriety in a cabinet designee helping to line up some future business with the fund that the Labor Department says corruptly bankrolls Las Vegas mobsters.

Just before leaving Atlanta six months ago, Mr. Lance must have had cause to worry about his financial house of cards. He turned to another Democratic banktician, J. Robert Abboud, the go-go boss of the First National Bank of Chicago, who has replaced his mentor, the late Mayor Daley, as the city's most powerful man.

Mr. Abboud must have been delighted to bail out a man who would be part of the President's quadriad, and whose ambitions include becoming chairman of the Federal Reserve. On Jan. 6, 1977, prior to his Jan. 11 trip to Washington, Mr. Abboud refinanced the $2.7 million Manufacturers Hanover loan that enabled Mr. Lance to own his stock—adding another $725,000.

Why? Mr. Lance (give him credit, he answers his phone) says, "First Chicago is moving aggressively in the Atlanta area."

I see a more sinister motive. First Chicago's Abboud knows all about bad real estate loans, and should have known that Mr. Lance's assets would shrink when the bad loans were audited by a successor. Here was Mr. Abboud's chance to gain life-and-death financial control over the man closest to the President.

The central question, which Senators Ribicoff and Percy do not see, is this: Was the President's most powerful cabinet member given a "sweetheart loan"? Did Mr. Lance's assets include his closeness to President Carter? And why did he need that extra money in the refinancing?

One source who has been close to the refinancing passes the word that the stories of Mr. Lance's need for funds to meet interest payments may be off the track—that the Abboud-Lance loan is so favorable that it defers interest payments. Such special arrangements are denied to most cabinet borrowers.

Here we have a situation in which the man in charge of the nation's books is deeply, dangerously in hock; who goes home every night not knowing whether the Labor Department will find out about his teamster connections, or the S.E.C. will look into his assurances to 45 people about a stock issue, or the bank examiners and First Chicago stockholders will expose a "sweetheart loan," or the man on whom he depends for financial solvency will exert some subtle pressure for political advantage.

Jimmy Carter's Broken Lance is a walking conflict-of-interest. The complaisant Senate subcommittee now glancing at his wheeling and dealing should stop making an exception and start making an example.

The members of the so-called Georgia Mafia in the White House were appalled by Safire's attack on the President's friend. However, instead of reexamining the facts, they pressed for full speed ahead with the move to give Lance more time to sell his bank stock.

Four days after the first Safire column was published, the Senate committee gave him what it called its "Good Housekeeping seal of approval" and the chairman, Senator Abraham A. Ribicoff of Connecticut, told him, "You have been smeared from one end of the country to the other and, in my opinion, unjustly."

Safire dug up more detail on Lance's affairs than the *Times* was publishing on Page 1 and ripped into the Georgia banker in several other columns on the case. He was ahead of the pack in a number of instances, stimulating both the *Times*'s reporting and that of the opposition.

Despite a favorable report on August 18 by the Controller of the Currency, which caused President Carter to exclaim, "Bert, I'm proud of you," the press inquiry continued to disclose embarrassing material about Lance. And at last the Senate Governmental Affairs Committee called new hearings in the affair.

Lance was given a chance to clear himself before the committee on Sept. 15, 16, and 17, admitting nothing and denying everything, but in the end he had to resign. President Carter, tears in his eyes, went on national TV on Sept. 21 to announce the decision and concluded, "Bert Lance is my friend . . . a great and honorable man. . . . Nothing I have heard or read has shaken my belief in Bert's ability or his integrity." [3]

When the Pulitzer Prize Juries met in the spring of 1978, however, Safire's name did not lead all the rest. Far from it. He wasn't even mentioned in the report of the Commentary Jury, before which his exhibit was placed. Instead, the jurors sent the names of Gary Deeb, *Chicago Tribune* TV critic, Mike Royko, *Chicago Daily News* columnist, and John Leonard, one of the *New York Times*'s stable of book critics and a general commentator on the literary scene, to the Pulitzer Prize Board.

The Board, however, was not impressed. Instead, with a few dissents, its members voted to give the 1978 Pulitzer Prize for Commentary to William Safire for his disclosures about Bert Lance. And so it was ordained. [4]

While Safire went on to other triumphs, Lance's fortunes continued to decline. On April 26, 1978, he was accused by the Securities and Exchange Commission of civil fraud and "unsafe and unsound banking practices and irregularities." While Lance made no admissions of any kind, he did agree not to violate in future actions the laws cited in the complaint. Subsequently, he was indicted in Georgia, pleaded innocent and went to trial blaming the press for his predicament. He was eventually cleared.

[3] *New York Times*, Sept. 22, 1977, p. 1.
[4] From my knowledge of the Pulitzer Board's actions, following a discussion with several of its members.

THE FLOATING DOLLAR
Pulitzer Prize for Editorial Cartooning, 1972

A COMMENT ON THE VALUE OF THE DOLLAR BY JEFF MACNELLY IN THE
RICHMOND NEWS-LEADER

33. *MERRIMAN SMITH SEES ASSASSINATION* *OF PRESIDENT KENNEDY IN DALLAS*

The UPI's White House Correspondent Writes the Story
of a Great and Poignant National Tragedy on Nov. 22, 1963

Merriman Smith, a sallow-faced, moustached Georgian who had covered the White House for 22 years, briskly took his place beside the driver of the fifth car of the Presidential motorcade in Dallas on the morning of November 22, 1963.

He was a privileged character, both as the senior White House correspondent and the representative of United Press and its successor organization, United Press International. Wire service people always had to be closest of all the press to the President because they worked on a deadline every minute.

Smith *was* close that day, as always, for he was a part of the pool that covered the President for all media. He had a particular advantage over his chief rival, the Associated Press correspondent, and the two other pool reporters who rode in the rear seat. For he noted that there was a radio telephone built into the car and the set was within easy reach in the front seat near a Presidential press secretary who was squeezed in with him and the driver.

It was a beautiful morning in Dallas—76 degrees and glowing with the garish brightness of the Texas sun. Nobody in the press crowd could imagine anything happening to President John Fitzgerald Kennedy, his wife, Jacqueline, Governor John B. Connally of Texas, and Mrs. Connally, the occupants of the lead car.

The President and Mrs. Kennedy had flown to Dallas that morning from Fort Worth in Air Force One, the Presidential jet, and at 11:50 A.M. were ready to leave Love Field for the Trade Mart, eleven miles away, where the President was to speak. The President and the First Lady were in the back seat, waving to the friendly Texans about them, and Governor and Mrs. Connally were sitting on the jump seats. Also in the processional was the most prominent Texan of them all, the Vice President, Lyndon Baines Johnson.

Merriman Smith was then 50 years old. He worked with the quickness and agility of an acrobat and the pent-up energy of a locomotive racing along under a full head of steam. From his vantage point in the fifth car, he saw the President's open limousine roll off slowly and fidgeted until the press pool car got under way. The other correspondents were in a press bus that was going directly to the Trade Mart, so there was more than usual pressure on Smith and the others in the pool to get things first and get them right.

It didn't bother him. He was used to pressure. He had handled every kind of news story that events had conspired to throw at him through a succession of small and dreary newsrooms in Georgia and during his long service with UP and UPI beginning 1936. As an old pro, he was ready for anything.

Smith noted the applauding crowds along the route of the Presidential motorcade but saw nothing unusual until the lead car rolled past the old court house and turned right around an open-faced triangle called Dealey Plaza. In front of a depressingly ugly red-orange brick building, the Texas School Book Depository, the motorcade turned left along Elm Street and headed for the new Stemmons Freeway. That would be the final stage of the 45-minute trip.

It was just 12:30 P.M. The motorcade was doing only 11 miles an hour and the press pool car was 150 to 200 yards behind. Suddenly Smith and the other pool reports heard three loud noises—they could have been shots—they could have been a series of backfires from an exhaust.

Smith knew instinctively that someone had shot at the President and reached for the radio telephone. There was a short, sharp struggle with another pool reporter but the wiry Smith won out and phoned in the first bulletin. This is the essence of what he did and how he did it that day in Dallas when President Kennedy was assassinated—a classic story that was written hours afterward and was moved on the UPI "A" wire early next morning:

"ONE SEES HISTORY EXPLODE . . ."

By Merriman Smith

From the United Press International File, Nov. 23, 1963

WASHINGTON, Nov. 23 (UPI)—It was a balmy, sunny afternoon as we motored through downtown Dallas behind President Kennedy. The procession cleared the center of the business district and turned into a handsome highway that wound through what appeared to be a park.

I was riding in the so-called White House press "pool" car, a telephone company vehicle equipped with a mobile radio telephone. I was in the front seat between a driver from the telephone company and Malcolm Kilduff, acting White House press secretary for the President's Texas tour. Three other pool reporters were wedged in the back seat.

Suddenly we heard three loud, almost painfully loud, cracks. The first sounded as if it might have been a large firecracker. But the second and third blasts were unmistakable. Gunfire.

The President's car, possibly as much as 150 or 200 yards ahead, seemed to falter briefly. We saw a flurry of activity in the Secret Service follow-up car behind the Chief Executive's bubble-top limousine.

Next in line was the car bearing Vice President Lyndon B. Johnson. Behind that, another follow-up car bearing agents assigned to the Vice President's protection. We were behind that car.

Our car stood still for probably only a few seconds, but it seemed like a lifetime. One sees history explode before one's eyes and for even the most trained observer, there is a limit to what one can comprehend.

I looked ahead at the President's car but could not see him or his companion, Gov. John B. Conally of Texas. Both men had been riding on the right side of the bubble-top limousine from Washington. I thought I saw a flash of pink which would have been Mrs. Jacqueline Kennedy.

Everybody in our car began shouting at the driver to pull up closer to the President's car. But at this moment, we saw the big bubble-top and a motorcycle escort roar away at high speed.

We screamed at our driver, "Get going, get going." We careened around the Johnson car and its escort and set out down the highway, barely able to keep in sight of the President's car and the accompanying Secret Service follow-up car.

They vanished around a curve. When we cleared the same curve, we could see where we were heading—Parkland Hospital, a large brick structure to the left of the arterial highway. We skidded around a sharp left turn and spilled out of the pool car as it entered the hospital driveway.

I ran to the side of the bubble-top.

The President was face-down on the back seat. Mrs. Kennedy

made a cradle of her arms around the President's head and bent over him as if she were whispering to him.

Gov. Connally was on his back on the floor of the car, his head and shoulders resting in the arms of his wife, Nellie, who kept shaking her head and shaking with dry sobs. Blood oozed from the front of the Governor's suit. I could not see the President's wound. But I could see blood spattered around the interior of the rear seat and a dark stain spreading down the right side of the President's dark gray suit.

From the telephone car I had radioed the Dallas bureau of UPI that three shots had been fired at the Kennedy motorcade. Seeing the bloody scene in the rear of the car at the hospital entrance, I knew I had to get to a telephone immediately.

Clint Hill, the Secret Service agent in charge of the detail assigned to Mrs. Kennedy, was leaning over into the rear of the car.

"How badly is he hit, Clint? I asked.

"He's dead," Hill replied curtly.

I have no further clear memory of the scene in the driveway. I recall a babble of anxious voices, tense voices—"Where in hell are the stretchers . . . Get a doctor out here . . . He's on the way . . . Come on, easy there." And from somewhere, nervous sobbing.

I raced down a short stretch of sidewalk into a hospital corridor. The first thing I spotted was a small clerical office, more of a booth than an office. Inside, a bespectacled man stood shuffling what appeared to be hospital forms. At a wicket much like a bank teller's cage, I spotted a telephone on the shelf.

"How do you get outside?" I gasped. "The President has been hurt and this is an emergency call."

"Dial 9," he said, shoving the phone toward me.

I took two tries before I successfully dialed the Dallas UPI number. Quickly I dictated a bulletin saying the President had been seriously, perhaps fatally, injured by an assassin's bullets while driving through the streets of Dallas.

Litters bearing the President and the Governor rolled by me as I dictated, but my back was to the hallway and I didn't see them until they were at the entrance to the emergency room about 75 or 100 feet away.

I knew they had passed, however, from the horrified expression that suddenly spread over the face of the man behind the wicket.

As I stood in the drab buff hallway leading to the emergency ward trying to reconstruct the shooting for the UPI man on the other end of the telephone and still keep track of what was happening outside the door of the emergency room, I watched a swift and confused panorama sweep by me.

Kilduff of the White House press staff raced up and down the hall. Police captains barked at each other: "Clear this area." Two priests hurried in behind a Secret Service agent, their narrow purple stoles rolled up tightly in their hands. A police lieutenant ran down the hall with a large carton of blood for transfusions. A doctor came in and said he was responding to a call for "all neurosurgeons."

The priests came out and said the President had received the last sacrament of the Roman Catholic Church. They said he was alive, but not conscious. Members of the Kennedy staff began arriving. They had been behind us in the motorcade but hopelessly bogged for a time in confused traffic.

Telephones were at a premium in the hospital and I clung to mine for dear life. I was afraid to stray from the wicket lest I lose contact with the outside world.

My decision was made for me, however, when Kilduff and Wayne Hawks of the White House staff ran by me shouting that Kilduff would make a statement shortly in the so-called nurses' room a floor above and at the far end of the hospital.

I threw down the phone and sped after them. We reached the door of the conference room and there were loud cries of "Quiet!" Fighting to keep his emotions under control, Kilduff said, "President John Fitzgerald Kennedy died at approximately one o'clock."

I raced into a nearby office. The telephone switchboard at the hospital was hopelessly jammed. I spotted Virginia Payette, wife UPI's Southwestern division manager and a veteran reporter in her own right. I told her to try getting through on pay telephones on the floor above.

Frustrated by the inability to get through the hospital switchboard, I appealed to a nurse. She led me through a maze of corri-

dors and back stairways to another floor and a lone pay booth. I
got the Dallas office. Virginia had gotten through before me.

Whereupon I ran back through the hospital to the conference
room. There Jiggs Fauver of the White House transportation staff
grabbed me and said Kilduff wanted a pool of three men
immediately to fly back to Washington on Air Force One, the
Presidential aircraft.

"He wants you downstairs and he wants you right now," Fauver
said.

Down the stairs I ran and into the driveway, only to discover
Kilduff had just pulled out in our telephone car.

Charles Roberts of *Newsweek* magazine, Sid Davis of Westinghouse Broadcasting and I implored a police officer to take us to
the airport in his squad car. The Secret Service had requested that
no sirens be used in the vicinity of the airport, but the Dallas
officer did a masterful job of getting us through some of the worst
traffic I've ever seen.

As we piled out of the car on the edge of the runway about 200
yards from the Presidential aircraft, Kilduff spotted us and
motioned for us to hurry. We trotted to him and he said the plane
could take two pool men to Washington; that Johnson was about
to take the oath of office aboard the plane and would take off
immediately thereafter.

I saw a bank of telephones beside the runway and asked if I had
time to advise my news service. He said, "But for God's sake,
hurry!"

Then began another telephone nightmare. The Dallas office
rang busy. I tried calling Washington. All circuits were busy.
Then I called the New York bureau of UPI and told them about
the impending installation of a new President aboard the airplane.

Kilduff came out of the plane and motioned wildly toward my
booth. I slammed down the phone and jogged across the runway. A
detective stopped me and said, "You dropped your pocket comb."

Aboard Air Force One, on which I had made so many trips as a
press association reporter covering President Kennedy, all of the
shades of the larger main cabin were drawn and the interior was
hot and dimly lighted.

Kilduff propelled us to the President's suite two-thirds of the way back in the plane. The room is used normally as a combination conference and sitting room and could accommodate eight or ten people seated.

I wedged inside the door and began counting. There were 27 people in this compartment. Johnson stood in the center with his wife, Lady Bird. U.S. District Judge Sarah T. Hughes, 67, a kindly faced woman, stood with a small black Bible in her hands, waiting to give the oath.

The compartment became hotter and hotter. Johnson was worried that some of the Kennedy staff people might not be able to get inside. He urged people to press forward, but a Signal Corps photographer, Capt. Cecil Stoughton, standing in the corner on a chair, said if Johnson moved any closer it would be virtually impossible to make a truly historic photograph.

It developed that Johnson was waiting for Mrs. Kennedy, who was composing herself in a small bedroom in the rear of the plane. She appeared alone, dressed in the same pink wool suit she had worn in the morning when she appeared so happy shaking hands with airport crowds at the side of her husband.

She was white-faced and dry-eyed. Friendly hands stretched toward her as she stumbled slightly. Johnson took both of her hands in his and motioned her to his left side. Lady Bird stood at his right, a fixed half-smile showing the tension.

Johnson nodded to Judge Hughes, an old friend of his family and a Kennedy appointee.

"Hold up your right hand and repeat after me," the woman jurist said to Johnson.

Outside a jet could be heard droning to a landing.

Judge Hughes held out the Bible and Johnson covered it with his large left hand. His right arm went slowly into the air and the jurist began to intone the Constitutional oath: "I do solemnly swear I will faithfully execute the office of President of the United States. . . ."

The brief ceremony ended when Johnson, in a deep firm voice, repeated after the judge, ". . . and so help me God."

Johnson turned first to his wife, hugged her about the shoulders and kissed her on the cheek. Then he turned to Kennedy's widow, put his left arm around her and kissed her cheek.

As others in the group—some Texas Democratic members of the House, members of the Johnson and Kennedy staffs—moved toward the new President, he seemed to back away from any expression of felicitation.

The two-minute ceremony concluded at 3:38 P.M. EST, and seconds later the President said firmly, "Now let's get airborne."

Col. James Swindal, pilot of the plane, a big gleaming silver and blue fan-jet, cut on the starboard engines immediately. Several persons, including Sid Davis of Westinghouse, left the plane at that time. The White House had room for only two pool reporters on the return flight and those posts were filled by Roberts and me, although at the moment we could find no empty seats.

At 3:47 EST, the wheels of Air Force One cleared the runway. Swindal roared the big ship up to an unusually high cruising altitude of 41,000 feet, where at 625 miles an hour, ground speed, the jet hurtled toward Andrews Air Force Base outside Washington.

When the President's plane reached operating altitude, Mrs. Kennedy left her bedchamber and walked to the rear compartment of the plane. This was the so-called family living room, a private area where she and Kennedy, family and friends, had spent many happy airborne hours chatting and dining together.

Kennedy's casket had been placed in this compartment, carried aboard by a group of Secret Service agents.

Mrs. Kennedy went to the rear lounge and took a chair beside the coffin. There she remained throughout the flight. Her vigil was shared at times by four staff members close to the slain chief executive—David Powers, his buddy and personal assistant; Kenneth P. O'Donnell, appointments secretary and key political adviser; Lawrence O'Brien, chief Kennedy liaison man with Congress, and Brig. Gen. Godfrey McHugh, Kennedy's Air Force aide.

Kennedy's military aide, Maj. Gen. Chester V. Clifton, was busy most of the trip in the forward areas of the plane, sending messages and making arrangements for arrival ceremonies and movement of the body to Bethesda Naval Hospital.

As the flight progressed, Johnson walked back into the main compartment. My portable typewriter was lost somewhere around the hospital and I was writing on an oversized electric typewriter which Kennedy's personal secretary, Evelyn Lincoln, had used to type his speech texts.

Johnson came up to the table where Roberts and I were trying to record the history we had just witnessed.

"I'm going to make a short statement in a few minutes and give you copies of it," he said. "Then when I get on the ground, I'll do it over again."

It was the first public utterance of the new Chief Executive, brief and moving:

"This is a sad time for all people. We have suffered a loss that cannot be weighed. For me it is a deep personal tragedy. I know the world shares the sorrow that Mrs. Kennedy and her family bear. I will do my best. That is all I can do. I ask for your help, and God's."

When the plane was about 45 minutes from Washington, the new President got on a special radio telephone and placed a call to Mrs. Rose Kennedy, the late President's mother.

"I wish to God there was something I could do," he told her. "I just wanted you to know that."

Then Mrs. Johnson wanted to talk to the elder Mrs. Kennedy.

"We feel like the heart has been cut out of us," Mrs. Johnson said. She broke down for a moment and began to sob. Recovering in a few seconds, she added, "Our love and our prayers are with you."

Thirty minutes out of Washington, Johnson put in a call for Nellie Connally, wife of the seriously wounded Texas Governor.

The new President said to the Governor's wife:

"We are praying for you, darling, and I know that everything is going to be all right, isn't it? Give him a hug and a kiss for me."

It was dark when Air Force One began to skim over the lights of the Washington area, lining up for a landing at Andrews Air Force Base. The plane touched down at 5:59 P.M. EST.

I thanked the stewards for rigging up the typewriter for me, pulled on my raincoat, and started down the forward ramp. Roberts and I stood under the wing and watched the casket being lowered from the rear of the plane and borne by a complement of armed forces body bearers into a waiting hearse. We watched Mrs.

Kennedy and the President's brother, Atty. Gen. Robert F. Kennedy, climb into the hearse beside the coffin.

The new President repeated his first public statement for broadcast and newsreel microphones, shook hands with some of the government and diplomatic leaders who turned out to meet the plane, and headed for his helicopter.

Roberts and I were given seats on another 'copter bound for the White House lawn. In the compartment next to ours in one of the large chairs beside a window sat Theodore C. Sorensen, one of Kennedy's closest associates with the title of special counsel to the President. He had not gone to Texas with his chief but had come to the air base for his return.

Sorensen sat wilted in the large chair, crying softly. The dignity of his deep grief seemed to sum up all of the tragedy and sadness of the previous six hours.

As our helicopter circled in the balmy darkness for a landing on the White House south lawn, it seemed incredible that only six hours before, John Fitzgerald Kennedy had been a vibrant, smiling, waving and active man.

While Smith was writing his story, Lee Harvey Oswald, the 24-year-old rifleman who was seen leaving the Texas School Book Depository, already was in custody. Police had traced him to the corner of Tenth Street and Patton Avenue, where he had shot and killed Patrolman J. D. Tippett, who had sought to question him at 1:10 P.M.

A few minutes later, Oswald was arrested in a nearby movie house, the Texas Theatre. And at 11:20 A.M. on Sunday, November 24, he was shot and killed by Jack Ruby, a 52-year-old night club owner, in the basement of the Dallas city jail while television recorded the second assassination for 50 million witnesses.

Smith was awarded the Pulitzer Prize for National Reporting in 1964. He continued as the White House correspondent for UPI, surviving to cover six Presidents in 30 years. But in 1968, he fell ill, and on April 13, 1970, at the age of 57, he ended his own life with a shot in the head.[1]

[1] Smith's suicide, *New York Times*, April 14, 1970; main sources for the Kennedy assassination, in addition to the Smith account, are the Warren Commission Report; *Four Days: The Historical Record of the Death of President Kennedy*, compiled by UPI and the American Heritage magazine (New York, 1964); *The Torch Is Passed*, the AP story of the death of the President (New York, 1964); the *Columbia Journalism Review* (Winter 1964); the *Quill* (January 1964), an assessment by John Tebbel.

THE ASSASSINATION OF LEE HARVEY OSWALD
Pulitzer Prize for News Photography, 1964

ROBERT H. JACKSON OF THE DALLAS TIMES-HERALD PHOTOGRAPHS JACK
RUBY AS HE SHOT AND KILLED LEE HARVEY OSWALD, UNDER ARREST FOR
THE ASSASSINATION OF PRESIDENT KENNEDY, IN DALLAS

VIII. CIVIL RIGHTS BATTLE
STRAINS THE NATION

When Joseph Pulitzer's *New York World* exposed the Ku Klux Klan as a menace to American society in 1921, it set a pattern for American journalism and the nation as well. For in this century, more often than not, the journalists have served as the first line of defense against the forces of hate and intolerance when duly constituted authority failed.

The records of the Pulitzer Prizes bear witness to this phenomenon of our times. In sheer numbers, it is true that more awards have gone to exposés of governmental corruption at all levels and to war correspondence. But the prizes that have had the most lasting influence on both the profession and the society as a whole are those bestowed upon reporters, editors, and newspapers in the long struggle for civil rights.

The Ku Klux Klan is a case in point. A few hard-headed promoters, cashing in on the willingness of the ignorant and the foolhardy to enlist in a white supremacy movement, revived the Klan in the let-down of public spirit in America after World War I. While it was not at all like the Klan of the Reconstruction era, it found thousands of recruits in the South and quickly spread in the industrial North wherever anti-black, anti-Catholic, and anti-Jewish sentiment could take root.

Once the *World* revealed the Klan's true origins and its money-making intent, and received a Pulitzer Prize as recognition of its public service, many other news organizations joined in the attack.

For by this time, the Klan had developed powerful political bases in many states and was of particular importance in Texas, Oklahoma, Indiana, Oregon, and Maine. While many a politican walked in fear of the hooded order, the more courageous editors did not.

In the earliest years of the Pulitzer awards, therefore, the moral war against the Klan was a matter of major concern to those who sat in judgment on the performance of the American press. In addition to the *New York World*, the *Memphis Commercial Appeal* in 1923, the *Columbus* (Ga.) *Enquirer Sun* in 1926, and the *Indianapolis Times* in 1928 all were awarded the Pulitzer gold medal for public service for attacks on the power of the Klan.

The editorial writers, too, won recognition for attempting to sway public opinion against racial violence and lynch law, particularly in the South. Among the noteworthy editorial awards were those given to Grover Cleveland Hall of the Montgomery (Ala.) *Advertiser* in 1928 for rebuking the hate-mongers and the floggers, and Louis Isaac Jaffe of the *Norfolk Virginian-Pilot* in 1929 for his successful campaign for strong legal measures to halt lynching in Virginia.

Once the power of the Klan was broken, however, there was a hiatus in the interest of American journalism in the nation's racial problems. And this, too, is reflected in the Pulitzer records. Now and then, prizes were awarded for outstanding journalism that dealt with racial intolerance. Two small North Carolina weeklies, the *Whiteville News Reporter* and the *Tabor City Tribune*, shared a public service award in 1953 for attacking a post World War II attempt to revive the Ku Klux Klan in their state.

In national reporting, Edward Folliard of the *Washington Post* won a prize in 1947 for exposing a hate group called the Columbians. And among editorial writers, Hodding Carter, editor of the *Delta Democrat-Times* of Greenville, Miss., was recognized for attacking intolerance practiced against Japanese-Americans, his award coming in 1946, directly after a Japanese-American combat unit had been cited for valor in World War II.

But until the Supreme Court's 1954 school desegregation decision, wars and political corruption were more important to a large area of the American press than racial problems. Nor did the new-born art of television journalism break out of the established pattern of news priorities.

The tube did demonstrate its power when Edward R. Murrow launched an assault on Senator Joseph R. McCarthy, Jr., who used an anti-Communist crusade in the early 1950s as a pretext to violate the rights of defenseless citizens. But when McCarthy at last was overthrown, television seldom evinced interest in the racial conflict until the black ghettos of America burst into flames.

It remained for the press, in large part, to cover the school desegregation crisis—to explain and to persuade, and above all to try to calm public outcries against the Supreme Court's decision. Here, the record of the Pulitzer Prizes reads like a fever chart; for, whenever the racial struggle broke into violence, there were reporters and editors who had to find a way to tell the story to their people under deadline pressure. There were photographers and cartoonists who had to illustrate it. And there were publishers who had to summon up the courage to authorize the printing of a lot of material that was certain to antagonize many readers and advertisers.

In the 18 annual announcements of Pulitzer awards from 1957 through 1974, there were no less than 13 prizes arising from the coverage of the racial crisis—investigation of its causes or commentary that was intended to ease tensions. All save three were won by Southern journalists and Southern newspapers.

The list of winners reads like an honor roll of American journalism.

In 1975, it was Buford Boone with his reasoned appeals to halt the riots over the desegregation of the University of Alabama.

In 1958, Harry Ashmore of the *Arkansas Gazette* and Relman Morin of the Associated Press were telling the story at Little Rock when the first black students entered Central High.

In 1959, it was Ralph McGill in Atlanta, calling on the South to abjure and condemn further violence, and Mary Lou Werner of the *Washington Star*, calmly covering the uproar over desegregation in Virginia schools.

In 1960, it was Lenoir Chambers crying out in the *Norfolk Virginian Pilot* for public understanding of school desegregation.

In 1963, it was Ira B. Harkey, Jr., and, a year later, Hazel Brannon Smith, both fighting against racial injustice in their home state of Mississippi.

In 1966, when Watts went up in flames, it was the *Los Angeles Times;* in 1967, Eugene Patterson of the *Atlanta Constitution*, and in 1968, the *Detroit Free Press* covering the worst riots in the city's history.

In 1971, it was Buddy Davis of the *Gainesville Sun*, calling for the peasceful desegregation of Florida's schools; and in 1972, John Strohmeyer of the *Bethlehem* (Pa.) *Globe-Times* campaigning to reduce racial tensions in his own city.

In 1974, it was the *Boston Globe*, throwing all its resources into the coverage of the massive struggle over school busing.

For every prize winner, however, there were many to whom the racial struggle presented a terrible problem—a problem that had to be dealt with somehow beyond hope of special honors or even a small sign of public gratitude. Indeed, to some, the mere publication of an article about a racial incident could involve threats of retribution followed by blows, beatings, shattered glass windows in newspaper offices and even bullets.

It would be pleasant to report that the American press as a whole distinguished itself in such extremities but it would not be true. Not even a majority of the nation's newspapers, North or South, called for fealty to the law once the Supreme Court had spoken. The ones who did, particularly in the South, showed extraordinary courage. And the wonder of it is not that there were so few, but that a hard-bitten core of responsible journalists in every Southern state did stand up to be counted on the side of fairness in race relations.

By their example, they undoubtedly prepared the journalists of the North for their own ordeal by riot and firebomb when the mob spirit swept across the Mason-Dixon Line to the black ghettos beyond. For those who thought quite mistakenly that the struggle would be confined to the South, there was a terrible awakening. For as events demonstrated, the racial issue was to remain a flash point for American journalism throughout this century.

In this section, there are vivid and unforgettable illustrations of how some of the great ones measured up to their responsibilities during two decades of the sternest testing in American history. It

"STAND BACK EVERYBODY! HE'S GOT A BOMB.!!"

Pulitzer Prize for Editorial Cartooning, 1964

AS PAUL CONRAD, THEN OF THE DENVER POST, SAW ALABAMA'S
RESISTANCE TO SCHOOL DESEGREGATION

was an era that tried the strength of the nation; had it not been able to withstand the tension and the torment of the multitudes, the whole fabric of our society might have been torn apart.

34. RALPH MCGILL LEADS THE FIGHT
FOR CIVIL RIGHTS IN THE SOUTH

The Atlanta Constitution's Editor Attacks Bigots
Who Bombed a Jewish Temple and a High School

Ralph McGill represented the best in American journalism. There was nothing that angered him more than injustice, nothing he despised more than a lie. To his friends, he gave his devotion and unflinching loyalty, sometimes to the point of rashness. And when he embraced a cause, he flung himself into the struggle with bravery and passion regardless of consequences.

For much of his career as the editor and later the publisher of the *Atlanta Consititution*, his was the great liberal voice of the South. And though he was bitterly attacked, often threatened and even had shots fired at the home where he cared for his wife in her long illness, he never once retreated from advocating what he believed was right.

For a Southern journalist of such character, it was foreordained that he would lead in the massive effort to desegregate the public schools, insure voting rights to all citizens, and otherwise bring the fullness of civil rights to the South's blacks who had been denied them for so long.

Even before America was flung into World War II by the Japanese attack on Pearl Harbor, McGill was writing about the various court suits that were being brought to desegregate the nation's public schools. But few paid attention to him.

Still, out of a sense of responsibility and an awareness of the coming social conflict, he persisted. A year before the Supreme Court took up the crucial suit, Brown vs. Topeka (Kansas) Board of Educaiton, he wrote a column in the *Constitution* entitled, "One of These Days It Will Be Monday." It was an explicit warning that a landmark decision in the school case could be expected on a Monday when the high court customarily issued its major rulings.

That Monday came on May 17, 1954, when the court, in a unanimous opinion delivered by Chief Justice Earl Warren, struck down the doctrine of "separate but equal" treatment for black children in the schools that had been ordained in the case of Plessy vs. Ferguson. Acting on the case of Linda Brown, who had been refused admission to a Topeka elementary school because she was black, the Warren court held that the unequal treatment of black children violated the 14th amendment of the Constitution, which guarantees equal protection under the law to all citizens.

McGill commented sadly, "None of those whose duty it was to cope with the effect of it had done any preliminary planning or educating. It could be seen, too, that we were all caught in it, white and colored, the haves and the have-nots."[1]

McGill had the strength and intestinal fortitude to stand up under pressure, once he had made a policy decision. And he needed it, for his pro-desegregation arguments in the *Atlanta Constitution* made him a ready target for every bigot with a knife, a club, or a gun. Yet, even to those who admired him, he was an unlikely crusader—a kindly and generous man who delighted in having a good time, enjoyed convivial companionship, and was unsurpassed as a crowd-pleaser and story-teller.

Nothing in his early career indicated that he would emerge as a champion of the weak, the defenseless and the poor. He had been born in Tennessee in 1898, majored in football more than anything else while he was at Vanderbilt, quit school to serve in World War I, and became a sports writer thereafter for the *Nashville Banner* in 1922. It was only when he came to the *Atlanta Constitution* in 1931 that he began to broaden his vision. Within seven years, he left a comfortable job as sports editor of the *Constitution* to become the executive editor of the paper, but soon found that his brand of liberalism did not sit well with the Ku Klux Klan. Despite demonstrations against him by hooded and robed Klansmen, he took over as editor of the *Constitution* in 1942; from then on, his was invariably the first voice to be raised against intolerance, hate, and imprisonment of the human spirit.

Once desegration of schools was legally ordained in the South, he was caught up in the flow of events. He came to know and admire the young and forthright pastor of the Ebenezer Baptist Church in Atlanta, the Rev. Dr. Martin Luther King, Jr., who beat down Birmingham's "back-of-the-bus" segregation law against blacks with a 1955-56 bus boycott.

In his column, McGill was among the first to support King's devotion to

[1] Ralph McGill, *The South and the Southerner* (Boston: Little, Brown, 1959, 1963) pp. 24-25, 170-171. Characterization of McGill from my own memories of him; other details from Harold H. Martin, *Ralph McGill, Reporter*, (Boston: Atlantic Monthly Press, 1973).

the principle of nonviolent protest and worked incessantly to calm the passions of those who opposed them both. There were many, indeed, who declared long afterward that without McGill's humanitarian approach and his appeal to reason, Atlanta could well have become a major battleground of the civil rights movement.

Instead, the focus of the struggle swung from Birmingham to Tuscaloosa where, in 1956, a four-day riot forced the withdrawal of the first black student to be admitted to the University of Alabama, Autherine Lucy. After that crisis, Buford Boone of the *Tuscaloosa News* was awarded a Pulitzer Prize in 1957 for helping to bring a hysterical community back to its senses.

Then came Little Rock, when President Eisenhower had to send federal troops to all-white Central High School in 1957 in order to protect the first black students there from the wrath of Arkansas Governor Orval Faubus and his riotous adherents. This time it was Harry S. Ashmore, executive editor of the Arkansas Gazette, who wrote in an editorial on Sept. 9, 1957:

"We are going to have to decide what kind of people we are—whether we obey the law only when we approve of it, or whether we obey it no matter how disasteful we may find it. And this, finally, is the only issue before the people of Arkansas."

It was the only issue, too, for Ralph McGill; when Ashmore and the *Arkansas Gazette* both won Pulitzer Prizes in 1958 for their leadership and courage under fire, the great Georgian led the applause.

McGill paid a heavy price for his championship of an unpopular cause. He was condemned repeatedly as a traitor to the South. His home became even more of a target for his opponents and he seldom could relax his guard wherever he went. Someone with less courage and dedication would have steered a more moderate course, but it was not in his character to retreat.

He watched the course of events in the South with mounting anger, even reproaching those of his own profession for their timidity. And then, in mid-October of 1958, he came home from a trip just after a fine new high school at Clinton, Tenn., had been destroyed by fanatical bombers in a protest against desegregation. The first news his wife gave him dealt with that outrage in his native state and still another bombing in Atlanta that had destroyed The Temple, home of the city's largest Jewish congregation.

Utterly appalled, McGill went to his typewriter and in 20 minutes wrote an editorial that ran in the *Constitution* next day, and in scores of other papers, North and South, on succeeding days. It was among the best, and certainly one of the most effective, that he ever did in more than four decades of newspaper work:

"ONE CHURCH . . . ONE SCHOOL"

By Ralph McGill

From the Atlanta Constitution, Oct. 13, 1958

Dynamite in great quantity early Sunday, Oct. 13 ripped a beautiful temple of worship in Atlanta. It followed hard on the heels of a like destruction of a handsome high school at Clinton, Tennessee.

The same rabid, mad-dog minds were, without question, behind both. They are also the source of previous bombings in Florida, Alabama, and South Carolina. The schoolhouse and the church were the targets of diseased, hate-filled minds.

Let us face the facts. This is a harvest. It is the crop of things sown.

It is the harvest of defiance of courts and the encouragement of citizens to defy the law on the part of many Southern politicians. It will be the acme of irony . . . if any of four or five Southern governors deplore this bombing. It will be grimly humorous if certain state attorneys general issue statements of regret. And it will be quite a job for some editors, columnists, and commentators, who have been saying that our courts have no jurisdiction and that people should refuse to accept their authority, now to deplore.

It is not possible to preach lawlessness and restrict it. . . .

When leadership in high places . . . fails to support constituted authority, it opens the gates to all those who wish to take the law into their hands. . . .

The extremists of the citizens' councils, the political leaders who in terms violent and inflammatory have repudiated their oaths and stood against due process of law have helped unloose this flood of hate and bombing.

This, too, is a harvest of those so-called Christian ministers who have chosen to preach hate instead of compassion. Let them now find pious words and raise their hands in deploring the bombing of a synagogue.

You do not preach and encourage hatred for the Negro and hope to restrict it to that field. It is an old, old story. It is one repeated over and over again in history. When the wolves of hate are loosed on one people, no one is safe. . . .

This series of bombings is the harvest, too, of something else.

One of those connected with the bombing telephoned a news service early Sunday morning to say the job would be done. It would be committed, he said, by the Confederate Underground.

The Confederacy and the men who led it are revered by millions. Its leaders returned to the Union and urged that the future be committed to building a stronger America. This was particularly true of General Robert E. Lee. Time after time he urged his students at Washington University to forget the War Between the States and to help build a greater and stronger union.

For too many years now we have seen the Confederate flag and the emotions of that great war become the property of men not fit to tie the shoes of those who fought for it. Some of these have been merely childish and immature. Others have perverted and commercialized the flag by making the Stars and Bars, and the Confederacy itself, a symbol of hate and bombings.

For a long time it has been needful for all Americans to stand up and be counted on the side of law and the due process of law—even when to do so goes against the personal beliefs and emotions. It is late. But there is yet time.

The editorial was among a collection of McGill's work that was proposed for a Pulitzer Prize the following year. It had much to do with his selection as the winner of the 1959 Pulitzer Prize for Editorial Writing. After he was told of the award, he said: "I never thought I'd make it."

When he was asked to join the Pulitzer Prize Board two years later, as tensions in the South continued to mount, it was a rare recognition of a journalist who stood for principle and a tacit encouragement to other Southern journalists who were in the forefront of the struggle for civil rights. He remained a member of the Board until his death in 1969.

At a time when many another Southern city was contorted with hate and paid a terrible penalty in casualties and destruction of property, McGill could look with satisfaction on the hope of something better that he had helped to create in Atlanta. He wrote:

CONFRONTATION
Pulitzer Prize for Feature Photography, 1976

AN ANTIBUSING DEMONSTRATOR FACES LOUISVILLE POLICE—ONE OF MANY
PHOTOS OF THE LOUISVILLE SCHOOL CRISIS IN THE PORTFOLIO OF THE
PHOTOGRAPHIC STAFF OF THE LOUISVILLE COURIER-JOURNAL AND TIMES

"The greatest of all compensations was to be one of the many who worked long and patiently at the arduous job of seeing to it that the people of Atlanta know the facts and the alternatives. To see the golf courses, transportation, eating places, libraries, and schools desegregated without incident but rather with understanding and good manners was a warm and rewarding experience. There is almost an ecstasy which is quite indescribable in seeing, and feeling, a city slowly but surely reach a decision and act on it. For a time, one lives a shared existence which is deeply rewarding." [2]

It was no mere accident that Atlanta became the first city in the South, and indeed in the entire nation, to honor the Rev. Dr. Martin Luther King, Jr., in 1965 when he won the Nobel Peace Prize. The ceremony was a symbol of the change that McGill had helped to bring about through patience and courage and a rare devotion to principle.

35. HAYNES JOHNSON RETRACES THE MARCH FROM SELMA TO MONTGOMERY, ALA.

The Washington Star's Correspondent Sees Evidence That the "Old Days" in the South Are Gone Forever

Before the demonstration for civil rights on August 29, 1963, in which 200,000 people participated in Washington, D.C., the Rev. Dr. Martin Luther King, Jr., climaxed his greatest speech with these familiar lines:

"I have a dream . . . I have a dream that this nation will rise up and live out the true meaning of its creed, 'We hold these truths to be self-evident: that all men are created equal. . . .'"

The passage of the Civil Rights Act of 1964, which forbade discrimination in voting, public accommodations, and employment, was a long step toward the realization of that dream. And yet, Dr. King knew perfectly well that much more remained to be done, that many years would pass, and others would have to take up the battle for him to insure the translation of his vision into reality. And so, in 1965, he took his crusade into the most hostile territory in the South, Governor George C. Wallace's Alabama, and led a march from Selma to Montgomery to stimulate black voter registration.

It was a spectacular news story, which was featured on television's evening news programs and the front pages of the nation's newspapers for

[2] Ralph McGill, *The South and the Southerner*, p. 297.

days on end. But after it was all over, many wondered what it really had accomplished. Haynes Johnson, a reporter for the *Washington Star*, went back to Selma to find out in the summer of 1965.

Johnson was 34 at the time, and a newspaperman's newspaperman. He had literally been born into the business. His father was Malcolm (Mike) Johnson of the *New York Sun*, winner of a 1949 Pulitzer Prize for Reporting for a dramatic series, "Crime on the Waterfront."

Haynes Johnson, born in New York City in 1931, was educated at the University of Missouri's journalism school and did graduate work at the University of Wisconsin. He joined the *Washington Star* in 1957, where he covered everything from an earthquake in Chile to the "Bay of Pigs" fiasco in Cuba, handled rewrite and desk work, and did the lead story in the paper on President John F. Kennedy's assassination in 1963. He was, therefore, a seasoned journalist when he returned to Selma for an estimate of where the civil rights movement was going and what it had accomplished by the middle of that turbulent decade.

This is the substance of his report:

"THE DEEP SOUTH WILL NEVER BE THE SAME"

By Haynes Johnson

From the Washington Star, July 26, 1965

SELMA, Alabama—A new sign stands near the spot where the Rev. Martin Luther King, Jr., led the marchers into the street and down the long road to Montgomery last spring. It reads: "FORWARD EVER—BACKWARD NEVER."

Today that sign is more an expression of hope than a statement of fact. While stoutly maintaining their faith in themselves and in the civil rights movement, Negroes are shocked and divided.

The spirit and singleness of purpose they showed when Selma became a byword around the world have been shattered by bickering and scandal. While the victory they scored last spring remains untarnished, the drive to build on it by improving their lot in life has slowed.

Their leaders are struggling to regain precious momentum, but many of those who followed them so patiently are frankly bewildered and disillusioned. Selma's Negro community is, in fact, in an hour of new and more subtle crisis—a tragic crisis when it is contrasted with the soaring hopes and selfless devotion they and their friends demonstrated here such a short time ago.

This reporter returning to Selma finds none of this on the surface. Selma slumbers in the summer heat as if the exciting days of springtime had never occurred. Women with parasols stroll past the small stores. The streets are quiet; there is little movement. Across the Alabama River the hot wind plays across the cotton fields.

Now there are no demonstrators, no barricades, no jeering or chanting crowds, no troopers or armed posses. Now, Selma, Ala., seems merely another trading center in the heart of the black belt of the rural South.

There is no discernible change in the racial climate of the city. The Negroes have scored no real advances in their areas of greatest need—employment, housing, and education. They are discovering that these goals are easier to express than to achieve.

To be sure, there have been some improvements in the Negro position. Volunteer workers of both races are teaching students and adults in improvised classrooms. Leaders of the white and Negro communities have met in an attempt to begin meaningful communications. The Negroes are continuing their voter registration work. More than 20,000 books have been collected from across the country for a Negro library.

And above all is a historical fact: As a result of what the Selma Negroes and their white friends did last spring, the Deep South will never be the same again. The demonstrations and the march lifted the spirits of Negroes everywhere.

In part, the present dispirited mood in Selma may reflect an inevitable letdown from an emotional peak—what happens when the cheering stops.

It has been aggravated, however, by some specific incidents— the arrest of one of the most prominent local Negro leaders of the protest movement on charges of embezzling civil rights funds and the morals conviction of another Negro who assumed a position of leadership during the demonstrations. . . .

Economically, the outlook for the Negro is still bleak. There are few jobs. There are still no street lights in the Negro sections. The housing and plumbing are abysmal. The streets are still unpaved. The wages are still below any reasonable minimum. In Selma, a Negro who earns $50 a week is a wealthy man.

And outside Selma, in the farmland through which the marchers made their way, the conditions are worse.

After the march some of the Negroes who came to the side of the road to cheer and wave suffered retaliations. Others appear to have been forgotten.

Mrs. Carrie Beaton, 39, sat on the porch of her shack surrounded by children and said: "Ain't nobody come to see us no way." Even if they had, she said, "It wouldn't make no difference."

But she, like all the Negroes one talks to, takes great pride in the Selma movement and the march. "It was real good," she said.

Across the field from one of the campsites used on the march, a Negro woman who operates a grocery told how a bakery in Montgomery refused to sell her bread for her store. "The bread man said the white man came to them and told them they better not sell us the bread," she said. "And they said we aren't going to have any school for the little children."

Now the bread deliveries have resumed; things have returned to normal along the Jefferson Davis Highway to Montgomery. But for Selma and Dallas County, as well as the other rural centers of the South, the old days and ways, it seems clear, will never come again.

Haynes Johnson won the Pulitzer Prize in National Reporting in 1966 for his probing analysis of the march to Montgomery and the hope it raised in what was then an essentially divided black community. His father was delighted; it isn't often, in the annals of the Prizes, that there have been two winners in the same family. Today, Haynes Johnson is a member of the staff of the *Washington Post*.

IN MOURNING
Pulitzer Prize for Feature Photography, 1969

MONETA J. SLEET, JR., OF EBONY MAGAZINE, SERVING AS ONE OF THE POOL PHOTOGRAPHERS FOR THE AMERICAN PRESS, TOOK THIS PICTURE OF CORETTA SCOTT KING AND HER DAUGHTER, BERNICE, AT FUNERAL SERVICES FOR HER HUSBAND, THE ASSASSINATED REV. DR. MARTIN LUTHER KING, JR., AT ATLANTA'S EBENEZER BAPTIST CHURCH ON APRIL 9, 1968 (Copyright 1968 by Moneta J. Sleet, Jr. and *Ebony* magazine. Used by permission.)

36. THE LOS ANGELES TIMES REPORTS
THE FIVE-DAY RIOTS IN WATTS

An Eyewitness Tells of Arsonists Tossing Molotov Cocktails
into Stores and Shouting a Slogan, "Burn, Baby, Burn."

One of the worst riots in American history swept through the predominantly black Watts area of Los Angeles for five terrifying days and nights in the summer of 1965.

Between August 11 and 16, at least 35 persons died, hundreds were injured, many thousands were left homeless, and a large section of Watts was gutted by fire. Damage was put at more than $200 million and Watts took years to recover.

With 21,000 National Guard troops and local police waging what amounted to a guerrilla war with the rioters, anybody who tried to find out what was happening became a likely target in the confusion. And this was particularly true of the reporters and photographers of the *Los Angeles Times* who covered the agony for all five days. They were always in danger, and often without sleep or even food.

The despair and the agony of that period are best exemplified in a brief Page 1 editorial run by the Times on the fourth day of the rioting, Sunday, August 15, which began:

"There are no words to express the shock, the sick horror, that a civilized city feels at a moment like this.

"It could not happen in Los Angeles. But it did. And the shameful, senseless, bloody rioting continues unabated after the four ugliest days in our history.

"Decent citizens everywhere, regardless of color, can only pray that this anarchy will soon end."

Despite a disaster proclamation from the Governor's office and the imposition of an 8 P.M. curfew that was ordered beginning Saturday night, August 14, there seemed to be no end to the anarchy.

A five-year-old black boy was killed by a sniper's bullet in his own back yard, the *Times* reported in its lead story, and firemen who tried to control a blaze in the area at midnight were pinned down by firing from nearby houses and buildings.

"A huge section of the Negro area was in flames," the *Times* said.

And what of the rioters? Robert Richardson, then a 24-year-old advertising salesman for the *Times*, became an involuntary eyewitness to terror when he turned reporter. Because he was black, perhaps there was some feeling at the *Times* that he might not be in such great danger in the disaster area. But on Friday night, August 13, he also became a target. Here is his story, in essential part, as it appeared on page 1 of Sunday's *Times*:

"BURN, BABY, BURN!"

By Robert Richardson

From the Los Angeles Times, August 15, 1965

Negro arsonists raced autos through otherwise deserted Los Angeles streets, flinging Molotov cocktails into store after store and shouting a hip slogan borrowed from a radio disc jockey:

"Burn, baby, burn!"

It was an eerie scene Friday night. Streets crowded with hundreds of rioters the night before were debris-littered but empty. Lighted windows were few. It was almost like a ghost town.

But new flames continued to shoot up. Speeding cars crisscrossed the area. Occupants exchanged the now familiar one, two, or three-finger salute and shouted the grim slogan:

"Burn, baby, burn!"

(One finger meant he was a Watts man, two a Compton man, and three meant a man from the Willowbrook area.)

The rioters were burning their city now, as the insane sometimes mutilate themselves.

A great section of Los Angeles was burning and anyone who didn't return the crazy password was in danger.

I, too, learned to shout, "Burn, baby, burn!" after several shots were fired at me. Luckily, none of the bullets hit my car and, luckier still, none hit me.

At Holmes Avenue and Imperial Highway, I saw a looted Safeway Store all but destroyed by fire.

At 120th Street and Central Avenue, a Shoprite Market was burning.

Other stores were burning near Manchester Avenue and Broadway with no one apparently paying the least attention. I saw nobody near them.

Near Vernon and Central Avenues, several stores were burning over a six-block area from north to south. All had been looted. People had carried off everything.

It seemed almost a miracle that the riot spent itself and died out on August 16, but a horrified city then had to face up to the consequences of the disaster. Why had it happened? Who had been responsible for the wanton killing, the looting, the burning? What could be done to avert a recurrence?

Tucked away among the pages of the news accounts was this thoughtful editorial:

WHO WILL NOW SHARE THE LOAD?

From the Los Angeles Times, August 16, 1965

One hundred years after the Emancipation Proclamation, the American Negro, most classically underprivileged of all U.S. minorities, has won his battle for civil rights and lawful freedoms.

His victory came through the selfless efforts of a heavy Congressional majority which passed the Civil Rights Act of 1964.

It appeared this summer that the moment had arrived for consolidation of these overdue gains, for application in fact of these legal principles.

Meanwhile responsible leaders of the general public, headed by President Johnson, and of the national Negro community urged that Negroes proceed in orderly fashion to secure still other advantages so long denied them: better education, better jobs, better housing.

With ironic prophecy, in a column written on the eve of Los Angeles's racial holocaust, Roy Wilkins of the NAACP wondered: "Will Negro citizens now pitch in for the unglamorous work, out of the spotlight, that will prepare and send the individual Negro through the doors that have been opened?"

He concluded: "The sober majority in the Negro community and in its leadership will distinguish itself in the degree that it adapts to the new era."

Now that a precarious peace has been established in the ravaged area, certain basic truths should be recognized:

—What happened here was not the doing of the Negro majority

in Los Angeles. Far from it. Innocent Negroes were among the saddest victims of the burning and looting.

—It would be wrong to allow the riots to impede steady progress on the civil rights front.

Nevertheless, in the white heat of emotions generated in recent days, there will be a tendency for some to lash out against the Negro community in general, against the "situation" that let all this develop.

A terrible responsibility rests upon white and Negro leaders alike, to chart both the immediate and the long-range courses that must be followed if we are to emerge from the present crisis without precipitating another.

To a sobering degree, this burden falls upon the spokesman for the Negro community, whose voices have not always contributed to the understanding so badly needed today.

Even by inference, none should condone the criminal terrorism or dismiss it as the inevitable result of economic or sociological pressures.

President Johnson said it well: "There is no greater wrong in our democracy than violent, wilful disregard of law. If men live decently, it is because obedience to legal process saved their lives and allowed them to enlarge those lives."

In his speech at Howard University, a predominantly Negro institution, Mr. Johnson looked ahead to "the next great battle in the civil rights movement"—"to shatter forever not only the barriers of law and public practice but the walls which bound the conditions of man by the color of his skin."

That effort, tragically, may have been set back to an incalculable degree.

It need not necessarily be so. But only the genuine, whole-souled effort of those concerned, whatever their ethnic origin, will determine whether we can abandon narrow racial policies in favor of an enlightened area-wide approach to this crushing problem.

This was what a Pulitzer Prize jury thought of the *Los Angeles Times*'s coverage of the Watts disaster:

"Here was a superb example of a large newspaper using all its resources to cover a local event that assumed world importance. There was the immediate reporting of a continuously explosive situation. There were editorials articulating the need for action to restore law and order. There was exploration of the causes of the rioting and a search for solutions. Finally, there was a series of seven articles, "The View from Watts," telling the entire community—though some of this material was repugant and inflammatory—what the inhabitants of Watts thought about the rioting and the reasons for it."

The Pulitzer Prize Board showed no hesitation in giving the *Los Angeles Times* staff a Pulitzer Prize in Local Reporting for 1966 for the Watts story.

37. EUGENE PATTERSON PROTESTS TWO OUTRAGES IN THE SOUTH

The Atlanta Constitution's Editor Criticizes a Refusal to Seat Julian Bond and the Shooting of James Meredith

Eugene Patterson, a soft-spoken and kindly man with a glint of cold steel in his eyes, carried on the tradition of Ralph McGill as editor of the *Atlanta Constitution*. In their broad outlook and their championship of civil rights, they were very much the same. But Patterson was not as patient as his predecessor.

McGill really wanted to be friends with almost anybody who seemed willing to listen to reason; Patterson, for his part, was a good deal more selective and probably more efficient. But both, in whatever editorial position they took in the *Constitution*, never let themselves be deterred from principle either by fear or expediency.

This was why, in the winter of 1966, Patterson was among the first to protest the exclusion of Julian Bond, a black critic of the Vietnam War, from the Georgia Legislature even though the *Constitution* then was still a supporter of the war policy. It was also the reason, when James Meredith was shot by a sniper in the spring of that year, that Patterson mourned for what he called the "sick soul" of the South.

Like McGill, Patterson was a Southerner (born in Adel, Ga., in 1923), but unlike McGill, who had his doubts about journalism education, Patterson was a journalism graduate of the University of Georgia in 1943. He won the Silver Star and the Bronze Star with Oak Leaf Cluster for gallantry in action in World War II while a platoon leader in the 10th Armored Division in Europe.

After the war, he became a reporter on small papers in Texas and Georgia and in 1948 joined United Press, which later became United Press International. Eventually he became UPI's New York night bureau manager and manager and chief correspondent for the United Kingdom in London. He became executive editor of the *Constitution* and *Atlanta Journal* in 1956 and was named editor in 1960.

Here was his climactic editorial in the Julian Bond case:

IN DEFENSE OF JULIAN BOND

By Eugene C. Patterson

From the Atlanta Constitution, Jan. 10, 1966

Unsurprisingly, the United States Supreme Court was unanimous in saying that the Georgia Legislature erred when it refused to seat Representative Julian Bond last January.

So the matter is over and nobody is hurt but the people of the state. Their Legislature brought down on them a lasting embarrassment by permitting political hotheads to stampede it into an untenable position.

A representative elected by the people was turned away from his seat because he had said unpopular (and, we think, unsupportable) things against United States policy in Vietnam.

But this represented the spectacle of an attempted punishment of Representative Bond by many legislators who for years had said unpopular and insupportable things against United States racial policy without losing THEIR seats.

Even the two federal cricuit judges who tried to affirm the Legislature's expulsion of Mr. Bond, and who were reversed by the unanimous Supreme Court, specified that they weren't saying the Legislature had chosen the "wisest course."

But they felt compelled to give the Legislature free rein in determining the qualifications of its members so long as it acted rationally; and the two judges decided it wasn't irrational for the Legislature to reject Mr. Bond since they felt he had called for "action" to violate a law—the Selective Service Law.

The Supreme Court discerned no such "call to unlawful refusal" on Mr. Bond's part. It noted the statement of the Student Nonviolent Coordinating Committee, which Bond supported, said: "We are in sympathy with and support the men in this country who are unwilling to respond to a military draft." This statement was "at worst unclear on the question of the means to be adopted to avert the draft," the high court ruled. Moreover, Mr. Bond modified it to say he was only talking about "Congressionally outlined" alternatives to military service.

This supplementary statement tended "to resolve the opaqueness in favor of legal alternatives to the draft," the Supreme Court said. Thus, it reversed the lower court finding and held that the Legislature had "violated Bond's right of free expression under the First Amendment."

The Supreme Court wisely repeated its view that debate on public issues in this country should be "uninhibited, robust, and wide open."

The net results of this controversy, which the Legislature never should have initiated, have been to make Julian Bond famous, spread his views, revive SNCC, and damage Georgia's claim to being a state of wisdom, justice, and moderation. That was a mighty poor return on one day's blowoff in the Legislature.

The editorial about James Meredith, who had created a crisis by seeking admission to the University of Mississippi, was written at an even more difficult period in the conflict of the 1960s over race relations in the United States. The South was disturbed over the Selma-to-Montgomery march and its consequences. The Watts area of Los Angeles had gone up in flames and smaller riots had broken out in other communities.

Against this background, Meredith announced that he was undertaking a solitary march from Memphis, Tennessee, to Jackson, Mississippi, to promote black voter registration. This was quite a different man from the solitary black student who had enrolled at the University of Mississippi in 1962 and caused federal troops to be called out to protect his rights. Following his graduation from Ole Miss, he had gone on to Columbia Law School and on April 19, 1972, had returned to his alma mater in Mississippi as a guest lecturer on the history of the state.

As a national figure in the civil rights movement, he was extensively covered but he didn't get far on his march. On June 6, 1966, he was ambushed as he walked along a half-deserted highway with only reporters, photographers, and a few curious bystanders as witnesses. His wounds turned out not to be serious.

This was Patterson's editorial on the case:

THE SHOOTING OF JAMES MEREDITH

By Eugene Patterson

From the Atlanta Constitution, June 7, 1966

"Oh!" cried James Meredith as the gunshots beat him down to the Mississippi pavement. "Oh!" Cry it for the white South, bleeding brother. You can only die with a torn body. The white South must live with its sick soul.

"We're no different," the white Southerner wants to say.

Aren't we?

The savage difference is there to look at. See whose face is reflected in the puddle of blood.

"But people get shot anywhere," we want to say. Yes, the President himself was shot by a madman.

But the savage difference that does still shamefully separate the South from other regions is that nobody expected the President to be shot.

Meredith expected he would be.

The President went to Dallas, confident that he would live. Meredith walked into Mississippi fearing he would be killed.

That is the fear Negro Southerners must always remember, and a fact the white South has tried to forget. It will not be forgotten.

What a terrible weight rests on this land. Not primarily because some weak, inflamed mind turned murderous. That can happen anywhere.

What does not happen anywhere but in the South is the sustained inflammation of those weak, uncomprehending minds by men who know better.

That is the savage difference. That is the unspeakable concern.

Every Negro in the South has had to live like Meredith, day in, day out, with knowledge of the danger those weak minds present to his life.

When Negroes have turned to the strong white minds of the South for safety, what have those minds offered? Have they reduced the inflammation with calm counsel, powerful example, concerned votes?

No. The majority have not. They have listened when racists orate, be they parlor brand or stump; they have used power and substance to install emotion-searing demagogues in office; they have closed their own doors to Negroes instead of setting examples of open minds; they have conversed agreeably about conservatism and the Constitution while the Negro has run for his life.

That was the point of Meredith's walk into Mississippi. He was angry with himself for being afraid. He felt less than a man. So he walked down the road and presented his life. His safety at that moment passed into the keeping of the strong white mind of the South.

That mind had shirked its duty. Not just to Meredith. To itself. It had evaded, alibied, caviled and quit; it had sought to justify, not rectify, the fearful plight of the Negro. And by the power of its honored example, it had loaded the gun of the weak man.

The gunman pulled the trigger. That much could have happened anywhere. The savage difference lies in the rest of us, and we won't even be arrested. We have only to live with the knowledge until, in God's own time, we assume responsibility.

For these and other editorials in similar vein, Eugene Patterson was awarded the Pulitzer Prize in Editorial Writing for 1967. He went on to become the managing editor of the *Washington Post* and, later, the president and editor of the *St. Petersburg* (Fla.) *Times and Evening Independent*. He presided over a campaign that exposed the bizarre methods and intimidating practices of the Church of Scientology in Clearwater, Fla., and brought the 1980 Pulitzer Prize for National Reporting to two reporters for the *St. Petersburg Times*, Bette Swenson Orsini and Charles Stafford.

38. THE FREE PRESS COVERS DETROIT'S RIOT AND ASKS, "WHY DID 43 PEOPLE DIE?"

The Staff Reports on the City's Worst Disaster,
Then Investigates Troops, Police, and Itself

The climax of America's racial troubles came in the pitiless heat, the despair and sheer desperation of the summer of 1967. Nothing like it had ever happened in this nation.

Every municipal official in the country had been warned against complacency by the Watts riot two summers before. And yet, when Newark went up in flames on July 12–17, with 26 dead and more than 1,500 injured, the authorities were caught unprepared. The same thing happened shortly afterward to a lesser extent in New York's Harlem, where more than a million blacks and Hispanics lived in dreadful conditions.

There was sporadic violence in smaller cities, enough to show that every black ghetto in the land was a tinderbox of crushed hopes and frustration. And then, without warning, Detroit blew up in what the *Free Press* described as nothing short of modern civil war.

Between July 23 and 30, there was incessant rioting, looting, and burning in the city's ghetto, where most of its black population existed. The casualties were enormous—43 dead, hundreds more injured, and somewhere between 5,000 and 7,000 people left homeless.

This was not a riot that Detroit police could have handled alone, even if they had been forewarned. Before it was over, 4,700 U.S. Army paratroops and 8,000 National Guardsmen were patrolling the streets and enforcing order.

The *Free Press* and the *News*, Detroit's two fine newspapers, responded to the extraordinary challenge by putting everything they had—staff, resources, equipment and funds—into an unprecedented effort to bring a devastated community accurate and comprehensive coverage of the riots. Neither paper spared itself; nor, for that matter, did any reporter, writer, photographer, or editor catch any more than a few hours' sleep now and then during that long and appalling week and a day.

Long before it was over, the *Free Press* did something of major significance in addition to its news coverage. Its editors decided to embark at once on a massive study of the city, the riot victims, the police, the troops, and the news people themselves to try to find out what went wrong—and why.

"Why," the Free Press asked, "did 43 people have to die? Were these deaths avoidable? Could any of these lives have been saved?"

It was a tough series of questions to ask in the middle of such disaster coverage and at first it seemed that they would be almost impossible to answer. For, as Frank Angelo, managing editor of the *Free Press*, said, "The first calamity of the Detroit riots was truth."

As the reporters learned all too quickly, official voices were beyond belief. And in the streets, rumors and half-truths and outright lies were spread by perfectly well-meaning people.

"The city seemed divided at its roots," Angelo wrote. "In the white community, there was a general view of the riot as an all-Negro uprising in which only lawbreakers had been killed. From the black point of view, there was fear that the riots had been used as a white excuse for murder. On both sides, even moderate men had difficulty agreeing on a single version of the facts. The need for an accurate, unbiased record was obvious." [1]

And so, after the rioting finally flared out, the men and women who had not spared themselves in the coverage of the tragedy were assigned to investigate it as impartially as was humanly possible. They worked for five weeks, seven days a week, seldom less than 12 hours a day, to produce a 24,000-word report that spread over five pages of the paper. What appears here is a synopsis, based on the *Free Press*'s conclusions:

WHY DID DETROIT'S 43 DIE?

By the Detroit Free Press

From the Detroit Free Press, September 3, 1966

In the space of eight silent days and bullet-broken nights, 43 persons died or were fatally wounded on the streets of Detroit. They are explained as victims of riot, the casualties of modern civil war.

Even now, it is difficult to arrive at more satisfactory explanations. It is tempting indeed to conclude that only the riot itself can be blamed for creating the situations in which it was pathetically easy to die.

Thirty-six hours after the riot began, something more than 3,000 armed men were assigned or had access to a single 20 by 20 block area on the near West Side, a concentration of firepower paralleled only by a major military invasion force.

Hundreds of regular Army paratroopers were stationed on the East Side of Detroit. In the Inner City, city and state police and National Guardsmen patrolled in Scout cars, paddy wagons, expressway cruisers, jeeps, trucks, personnel carriers, and tanks. The armament ranged from service revolvers and M-1 rifles to privately owned sporting arms, short-barreled repeating shotguns, carbines, and machine guns of up to .50 caliber.

Numbers alone made it inevitable that confrontations would occur, that incidents would result, that mistakes would be made

---

[1] The quotations from Frank Angelo are extracted from a letter that accompanied the submission of the *Detroit Free Press*'s exhibit in the Pulitzer Prizes for 1968.

and that, ultimately, someone would die. There were too many guns and too many people for it to be otherwise.

Now the central questions are simple though the answers are not:

—How many of the 43 deaths were necessary?

—How many could have been prevented?

The answers are individual, based on more than five weeks of independent investigation by a team of *Free Press* reporters assigned to examine every riot-connected death.

The conclusion reached in that investigation is inescapable:

The majority of the riot victims need not have died. Their deaths could have been—and should have been—prevented.

Fate's selection of those who would die followed no pattern and the riot victims do not fit easily into categories and classifications. Among them are the most innocent—a four-year-old girl killed by a wanton bullet—and the most guilty—a drunken sniper who died trying to take another's life. Equally various were the ways in which they died.

Eighteen of the riot victims were shot and killed by Detroit police and, of that number, 14 have been confirmed as looters in the *Free Press* investigation. The other four are a sniper, a possible but unconfirmed arsonist, and two of the three men shot and killed in the Algiers Motel.

At least six of the victims were killed by the National Guard, five of them innocent, the victims of what seem now to be tragic accidents.

In five more cases, both police and National Guardsmen were involved and it is impossible to say definitely whose bullets were fatal. Four of these five victims were innocent of any wrongdoing.

Two more persons, both looters, were shot and killed by store owners. Three more were killed by private citizens; murder warrants have been issued in two of those cases and a warrant decision is pending in the third.

And two looters died when fire swept the store from which they were stealing.

Two additional victims, one a fireman and the other a civilian, were killed by electric power lines.

Five deaths remain. They are a 19-year-old boy killed accidentally by an Army paratrooper; a 23-year-old white woman shot by an unknown gunman; a Detroit fireman killed by either a hidden sniper or a stray bullet of the National Guard; a policeman shot as a fellow-officer struggled with a prisoner; and the third victim of the Algiers Motel slayings, whose assailant is not known.

Hindsight is easy. The fires have gone out and the streets are quiet and, in the midst of normalcy, the temptation to insist that logic and order and common sense should have prevailed throughout the riot is overwhelming, but impossible to tolerate.

No one who drove those gutted streets at midnight, when the fires still burned and the shadows hung and moved in vacant doorways, when frightened voices cried "Halt!" into the silence and footsteps crunched on broken glass, will contend that men could have behaved rationally in those awful hours.

With that qualification accepted and understood, here are the general conclusions of the five-week investigation into the riot deaths:

—Both the number of snipers active in the riot area and the danger that snipers presented were vastly overstated. Only one sniper is among the riot victims and only three of the victims may possibly have been killed by snipers, two of them doubtful. In all, some 31 persons were arrested and charged with sniping; none of these cases has gone to trial.

—In the 43 deaths, criminal intent may possibly be an element in only seven—the three Algiers Motel deaths, three killings by civilians, and one case, that of William Dalton, still unresolved. *Free Press* investigators found no evidence of deliberate or preconceived killings in the cases remaining.

—In retrospect, the performance of Michigan State and city policemen seems generally restrained and impressive. The fact that 4,400 city policemen worked for at least five days in the midst of chaos without more bloodshed is significant. There are individual instances of poor judgment, it is true, and several regrettable instances where officers may have fired too soon, though they acted legally.

One major critical observation must be made. Both city and Army authorities acted to try to keep the death toll at a minimum, though they did so in different ways. In both cases, their efforts were not successful and permitted unnecessary deaths.

At 11:20 Monday night, within hours after the National Guard had come under federal control, Lt. Gen. John Throckmorton, the commanding officer, issued a general order commanding all troops under his control to unload their weapons and to fire only on the command of an officer.

Throckmorton's regular Army troops obeyed that order; only one person was killed in paratrooper territory in the five days that followed.

The National Guard did not obey, in many cases because the order was improperly disseminated and was never made clear to the men on the street. As a result, the Guard was involved in a total of 11 deaths in which nine innocent people died.

Military discipline and attention to Throckmorton's order could have avoided these deaths.

It took many more weeks to restore calm to a shattered community and begin the long and arduous process of rebuilding. And years were to pass before the lawsuits and criminal trials growing out of the disaster were concluded. One case—the alleged slaying of three persons in the Algiers Motel by law enforcement officers who contended they were snipers— attracted nationwide interest.

The spring following the riots, when the Pulitzer Prize deliberations began, two local reporting juries working separately singled out the *Detroit Free Press*'s coverage for a prize. The general local reporting jury commended the spot news coverage while the investigative reporting jury praised the long inquiry into the cause of the riots.

The Pulitzer Prize Board, combining the two reports, awarded the *Detroit Free Press* the 1968 Pulitzer Prize for General Local Reporting "for its coverage of the Detroit riots of 1967, recognizing both the brilliance of its detailed spot news staff work and its swift and accurate investigation into the underlying causes of the tragedy."

Such double-barreled awards have seldom been made in the history of the prizes. The *Free Press*'s work, as a result, stands in a class by itself in the archives of the Pulitzer Prizes.

39. THE GLOBE FACES BLOWS AND BULLETS
IN COVERING BOSTON'S SCHOOL CRISIS

Anti-Busing Forces Besiege Newspaper Over Court Order
That Brings Many More Blacks to South Boston Classrooms

When school busing came to Boston, there was hell to pay.

Nowhere, not even in the deep South, was there so much hysteria, so many ugly threats, so violent a mob reaction as there was among the people of South Boston.

When the first buses bore black children into South Boston's schools in compliance with a Federal Court order, they were stoned and nine black children and a monitor were hurt.

When Senator Edward M. Kennedy tried to calm tempers at an anti-busing rally, he was jeered and pelted with tomatoes and eggs. And some in the mob yelled at him: "You're a disgrace to the Irish."

"They're expressing their frustration," Kennedy said later, his hands trembling. "They're not bigots. They care about the safety of their children and the education at the end of the line."

Bigots or not, the people of South Boston created a storm that swept with fury across the entire city and imperiled the chances of successful integration in other Northern cities.

At the *Boston Globe*, the city's dominant newspaper, the immediate decision was to uphold the law and support the busing order that had been issued in mid-1974 by Federal Judge W. Arthur Garrity, Jr. Thomas Winship, the editor, said there were no other way the paper could go despite the temper of the people in a very large section of the city.

But together with editorial support for school busing as a means of achieving integration, Winship determined that the *Globe* would be fair, that the *Globe* would report all sides of the controversy in the news columns without partisanship, that the *Globe* would tell the story in all honesty and at length. He wrote:

"With neighborhood pitted against neighborhood, with organizations and even households divided, with the city's leadership faltering, the *Globe* set as its goal the difficult task of providing all the people, whatever their views, with credible information on what was happening and why."

The people at the *Globe* knew what was coming and prepared for the worst.

They got it. First came bombs threats, then broken windows. Up went newly installed steel shutters. Next came 11 shots from a battery of rifles that thudded into the beleaguered building.

The anti-busing forces were outraged over what they felt was a betrayal. They hijacked newspapers, blocked the *Globe*'s trucks, demonstrated in front of the building.

If the paper expected support from the frightened black community, its hopes were soon dashed. For even the blacks muttered that the Globe was not on their side in its news columns; they weren't looking for just fairness, they wanted the whole newspaper but they didn't get it.

Do not look for elegant writing in the *Globe*'s reportage. What went into the paper, day after day and week after week, was the guts of the best kind of newspaper journalism in this land—an unemotional, impartial, immensely detailed and thoroughly honest and accurate report of what was going on in the schools, the streets, the entire community.

You will not find reporters parading their hardships here as they struggled to do their work in the face of enormous difficulties. Nor will you hear that rewrite people and editors had to produce and clear copy minutes before deadline, edition after edition, and still make it read well. No one has ever been able to describe fittingly the miracle by which a good newspaper is able to do these things under pressure, nor do most readers know or even care.

Here is an example, reproduced in large part except for the long lists of names and other identification of victims, of what the *Globe* covered and how it appeared in the paper:

"ALWAYS THE LITTLE PEOPLE GET HURT"

By James Ayres

From the Boston Globe, Dec. 12, 1974

A clash between police and a crowd of 1,500 persons outside South Boston High School yesterday, after a white student was stabbed inside the school, led to the closing of seven public schools in South Boston and Roxbury High School for the remainder of the week.

The victim of the stabbing early yesterday morning—Michael Faith, 18, of South Boston, a senior—was on the danger list at Boston City Hospital last night with a wound in his abdomen. His condition following surgery was described as stable.

His mother, Mrs. Lorraine Faith, said, "I'm heartsick, I'm worried and I'm disgusted. It is a disgrace. If people knew what was happening they would leave the state. Always the little people get hurt. My children will never, never go back to that school. Never."

Boston Police said that James A. White, 18, of Roxbury, a black senior at the high school, was charged with assault and battery with a dangerous weapon in South Boston District Court and was released from Charles Street Jail after $500 bond was posted.

Boston School Supt. William F. Leary ordered classes canceled at the eight schools today and tomorrow because of the day's events, which included:

—The arrests of three white men for assaulting police officers outside South Boston High School during a clash between area residents and police, including six mounted police, during which soft drink cans, grapefruit, sidewalk bricks, and stones were thrown.

—Eleven civilians and 14 police officers were treated at Boston City Hospital and released following the confrontation outside the high school on G Street. Lt. Robert Bradley of the Tactical Patrol Force said nine additional police officers reported they had sought hospital treatment.

—Windows of cars, police cruisers, and school buses were smashed near the high school, and the cruiser of Supt. Joseph Jordan, chief of field services, was overturned at the height of the clash. Boston Police reported five cruisers were "severely damaged."

—One hundred thirty-one black students were trapped inside the high school until they were led out the back to buses waiting at Thomas Park while three decoy school buses at the front of the building on G Street distracted the attention of demonstrators.

—Supt. Jordan said that the police force in South Boston was increased from 93 to 325 officers after the stabbing occurred in a second-floor corridor at 9:40 A.M. while students were going to second-period classrooms.

—A walkout by about 400 white students at Roslindale High School over a scuffle between a white female student and a black male student Tuesday caused police to enter the building for the second time since the school opened under the court-ordered busing plan Sept. 12.

—Judge W. Arthur Garrity, Jr., author of the order, said yesterday he will direct that one of every five teachers in the Boston school system be black.

—Boston NAACP President Thomas I. Atkins said last night that his organization will go to Federal Court to respond "to what happened in South Boston."

Dr. Irwin Hirsch, associate director of surgery at Boston City Hospital, said last night that Faith "is expected to recover adequately barring unforeseen difficulties."

After the stabbing, Headmaster William J. Reid ordered the 380 white students dismissed for the day to prevent a clash between white and black students.

Police called for reinforcements when the dismissed white students attempted to break through the police lines to reenter the building. More police were called as word of the stabbing spread throughout the community.

Supt. Jordan said: "That was really an angry, hostile crowd, a mob."

Tension reached a peak when a unit of mounted police attempted to force the crowd from G Street to clear the way for buses to take the 131 black students out of the school.

Fruit, eggs, bricks, and stones were hurled by the crowd, many of whom were sitting or lying on the street chanting and shouting racial epithets.

Six mounted officers charged the group, which broke up and ran down East Seventh Street as motorcycle officers moved in with three decoy buses.

As the crowd engaged police in front of the building, stoning the decoy buses, heavily guarded buses arrived at Thomas Park at the rear of the building and all the black students boarded the buses by 2:15 P.M.

For its massive and balanced coverage of the Boston school desegregation crisis, the *Globe* won the Pulitzer Prize Gold Medal for Public Service in 1975. The jurors wrote in their recommendation that the paper

THE SOILING OF OLD GLORY
Pulitzer Prize for News Photography, 1977

STANLEY FORMAN OF THE BOSTON HERALD AMERICAN SHARED THE PRIZE
FOR THIS PICTURE, MADE DURING AN ANTI-BUSING DEMONSTRATION IN
BOSTON IN 1976. IT SHOWS A WHITE DEMONSTRATOR CHARGING WITH THE
FLAG AGAINST A BLACK LAWYER WHO HAPPENED TO BE PASSING BY

had given "an impressive demonstration of public service" and had "withstood pressures from both pro- and anti-busing forces to put the issue into perspective and inform the public impartially."

Good journalism also turned out to be good business, for despite all the boycotts and hostility toward the *Globe* throughout the crisis its circulation increased—even in South Boston. The paper also gained a national reputation, which was enhanced in 1980 when its staff people won three Pulitzer Prizes.

But Boston's school crisis, far from being dispelled, flared up again from one year to the next as late as the fall of 1979. School busing remained a political issue, although it did not appear to interfere with the administration of Mayor Kevin White, who was re-elected.

The courts, throughout, acted with reserve in handling the cases of youthful offenders in the schools. The accused youth in the 1974 stabbing case, for example, was not brought to trial for almost a year after the incident outside South Boston High school. The youth, James White, pleaded guilty before Suffolk Superior Court Judge Robert Sullivan and was given a suspended sentence of five to seven years plus three concurrent years on probation.

Michael Faith, who was stabbed in the incident, said later that he had suffered damage to his lung and liver and that, as a result, he had been rejected for military service. It was as his mother had said, "Always the little people get hurt."[1]

[1] Michael Faith's report in the *Boston Herald American*, Aug. 16, 1975; the White sentencing in the *Boston Globe*, Oct. 2, 1975.

IX. COLUMNISTS AND CRITICS
GAIN NEW INFLUENCE

When Walter Lippmann summarized his eight-hour interview with Soviet Premier Nikita S. Khrushchev at Sochi in 1961, he wrote of Soviet relations with Iran as follows:

"Speaking of Iran, which he [Khrushchev] did without my raising the subject, he said that Iran had a very weak Communist Party but that nevertheless the misery of the masses and the corruption of the government was surely producing a revolution. . . . It would be fair to conclude that he is not contemplating military intervention and occupation—'Iran is a poor country which is of no use to the Soviet Union'—but that he will do all he can by propaganda and indirect intervention to bring down the Shah." [1]

Lippmann's perception of Soviet policy toward Iran was accurate, as events surrounding the overthrow of the Shah demonstrated years later. What he could not have foreseen was the Soviet decision to use its own troops to invade Afghanistan—but the State Department of this era missed that one, too.

What Lippmann produced in 1961 was an important document about Soviet intentions, not only toward Iran, but also toward the more important East-West issues—the two Germanies, the Mideast, and Cuba. He had the prestige, knowledge, and ability to do it. He also had a unique insight into foreign affairs, developed over 50 years, and a comprehension of the meaning of events.

It was with good reason, therefore, that the Pulitzer Prize Board

[1] *New York Herald Tribune*, April 18, 1961.

awarded Lippmann the international reporting prize for 1962, not only for his Khrushchev interview, but also for his "long and distinguished contribution to American journalism." This was his second such recognition, his first having come in 1958 in the form of a special award for his distinguished commentary at that time. He was proposed for at least three other prizes, as the Pulitzer records show, but disqualified himself from consideration while he worked for Pulitzer's *New York World* on the ground that he was a Pulitzer employee.[2] Others in the same situation never let such scruples deter them from entering the competition.

Lippmann's influence in journalism has continued since his death in a number of ways. He had a decided effect on the thinking of his contemporaries in American journalism, especially in the nation's capital, and he also dignifed and expanded the revival of personal journalism in the United States to a considerable degree. It was his example that eventually led to the establishment of separate prizes for criticism and commentary.[3]

Although there is still a broad area of mistrust in American public life (and among numerous editors as well) of the power of commentators and critics published by influential newspapers, they have restored the personal element in American journalism and strengthened it.

Such columnists as David S. Broder of the *Washington Post*, Mary McGrory of the *Washington Star*, Vermont Connecticut Royster of the *Wall Street Journal*, and James Reston and Anthony Lewis of the *New York Times* have an influence far beyond that of the newspapers in which they are published. All won their Pulitzer Prizes, not because of the showcases in which they were presented, but rather because what they themselves had to say was important to the people of their time.

This kind of personal journalism, so different from the political machinations and self-promotion of Horace Greeley, William Randolph Hearst, and some of the other personal journalists of another day, has attracted a growing audience. But it is seldom that the size of a commentator's readership can be equated with

[2] John Hohenberg, *The Pulitzer Prizes* (New York: Columbia University Press, 1974) p. 40.

[3] Ibid., pp. 302, 306, 369.

his demonstrable influence. Lippmann, for example, never had more than a fraction of the audience of a gossip columnist like Walter Winchell, but Lippmann's elite readership in all probability would have considered Winchell an unmitigated nuisance who had to be suffered for the sake of the First Amendment.

Nor is a commentator's influence confined to his immediate audience. People who don't know a discus from first base, and think rather hazily that a marathon is some new dance craze, may sometimes be discovered perusing Red Smith on a sports page for the sheer joy of reading a master of the English language. Also, some of the readers of Walter Kerr, the drama critic of the *New York Times*, may never have seen a Broadway show. And those who regularly turn to Alan M. Kriegsman, dance critic of the *Washington Post*, may not know a time step from a *pas de deux*.

A columnist, moreover, is able at times to make disclosures that escape the attention of the most vigilant news organization. This was the case when Jack Anderson revealed the American "tilt" toward Pakistan in the Indo-Pakistan War, and when William Safire inquired into the chaotic banking affairs of Bert Lance during the Carter administration.

The columnists and critics whose work is presented in this section have been among the leaders of their special journalistic fields for many years. Each is represented by a single distinguished, if relatively brief, work selected from the respective Pulitzer Prize exhibits that won them the accolade of their peers.

40. RICHARD L. STROUT OF THE MONITOR
REPORTS ON 11 AMERICAN PRESIDENTS

The Commentator Watches Washington Pass in Review
for 55 Years and Wins a Pulitzer Prize at 80

Richard L. Strout is a walking encyclopedia of the modern American Presidency. He is also a very special writer for the *Christian Science Monitor*.

When he won a Pulitzer Prize Special Award at 80 years of age in 1978, he had been covering Washington for 55 years and working for the *Moni-*

'O beautiful for spacious skies
For amber waves of grain ...'

Pulitzer Prize for Editorial Cartooning, 1976

TONY AUTH COMMENTS IN THE PHILADELPHIA INQUIRER ON SOVIET
PREMIER BREZHNEV'S PLEASURE OVER HIS DEAL FOR AMERICAN WHEAT

Pulitzer Prize for Editorial Cartooning, 1979

tor for 57. He had reported on the deeds and misdeeds of 11 American Presidents who had served a total of 15 terms—every one from the 29th, Warren Gamaliel Harding, to the 39th, James Earl Carter, Jr.

In addition to covering the news of the day, he also had been writing a column of widely read commentary for the *Monitor* for 44 years and a separate column for the *New Republic* under the pseudonym, "T.R.B." For many years, he had been regarded as one of the most influential, as well as one of the most respected, members of the Washington press corps.

Strout came to the *Monitor* in 1921 by way of Cohoes, N.Y., where he was born in 1898, the Flatbush section of Brooklyn, where he grew up, and Harvard, where he took his bachelor's and master's degrees. He had had brief experience in the business on two British publications and the *Boston Post* before he came to the *Monitor* as a copy editor.

But once he landed in the *Monitor*'s newsroom, he stayed on for his entire professional life. In 1923, he was temporarily assigned to the *Monitor*'s Washington bureau and became a fixture there in 1924. Fifty-three years later, here is how he remembered his arrival in the nation's capital:

MR. STROUT GOES TO WASHINGTON

By Richard L. Strout

From the Christian Science Monitor, July 1, 1977

It is two days after Christmas, 1924, and great changes are occurring. I am married. My salary is $60 a week. I am assigned to the Washington bureau permanently. It is time to leave Boston.

One last look at the emptied apartment at 19 Huron Avenue, Cambridge. We sigh. We just moved in and now we are moving out, with the minister's family below and the landlady above. It has seemed a bit extravagant to pay $12 a week rent for this place since the rooms aren't large and the coal is extra. Calvin Coolidge, our frugal President, still maintains his half of a two family house at Northampton, Mass., and pays only $32 a month.

The car waits, the Model T we affectionately call "Southard." Have I thought of everything? I have unstrapped the top and pulled it forward with its braces, like a concertina. I have snapped in the side curtains with the celluloid windows.

I have bought a new tire and inner tube, $13; bolted the spare on the rear; inflated the tires to 40 pounds; filled the tank under the front seat with nine gallons (measured with a dipstick); and bought oil, alcohol, and $1.50 worth of Can't Leak. Grease cups are filled, steering knuckles oiled.

Normally, "Southard" dreams through the winter, jacked up on fruit crates, radiator drained. Now she must face the elements, carrying some of our hardier goods lashed to the running board.

I crouch in front in the street, pull the finger ring of the choke wire coming through the radiator, and turn the crank—an explosion, a machine gun chatter, a roar. The whole car vibrates.

Off we trundle. There's no heater, of course, or windshield wiper, or directional signal; the roads aren't center-lined or routes numbered; we wear woolens, scarves, mittens, overcoats. We look at each other and exclaim how snug we are.

My account book tells the story: two gallons of gas at Worcester, seven more at New Haven, plus a pint of alcohol. We pay visits and spend the night at Bridgeport (Stratfield Hotel, $4). More gas, more alcohol; we are making almost 17 miles to the gallon.

It's colder Sunday—10 above. "Cold snap," says the paper before I put it on the floor for added insulation. The wind whistles through the flaps. We start at 11, cross Dyckman's Ferry at 2, reach Trenton at 6 P.M. (Hotel Driscoll, $4.50).

If you fault our slowness, remember the Ford joke of the day: "What does the Model T use for shock absorbers?" Answer: "The passengers.

"Southard" has two forward speeds, Low and High, but it can go direct from High into Reverse, which is a marvel even today. At one point as we labor up a grade, I look between the floorboards and see the muffler—red hot. "Southard" runs better with her radiator boiling, as it usually is.

Now it is the third day and we approach Washington in the evening. The road isn't lighted. Are we on course? Aim the car directly at the sign post and race the motor for more light; it's like a flashlight. Yes, the arrow points ahead.

We reach Washington at 9. and go to a boarding house. I report for work next day. In the White House live Calvin Coolidge and Alice and I can park "Southard" in the Ellipse behind the White House all day, free.

Actually, Strout had begun work at the *Monitor* on June 13, 1921, at $40 a week on a "temporary assignment." More than a half century later, he wrote, "Like the bell from the Paul Revere Foundry in the steeple of the All Souls Unitarian Church in Washington, D.C., that came with a one-year guarantee, I'm still functioning."

When Strout came to Washington, there were 107 million people in the United States as against more than 220 million today. The postage, he recalled, was only two cents for a first-class letter "and if a youth kissed a girl it was understood as a proposal of marriage."

"There have been seven amendments [to the Constitution] and 11 Presidents since," he went on. "The great granite structure on Pennsylvania Avenue next to the White House is no longer called the 'State, War, and Navy Building' after the three government departments it simultaneously housed. There is a huge FBI building on the avenue bigger than the office of the Department of Justice which it serves.

"There have been more subtle alterations, too, in Washington and the nation. People no longer leave their doors unlocked when they visit neighbors. Many of the things everyone in 1921 knew couldn't be done have been done—not easy things like putting a man on the moon but more difficult feats: ending school segregation, electing a Roman Catholic President, discussing birth control publicly, edging toward a world community."

Strout watched history in the making during his years in Washington. He remembered waiting before the White House on the night of Dec. 7, 1941, after the Japanese had bombed Pearl Harbor and hearing the crowd trying to sing "The Star-Spangled Banner"; watching the great American troop landings on D-Day in Normandy; seeing the wire service flash of President Kennedy's assassination; hearing Jimmy Carter tell how he had been born again while campaigning for the Presidency.

"Always progress intrudes," Strout concluded. "You can't stop it. The earth shrinks. Change accelerates. The most exciting thing is around the corner. Still, we hold our breaths and accept the acerb wisdom of E. B. White's cautious definition: 'Democracy is the recurrent suspicion that more than half the people are right more than half the time.'" [1]

In the fullness of his 80 years, Richard L. Strout was honored, in the words of his Pulitzer citation, "for distinguished commentary from Washington over many years as staff correspondent for the *Christian Science Monitor* and contributor to the *New Rupublic*."

---

[1] Column, *Christian Science Monitor*, March 1, 1977.

41. RED SMITH WATCHES MUHAMMAD ALI BEAT DOWN A GALLANT JOE FRAZIER

The New York Times's Sports Columnist Salutes the Comeback of a Champion at Manila

Red Smith once wrote of Grantland Rice, his friend and colleague for more than half a century in the press boxes of the sports arenas:

"He loved beauty but knew poetry was where you found it. There was laughter in him and a warm sense of the ridiculous. He could jeer gently as well as cheer."[1]

The description could easily have fitted Red Smith himself, but few except his friends would have recognized it. For despite his prominence as a sports writer, this small, neat, rather dignified man was modest and self-effacing to an unheard of degree. Like the unexplained presence in his columns—the passerby, the stranger who paused for a moment, the disembodied questioner—he liked to live as well as write in the third person.

Thousands in the grandstand knew celebrities like Bill Corum, with his nervous chuckle and his pot belly; Bob Considine, with his eagle's-beak poker face and laughing eyes; Damon Runyon, with the solemn look of a preacher and a quick wit that could bowl over an unsuspecting opponent with the snap of a Jack Dempsey left jab. But Red Smith, the little fellow with the big eyeglasses and the cheerful smile, seemed to be shoved into the background like somebody's uncle from Yakima, Wash., who didn't belong.

Of course, he did belong. If he had wished, he could have owned the press box. And that says something about this mild-mannered graduate of Notre Dame who somehow ventured into the roughest, pushiest, and least considerate compartment of American journalism. He always seemed content to let everybody else hog the best seats in the arena but his was the story that everybody was talking about next day.

Like Martene W. Corum, the sports columnist who clung with desperation to the name of Bill, Walter Wellesley Smith always preferred to be called Red, even after his brick-colored hair had turned into a lackadaisical gray wisp.

---

[1] The remarks about Grantland Rice are taken from a memorial lecture by Red Smith at the Columbia Graduate School of Journalism, reported in *Editor & Publisher* (Feb. 7, 1959).

He was born in 1905 in a sports town, Green Bay, Wis., dabbled in sports writing while at Notre Dame, and began working as a sports writer at the *Milwaukee Sentinel* after his graduation in 1927. He was with the *St. Louis Star* from 1928 to 1936, the *Philadelphia Record* from 1936 to 1945, the *New York Herald Tribune* from 1945 until it folded in 1966, and from then on with the *New York Times*, which syndicated his work.

Almost any column of Red Smith's deserves to be reprinted, but this one about the Ali-Frazier fight in Manila is a classic:

JOE WAS STILL COMING IN

By Red Smith

From the New York Times, Oct. 1, 1975

MANILA, Wednesday, Oct. 1—When time has cooled the violent passions of the sweltering day and the definitive history is written of the five-year war between Muhammad Ali and Joe Frazier, the objective historian will remember that Joe was still coming in at the finish.

For more than 40 minutes, the former heavyweight champion of the world, who was now the challenger, attacked the two-time champion with abandoned, almost joyous, ferocity. For seven rounds in a row, he bludgeoned his man with hooks, hounding him into corners, nailing him to the ropes.

And then, when Ali seemed hopelessly beaten, he came on like the good champion he is. In the 12th round, the 13th, and all through a cruel 14th, Ali punched the shapeless, grinning mask that pursued him until Eddie Futch could take no more.

After 14 rounds of one of the roughest matches ever fought for the heavyweight championship, Frazier's trainer, Futch, gave up. At his signal, the referee stopped the fight with Ali still champion.

All three Filipino officials had Ali leading on points at the end, but in the *New York Times* book, Futch snatched defeat from the jaws of victory. On the *Times*'s two scorecards, Frazier had won eight of the first 13 rounds when he walked into the blows that beat him stupid. He lost while winning, yet little Eddie was right to negotiate the surrender. Frazier's $2 million guarantee wasn't enough to compensate him for another round like the last.

So now the saga ended. It began on March 8, 1971, when Ali and Frazier met for the first time, both undefeated as professionals, both with valid claims to the championship, both in the glory and strength of youth. That time Frazier won it all. They fought again on Jan. 28, 1974, when both were ex-champions and Ali got a debatable decision. Today's might have been debatable, too, if a decision had been needed.

It has been a series both men can remember with pride—and pride has been the spur for both. All three meetings were happenings, memorable chapters in the annals of the ring, and in many respects this was the best of the three. It will be some time before anybody knows whether the gross revenue from the live gate, closed circuit and home television around the world will equal the $20 million drawn for their first encounter, but this day's business in the Philippine Coliseum may have broken all records for an indoor fight. Attendance was estimated at 25,000, with a gate of something like $1.5 million at $333 tops.

If a price can be put on the suffering of brave men, this returned a dollar in pain for every dollar involved. Curiously, the winner's suffering was the greater. Not many men could have stood up under the punishment Ali took from the fifth round through the 11th.

Yet Ali not only endured when he had taken all that Frazier could deliver, but he also had enough to win.

Say what one will about this noisy extrovert, this swaggering, preening, play-acting slice of theatrical ham: the man is a gladiator. He was a callow braggart of 22 when Sonny Liston surrendered the title to him 11 years ago. At the ripe age of 33, he is a champion of genuine quality.

Whatever can be said to Ali's credit must be said with equal emphasis about Joe Frazier. This man was a good champion in his own right. He is the best man Ali ever fought, an opponent who searched Ali's inner depths and brought out qualities Ali never had to reveal to any other man.

It was Joe, rather than Muhammad, who made this a great fight. In the early rounds, Ali made half-hearted attempts to strut and posture the way he has done against men like Joe Bugner and Chuck Wepner, but Frazier's persistent advance brooked no such nonsense. Ali's faster hands and circling retreat held Joe off for a while. Joe was remorseless, though, and single-minded.

He brushed pawing gloves aside, rolled in under punches, bore straight ahead and slugged, and by the fifth round he was getting the message across. It was hook, hook, hook—into the belly to draw Ali's hands down, then up to the head against the ropes.

He beat the everlasting whey out of Ali. His attack would have reduced another man to putty. The guy in the white trunks was not another man. He was the champion and this time he proved it.

Ali kept proving it until he retired on June 27, 1979, and he had enough left to attempt a comeback in 1980. At that time, Red Smith was still a champion in his own line of work and he had a piece of paper somewhere around the house, if he remembered to put it away, that attested to his Pulitzer Prize for Commentary in 1976.

The jury that recommended him said his work was "marked not only by the professional craft of the specialist but also by a humor and a humanism that bring universal interest to that specialty."

The report concluded:

"In an area heavy with tradition and routine, Mr. Smith is unique in the erudition, the literary quality, the vitality, and the freshness of viewpoint he brings to his work and in the sustained quality of his columns."

Being Red Smith, he probably thought the judges were just being nice to him that day.

42. DAVID BRODER TOLLS A REQUIEM
FOR HUMPHREY'S PRESIDENTIAL DREAM

The Washington Post's Commentator Concludes
That the Senator's 25-Year Quest Is Over

In the hearts and minds of that elite group of professional nay-sayers known as the Washington press corps, nobody can replace Walter Lippmann as their spiritual preceptor. But David Broder of the *Washington Post* comes close.

While others were trumpeting President Nixon's invincibility in the Presidential campaign of 1972 against Senator McGovern, Broder observed quietly that the President was feared and mistrusted, adding:

"My guess is that the results [of the election] are going to be ambiguous because the public attitude toward governmental power is equivocal and contradictory."[1]

His forecast, as events demonstrated, was conservative in the extreme. The outcome was so ambiguous, in the light of the Watergate relevations, that the President was forced to resign despite his record-breaking electoral victory.

Again, when the press began raising a clamor against President Carter after he had been in office only a few months, Broder wrote:

"It looks like a classic case of overreaction. Objectively, it is hard to see why there should be so much hand-wringing. . . . The criticisms being shouted now are not different from those catalogued in this space last June."[2]

Temporarily, at least, the tumult quieted down. But as Carter approached the decisions of the 1980 Presidential campaign, Broder was warning that he was in deep trouble long before the shadows of the Iranian crisis and inflation began to darken the Georgian's political future.

Broder is neither a seer nor a great stylist, and he is generally kinder to politicians than they deserve. But he is also a painstaking and usually accurate reporter. As a result, his sober and quietly stated judgments have much the same kind of impact on many in the Washington press corps and the Washington news media in general that Lippmann's had. This, magnified by the national and international attention Broder commands, increases his influence a hundred-fold.

There are some who credit Broder with the power to set a trend of press comment, but he would of course be the first to deny it. He is, nevertheless, one of a rather small group of Washington editors and correspondents whose judgments generally have a majority following in the profession.

This is by no means a companion to the hard-line conservative scare story about a tiny group of men in New York who decide each day what the nation shall think by arranging for a certain sequence of news for print and broadcast use. Nor is it an echo of the equally picturesque conservative vision of a liberal press (three networks, *Washington Post*, *New York Times*, *Time*, and *Newsweek*) that casts all the news media in a liberal-to-radical mold.

The influence of correspondents like Broder, Hedrick Smith of the *New York Times*, Jack Nelson of the *Los Angeles Times*, Richard L. Strout of the *Christian Science Monitor*, and a few others is based primarily on

[1] *Washington Post*, Nov. 5, 1972.
[2] *Washington Post*, Oct. 24, 1977.

respect for their judgment, their reporting, and their sources. As the leaders in their profession, they are bound to have a following.

The key to Broder's position in the nation's capital is that he has been chosen, in a poll of political correspondents, as the most respected political writer in the country. However, he didn't qualify for that honor by sitting in an office, reading newspapers, and watching TV.

Broder's early background was centered in Illinois—born on Chicago Heights in 1939, educated in Chicago (he likes to recall that he was refused admission to the Columbia Graduate School of Journalism), and a reporter beginning in 1953 on the *Bloomington Pantagraph*. From 1955 to 1960, he worked on the *Congressional Quarterly* and for five years until 1965 worked on the *Washington Star*. Then he went to the *New York Times* for a year. His rise to eminence as a political writer and commentator began in 1966 when he joined the *Washington Post*.

There is an element of compassion and throughtfulness about Broder's political commentary that is all too rare in Washington—or anywhere else for that matter. Instead of the tough-guy, this-is-the-way-it-is approach so favored by most of the think-piece writers, Broder is one of the relatively few commentators who instinctively regard politicians and office-holders as human beings and not incipient con artists, crooks, and worse.

In an age in which trust in public officials has sunk to a low previously reserved for used car salesmen, the *Washington Post*'s political columnist invariably shows both patience and sympathy toward those who aspire to high public office. These traits are particularly in evidence in the following estimate of the fortunes of Hubert Horatio Humphrey, who pursued the shining mirage of the Presidency for 25 years:

THE END OF THE TRAIL FOR HHH

By David S. Broder

From the Washington Post, June 6, 1972

HOUSTON—Unless all signs and portents are wrong, today may mark the end of Hubert H. Humphrey's hopes for the Presidency. The quest began a quarter-century ago, in his own mind, and has been actively pursued for twelve years, but it is hard to see how it can survive the predicted [primary election] defeats in California and New Jersey.

If a man finds himself beaten by such diverse personalities as John Kennedy, Richard Nixon, and George McGovern, maybe the conclusion is that he was never meant to be President. Considering the chronic difficulty Humphrey has had in organizing all his campaigns for the White House, it may be that he was foredoomed to failure by his own shortcomings.

But looking back at the Humphrey career, the fateful moment appears to have come that August afternoon in 1964 when Lyndon Johnson summoned him down from Atlantic City and offered him the Vice Presidential nomination.

Humphrey accepted, of course, just as any Democratic senator (except Mike Mansfield) would have, had the prize been offered him. It's forgotten now, but Gene McCarthy and Bob Kennedy were eager to be Johnson's running mate in that year of Democratic destiny, and George McGovern would have jumped at the chance, too, had the President's eye chanced to fall on the then obscure freshman senator from South Dakota.

If Johnson had passed over Humphrey and picked, say, the other passenger on the plane from Atlantic City, Tom Dodd, then the history of the last two Presidential campaigns might have been different.

Humphrey then would have been another senator from 1965 to 1968, free to make his own judgments about the Vietnam War and to join McCarthy, Kennedy, and McGovern, if he wished, in their gradual shift to a position of vocal criticism of the President's policies.

Instead, as Vice President, he embraced those policies with the unbounded enthusiasm he brings to any cause in which he is involved. They carried him down to defeat in 1968 and the memory of the 1968 travail dogged his campaign this year.

One can argue, as McCarthy did in 1968, that even as Vice President, Humphrey could have dissented by silence when Johnson attempted to sell the American public on the escalation of the war. But Humphrey has never found a way to be silent or half-hearted about any enterprise on which he embarks.

That enthusiasm betrayed him as Vice President, as it sometimes betrayed him in this campaign—in speeches that exhausted his listeners and rhetoric that promised far more than he could ever fulfill.

Humphrey can be faulted for his excesses, but they are the excesses of a generous spirit, not an angry or embittered heart. His exaggerations are like a lover's lies—and at 61, Humphrey is still engaged in a reckless love affair with his country and, indeed, all of life.

Even in these last days of adversity, knowing as well as anyone what likely awaits him, his energy and spirit have been irrepressible. Helen Bentley, a San Francisco television interviewer, got him talking the other morning about what he'd like to do if he had a day off.

The answer, in typical Humphrey fashion, was that he'd like to see a baseball game, attend an opera, talk to a prize figher and a scientist, and watch an actor at work.

"I enjoy life," Humphrey told the stunned interviewer. "It's a delight. You only live a short time. You ought to enjoy every fleeting moment."

He means it, too.

Humphrey's political life seems fated to end in disappointment, but it's still been a remarkable career. He's left his mark on this land he loves, and made it a better place for millions. Not even Humphrey has found a way to exaggerate his own contributions, from medicare to civil rights to disarmament to education.

Fortunately, neither his service nor his enthusiasm is ended. He has more energy than most men half his age, and the voters of Minnesota, who long ago accepted Hubert Humphrey for the man he is, with all his faults and all the strengths of his free spirit, have the good sense to keep him working.

Hubert Horatio Humphrey, born May 27, 1911, in Wallace, S. D., and elected to the United States Senate in 1949, died of cancer January 12, 1978, in Waverly, Minn., without achieving his life's dream—the Presidency of the United States. President Carter led the nation in public tribute to a remarkable career.

David Broder, who so clearly foresaw the end of Humphrey political career, was awarded the Pulitzer Prize for Commentary in 1973.

43. WALTER KERR SEES ZERO MOSTEL
AS A GREAT NATURAL COMIC FORCE

The New York Times's Drama Critic Pays Tribute
to One of the World's Funniest Actors

When a vintage musical called *Going Up* opened on Broadway, Walter Kerr reported in the *New York Times*, "It had its charms but not enough of them." Of the avant-garde dramatist Samuel Beckett, he concluded, "Beckett had a message. The message was that there was no message." As for avant-garde movements in general, he recognized that they often begin as literary revolutions but peter out "when their own *Finnegan's Wake* exhausts them."

Such judgments as these have led many of the readers of the *New York Times*, in which Kerr mainly writes his comments, to regard him as the All-America Drama Critic. He can plunge right through the center, as he did in a minor play by a new dramatist, Albert Innaurato, demanding, "At what point did the contemporary world, enlightened as it is, come to regard sex as poison, deadly no matter what the dosage?" Or he can do a neat end run, as witness his commentary on a joint performance by Mary Martin and Ethel Merman: "Ethel Merman is the bonfire and Mary Martin is the smoke. They go very nicely together, if you're in a mood to burn up the town."

Then, too, when he is working with a brilliant receiver, he can score almost every time with lightning thrusts. For example, on Bette Davis: "She had to beat the living daylights out of Hollywood to prove how vulnerable she was." Or on the British actor John Wood in a Molière classic: "When you've seen one *Tartuffe* you haven't seen them all." And this, on Ethel Merman all by herself: "Ethel Merman hollering her heart out to get *Gypsy* going and damn near stopping ours." And still another, on viewing Irene Worth in *The Cherry Orchard* with open admiration: "Miss Worth sits at the lip of the apron and commands the universe itself to be still while she ever so slowly tears a letter from her lover into two equal halves—the severing of the last shred of paper has the force of the guillotine, resolutely faced."

Sometimes, when he falls prey to sentimentality, a usually deadly Broadway weakness, he can recover very quickly and punt out of danger as he did following the opening of a 1979 musical called *Sugar Babies*. After a nostalgic salute to burlesque, he termed the show a "grinning, leering, warmly innocent and altogether delightful tour of burlesque circuits that flourished before the Great Depression and the strippers took over. The sketches . . . go right back to Aristophanes, although Aristophanes was slightly more lyrical and decidedly dirtier."[1]

Kerr is something more than a drama critic. He is also a teacher, a playwright of sorts, and the husband of a writer of Broadway comedies, Jean Kerr. He came to Broadway by way of Evanston, Ill., where he was born in 1913; Northwestern University, with a degree in speech in 1937, and Catholic University in Washington, D.C., where he taught drama. His first job as a drama critic was for *Commonweal*, 1950–1952, and for 15 years thereafter his criticism graced the pages of the *New York Herald Tribune* until its demise.

In the *New York Times* since 1967, Kerr has served as both critic and catalyst of the American theater. Some of his judgments have made him enemies; the producer, Joseph Papp, once complained publicly that Kerr seemed to have it in for Papp's productions, which was demonstrably far from the truth. But Kerr has also encouraged talent and saluted genius, as he did when Zero Mostel once again appeared on Broadway in a revival of *Fiddler on the Roof*.

This was a show that had played seven years on Broadway in its original production, in which Mostel had created the role of Tevye, the milkman. There had been Tevyes since—in London, Paris, Tel Aviv, even Tokyo (and in Japanese, at that)—but the greatest Tevye of them all was the stout, grimacing comic who had been born Samuel Joel Mostel in Brooklyn, the son of a rabbi.

Here was Kerr's appreciation of Zero Mostel:

WHEN A GREAT ACTOR PLAYS THE FOOL

By Walter Kerr

From the New York Times, January 16, 1977

I am sorely tempted to pronounce Zero Mostel simply unreviewable and let it go at that. What is one to say of him? That he is a magnificent, wholly legitimate actor capable of tearing your heart out as he bends himself double, brow pouring sweat, over the milk cart he must push on alone?

No, you can't quite say that, indelible as the image is in *Fiddler on the Roof*, because just a few minutes earlier in the same *Fiddler*

---

[1] The quotations from Kerr's critiques are in the Pulitzer Prize exhibit that was entered for him with the exception of the one about *Sugar Babies*, which was taken from his column in the *New York Times* entertainment section on Oct. 21, 1979.

on the Roof he has been bringing down the house with a cross-eyed grimace—tongue lolling wildly—contorted enough to resurrect vaudeville, burlesque, and possibly the commedi dell'arte in one great swivel of his head. The swivel undercuts the sweat, the seriousness on the second image can't be taken at face value because of what the man has so recently been doing with his face.

What then? Do you treat him as a clown, almost as a king among clowns, because the manic impulse to which he so frequently surrenders is, for him, irresistibly real, a seizure rather than a posture, an inspiration from his *daimon* rather than a reflex acquired during long years of stand-up entertaining? God knows he is one of the four or five funniest men left alive; it is scarcely a year since I saw the man do ten minutes at a banquet that left me gasping with admiration whenever I could stop laughing. But in *Fiddler* he is playing Sholom Aleichem's Tevye, Tevye the dairyman with all those daughters to marry off sensibly; Tevye, the intimate of God with whom he is candid but to whom—as he points out—he never complains. ("After all, with Your help, I'm starving to death.") Wryness, yes. But crossed eyes, cap and bells?

The professional fool intercepts the great actor, the role the actor is playing inhibits the fool—somewhat. And you can, as a reviewer, point out the contradiction, the quarrel of styles. What you will still not have done is account for the effect Mr. Mostel imposes upon the yielding Winter Garden stage, upon the *shtetl* folk around him who live in designer Boris Aronson's lovely floating spill of houses along a backdrop that threatens sunset, upon the audience. It is not that he is good, not that he is funny, not that he is one where he ought to be the other. It is simply that he is there.

Zero Mostel is a mighty presence rather than a completely honest performer, so enormous in his nimble bulk and so violent in his willed impact that he doesn't invite judgment; he defies it, successfully. You can measure what he's doing, if you want to; but it's not going to get you anywhere, he's going to roll right over on you no matter what. And so you surrender, agree to let him dictate terms, and simply watch him.

You watch him do things that Sholom Aleichem would surely approve; tilt a sad head toward one weary shoulder not because he has a crick in the neck but because his eyes have opened so wide so often at the world's unexpected ways that they've grown topheavy, developed a list; wring out a wet sleeve as though the elements themselves had planned this injustice, while glancing at God to let Him know *he* knows just who perpetrated the joke; try desperately and helplessly to keep a stern finger pointed at the impoverished young tailor who'd like to marry his eldest daughter while that same daughter strokes his beard and begs him to reconsider his wrath. Even this behemoth, properly handled, can be tamed, touchingly.

You watch the actor do things that might have brought a bemused shrug from his original author, since even authors understand that adaptations for the musical stage must be given a little leeway; hold his head during a hangover and then wince mightily as his wife claps her hands in joy at a piece of welcome news; lapse into an unintelligible prayer as a means of silencing the woman he married long before youngsters were making marriage a matter of love; find himself utterly immobilized because he is standing on his own nightgown. And you watch him, listen to him, engage in familiar routines that haven't much to do with folkways; nearly strangle on a drink and then pronounce it "very good"; camp a bit by rolling his belly during an otherwise charming marriage dance; pursue the intimidated tailor in circles until, losing him, he lifts a tablecloth to see if *that's* where he's hiding.

Whatever is done is done with such almost indifferent authority that it seems irreversible, like a landslide. One hesitates to raise questions about natural forces. Mr. Mostel *is* a natural force, going its own predetermined and quite conscienceless way, effortlessly brushing aside such obstacles as present themselves, using up all the oxygen in the immediate vicinity. The performer never seems to be contriving effects calculated to please us; he seems simply to exist, to let who will issue challenge. With the heft of Mount Rushmore and the wingspread of a giant Condor, the man goes by, lifting one finger in acknowledgment of God and the rest of us. No, he doesn't go by. He happens. He will happen again and we will go to watch him again. It's like that.

A little less than eight months after Kerr's tribute was published, Zero Mostel died, Sept. 8, 1977, of a cardiac arrest at the age of 62. He had been playing Shylock in Arnold Wesker's play, *The Merchant*, which was being tried out in Philadelphia.

Kerr was awarded the Pulitzer Prize for Criticism in 1978. The piece about Zero Mostel was prominent among the examples of his work that were submitted to the Pulitzer judges.

44. MARQUIS CHILDS PONDERS MAN'S FATE IN A WORLD MARRED BY POLLUTION

A St. Louis Post-Dispatch Columnist Reviews a Film,
"Can Man Survive?"—and Can't Help Wondering

For more than 40 years, Marquis William Childs covered Washington, mainly as a member of the Washington bureau of the *St. Louis Post-Dispatch* and later as its chief.

He was Iowa-born (in 1903), received a degree in 1923 from the University of Wisconsin School of Journalism and, after brief service with the United Press in Chicago, joined the *Post-Dispatch* in 1926. He reported on nine Presidents of the United States, wrote about them in his syndicated column, and was so greatly respected by his colleagues that they made him president of their Gridiron Club in 1957.

Like Walter Lippmann, Arthur Krock, and Richard L. Strout, he was the standard-bearer of an older generation of Washington correspondents who never let themselves be confined merely to politics and the day-by-day news of the nation's capital. In his work for the *Post-Dispatch*, and during the ten years he wrote a column for the United Features Syndicate (1944–1954), he commented broadly on American life.

When a new Pulitzer Prize was established in 1970 for commentary, a jury considered almost 100 entries and concluded that "this award—especially in its first presentation—should go to someone distinguished for writing broadly in the field of public affairs."

It was not a surprise, therefore, that the jury recommended Childs. As its chairman wrote: "This man's high quality of work and his own distinguished standing and reputation need no documentation here."

Tucked away among the ten representative columns that were entered for him in the Pulitzer competition was a thoughtful essay based on a film about man's survival. It is typical of his broad interest in conservation and of his concern for the future of the nation.

SAVING MAN FROM HIMSELF

By Marquis Childs

From the St. Louis Post-Dispatch, July 1, 1969

NEW YORK—One of the city's great museums is the American Museum of Natural History. For its hundredth anniversary the museum has an exhibit that would have startled the daylights out of the supremely confident establishment figures who provided the millions for one of the most comprehensive collections of man's past and present on this troubled planet.

It is called, "Can Man Survive?" With films, sound tracks, and blown up photo montage, the despoiling of the elements fundamental to life—air, earth, and water—is shown is appalling detail.

Here is industry belching out vile fumes and dense smoke—133,000,000 tons of aerial garbage a year, says the sound track. Waste poured into rivers big and small that are hardly more than sewers.

The consequences of the population explosion are shown in the dire proliferation of peoples far beyond the food supply in many parts of Asia and Latin America. The films of Asians on the ragged edge of starvation are strong stuff, hardly conducive to sitting down to that full dinner with complacent disregard for one's fellow man. Teeming millions move before the camera looking like lemmings swayed by herd instinct.

In the latter part of the exhibit, the sound track blares out the defiant words of the individualist challenging any restraints on his right to exploit air, earth, or water falling under his domain. "Why can't I do what I want to with my own land?" "Who's going to tell me how to run my plant?" "Why shouldn't we try to get ahead of the Russians?"

The overwhelming impact is of the destruction of the vital oxygen in the air and the fresh water essential to all animal and plant life. In a few decades technological man has begun to undermine the elements built up over millions of years since the first animate creatures crawled out of the slime. The answer posed by the exhibit must be a hesitant maybe yes, maybe no.

With a jolt, this country has begun to wake up to a realization of how far down the road to devastation we have gone. The first small steps are being taken to reverse the trend. But as an answer to "Can Man Survive?" they are only the most tentative footprints in the wasteland.

The bureaucracies have been created in Washington to clean up the rivers and restore the balance in the polluted air of our cities. The Federal Water Pollution Control Administration is housed in the Department of the Interior. Secretary Walter Hickel has testified that the administration could effectively spend $600 million a year in grants to build sewage disposal plants. This is almost $400 million more that the request in the budget for the coming fiscal year.

The estimate of leaders of the cleanup drive—Senator Edmund Muskie of Maine in the forefront—is that between 1969 and 1973 alone it will take $10 billion to make a substantial advance. At the rate of $214 million a year, which is the budgetary request, you can see how far we'll get in four years.

Most states, which pay 40 percent of the construction cost for sewage plants as against 60 percent from the federal grant, put the cleanup cost much higher than the federal estimates. This is particularly true in the big-city states where industry adds a constant stream of pollution to the raw sewage flowing into the rivers.

Here in New York State, the federal estimate is $1 billion. The state's own estimate is more than twice that amount. For Pennsylvania, the Federal Water Pollution Administration puts the cost at $331 million, the state at $454 million. Maine, where the vision is of sparkling streams and lakes, sets a goal of $148 million as against the federal estimate of $47 million.

The National Center for Air Pollution Control is in the Department of Health, Eduction, and Welfare. The request in the budget for next year is $95,800,000. As with water, that is woefully inadequate when measured against the cost of doing a job that will begin to remove the poisons that millions breathe each day. "Can Man Survive?" shows how these poisons harass the city dweller and help fill up the hospitals with victims of respiratory diseases.

Senator Gaylord Nelson of Wisconsin, a valiant champion of clean environment, tells a story of how the animals of the earth held a congress to charge man with destroying their world. They voted with one exception to find man guilty as charged. The exception was the dog. "Pay no attention to him," said the presiding officer. "He's an Uncle Tom."

45. RUSSELL BAKER FINDS WASHINGTON IS SOLEMN BUT NEW YORK IS SERIOUS

The New York Times's Resident Humorist Dissects
the Fine Art of Being Funny in a Daily Paper

Ever since Mark Twain wrote for the *Territorial Enterprise*, there has been a pleasant myth in our literature about the prevalence of humor in American journalism. Unfortunately, it isn't so. Pick up any newspaper and you'll find, on the whole, that the comic art, if any, is confined to the funny page and not many of the current strips are all that humorous. As for television. the appalling notion that slick-haired announcers can liven up the news by making sick jokes about it is one of the very real tragedies of American journalism.

The point has been recognized within the profession for as long as newspapers have been published. It is never easy to be funny in print, whatever the circumstances. And to write a humorous column for a daily newspaper for any length of time is an extraordinary achievement. The career of Russell Baker of the *New York Times* is a case in point.

Like his fellow humorist, Art Buchwald of the *Washington Post*, Baker hadn't the faintest idea of making humor his specialty when he became a journalist. His background is Southern—born in 1925 in Loudoun County, Virginia, and educated at Johns Hopkins University in Baltimore. After service in the U.S. Navy, he began quite conventionally as a reporter for the *Baltimore Sun* from 1947 to 1954, then switched to the *New York Times*'s Washington Bureau. For the better part of eight years, he covered the White House and often was a part of the traveling press entourage of Presidents Eisenhower and John F. Kennedy.

The turn in his career came in 1962 when he began writing a three-times-a-week column for the *Times*. It was part humor, part social criticism, and as time went on the two became so intertwined that sometimes it was difficult to tell when Baker was being serious about humor or when he was making fun of being solemn. He discusses the point in the following column:

WHY BEING SERIOUS IS HARD

By Russell Baker

From the New York Times, April 30, 1978

Here is a letter of friendly advice. "Be serious," it says. What it means, of course, is, "Be solemn." The distinction between being serious and being solemn seems to be vanishing among Americans, just as surely as the distinction between "now" and "presently" and the distinction between liberty and making a mess.

Being solemn is easy. Being serious is hard. You probably have to be born serious, or at least go through a very interesting childhood. Children almost always begin by being serious, which is what makes them so entertaining when compared to adults as a class.

Adults, on the whole, are solemn. The transition from seriousness to solemnity occurs in adolescence, a period when Nature, for reasons of her own, plunges people into foolish frivolity. During this period, the organism struggles to regain dignity by recovering childhood's genius for seriousness. It is usually a hopeless cause.

As a result, you have to settle for solemnity. Being solemn has almost nothing to do with being serious, but on the other hand, you can't go on being adolescent forever, unless you are in the performing arts, and anyhow most people can't tell the difference. In fact, though Americans talk a great deal about the virtue of being serious, they generally prefer people who are solemn over people who are serious.

In politics, the rare candidate who is serious, like Adlai Stevenson, is easily overwhelmed by one who is solemn, like General Eisenhower. This is probably because it is hard for most people to recognize seriousness, which is rare, especially in politics, but comfortable to endorse solemnity, which is as commonplace as jogging.

Jogging is solemn. Poker is serious. Once you can grasp that distinction, you are on your way to enlightenment. To promote the cause, I submit the following list from which the vital distinction should emerge more clearly:

(1) Shakespeare is serious. David Susskind is solemn.

(2) Chicago is serious. California is solemn.

(3) Blow-dry hair stylings on anchor men for local television news shows are solemn. Henry James is serious.

(4) Falling in love, getting married, having children, getting divorced, and fighting over who gets the car and the Wedgewood are all serious. The new sexual freedom is solemn.

(5) *Playboy* is solemn. *The New Yorker* is serious.

(6) S. J. Perelman is serious. Norman Mailer is solemn.

(7) The Roman Empire was solemn. Periclean Athens was serious.

(8) Arguing about "structured programs" of anything is solemn. So are talking about "utilization," attending conferences on the future of anything, and group bathing when undertaken for the purpose of getting to know yourself better, or at the prescription of a swami. Taking a long walk by yourself during which you devise a foolproof scheme for robbing Cartier's is serious.

(9) Washington is solemn. New York is serious. So is Las Vegas, but Miami Beach is solemn.

(10) Humphrey Bogart movies about private eyes and Randolph Scott movies about gunslingers are serious. Modern movies that are sophisticated jokes about Humphrey Bogart movies and Randolph Scott movies are solemn.

Making lists, of course, is solemn, but this is permissible in newspaper columns because newspaper columns are solemn. They strive, after all, to reach the mass audience and the mass audience is solemn, which accounts for the absence of seriousness in television, paperback books found on airport bookracks, the public school systems of America, wholesale furniture outlets, shopping centers, and American-made automobiles.

I make no apology for being solemn rather than serious. Nor should anyone else. It is the national attitude. It is perfectly understandable. It is hard to be Periclean Athens. It is hard to be Shakespeare. It is hard to be S. J. Perelman. It is hard to be serious.

And yet, one cannot go on toward eternity without some flimsy attempt at dignity. Adolescence will not do. One must make the effort to resume childhood's lost seriousness and so, with the best of intentions, one tries his best, only to end being vastly, uninterestingly solemn.

Writing sentences that use "one" as a pronoun is solemn. Making pronouncements on American society is solemn. Turning yourself off when pronouncements threaten to gush is not exactly serious, although it shows a shred of wisdom.

Russell Baker was awarded the Pulitzer Prize for Commentary in 1979. The jury wrote of him: "While famed as a humorist, he makes incisive points with or without satire. He is one of our era's greatest social critics without many of his readers being aware of it." Mark Twain himself could not have written a better definition of the function of the humorist in American journalism.

X. THE PRESS EXAMINES
OUR LEGAL SYSTEM

The nomination of Clement F. Haynesworth, Jr., to the United States Supreme Court in 1969 won universal approval from his fellow lawyers and judges.

The South Carolinian, who had ascended to the United States Court of Appeals of the 4th Circuit, also drew the endorsement of the *Chicago Daily News* on Aug. 19, the day after his name had been submitted by President Nixon to the Senate for a favorable vote.

"His personal reputation is impeccable," the *News* editorialized, "his professional qualifications are of the highest."

William J. Eaton, a member of the *News*'s Washington bureau, did what amounted to a "puff" piece about Hynesworth on page 3 of the *News* that same day, calling him "a jurist with charm and great dignity."

Eaton did mention in passing an allegation that Haynesworth had been involved in 1963 in a conflict of interest in connection with a case then pending before the appeals court. But, he added, the then Attorney General of the United States, Robert F. Kennedy, had dismissed the matter.

That should have settled everything and, for the average reporter, it would have. But Eaton wasn't an average reporter. He was a devoted, painstaking and conscientious investigator who took nothing for granted; at 39, he knew his way around Washington as well as his native Chicago. With bachelor's and master's degrees in journalism from Northwestern University, he had served his apprenticeship on the *Evanston* (Ill.) *Review* and the United Press. The, after winning a Nieman Fellowship at Harvard, he became a member of the *Chicago Daily News*'s Washington bureau.

On the day he finished his "puff" piece about Judge Haynesworth, he decided to look into the 1963 case on his own. What he learned from a lawyer who had been involved in the transaction sent him scurrying next day to the headquarters of the Securities and Exchange Commission in Washington. There, he went through the files of a vending machine company, in which Judge Haynesworth had owned stock, and took some photostats of pertinent papers back to the *News* bureau. On August 23, he broke a banner headline story in the *News* that began:

"WASHINGTON—U.S. Appeals Court Judge Clement F. Haynesworth, Jr., owned vending machine company stock, later sold for approximately $450,000, when he ruled in favor of a giant textile firm that did business with the vending company.

Records on file with the Securities and Exchange Commission show that Haynesworth swapped 18 shares of Carolina Vend-a-matic Co., a one-seventh interest, for 14,173 shares of Automatic Retailers of America stock on April 8, 1964. Closing price of ARA stock was $32.25 on that day. . . ."

The story went on to point out that the Carolina firm had doubled its business in 1963 by supplying food for mills owned by Deering, Milliken & Co., and that Haynesworth was still a Carolina stockholder when he provided the swing vote in a 3–2 appeals court decision in favor of a company owned by Deering, Milliken that had shut down rather than deal with the Textile Workers of America (AFL-CIO). Haynesworth stoutly denied to Eaton that he had acted improperly in voting that the mill was correct in refusing to deal with union and pointed out that he had "immediately" sold the vending machine stock thereafter.

Nevertheless, Eaton's story led to a full-scale investigation of Judge Haynesworth's affairs by the Senate Judiciary Committee and ultimate rejection by the Senate of the Haynesworth nomination. Eaton won the Pulitzer Prize for National Reporting in 1970.

With the demise of the *Daily News*, a once-great paper that had gone into a decline, Eaton joined the Washington bureau of the *Los Angeles Times*.

He is not by any means the only reporter in the annals of the Pulitzer Prizes who has won distinction by scrutinizing the courts; nor, for that matter, is the *Chicago Daily News* the only newspaper that has supported such high-level investigations. It is one of the most enduring characteristics of Pulitzer winners.

As early as 1927, John T. Rogers of the *St. Louis Post-Dispatch* won an award for an investigation that led to the impeachment of a federal judge in Illinois. And in 1929, another Pulitzer paper, the *New York Evening World*, won the public service gold medal in large part because of its inquiry into the activities of ambulance-chasing lawyers and politically corrupt municipal courts. In 1940, S. Burton Heath of the *New York World-Telegram*, in a brilliant one-man investigation, turned up evidence that led to the resignation, trial, and imprisonment of Federal Judge Martin T. Manton in a spectacular fraud case.

The *Sacramento Bee* in California also won a public service prize in 1935 for campaigning against machine politics in the appointment of two Federal judges in Nevada. So did the *Boston Globe* in 1966 for a series that prevented confirmation of a candidate for a Federal judgeship in Massachusetts.

Another Pulitzer Prize winner, William Lambert, disclosed in *Life* magazine in 1969 that a member of the United States Supreme Court, Abe Fortas, had accepted but returned a check from a convicted industrialist's family foundation. Although Justice Fortas denied intervening in the industrialist's case, he later resigned from the high court.

The activities of Pulitzer Prize winners in police matters, particularly in the investigation of corruption in official ranks, have attained even wider scope. In many of the largest cities of the land, and a number of smaller ones, such inquiries are regarded as a logical and necessary part of the "watchdog" function of a free and independent press. The Pulitzer Prizes testify to the quality of the work that has been done over more than six decades, and especially in the 1960s and 1970s, the period with which this volume is primarily concerned.

The following individual articles, series, and editorials testify to the results of the press's long stewardship over the administration of justice in the United States.

46. THE PHILADELPHIA INQUIRER REVEALS
POLICE BRUTALITY ON A MASSIVE SCALE

A Pattern of Violence Against the Legal Rights
of Minorities Is Disclosed by an Investigation

A home-made firebomb—a gasoline-filled bottle—was hurled into the Philadelphia home of Radames Santiago on Oct. 5, 1975, killing Santiago's wife, three children, and a youthful house guest.

Based on the testimony of six neighbors, Philadelphia detectives arrested a somewhat retarded auto mechanic, Robert "Reds" Wilkinson, and obtained from him a signed confession that he had set the blaze.

Wilkinson was sent to jail for 15 months.

On the surface, it appeared to be an open-and-shut case. But two reporters for the *Philadelphia Inquirer*, Jonathan Neumann and Jan Schaffer, were convinced that Wilkinson was innocent and began their own investigation.

In a series of articles in the *Inquirer*, they demonstrated that the six neighbors who testified against Wilkinson had been threatened or actually beaten by some of the detectives who interviewed them.

Wilkinson, moreover, was unable to read and said he signed the confession after his hands had been whipped with a blackjack, his body had been stomped upon and his life had been threatened. He had been told, he went on, that he would never again see his wife and child unless he confessed to a series of murders that he had never committed.

In the same state court in which he was convicted, Wilkinson was cleared of all charges and freed in 1977. And in Federal court nearby, David McGinnis, a neighbor, not only confessed to the fire-bombing but plea-bargained for a 22-year prison term. Ronald Hanley, an accomplice, was convicted and sentenced to a life term.

What of the six Philadelphia detectives involved in the case? Not even the most optimistic editors of the *Philadelphia Inquirer* believed that very much could be done about them because the political system in the city seemingly had made them immune.

The system was formulated by one man, Frank Rizzo, the then mayor of Philadelphia. He had been a tough cop. He had fought his way through the ranks to become police commissioner. And in 1971 he had become mayor on a "law-and-order" platform that was clearly aimed at blacks and other minorities in the city.

Rizzo didn't care who knew it. He was outspokenly racist in his views of what his police could and could not do. And that was how he appealed for white support in his various political campaigns.

For years there had been attempts to force the Philadelphia police to moderate their treatment of minority prisoners. The *Inquirer* had tried it several times, always producing evidence but never getting very far with the obdurate Rizzo.

But with the Wilkinson case, the *Inquirer* decided to try again. Neumann and another reporter, William K. Marimow, put together a series on police brutality called "The Homicide Files" in 1977 that detailed how suspects were handcuffed to metal chairs and beaten with brass knuckles, lead pipes, and blackjacks.

The series constituted the most serious challenge in Rizzo's tenure as mayor. This is a digest of the first article:

THE HOMICIDE FILES

By Jonathan Neumann and William K. Marimow

Copyright 1977 by the Philadelphia Inquirer, April 24, 1977

It can be said with certainty that two things happened in the 22 hours between Carlton Coleman's arrest and his arraignment last October.

One is that he was interrogated by homicide detectives. The other is that his health went from good to poor. When it was all over, he spent the next 28 days hospitalized for injuries of the abdomen, arms, shoulders, chest, calf, spine, and back.

Medical problems are not rare among those interrogated by the Philadelphia Police Department's 84-member homicide division. In fact, a four-month investigation by the *Inquirer* has found a pattern of beatings, threats of violence, intimidation, coercion, and knowing disregard for constitutional rights in the interrogation of homicide witnesses and suspects.

The study shows that many homicide detectives, in beating or coercing suspects and later denying it under oath, have come to accept breaking the law as part of their job.

As a result of those practices, the *Inquirer* has found, there are cases in which murders have remained unsolved, killers have gone free, and innocent men have been imprisoned.

From 1974 through April 1977, judges of the Common Pleas Court have been asked to rule in pretrial hearings on the legality of police investigations in 433 homicide cases. Those rulings require the judge to decide who is telling the truth—the police or the suspect. In most cases, the judge believes the police.

In 80 of those cases, however, judges have ruled that the police acted illegally during homicide interrogations. The judges found in many cases that police had used either physical or psychological coercion. In some cases, the victims' injuries were documented by X-rays, medical records, and photographs.

Extensive interviews with homicide detectives and prosecutors who work with detectives every day confirm these findings. The interviews—including some with detectives who frequently have been accused of beatings—make it clear that top officials in the Police Department know of and tolerate the coercive measures.

The illegal interrogations follow a pattern:

—They are conducted by teams of detectives in tiny rooms at Police Headquarters—known as the Roundhouse—at Eighth and Race Streets. The suspect or witness is often handcuffed to a metal chair, which is bolted to the floor. Some of these sessions have lasted 24 hours.

—Some of the techniques used in the beatings leave no severe marks. Those techniques include placing a telephone book on a suspect's head and hammering it with a heavy object; beating his feet and ankles; twisting or kicking his testicles, and pummeling his back, ribs, and kidneys.

—Other techniques do leave marks. Testimony about interrogations that judges have ruled illegal has shown that suspects have been beaten with lead pipes, blackjacks, brass knuckles, handcuffs, chairs, and table legs. One suspect was stabbed in the groin with a swordlike instrument.

—The detectives make use of one-way mirrors through which the interrogation rooms can be observed. Suspects and witnesses have testified that they were forced to watch beatings through such windows and were told they would receive the same treatment unless they cooperated.

"What we're living in at the Roundhouse," a former homicide detective said, "is a return to the Middle Ages. All this nonsense about the 'thin blue line between society and the underworld,' it's bull——. Police are breaking the law every day and they know it."

Why are the detectives doing this?

The main reason, detectives say, is outrage—outrage at the heinousness of the crimes they investigate and outrage at a court system that allows murderers to "walk," or go free.

"It's a fight every day," one detective said. "The homicide detective must fight the lawyers, the judges, the Supreme Court—and he must fight crime."

But there is also another reason: money.

To get a statement from a suspect, a detective often works around the clock—and that means overtime. Once he gets a statement, he becomes a court witness and court time means more overtime.

City payroll records show that the average homicide detective got $7,575 in overtime pay last year. One more than doubled his base pay, earning a total of $36,293, which is higher than the salary of Police Commissioner Joseph F. O'Neill.

Does the Police Department care that murder cases are lost because illegal "confessions" have been thrown out?

As individuals, the police care very much. But their concern does not carry over into the department's official gauge of its effectiveness—the rate at which murder cases are "cleared." A "cleared" case is one in which somebody is charged with the crime but not necessarily convicted.

The department is proud that it has "cleared" nearly 87 percent of its cases in recent years. But 20 percent of the homicide defendants who went to court last year were acquitted or were freed because the district attorney's office dropped the charges for lack of evidence.

An example of a murder that was "cleared" but apparently not solved is the Santiago firebombing case. As the *Inquirer* has reported, the police rounded up seven neighbors, beat the men, threatened the women, and forced them to sign false statements implicating Robert (Reds) Wilkinson in five murders. He was convicted, but the verdict was overturned when another man, David McGinnis, confessed.

Why are homicide detectives not forced to obey the law?

No homicide detective has been prosecuted in recent years, if ever, for a crime committed during an interrogation. This apparent immunity can be explained in part by the detectives' close working relationship with the district attorney's office. . . .

That was just the beginning. During 1977 and 1978, the *Inquirer* identified 65 members of the Philadelphia police force who had been accused of criminal violence.

A judge in Philadelphia Common Pleas Court in 1977 threw out the confession in the Carlton Coleman case (he had been charged with shooting an off-duty policeman) on the ground that it had been obtained through illegal coercion. All charges against Coleman were subsequently dropped.

In 1978, the six homicide detectives identified in connection with false accusations made in the Reds Wilkinson case went on trial and were convicted of civil rights violations. In 1979, they began serving 15 months at a Florida federal prison—the first such convictions in Rizzo's regime.

The fabled immunity of Rizzo's police had finally been smashed. And while some defendants won dismissals, others continued to be involved in long federal proceedings.

The Department of Justice even tried to lodge a civil rights suit against the entire Philadelphia police force in 1979 but it was thrown out by a federal judge who ruled that Congressional sanction should have been obtained for so drastic a move.

However, the continued federal investigation was a reminder to Philadelphia police that they were being closely watched.

Mainly for political reasons, the action in state courts was not as effective as the federal inquiry. Out of 16 arrests in police civil rights violations, there was one guilty plea, one finding of guilt, six acquittals, two mistrials, and continuing legal action in the rest.

But when Mayor Rizzo went out of office in 1979, at the end of his second term, there was some assurance that his successor, William Green, would institute the police reforms for which the *Inquirer* had campaigned for many years.[1]

The *Inquirer* was awarded the Pulitzer Prize gold medal for public service in 1978.

47. NEWSDAY FOLLOWS THE HEROIN TRAIL FROM TURKEY AND FRANCE TO THE U.S.

A Vast Machine of Illegal Narcotics Smugglers Is Exposed in a 13-Country, 3-Continent Inquiry

Dope peddlers appeared outside high schools in some of the most exclusive Long Island communities early in the 1970s. And they weren't selling marijuana. What they were offering to school children was infinitely more dangerous—a hard, habit-forming drug, heroin.

It wasn't long before alarmed parents began complaining to anybody who would listen. But the law enforcement machinery was glacially slow in its response. Where was the evidence? What is the substance of the complaint? Who is going to bring the charges? Of course, all the legal niceties had to be observed—and nothing was done about the suddenly increased flow of heroin.

Nothing, that is, until the story reached *Newsday*, Long Island's largest and most influential newspaper. It didn't take the paper's management long to decide it had to do something. Big Bob Greene, the paper's star investigative reporter, was called in and told to find the source of the heroin no matter where the trail led or how long it took, to expose the illegal traffickers, to develop evidence that could be used in a massive prosecution, and above all to name names.

This was far from a small undertaking. Before Greene's inquiry was

---

[1] Notes on the *Inquirer*'s investigation: The original story of the auto mechanic's conviction was published Dec. 5, 1976. The "Homicide Files" series was published April 24–27, 1977. The Federal government's action against the Philadelphia police is detailed in Page 1 articles in the *New York Times* for Aug. 13 and 14, 1979, and a third interpretive piece on Page A-21 in the *Times* for Aug. 16, 1979. See also the *Inquirer* for Aug. 13 and 14, 1979. The Associated Press file for Oct. 31, 1979, carried the dismissal of the suit. Jonathan Neumann, who shifted to the *Washington Post*, wrote an article Aug. 14, 1979, for that newspaper headed: "Philadelphia Police: 'Toughest in the World.'" Conviction of the six homicide detectives was reported in the Associated Press file for Oct. 23, 1979. I am also indebted to William Marimow for a long and detailed summary of the *Inquirer*'s investigation dated Oct. 31, 1979.

complete, the newspaper was to spend $300,000 in an effort to slow down, if it couldn't break, the heroin traffic on Long Island. *Newsday* reporters were to travel in 13 countries on three continents during their six-month investigation. They were to interview the producers of the raw product, the chemists, accountants, wholesalers, and even some of the major figures in this world-wide ring of illicit narcotics smugglers.

Alicia Patterson, who had founded *Newsday* in a Long Island garage in 1940 and spurred its growth into the 10th largest paper in the country, would have been proud of the scope of the "Heroin Trail" investigation. She had presided over the winning of the newspaper's first Pulitzer Prize for Public Service in 1954. Another had been awarded in 1970, but this campaign was the largest the staff had ever undertaken.

A total of 13 reporters left the United States on June 4, 1972, fanning out to Turkey, France, Mexico, Canada, and nine other countries. They did not return until Dec. 12, 1972. During the interim, the Turkish task force studied opium farming and the very large smuggling network that subsisted on it; in France, another detachment tested the links between French officialdom and the French racketeers who presided over the manufacture of heroin from opium. Elsewhere, the remainder of the staff traced the shipment, processing, and packaging of heroin for the American retail trade.

Their 32-part series, entitled "The Heroin Trail," was published from Feb. 1 through March 4, 1973. This is the substance of one of the key stories in the investigation:

THE TURKISH CONNECTION

From Newsday, Garden City, N.Y., Feb. 4, 1973

The Istanbul narcotics merchants are big businessmen.

They legitimately own hotels, restaurants, shipping lines, night clubs, expensive houses, and other property. Most of their holdings are financed by their profits from their narcotics dealings.

Some have been jailed at one point or another; others have not. Many associate with members of the Turkish establishment; business, social, political, and governmental leaders. There are more than 50 patrons (in Turkey, a big shot who plans and finances smuggling) in the country.

The direct market for Turkish morphine base is the Mediterranean coast of France, where a loose group of gang leaders, most of them Corsican, convert the base to heroin.

The French gang leaders, who have a working relationship with the Sicilian Mafia, are called caids (pronounced ca-yeeds), an Arab word meaning lesser chieftains.

A typical shipment works like this: A caid contacts a patron by phone, or telegram, using a prearranged code, and orders a shipment, which will be picked up either in France or at some spot closer to Istanbul. If much discussion is required, the caid sends a representative to Turkey or some city like Munich, Vienna, or Beirut to meet the patron or his representative.

When the deal is made, the patron either finances the whole shipment or takes in other patrons to share the risk.

Then he sends representatives into Anatolia (in Asiatic Turkey) to collect the morphine base from regional middlemen, or opium from village headmen if it hasn't been converted. In some instances, patrons will finance the laboratory costs for conversion. On the other end, the patron hires smugglers, who move the base out of Turkey for a fixed fee or a percentage of the shipment.

The price the French caids pay on delivery is determined by supply and demand. If the supply flow has been interrupted by too many law enforcement seizures or if there has been a bad opium crop in Turkey, the price is higher. If the flow is steady, prices are lower.

If the morphine base is less then 80 percent pure, the price also is lower. The Istanbul patrons almost always accept the assessments of the French underworld chemists, who set the 80 percent standard. The French, in turn, want to keep doing business so they are usually accurate in their assessments.

Within this framework, the Istanbul patron pegs his own prices, based on the risks involved. For example, if the French caid accepts delivery of the morphine base in Istanbul, handling the rest of the smuggling himself, the price is lower. The farther the patron must smuggle the base, the higher the price.

We were in Turkey three months and spent much of our time gathering information about the patrons. We picked up scraps here and there—in bars, expensive restaurants, hotel lobbies, musty apartments, and whorehouses.

It was useful information but limited. We had an opportunity to talk first-hand with one of the biggest patrons but we declined when our contact asked that we provide $40,000 in cash as an incentive to conversation.

We had a second opportunity. It was a wet, late-summer afternoon in our small villa on the outskirts of Istanbul. The rain sloshed off the slanted roof and swept through the shrub-filled garden. The doorbell rang. A tall Turk, solidly built, came in. He looked to be in his late 40s, wearing wrap-around sun glasses, his dark hair combed straight back. His left thumb was lopped off at the bottom joint.

He was willing to talk about everyone but himself. That was all right. We knew about him:

"OFFICIAL REPORT: FOR POLICE BACKGROUND ONLY—Subject is highly knowledgeable. He has masterminded drug shipments out of Turkey over a period of 25 years. He is a university graduate with a sophisticated background in chemistry. He is a social and business acquaintance of most of Istanbul's big narcotics patrons. Subject comes from an excellent family and is closely related to several people who hold high government office. Through the years, subject has become a specialist in the chemistry of opiates and, until the death penalty was instituted for manufacture of heroin in Turkey in 1951, he illegally manufactured and exported the drug. Now he runs a legitimate export-import business. But he still occasionally arranges and finances illegal shipments of morphine base out of Turkey."

We sat around the dining room table. He chain-smoked black market Kents and sipped hot tea with a lot of sugar. A precise man, he pulled from his jacket pocket a fistful of notepaper covered with his own notes in small, neat handwriting. "I put down everything on paper over the last few nights so I wouldn't forget anything," he explained.

He gave us names, places, routes, amounts, prices, problems. He explained how the system worked: "Everyone is in and out. One day you are handling a drug shipment. Another day it is guns. Almost always you are moving cigarettes. Sometimes, you take in partners; sometimes, you finance a whole shipment yourself. No one is always in drugs. And there is no chief because everyone is a chief."

The talk went on for several hours, mostly through an interpreter, though sometimes we spoke Turkish. Occasionally we would seek to break the tedium of note-taking by bringing up other matters. He would pause, then quickly reply: "Yes, Istanbul is a very interesting city but, getting back to the subject of this patron, he now lives at. . . ."

Some questions he resented, such as when we routinely asked the ages of various patrons we mentioned. "What the hell do you think I am?" he snapped. "Some kind of a statistician? I know these people. I work with them. Do you think I walk up to them and tell them that I won't share a deal until they give me the precise date of their births?"

Later, when we stopped pressing him, he readily gave ages and, on occasion, information about the political background of the patrons.

We told him we planned to check out everything he said. He smiled and replied that his information would prove to be accurate. Then he turned philosophic: "Yes, I read in the newspapers what heroin is doing to the youth of America. Tragic, tragic. Of course we don't have the problem here. What is the matter with your young people?"

We answered the question with another: "Well, if continued shipment of heroin to the United States is a tragedy, why are people still shipping it out of Turkey?"

His reply: "It is a very profitable business. The most profitable business in the world. Here in Turkey we would like to get more money (for morphine base). But unfortunately, the market is oversupplied."

The interview was over. He gathered up his handwritten notes and walked to the fireplace. He made a neat pile of the notes and ignited them with a gold-plated cigarette lighter. He watched until nothing was left but ash.

"If the wrong people found me with this, it would mean my death," he said.

No, he didn't want a cab. No, he didn't want us to have his telephone number. He said to contact him through the same person again. He left the house but paused at the garden gate, looking up and down the street. Then he walked away in the rain.

He came back two more times. Both times, he burned his notes.

The series did name names, and published pictures to go with the names. There were 54 Turks who were identified as some of the leaders of the illegal exportation of opium. More traffickers were named in France, some with alleged connections to the French government and secret service. But the biggest blast was reserved for the home-grown figures who were alleged heroin dealers in New York City and Nassau and Suffolk Counties on Long Island.

Congressional committees summoned *Newsday* reporters to testify. Arrests were made but, law enforcement in the dope traffic being notoriously laggard, the convictions did not measure up to the scope of the *Newsday* inquiry nor to the more than a hundred figures who were publicly identified as a part of the heroin network. The enormous publicity, however, did turn the spotlight on the racket and alert many a community to try to protect itself as best it could.

Newsday was awarded its third Pulitzer Prize gold medal for Public Service in 1974.

There is an epilogue to the story. Almost six years later, Bob Greene, who by that time had become an assistant managing editor of *Newsday*, took another long look at "The Heroin Trail" and concluded that the supply of Turkish heroin flowing to the United States had been sharply reduced.

This was not, however, because of any sudden spurt of conscience by the Turkish government or tightened law enforcement by the United States. Greene found that the Turks had become too greedy and charged astronomical prices for their product when legal opium growing ended in Turkey in 1973-74 under pressure from the American government. The heroin syndicate, having foreseen this problem, had begun switching its opium-growing operations to Mexico and established laboratories there for conversion of morphine base to heroin.

"The work of smuggling the heroin into the States from Mexico was undertaken by a vast syndicate which for years has been smuggling cocaine and marijuana into the U.S.," Greene wrote.

"This Mexican heroin has been supplemented with heroin smuggled from the Far East. There has been no diminution in the amount of heroin supplied to the U.S., but there has been a much higher profit for heroin dealers. Heroin grown in Mexico and smuggled into the States through existing smuggling organizations is far cheaper than Turkish heroin.

"In our series, we quoted Turks who said that if heroin growing stopped
in Turkey it would merely be grown some place else because the market
demand had not been eradicated. This has proved to be true." [1]

48. THE WALL STREET JOURNAL UNCOVERS
A $150 MILLION SALAD OIL FRAUD

Norman C. Miller Follows the Mystery of Allied Crude
and the Risky Adventures of Tino DeAngelis

Of all the law-breakers in the discouragingly large American catalogue
of crime, the most difficult to catch is the financial wizard who sells his
victims on "get-rich-quick" schemes. Because the losers often complain to
newspapers if they cannot stir up action by properly constituted
authorities, the press frequently becomes involved in such investigations.

One of the earliest Pulitzer Prizes was awarded to the *Boston Post* in
1921 for exposing the operations of Charles Ponzi, who defrauded small
investors and gambled illegally with millions of dollars in the frantic post-
World War I atmosphere. There is some question whether Ponzi ever
would have been caught if the newspaper had not begun an independent
investigation of his activities.

A similar case occurred in Texas in the 1960s when Oscar Griffin, Jr.,
editor of the weekly *Pecos Independent and Enterprise*, disclosed that
Billie Sol Estes, an Abilene entrepreneur, had bilked investors out of
millions of dollars by borrowing money on 15,000 anhydrous ammonia
tanks in Reeves County that didn't exist. Griffin won a Pulitzer Prize and
Estes went to jail for six and a half years. [2]

But an even bigger swindle, in which investors lost an estimated $150
million that had been put up to buy or finance the purchase of
nonexistent salad oil, was brought to public attention by the *Wall Street
Journal*. It was called the worst financial scandal since Ivar Kreuger, the
Swedish "match king," worked a $500-million swindle in the 1920s at the
expense of gullible friends in the international banking set.

[1] Letter from Bob Greene to author, Sept. 26, 1979.

[2] Griffin began his series Feb. 12, 1962, in the Pecos newspaper and won the
Pulitzer Prize for Special Local Reporting in 1963. The luckless Estes was caught
again for income tax fraud and sentenced to ten years in prison in Dallas in 1979.
See Associated Press for Aug. 6, 1979.

In this case, a painstaking inquiry by Norman C. (Mike) Miller of the *Wall Street Journal* paralleled an official investigation that had been undertaken into the bankruptcy of the Allied Crude Vegetable Oil Refining Company, the largest supplier in the country of edible oils for export. Only Miller came up with the story long before the financial community had begun to suspect the enormity of the fraud.

Miller was a young reporter at the time, a 1956 graduate of Penn State's journalism school and a U.S. Navy veteran. He had actually been on the job in the New York office of the *Journal* for only three years when he broke this story:

THE GREAT SALAD OIL SWINDLE

By Norman C. Miller

From the Wall Street Journal, Dec. 2, 1963

BAYONNE, N.J.—Law enforcement authorities investigating "the case of the missing salad oil" at a vast tank storage facility here suspect they have stumbled on a swindle that will make Billie Sol Estes' escapades look like a kindergarten exercise.

Two weeks ago Allied Crude Vegetable Oil Refining Corp., the nation's biggest supplier of edible oils for export, filed a bankruptcy petition. It had made heavy purchases on credit of contracts for the future delivery of soybean and cottonseed oil; when the prices of these products dropped on the New York Produce Exchange and Chicago Board of Trade and Allied's brokers demanded nearly $19 million to offset the decline in value of the contracts, Allied couldn't pay.

One result was the failure of a major Wall Street securities firm, Ira Haupt & Co., that had purchased some futures contracts on Allied's behalf. Another result was that major commodities dealers who believed they had soybean oil, cottonseed oil, fish oil, and other edible oils stored here in Allied's tanks, or in the connected tanks of other companies, suddenly began to check their inventories—and found much of their commodities missing.

It's now clear that vast quantities of these "missing" commodities will never be found, and for a simple reason: They don't exist and never did.

Dozens of major companies dealing in commodities unwittingly bought phantom goods. They, in turn, borrowed millions from banks by unknowingly using as collateral the phony warehouse receipts issued to them.

The losses will be staggering. Claims already announced total $41 million and other claims are still coming in. Sources close to the investigation estimate final losses will reach $100 million and possibly more. By contrast, Billie Sol Estes' swindle, through loans obtained by using nonexistent tanks of fertilizer as collateral, is estimated at much less.

Insurance may not cover all of the losses. Policies covering commodities in storage usually rule out payments for losses due to fraud. Some of the storage companies that operate interconnected tanks here—but not all of these firms—will be pressed for huge sums by holders of worthless warehouse receipts. There also may well be substantial losses by some of the commodities dealers and banks that bought or loaned money on goods that now are nowhere to be found.

Details of the fantastic story of how many American and foreign companies put up millions of dollars for nothing are still being unraveled by FBI men and other investigators. After two weeks, they're still searching through the murky labyrinth of complex dealings created to conceal facts.

At the core of the massive mess is Allied, whose president, Anthony (Tino) DeAngelis, has a history of difficulties with the Securities and Exchange Commission, the Internal Revenue Service, and the bankruptcy courts. Law enforcement authorities have uncovered information indicating that Allied sold non-existent edible oils with the help of certain employees of some tank storage companies here—employees who received payments from Allied in return for arranging the issuance of phony warehouse receipts. It should be noted, however, that most of the storage companies were not victimized by corrupt employees.

Three weeks later, on December 22, Miller produced another front page sensation for the *Journal* when he discovered that, as was the case in the Estes swindle, a lot of the tanks for the phantom salad oil also were figments of a fertile imagination.

When all the losses were totaled in the Allied bankruptcy, they exceeded $150 million. *Time* magazine labeled it "the biggest financial intrigue in nearly half a century" and the *New York Times* called it "the most sensational Wall Street story of the past generation."

Miller won the 1964 Pulitzer Prize for Local Reporting. As for Allied's presiding genius, Tino DeAngelis, he pleaded guilty on Jan. 8, 1965, in Newark Federal Court to three charges of circulating forged warehouse receipts in interstate commerce and to a fourth charge of circulating $100 million in forged warehouse receipts. He served seven years of a 20-year sentence and was paroled in 1972, when he went into the meat business and soon was boasting to a *Wall Street Journal* reporter that he could gross $100 million a year.[2]

49. HOWARD JAMES OF THE MONITOR SEES A "CRISIS IN THE COURTS"

The Reporter Finds Miscarriages of Justice on the Bench
In a Nationwide Tour To Assess Our Judicial Problems

At the height of national tensions over the Vietnam War and the riots in big city ghettos in the 1960s, the *Christian Science Monitor* assigned Howard James, chief of its midwestern bureau, to conduct a nationwide survey of the administration of justice in American courtrooms.

He traveled unobtrusively from one state to another, slipped into courtrooms in large cities and small ones, and later talked with judges about their problems and the reasons for some of their decisions. He wasn't looking particularly for bad judges, but he found some; a black robe, as he observed, doesn't actually make a judge. But he also found hard-working, conscientious judges who were perturbed by the vagaries of the system of justice under which they labored, by the appalling case overloads in most courts, by the antiquated procedures that often handicapped them in their conduct of trials.

Sometimes, James was able to effect changes merely by being present in a courtroom. In Pittsburgh, for example, he told the Chief Magistrate about some irregular bail bond practices that then were being conducted in the city's courts. The bondsmen at once were barred from courtrooms, bail amounts were cut, and defendants were permitted to pick a bondsman by telephone from a printed list.

[2] Jonathan Kwitny, "Tino DeAngelis Is Out of Prison and Running a Business of his Own," *Wall Street Journal*, Jan. 15, 1974, p. 1.

In another case, in Miami, James heard a judge sentence a 15-year-old Spanish-speaking youth to 10 days in jail for driving without a valid license. When James asked why, the judge remarked that the defendant was "only" a migrant worker's son. It later developed that the youth did have a valid learner's permit and was driving the family truck in an emergency. The judge, somewhat abashed, released the youth next day.

Another development came in Anderson, S.C., where jail records that had been restricted were opened to public inspection as a result of James's inquiry.

This is a digest of his first article:

A ROBE DOESN'T MAKE A JUDGE

By Howard James

From the Christian Science Monitor, April 12, 1967

It is 11:43 A.M. on a Wednesday in late February. Spring is edging into Louisville, Ky., and on the street people have shed their coats and are nodding and smiling.

But in the courtroom of Circuit Judge R—— there are no smiles. A middle-aged barber, accused of wounding a man, is worried. His freedom and future are at stake.

On the witness stand, his daughter, an attractive woman, tells the jury how the victim provoked the shooting by taunting her father and by getting youngsters to block the barber shop driveway to keep customers away.

As she testifies, an aging newsboy enters the courtroom and hawks papers.

With considerable rustling Judge R—— opens his newspaper to the comic page. After reading for several minutes he pulls the section out, folds it into a smaller square, and counts quietly to himself, apparently working the crossword puzzle.

The young woman seems nervous. She speaks rapidly.

Judge R—— looks up from his paper and tells her to slow down. There is a note of irritation in his voice when, a few minutes later, he again orders her to speak more slowly so the court stenographer can keep up.

The stenographer, who already has put down her pen and is checking her fingernails, says, "Oh, I gave up a long time ago."

When the defendant's daughter finishes, two other witnesses take the stand briefly. Judge R—— denies the prosecution request to let a woman use the chalk board to clarify her testimony.

At 12:38 P.M., the judge adjourns court for lunch until 2 P.M.

A visitor, after buying license plates in another office, has stopped by to watch. With adjournment, he rises to leave before the jury has departed. Judge R—— orders him stopped by a bailiff, brings him before the bench, and gives him a lecture on courtroom decorum.

What happened on this day in Louisville is unusual. But it is far from unique in the nation's state courts.

In criminal court in Manhattan a judge read his newspaper-sized law bulletin while holding hearings. Lowering a corner to listen now and then, he kept the paper in front of his face as defendants appeared before him. To those involved each case was an important matter, worthy of his full attention.

In Cincinnati, a new Common Pleas magistrate, Judge K——, was reading, ironically enough, copies of the *Journal of the American Judicature Society* during a narcotics trial. (It is the Judicature Society that has pioneered in improving the administration of justice. It should be mentioned, however, that there are judges, known for their brilliance on the bench, who manage both to read and rule with perception and without lapse of rapport with the cases before them).

Behind a bench in Manhattan, Judge S—— became furious with a defendant when the man's lawyer did not show up in court. The defendant said his attorney was in a higher court in another city. The judge refused to listen and raised the man's bail—putting him behind bars "until your attorney shows up."

He also ordered the man to phone his lawyer. The defendant button-holed another attorney and asked for help. When the other attorney tried, confirming that the first one was away, the judge shouted him down and stormed off the bench.

One recalls that Harry W. Jones, Cardozo professor of jurisprudence at Columbia University, once said, "Every multijudge trial court of general jurisdiction has at least one tyrant in residence."

Later that day, perhaps after thinking it over and learning that a newspaper reporter had been watching, the judge reversed himself.

In San Francisco Municipal Court, Judge F—— was hearing traffic cases. He argued with the defendants, seemed to have trouble reading police accident reports without help from his aides, and made sarcastic remarks.

When a woman with a Spanish accent, who was trailed by several children, said she couldn't pay an $18 traffic fine, he asked her if her husband worked. Upon her explanation that her husband had left her, Judge F—— demanded, "Why don't you throw him in jail?"

Later he did show some compassion by giving her a 30-day suspended sentence—but not before he had embarrassed her before her children and a court full of spectators.

When I asked others in the courthouse about Judge F——, I was told he was a brilliant criminal lawyer who "thinks he is above hearing traffic cases," but must, under the system, take a turn at it.

Today there are some 3,700 major trial judges in the United States (courts of general jurisdiction) and roughly 5,000 judges in the lower courts.

If my sampling is a fair indication (I simply sat down in courtrooms selected at random around the country and listened), perhaps half of these judges are, for one reason or another, unfit to sit on the bench. This is the same percentage given by several leading lawyers and judges who were interviewed.

"About half are good judges," says Joseph Harrison, a Newark, N.J., lawyer. "The others have various kinds of shortcomings."

Generalizations upset many judges. They prefer to have adverse publicity swept under the rug, for it might harm their image or their professional pride.

Many with high standards find it hard to believe that other judges can falter and fall. Even today some Oklahoma judges refuse to believe that members of their state Supreme Court took bribes, even though one has confessed and another is in prison.

Some judges fear that a public airing of dirty judicial laundry will further reduce respect for law and order.

Others, like Robert C. Finley, Chief Justice of the Supreme Court of the State of Washington, take a balanced view, arguing that while courts must be criticized and improved they are not beyond hope: "Otherwise our society would have broken apart long ago."

Certainly very few lawyers or laymen have followed a path as far-reaching as that taken by this reporter, who was assigned to sit in court rooms and listen and watch. Judges seldom visit other judges' court rooms. And only a handful of lawyers spend time in court, and that usually in a single city or section of the country.

Most judges have their own "kingdoms," with no one having power to make them work, keep them from becoming abusive or arbitrary, or correct other human failings. Appeals courts only rule on errors of law. Lawyers across the country say they are afraid to challenge judges because it will harm their practice and their clients. And in most cities the public doesn't know what is going on, nor does it care.

Yet many judges and lawyers point out that reform will not come from within. It will be up to laymen to make the changes.

After the conclusion of the 13-article series, James testified before a Senate subcommittee on proposed improvements in the nation's judicial machinery and stressed 100 recommendations to increase public confidence in the courts. He was awarded a Pulitzer Prize in National Reporting in 1968. In the same year, the *Riverside* (Calif.) *Press-Enterprise* won the Pulitzer Prize gold medal for Public Service for exposing corruption in the courts in connection with the handling of the property of an Indian tribe in California.

Then, as now, the examination of judicial conduct remains one of the enduring themes in the records of the Pulitzer Prizes.

50. *ST. PETERSBURG TIMES EXPOSES*
A STRANGE CULT IN FLORIDA

Bette Orsini and Charles Stafford Reveal
the Dark Side of Scientology's Work

Cults have always had a peculiar fascination for Americans. Some have turned out to be mere aberrations. Others have been designed by their promoters to be profit-making devices, preying on gullible believers. The worst have been criminal organizations, which practiced everything from assault and battery to murder.

None have shocked Americans more than the grisly end of the People's Temple, the creation of the demonic Rev. Jim Jones, who in 1979 sent 911 of his followers to death in the Guyana jungle by mass suicide and murder in his private hell, Jonestown.

It isn't often, considering that such cults cloak themselves in the respectable guise of religion, that a newspaper can expose them before they do major damage to a community. Nor do some newspapers even attempt it.

But from 1975 to 1979, the *St. Petersburg Times* campaigned successfully to expose the so-called Church of Scientology in nearby Clearwater, Fla., and helped produce the evidence on which nine of its leaders were jailed.

Leading off a 14-part series that ran in the newspaper from Dec. 16 to 30, 1979, Eugene Patterson, its president and editor, wrote:

"When a strange new force imbeds itself clandestinely in this community and sets out to harm people who raise questions about it, a newspaper has a particular duty to resist intimidation itself and inform citizens fully of what is going on."

One reporter in particular, Bette Orsini, was made a target by the Scientologists when she exposed their efforts to buy up secretly some of the best property in Clearwater. Thereafter, she was slandered and threatened and an attempt was made to ruin her husband, who wasn't even a journalist. Moreover, others in the *Times*, including Patterson and the late chairman of the paper's board, Nelson Poynter, were falsely accused of wrongdoing.

They were able, in the end, to beat down the Scientologists, although it took numerous court actions to do it. Here is a digest of the first article on the cult by the chief of the *Times's* Washington bureau:

"IN THE NAME OF RELIGION"

By Charles Stafford

From the St. Petersburg Times, Dec. 16, 1979

It was this time four years ago—this time of year when the old-time religion celebrates the birth of a child—that the new religion came to Clearwater.

It came sneaking into town: a religion with beliefs and practices so alien to the teachings of Jesus that are preached in Clearwater's Christian churches, so different from the law of the prophets that is taught in the city's synagogues.

Discovery of the true nature of Scientology began on July 8, 1977, when FBI agents pounded down doors of church offices in Los Angeles and Washington and carted away 48,149 documents. Many of these were copies of documents that agents of Scientology stole after infiltrating government agencies. Others were files of private organizations like the American Medical Association and the *St. Petersburg Times.*

Still others were internal documents of the Church of Scientology and these would reveal myriad dark secrets.

The documents disclose that the church came to Clearwater with a written plan to establish its program headquarters—its school of theology, so to speak—in the old Fort Harrison Hotel and take control of the city. They show that the United Churches of Florida was created as a front to protect church assets from seizure by the government.

They show that church officials conceived and carried out plots to discredit their "enemies"—the mayor who questioned their secrecy, reporters who investigated and wrote about Scientology, the editor and owner of the area's largest newspaper, even local police departments.

They underscore what a spokesman for the church told Clearwater High School students: "We step on a lot of toes. We don't turn the other cheek."

Government prosecutors (following conviction of nine defendants in Washington, D.C.) delivered this judgment:

"AND BRING ME THEIR HEADS SO I CAN SEE WHAT GOES ON INSIDE THEM"

A COMMENT BY HERBLOCK IN THE WASHINGTON POST ON THE SUPREME COURT'S RECENT DECISIONS IN FIRST AMENDMENT CASES. IT WAS HERBLOCK'S THIRD PULITZER PRIZE (Copyright 1978 by Herblock in the *Washington Post*. Used by permission.)

"The crimes committed by these defendants are of a breadth and scope previously unheard of. No building, office, desk or file was safe from their snooping and prying. No individual or organization was free from their despicable conspiratorial minds.

"In view of this, it defies the imagination that these defendants have the unmitigated audacity to seek to defend their actions in the name of 'religion.' That these defendants now attempt to hide behind the sacred principles of freedom of religion, freedom of speech and right to privacy—which principles they repeatedly demonstrated a willingness to violate with impunity—adds insult to the injuries which they have inflicted on every element of society."

There, in capsule form, you have the story of the Church of Scientology since it came to Clearwater four years ago.

For their exposé of the Scientology cult, Bette Orsini and Charles Stafford won the Pulitzer Prize for National Reporting in 1980.

51. THE LOS ANGELES TIMES PROTESTS
JUDICIAL SANCTIONS AGAINST THE PRESS

Philip F. Kerby Writes an Editorial About Judges
Who Claim the Power of Censorship Over the News

There is something about a Rocky Mountain man that fairly cries out for freedom. Perhaps it is the challenge of living in a rarefied atmosphere, of surmounting the perils that go with climbing into the white silence of snow fields and threatening crags. In any event, the strength of Philip F. Kerby's urge for freedom—freedom to speak, to write, to think, to worship—was what set him apart from many of the newspapermen of his day.

He came out of the Rockies—born in 1911 in Pueblo, Colorado; graduated in 1931 from a Pueblo high school, a beginning reporter the same year on the *Pueblo Star-Journal-Chieftain*. In his 45 years as a working newspaperman, he was active on the staff of the *Denver Post*, editor of *Rocky Mountain Life*, and, from 1967 to 1971, associate editor of the Nation. In the latter year he joined the *Los Angeles Times* and soon became its senior editorial writer.

For much of his career, Kerby wasn't any more concerned than the other newspaper people of his time over infringements on freedom of the press. There simply hadn't been any serious challenges to the First Amendment for much of the century. Except for Near v. Minnesota in 1931, in which the U.S. Supreme Court had upheld the immunity of the press from prior restraints on publication in other than extraordinary cases, there had been no landmark decisions in the courts.

But in 1971, the first year of Kerby's service on the *Los Angeles Times* editorial page, the federal courts restrained the *New York Times* and the *Washington Post* from publishing the Pentagon Papers for 15 days before the U. S. Supreme Court ruled against the government's contention that such disclosures would damage national security. After that dubious victory came the high court's 5-4 decision in Branzburg v. Hayes in 1972, which stripped reporters of First Amendment protection when properly constituted authorities demanded their confidential sources. The result was that reporters began going to jail for contempt of court for refusing to disclose their sources.

Next, judges began to impose gag orders on the news media ostensibly to insure the impaneling of an impartial jury in controversial cases. After a number of years with a scattering of such gag orders, in which judges assumed the prerogatives of editors, Kerby noted that there was a sudden increase in such rulings—13 in 1974, 14 in 1975. In the latter year, in Lincoln County District Court, Nebraska, the broadest kind of restriction was placed on all the news media in the state by judicial order to prevent dissemination of proceedings against an accused mass murderer. In the same year, federal judges ordered a new trial for the convicted kidnaper of a newspaper editor, Reg Murphy, on grounds of prejudicial publicity.

It was all that Kerby could stand. At the beginning of December 1975, he wrote this editorial:

THE COURTS SCRATCH FOR POWER

By Philip F. Kerby

From the Los Angeles Times, Dec. 3, 1975

The decision of a three-judge federal panel in the case of the abducted newspaper editor is simply absurd. But absurd as it is, the ruling is a logical extension of a ten-year trend toward judicial censorship.

More and more judges have developed an itch for more and more power, and they are scratching it at every opportunity. In doing so, they are willing to tear up the First Amendment, the primary guardian of all our liberties.

Consider the decision of the panel that handled the appeal of the man who abducted Reg Murphy, then editor of the *Atlanta Constitution* and now editor and publisher of the *San Francisco Examiner*. The judges ordered a new trial for the abductor, who was convicted of extortion on August 3, 1974. On what basis was a new trial ordered?

The court ruled that what it called prejudicial errors by the prosecution and pretrial publicity prevented a fair trial. Of the man's guilt, there was no doubt. He admitted abducting Murphy; the $700,000 ransom was found in the home of the defendant, who entered a plea of insanity.

The three judges objected to a closing argument by the prosecuting attorney, who asserted that acquitting the defendant would be a "blank check" for him to commit crimes against judge, jury, and community; while the judges objected to this bit of hyperbole as prejudicial to a fair trial, they dealt more extensively with pretrial publicity.

Sitting as judges but also as presumptive editors, the panel noted that the sensational crime attracted widespread coverage in the news media. This, they speculated, overwhelmed the jury and tainted the trial. The convicted extortioner's guilt evidently was the one thing the panel chose to ignore.

So now there will be a new trial, unless the order is overturned, and presumably there will be gag orders restricting information and a hunt for jurors who do not read, who do not see, and who are unaware of the world around them. Although Murphy is personally involved, his comment on the decision is hard to discount:

"I presume the judges would like the trial to be held on Guam or in the Bavarian Alps before a jury which speaks no English and knows no American customs."

The government is considering an appeal of the panel's decision, but the judiciary in the past decade has shown little inclination to limit its powers to impose censorship on the conduct of criminal proceedings.

This predisposition toward censorship is asserted in behalf of fair trials. But predictions of harm that publicity may cause are based on nothing more than speculation which, in turn, is based on no more than subjective judgment. . . .

We have reached a strange point in this country. The publicity generated not by the press but by the nature of monstrous crimes is used as an excuse by the courts to impose censorship on the public.

Under the rationale used by the federal court in Atlanta, all information about the Watergate conspiracy could have been suppressed once the Watergate burglars, the most petty actors in the sordid drama, were arrested and charged. The implications of this kind of judicial tyranny by the courts need to be thoroughly understood by the public.

Eight years ago, the chairman of a committee that studied the issue of press freedom concluded:

"The prospect, in this pretrail period, of judges of various criminal courts of high and low degree sitting as petty tyrants, handing down sentaences of fine and imprisonment for contempt of court against lawyers, policemen, reporters, and editors, is not attractive. Such an innovation might well cut prejudicial publicity . . . but at what price?"

The chairman of that committee was not an editor. He was Harold R. Medina, a senior judge on the U.S. Circuit Court of Appeals for the 2nd District.

The price is now clear. For the first time in the history of the country, the courts, the chief defenders of the Constitution and in utter disdain of that Constitution, have claimed the power of wide censorship over the American people, a censorship that strikes at the heart of democratic government.

The courts, no less than legislatures and executives, are accountable to the people, and must function in the sunlight of public exposure and scrutiny.

Kerby won the Pulitzer Prize for Editorial Writing in 1976, the year of his retirement from the *Los Angeles Times.* But of even more importance to him, the legal pendulum seemed to be swinging back in favor of the press that year. For on June 30, 1976, the Supreme Court by 9–0 held judicial gag orders unconstitutional in deciding an appeal from the Nebraska case decision. And on August 25, 1976, Reg Murphy's kidnaper,

William A. H. Williams, was found guilty in Key West for a second time and in the following month was sentenced to 50 years in prison.

But there was no tendency in the nation's newsrooms to celebrate. For in 1976, too, the Supreme Court refused to intervene in contempt convictions against four Fresno newspapermen and in the case of William T. Farr, all in California. It fell to the state courts to release them when they demonstrated, after limited periods in jail, that they would not disclose their sources. Then came the most sensational reversal of all, the jailing of M. A. Farber of the *New York Times* for 28 days in 1978 and the $250,000 fine levied aginst the *New York Times*, his employer, by a New Jersey jurist who had demanded Farber's sources in a murder trial. Once more, the high court refused to intervene.

There followed a series of cases in which the Supreme Court made it clear that where the right to a fair trial conflicted with the rights of a free press, the press would have to yield up its special privilege. Moreover, the most powerful judges in the land also held that the press could claim no greater protection from the law than any citizen.

This was the import of the high court's decision in Zurcher v. *Stanford Daily* in 1978, in which police were given the right to raid newsrooms without a warrant in a search for evidence of the commission of a crime. In Herbert v. Lando in 1979, the court ruled that journalists could have their inner thoughts explored by plaintiffs in libel cases. And in Smith v. Maryland, the judges declared that the police could force disclosure of records of journalists' telephone calls in connection with criminal inquiries, another 1979 decision.

But the case that brought the loudest outcry was the high court's decision in Gannett v. DePasquale, which ostensibly permitted the closure of pretrial hearings to the press but actually gave numerous judges the excuse to bar the press from proceedings in what formerly were called open courts. This created so much confusion that four of the high court's judges, including the Chief Justice, gave varying opinions off the bench on what it meant.

In response to a storm of protest in the press, the high court held on July 2, 1980, that press and public *did* have an almost absolute right to attend criminal trials in open court. While some legal authorities speculated that this also meant the court was weakening its position on the closure of pretrial hearings, nothing in the decision (Richmond Newspapers v. Virginia, No. 79-243) indicated that Gannett v. DePasquale was being set aside.

What one of the concurring opinions in the 7-1 Virginia decision did do was to bolster the belief of most journalists that the First Amendment gave them an absolute right to gather as well as to disseminate the news. Associate Justice John Paul Stevens wrote, in commenting on the case, that the Supreme Court had "never before . . . held that the acquisition of newsworthy matter is entitled to any constitutional protection whatsoever."

However, in the face of rejoicing by editorialists over a decision that favored the press, the more realistic commentators still had their doubts about the sweeping nature of the victory. As Tom Wicker wrote in the *New York Times*, "It remains to be seen whether the ruling in the latest [Virginia] case means that the court will recognize that claim [to gather as well as disseminate news] more generally on the question of open courtrooms."

The Virginia decision came at a time when legal authorities like Alan U. Schwartz were warning that it was a period of "dark caution for the press and therefore for the country." In any event, it was certain that the press would have need in the later years of the 20th century of all its talent, spirit, wealth, and strength.[1]

[1] Notes of sources for the above: Thomas I. Emerson, *The System of Freedom of Expression* (New York: Random House, 1970), p. 506 on Near v. Minnesota; Benno C. Schmidt, Jr., "The Nebraska Decision," in *Columbia Journalism Review* (November/December, 1976), p. 53; Farr case, *New York Times*, July 1, 1976; Fresno Four case, see UPI file dateline Fresno, Sept. 18, 1976; Murphy case, Associated Press file, Aug. 25 and Sept. 17, 1976; for Branzburg v. Hayes, 408 U.S. 665 (1972) and *New York Times*, June 30, 1972; Claude Sitton, "Can the First Amendment Survive?" *ASNE Bulletin* (February 1978), p. 17; Stanford v. Zurcher in *Editor & Publisher* (June 17, 1978), p. 9; Farber case in *News Media & the Law*, published by the Reporters Committee for Freedom of the Press, Vol. 2, no. 3 (October, 1978), p. 2; Herbert v. Lando in *News Media & the Law*, Vol. 3, no. 2 (May–June, 1979), p. 2; telephone case, same issue, p. 6; Gannett v. DePasquale, *UPI Reporter* (July 26, 1979); *New York Times*, Aug. 11, 1979, p. 43; *Editor & Publisher* (Aug. 18, 1979), p. 8 and (Oct. 13, 1979), p. 13; Alan U. Schwartz, "Danger: Pendulum Swinging—Using the Courts to Muzzle the Press," *Atlantic* (February 1977), p. 29 et. seq.; Richmond Newspapers v. Virginia, No. 79-243, in *New York Times*, pp. 1 and D15–16, July 3, 1980; Tom Wicker in *New York Times*, July 6, 1980, p. D17.

PULITZER PRIZES
IN JOURNALISM, 1959–1980

NOTE: *Pulitzer Prizes in Journalism, 1917–1958, with citations, are in* The Pulitzer Prize Story *(New York: Columbia University Press, 1959; paperback, 1971)*

MERITORIOUS PUBLIC SERVICE

1959 UTICA (N.Y.) OBSERVER-DISPATCH and the UTICA DAILY PRESS for their successful campaign against corruption, gambling and vice in their home city and the achievement of sweeping civic reforms in the face of political pressure and threats of violence. By their stalwart leadership of the forces of good government, these newspapers upheld the best traditions of a free press.

1960 LOS ANGELES TIMES for its thorough, sustained and well-conceived attack on narcotics traffic and the enterprising reporting of Gene Sherman, which led to the opening of negotiations between the United States and Mexico to halt the flow of illegal drugs into southern California and other border states.

1961 AMARILLO (Texas) GLOBE-TIMES for exposing a breakdown in local law enforcement with resultant punitive action that swept lax officials from their posts and brought about the election of a reform slate. The newspaper thus exerted its civic leadership in the finest tradition of journalism.

1962 PANAMA CITY (Florida) NEWS-HERALD for its three-year campaign against entrenched power and corruption, with resultant reforms in Panama City and Bay County.

1963 CHICAGO DAILY NEWS, for calling public attention to the issue of providing birth control services in the public health programs in its area.

1964 ST. PETERSBURG (Florida) TIMES for its aggressive investigation of the Florida Turnpike Authority which disclosed widespread illegal acts and resulted in a major reorganization of the State's road construction program.

1965 HUTCHINSON (Kansas) NEWS for its courageous and constructive campaign, culminating in 1964, to bring about more equitable reapportionment of the Kansas Legislature, despite powerful opposition in its own community.

1966 The BOSTON GLOBE for its campaign to prevent the confirmation of Francis X. Morrissey as a Federal District Judge in Massachusetts.

1967 The LOUISVILLE COURIER-JOURNAL for its successful campaign to control the Kentucky strip mine industry, a notable advance in the national effort for the conservation of natural resources; and
The MILWAUKEE JOURNAL for its successful campaign to stiffen the laws against water pollution in Wisconsin, a notable advance in the national effort for the conservation of natural resources.

1968 The RIVERSIDE (Calif.) PRESS-ENTERPRISE for its exposé of corruption in the courts in connection with the handling of the property and estates of an Indian tribe in California, and its successful efforts to punish the culprits.

1969 The LOS ANGELES TIMES for its exposé of wrongdoing within the Los Angeles City Government Commissions, resulting in resignations or criminal convictions of certain members, as well as widespread reforms.

1970 NEWSDAY, Garden City, New York, for its three-year investigation and exposure of secret land deals in eastern Long Island, which led to a series of criminal convictions, discharges and resignations among public and political officeholders in the area.

1971 The WINSTON-SALEM (N.C.) JOURNAL AND SENTINEL for coverage of environmental problems, as exemplified by a successful campaign to block a strip mining operation that would have caused irreparable damage to the hill country of northwest North Carolina.

1972 The NEW YORK TIMES for the publication of the Pentagon Papers.

1973 The WASHINGTON POST for its investigation of the Watergate case.

1974 NEWSDAY, Garden City, N.Y., for its definitive report on the illicit narcotics traffic in the United States and abroad, entitled, "The Heroin Trail."

1975 The BOSTON GLOBE for its massive and balanced coverage of the Boston school desegregation crisis.

1976 ANCHORAGE DAILY NEWS for its disclosures of the impact and influence of the Teamsters Union on Alaska's economy and politics.

1977 The LUFKIN (Tex.) NEWS, for an obituary of a local man who died in Marine training camp, which grew into an investigation of that death and a fundamental reform in the recruiting and training practices of the United States Marine Corps.

1978 The PHILADELPHIA INQUIRER, for a series of articles showing abuses of power by the police in its home city.

1979 POINT REYES LIGHT, a California weekly, for its investigation of Synanon.

1980 GANNETT NEWS SERVICE for its series on financial contributions to the Pauline Fathers.

LOCAL REPORTING, EDITION TIME

1959 MARY LOU WERNER of the *Evening Star*, Washington D.C., for her comprehensive year-long coverage of the integration crisis in Virginia which demonstrated admirable qualities of accuracy, speed and the ability to interpret the news under deadline pressure in the course of a difficult and taxing assignment.

1960 JACK NELSON of the *Atlanta Constitution*, for the excellent reporting in his series of articles on mental institutions in Georgia.

1961 SANCHE DE GRAMONT, *New York Herald Tribune*, for his moving account of the death of Leonard Warren on the Metropolitan Opera stage.

1962 ROBERT D. MULLINS of the *Deseret News*, Salt Lake City, for his resourceful coverage of a murder and kidnapping at Dead Horse Point, Utah.

1963   SYLVAN FOX, ANTHONY SHANNON, and WILLIAM LONGGOOD of
       the *New York World-Telegram and Sun,* for their reporting
       of an air crash in Jamaica Bay, killing 95 persons on March
       1, 1962.

       NOTE: *In 1963, this category became Local General and
       Local Special Reporting.*

LOCAL GENERAL REPORTING

1964   NORMAN C. MILLER, JR., of the *Wall Street Journal* for his
       comprehensive account of a multi-million dollar vegetable
       oil swindle in New Jersey.
1965   MELVIN H. RUDER of the *Hungry Horse News,* a weekly in
       Columbia Falls, Montana, for his daring and resourceful
       coverage of a disastrous flood that threatened his com-
       munity, an individual effort in the finest tradition of spot
       news reporting.
1966   The LOS ANGELES TIMES Staff, for its coverage of the Watts
       riots.
1967   ROBERT V. Cox of the *Chambersburg* (Pennsylvania) *Public
       Opinion* for his vivid deadline reporting of a mountain
       manhunt that ended with the killing of a deranged sniper
       who had terrorized the community.
1968   The DETROIT FREE PRESS for its coverage of the Detroit riots
       of 1967, recognizing both the brilliance of its detailed spot
       news staff work and its swift and accurate investigation into
       the underlying causes of the tragedy.
1969   JOHN FETTERMAN of the *Louisville Times* and *Courier-
       Journal* for his article, "Pfc. Gibson Comes Home," the
       story of an American soldier whose body was returned to his
       native town from Vietnam for burial.
1970   THOMAS FITZPATRICK, *Chicago Sun-Times,* for his article
       about the violence of youthful radicals in Chicago, "A Wild
       Night's Ride With SDS."
1971   The Staff of the Akron (Ohio) BEACON JOURNAL for its
       coverage of the Kent State University tragedy on May 4,
       1970.
1972   RICHARD COOPER and JOHN MACHACEK of the *Rochester*
       (N.Y.) *Times-Union* for their coverage of the Attica (N.Y.)
       prison riot.

1973   CHICAGO TRIBUNE for uncovering flagrant violations of voting procedures in the primary election of March 21, 1972.

1974   ARTHUR M. PETACQUE and HUGH F. HOUGH of the *Chicago Sun-Times* for uncovering new evidence that led to the reopening of efforts to solve the 1966 murder of Valerie Percy.

1975   The Staff of the XENIA (Ohio) DAILY GAZETTE for its coverage, under enormous difficulties, of the tornado that wrecked the city on April 3, 1974.

1976   GENE MILLER of the *Miami Herald*, for his persistent and courageous reporting over eight and one-half years that led to the exoneration and release of two men who had twice been tried for murder and wrongfully convicted and sentenced to death in Florida.

1977   MARGO HUSTON of the *Milwaukee Journal* for her reports on the elderly and the process of aging.

1978   RICHARD WHITT, the *Louisville Courier-Journal*, for his coverage of a fire that took 164 lives at the Beverly Hills Supper Club at Southgate, Ky., and subsequent investigation of the lack of enforcement of state fire codes.

1979   The SAN DIEGO (Calif.) EVENING TRIBUNE, for its coverage of the collision of a Pacific Southwest airliner with a small plane over its city.

1980   Staff of the PHILADELPHIA INQUIRER for coverage of the nuclear accident at Three Mile Island.

LOCAL REPORTING, NO EDITION TIME

1959   JOHN HAROLD BRISLIN of the *Scranton* (Pa.) *Tribune* and the *Scrantonian* for displaying courage, initiative, and resourcefulness in his effective four-year campaign to halt labor violence in his home city, as a result of which ten corrupt union officials were sent to jail and a local union was emboldened to clean out racketeering elements.

1960   MIRIAM OTTENBERG, of the *Evening Star*, Washington, D.C., for a series of seven articles exposing a used-car racket in Washington, D.C., that victimized many unwary buyers. The series led to new regulations to protect the public and served to alert other communities to such sharp practices.

1961   EDGAR MAY, *Buffalo* (N.Y.) *Evening News*, for his series of articles on New York State's public welfare services entitled, "Our Costly Dilemma," based on part on his three-month employment as a State case worker. The series brought about reforms that attracted nation-wide attention.

1962 GEORGE BLISS, *Chicago Tribune*, for his initiative in uncovering scandals in the Metropolitan Sanitary District of Greater Chicago, with resultant remedial action.

1963 OSCAR GRIFFIN, JR., who as editor of the *Pecos* (Texas) *Independent and Enterprise*, initiated the exposure of the Billie Sol Estes scandal and thereby brought a major fraud on the United States government to national attention with resultant investigation, prosecution and conviction of Estes.

LOCAL INVESTIGATIVE SPECIALIZED REPORTING

1964 JAMES V. MAGEE and ALBERT V. GAUDIOSI, reporters, and FREDERICK A. MEYER, photographer, of the *Philadelphia Bulletin* for their exposé of numbers racket operations with police collusion in South Philadelphia, which resulted in arrests and a cleanup of the police department.

1965 GENE GOLTZ of the *Houston Post* for his exposé of government corruption in Pasadena, Texas, which resulted in widespread reforms.

1966 JOHN ANTHONY FRASCA of the *Tampa* (Fla.) *Tribune* for his investigation and reporting of two robberies that resulted in the freeing of an innocent man.

1967 GENE MILLER of the *Miami Herald* whose initiative and investigative reporting helped to free two persons wrongfully convicted of murder.

1968 J. ANTHONY LUKAS of the *New York Times* for the social document he wrote in his investigation of the life and the murder of Linda Fitzpatrick.

1969 ALBERT L. DELUGACH and DENNY WALSH of the *St. Louis Globe-Democrat* for their campaign against fraud and abuse of power within the St. Louis Steamfitters Union, Local 562.

1970 HAROLD EUGENE MARTIN, of the *Montgomery Advertiser* and *Alabama Journal*, for his exposé of a commercial scheme for using Alabama prisoners for drug experimentation and obtaining blood plasma from them.

1971 WILLIAM JONES of the *Chicago Tribune* for exposing collusion between police and some of Chicago's largest private ambulance companies to restrict service in low income areas, leading to major reforms.

1972 TIMOTHY LELAND, GERARD M. O'NEILL, STEPHEN A. KURK-JIAN and ANN DESANTIS of the *Boston Globe* for their exposure of widespread corruption in Somerville, Massachusetts.

1973 THE SUN NEWSPAPERS OF OMAHA for uncovering the large financial resources of Boys Town, Nebraska, leading to reforms in this charitable organization's solicitation and use of funds contributed by the public.

1974 WILLIAM SHERMAN of the *New York Daily News* for his resourceful investigative reporting in the exposure of extreme abuse of the New York Medicaid program.

1975 The INDIANAPOLIS STAR for its disclosures of local police corruption and dilatory law enforcement, resulting in a cleanup of both the Police Department and the office of the County Prosecutor.

1976 CHICAGO TRIBUNE's staff members who uncovered widespread abuses in Federal housing programs in Chicago and exposed shocking conditions at two private Chicago hospitals.

1977 ACEL MOORE and WENDELL RAWLS, JR., the *Philadelphia Inquirer*, for their reports on conditions in the Farview (Pa.) State Hospital for the mentally ill.

1978 ANTHONY R. DOLAN, the *Stamford* (Conn.) *Advocate*, for a series on municipal corruption.

1979 GILBERT M. GAUL and ELLIOT G. JASPIN, *Pottsville* (Pa.) *Republican*, for stories on the destruction of the Blue Coal Company by men with ties to organized crime.

1980 STEPHEN A. KURKJIAN, ALEXANDER B. HAWES, JR., NILS BRUZELIUS, and JOAN VENNOCHI, the *Boston Globe* Spotlight Team, for articles on Boston's transit system.

NATIONAL REPORTING

1959 HOWARD VAN SMITH of the *Miami* (Fla.) *News* for a series of articles that focused public notice on deplorable conditions in a Florida migrant labor camp, resulted in the provision of generous assistance for the 4,000 stranded workers in the camp, and thereby called attention to the national problem presented by 1,500,000 migratory laborers.

1960 VANCE TRIMBLE, of the Scripps-Howard Newspaper Alliance, for a series of articles exposing the extent of nepotism in the Congress of the United States.

1961 EDWARD R. CONY, the *Wall Street Journal*, for his analysis of a timber transaction which drew the attention of the public to the problems of business ethics.

1962 NATHAN G. CALDWELL and GENE S. GRAHAM of the *Nashville Tennessean* for their exclusive disclosure and six years of detailed reporting, under great difficulties, of the undercover cooperation between management interests in the coal industry and the United Mine Workers.

1963 ANTHONY LEWIS of the *New York Times* for his distinguished reporting of the proceedings of the United States Supreme Court during the year, with particular emphasis on the coverage of the decision in the reapportionment case and its consequences in many of the States of the Union.

1964 MERRIMAN SMITH of United Press International for his outstanding coverage of the assassination of President John F. Kennedy.

1965 LOUIS M. KOHLMEIER of the *Wall Street Journal* for his enterprise in reporting the growth of the fortune of President Lyndon B. Johnson and his family.

1966 HAYNES JOHNSON of the *Washington Evening Star* for his distinguished coverage of the civil rights conflict centered about Selma, Ala., and particularly his reporting of its aftermath.

1967 STANLEY PENN and MONROE KARMIN of the *Wall Street Journal* for their investigative reporting of the connection between American crime and gambling in the Bahamas. (The prize is shared between the two reporters.)

1968 HOWARD JAMES of the *Christian Science Monitor* for his series of articles, "Crisis in the Courts" and
NATHAN K. (Nick) KOTZ of the *Des Moines Register* and *Minneapolis Tribune* for his reporting of unsanitary conditions in many meat-packing plants, which helped insure the passage of the Federal Wholesome Meat Act of 1967.

1969 ROBERT CAHN of the *Christian Science Monitor* for his inquiry into the future of our national parks and the methods that may help to preserve them.

1970 WILLIAM J. EATON, *Chicago Daily News*, for disclosures about the background of Judge Clement F. Haynesworth

Jr., in connection with his nomination for the United States Supreme Court.

1971   LUCINDA FRANKS and THOMAS POWERS, of United Press International, for their documentary on the life and death of a 28-year-old revolutionary, Diana Oughton: "The Making of a Terrorist."

1972   JACK ANDERSON, syndicated columnist, for his reporting of American policy decision-making during the Indo-Pakistan War of 1971.

1973   ROBERT BOYD and CLARK HOYT of the Knight Newspapers for their disclosure of Senator Thomas Eagleton's history of psychiatric therapy, resulting in his withdrawal as the Democratic Vice Presidential nominee in 1972.

1974   JAMES R. POLK of the *Washington Star-News* for his disclosure of alleged irregularities in the financing of the campaign to re-elect President Nixon in 1972 and
JACK WHITE of the *Providence Journal* and *Evening Bulletin* for his initiative in exclusively disclosing President Nixon's Federal income tax payments in 1970 and 1971.

1975   DONALD . L. BARLETT and JAMES B. STEELE of the *Philadelphia Inquirer* for their series "Auditing the Internal Revenue Service," which exposed the unequal application of Federal tax laws.

1976   JAMES RISSER of the *Des Moines Register* for disclosing large-scale corruption in the American grain exporting trade.

1977   WALTER MEARS of the Associated Press, for his coverage of the 1976 Presidential campaign.

1978   GAYLORD D. SHAW, *Los Angeles Times*, for a series on unsafe structural conditions at the nation's major dams.

1979   JAMES RISSER, the *Des Moines Register*, for a series on farming damage to the environment.

1980   BETTE SWENSON ORSINI and CHARLES STAFFORD, *St. Petersburg Times*, for their investigation of the Church of Scientology.

INTERNATIONAL REPORTING

1959   JOSEPH MARTIN and PHILIP SANTORA of the *New York Daily News* for their exclusive series of articles disclosing the brutality of the Batista government in Cuba long before its downfall and forecasting the triumph of the revolutionary party led by Fidel Castro.

1960   A. M. ROSENTHAL, of the *New York Times*, for his perceptive and authoritative reporting from Poland. Mr. Rosenthal's subsequent expulsion from the country was attributed by Polish government spokesmen to the depth of his reporting into Polish affairs, there being no accusation of false reporting.

1961   LYNN HEINZERLING, Associated Press, for his reporting under extraordinarily difficult conditions of the early stages of the Congo crisis and his keen analysis of events in other parts of Africa.

1962   WALTER LIPPMANN of the *New York Herald Tribune* Syndicate for his 1961 interview with Soviet Premier Khrushchev, as illustrative of Mr. Lippmann's long and distinguished contribution to American journalism.

1963   HAL HENDRIX, of the *Miami* (Florida) *News*, for his persistent reporting which revealed, at any early stage, that the Soviet Union was installing missile launching pads in Cuba and sending in large numbers of MIG-21 aircraft.

1964   MALCOLM W. BROWNE of the Associated Press and DAVID HALBERSTAM of the *New York Times* for their individual reporting of the Vietnam war and the overthrow of the Diem regime.

1965   J. A. LIVINGSTON of the *Philadelphia Bulletin* for his reports on the growth of economic independence among Russia's Eastern European satellites and his analysis of their desire for a resumption of trade with the West.

1966   PETER ARNETT of the Associated Press for his coverage of the war in Vietnam.

1967   R. JOHN HUGHES of the *Christian Science Monitor* for his thorough reporting of the attempted Communist coup in Indonesia in 1965 and the purge that followed in 1965–66.

1968   ALFRED FRIENDLY of the *Washington Post* for his coverage of the Middle East War of 1967.

1969   WILLIAM TUOHY of the *Los Angeles Times* for his Vietnam War correspondence in 1968.

1970   SEYMOUR M. HERSH, of the Dispatch News Service, Washington, D.C., for his exclusive disclosure of the Vietnam War tragedy at the hamlet of My Lai.

1971 JIMMIE LEE HOAGLAND of the *Washington Post* for his coverage of the struggle against apartheid in the Republic of South Africa.

1972 PETER R. KANN of the *Wall Street Journal* for his coverage of the Indo-Pakistan War of 1971.

1973 MAX FRANKEL of the *New York Times* for his coverage of President Nixon's visit to China in 1972.

1974 HEDRICK SMITH of the *New York Times* for his coverage of the Soviet Union and its allies in Eastern Europe in 1973.

1975 WILLIAM MULLEN, reporter, and OVIE CARTER, photographer, of the *Chicago Tribune* for their coverage of famine in Africa and India.

1976 SYDNEY H. SCHANBERG of the *New York Times* for his coverage of the Communist takeover in Cambodia, carried out at great risk when he elected to stay at his post after the fall of Pnom Penh.

1977 No award.

1978 HENRY KAMM, the *New York Times*, for his stories on the refugee "boat people" from Indochina.

1979 RICHARD BEN CRAMER, the *Philadelphia Inquirer*, for reports from the Middle East.

1980 JOEL BRINKLEY, reporter, and JAY MATHER, photographer, *Louisville Courier-Journal*, for stories from Cambodia.

EDITORIALS

1959 RALPH MCGILL, editor of the *Atlanta Constitution*, for distinguished editorial writing during 1958, as exemplified in his editorial, "One Church, One School. . . ." and for his long, courageous and effective editorial leadership.

1960 LENOIR CHAMBERS, editor of the *Norfolk Virginian-Pilot*, for his series of editorials on the school segregation problem in Virginia, as exemplified by "The Year the Schools Closed," published January I, 1959, and "The Year the Schools Opened," published December 31, 1959.

1961 WILLIAM J. DORVILLIER, *San Juan* (Puerto Rico) *Star*, for his editorials on clerical interference in the 1960 gubernatorial election in Puerto Rico.

1962 THOMAS M. STORKE of the *Santa Barbara* (California) *News-Press* for his forceful editorials calling public attention to the activities of a semi-secret organization known as the John Birch Society.

1963   IRA B. HARKEY, JR., editor and publisher of the *Pascagoula* (Miss.) *Chronicle*, for his courageous editorials devoted to the processes of law and reason during the integration crisis in Mississippi in 1962.

1964   HAZEL BRANNON SMITH of the *Lexington* (Miss.) *Advertiser* for steadfast adherence to her editorial duty in the face of great pressure and opposition.

1965   JOHN R. HARRISON of the *Gainesville* (Florida) *Daily Sun* for his successful editorial campaign for better housing in his city.

1966   ROBERT LASCH of the *St. Louis Post-Dispatch* for his distinguished editorial writing in 1965.

1967   EUGENE PATTERSON of the *Atlanta Constitution* for his editorials during the year.

1968   JOHN S. KNIGHT of the Knight Newspapers for distinguished editorial writing.

1969   PAUL GREENBERG of the *Pine Bluff* (Ark.) *Commercial* for his editorials during 1968.

1970   PHILIP L. GEYELIN, *Washington Post*, for his editorials during 1969.

1971   HORANCE G. DAVIS, JR., of the *Gainesville* (Fla.) *Sun*, for his editorials in support of the peaceful desegregation of Florida's schools.

1972   JOHN STROHMEYER of the *Bethlehem* (Pa.) *Globe-Times* for his editorial campaign to reduce racial tensions in Bethlehem.

1973   ROGER B. LINSCOTT of the *Berkshire Eagle*, Pittsfield, Mass., for his editorials during 1972.

1974   F. GILMAN SPENCER, editor of the *Trentonian*, of Trenton, N.J., for his courageous campaign to focus public attention on scandals in New Jersey's state government.

1975   JOHN DANIELL MAURICE of the *Charleston* (W. Va.) *Daily Mail* for his editorials about the Kanawha County schoolbook controversy.

1976   PHILIP P. KERBY of the *Los Angeles Times* for the editorials against government secrecy and judicial censorship.

1977   WARREN L. LERUDE, FOSTER CHURCH, and NORMAN F. CARDOZA of the *Reno* (Nev.) *Evening Gazette* and *Nevada*

State Journal, for editorials challenging the power of a local brothel keeper.

1978 MEG GREENFIELD, deputy editorial page editor of the *Washington Post*, for selected examples of her work.

1979 EDWIN M. YODER, JR., the *Washington Star*.

1980 ROBERT L. BARTLEY, *Wall Street Journal*.

CARTOONS

1959 WILLIAM H. (BILL) MAULDIN of the *St. Louis Post-Dispatch* for his cartoon, "I won the Nobel Prize for Literature. What was your crime?" published on October 30, 1958.

1960 No award.

1961 CAREY ORR of the *Chicago Tribune* for his long and distinguished career as an editorial cartoonist as exemplified by a cartoon captioned, "The Kindly Tiger," published on October 8, 1960.

1962 EDMUND S. VALTMAN of the *Hartford Times* for his distinguished editorial cartooning during the year, as exemplified by "What You Need, Man, Is a Revolution like Mine," published on August 31, 1961.

1963 FRANK MILLER, of the *Des Moines Register*, for his distinguished editorial cartoons during the year, a notable example of which showed a world destroyed with one ragged figure calling to another: "I said—we sure settled that dispute, didn't we!"

1964 PAUL CONRAD of the *Denver Post* for his editorial cartooning during the year.

1965 No award.

1966 DON WRIGHT of the *Miami News* for his editorial cartooning for 1965, as exemplified by his cartoon, "You Mean You Were Bluffing?"

1967 PATRICK B. OLIPHANT of the *Denver Post* for his cartoons during the year as exemplified by "They Won't Get *Us* To The Conference Table . . . Will They?" published February 1, 1966.

1968 EUGENE GRAY PAYNE of the *Charlotte Observer* for his editorial cartooning in 1967.

1969 JOHN FISCHETTI of the *Chicago Daily News* for his editorial cartooning during 1968.

1970   THOMAS F. DARCY, of *Newsday*, Garden City, New York, for his editorial cartooning during 1969.

1971   PAUL CONRAD of the *Los Angeles Times* for his editorial cartooning during 1970.

1972   JEFFREY K. MACNELLY of the *Richmond News-Leader* for his editorial cartooning during 1971.

1973   No award.

1974   PAUL SZEP of the *Boston Globe* for his editorial cartooning during 1973.

1975   GARRY TRUDEAU for his cartoon strip "Doonesbury," distributed by Universal Press Syndicate.

1976   TONY AUTH of the *Philadelphia Inquirer* for his editorial cartooning during the year, as exemplified by the cartoon, "O beautiful for spacious skies, For amber waves of grain," published on July 22, 1975.

1977   PAUL SZEP of the *Boston Globe.*

1978   JEFFREY K. MACNELLY, of the *Richmond News Leader.*

1979   HERBERT L. BLOCK of the *Washington Post* for the body of his work.

1980   DON WRIGHT, *Miami News.*

PHOTOGRAPHY

1959   WILLIAM SEAMAN of the *Minneapolis Star* for his dramatic photograph of the sudden death of a child in the street.

1960   ANDREW LOPEZ, of United Press International, for his series of four photographs of a corporal, formerly of Dictator Batista's army, who was executed by a Castro firing squad, the principal picture showing the condemned man receiving last rites.

1961   YASUSHI NAGAO, of *Mainichi*, Tokyo, for his photograph, "Tokyo Stabbing," distributed by United Press International and widely printed in American newspapers.

1962   PAUL VATHIS of the Harrisburg, Pa., bureau of the Associated Press, for his photograph, "Serious Steps," published April 22, 1961.

1963   HECTOR RONDON, photographer for the Caracas, Venezuela, newspaper, *La Republica*, for his remarkable picture of a priest holding a wounded soldier in the 1962 Venezuelan insurrection: "Aid From The Padre." The photograph was distributed by the Associated Press.

1964 ROBERT H. JACKSON of the *Dallas Times-Herald* for his photograph of the murder of Lee Oswald by Jack Ruby.

1965 HORST FAAS of Associated Press for his combat photography of the war in South Vietnam during 1964.

1966 KYOICHI SAWADA of United Press International for his combat photography of the war in Vietnam during 1965.

1967 JACK R. THORNELL of the Associated Press New Orleans bureau for his picture of the shooting of James Meredith in Mississippi by a roadside rifleman.

[NOTE: *In 1968 the Photography category was divided into two groups, Spot News Photography and Feature Photography.*]

SPOT NEWS PHOTOGRAPHY

1968 ROCCO MORABITO of the *Jacksonville Journal* for his photograph, "The Kiss of Life."

1969 EDWARD T. ADAMS of the Associated Press for his photograph, "Saigon Execution."

1970 STEVE STARR, of the Associated Press, Albany (N.Y.) Bureau, for his news photo taken at Cornell University, "Campus Guns."

1971 JOHN PAUL FILO of the *Valley Daily News* and *Daily Dispatch* of Tarentum and New Kensington, Pennsylvania, for his pictorial coverage of the Kent State University tragedy on May 4, 1970.

1972 HORST FAAS and MICHEL LAURENT of the Associated Press for their pictures series, "Death in Dacca."

1973 HUYNH CONG UT of the Associated Press for his photograph, "The Terror of War," depicting children in flight from a napalm bombing.

1974 ANTHONY K. ROBERTS, a free-lance photographer of Beverly Hills, Calif., for his picture series, "Fatal Hollywood Drama," in which an alleged kidnaper was killed.

1975 GERALD H. GAY of the *Seattle Times* for his photograph of four exhausted firemen, "Lull in the Battle."

1976 STANLEY FORMAN of the *Boston Herald American* for his sequence of photographs of a fire in Boston on July 22, 1975.

1977 NEAL ULEVICH of The Associated Press, for a series of

photographs of disorder and brutality in the streets of Bangkok, and

STANLEY FORMAN of the *Boston Herald American*, for his photograph of a youth using the flag as a lance in street disorders. A shared award of $500 each, and a certificate for each.

1978   JOHN H. BLAIR, special assignment photographer for United Press International, for a photograph of an Indianapolis broker being held hostage at gunpoint.

1979   THOMAS J. KELLY, III, the *Pottstown* (Pa.) *Mercury*, for a series called "Tragedy on Sanatoga Road."

1980   A photographer for United Press International (at present unnamed), "Firing Squad in Iran."

FEATURE PHOTOGRAPHY

1968   TOSHIO SAKAI of United Press International for his Vietnam War combat photograph, "Dreams of Better Times."

1969   MONETA SLEET, JR., for his photograph of Martin Luther King, Jr.'s widow and child, taken at Dr. King's funeral. (Mr. Sleet, of *Ebony* magazine, was one of several photographers representing the American press on this occasion.)

1970   DALLAS KINNEY, *Palm Beach Post*, West Palm Beach, Florida, for his portfolio of pictures of Florida migrant workers, "Migration to Misery."

1971   JACK DYKINGA of the *Chicago Sun-Times* for his dramatic and sensitive photographs at the Lincoln and Dixon State Schools for the Retarded in Illinois.

1972   DAVE KENNERLY of United Press International for his dramatic photographs of the Vietnam War in 1971.

1973   BRIAN LANKER of the *Topeka Capital-Journal* for his sequence on childbirth, as exemplified by his photograph, "Moment of Life."

1974   SLAVA VEDER of the Associated Press for his picture of the return of an American prisoner of war from captivity in North Vietnam.

1975   MATTHEW LEWIS of the *Washington Post* for his photographs in color and black and white.

1976   The LOUISVILLE COURIER-JOURNAL and TIMES photographic staff for a comprehensive pictorial report on busing in Louisville's schools.

1977 ROBIN HOOD of the *Chattanooga News-Free Press*, for his photograph of a disabled veteran and his child at an Armed Forces Day parade.

1978 J. ROSS BAUGHMAN, the Associated Press, for three photographs from guerrilla areas in Rhodesia.

1979 Staff photographers of the BOSTON HERALD AMERICAN for photographic coverage of the blizzard of 1978.

1980 ERWIN H. HAGLER, *Dallas Times Herald*, for a series on the Western cowboy.

CRITICISM-COMMENTARY

NOTE: *In 1970, as a result of the discontinuance of the Pulitzer Fellowship in Critical Writing, a new journalism category for distinguished Criticism or Commentary was added. A prize was awarded in each field, however, that year and in 1971, which led to its establishment as two separate categories in 1972.*

COMMENTARY

1970 MARQUIS W. CHILDS, *St. Louis Post-Dispatch*, for distinguished commentary during 1969.

1971 WILLIAM A. CALDWELL of the *Record*, Hackensack, New Jersey, for his commentary in his daily column.

1972 MIKE ROYKO of the *Chicago Daily News* for his columns during 1971.

1973 DAVID S. BRODER of the *Washington Post* for his columns during 1972.

1974 EDWIN A. ROBERTS JR., of the *National Observer* for his commentary on public affairs during 1973.

1975 MARY MCGRORY of the *Washington Star* for her commentary on public affairs during 1974.

1976 WALTER WELLESLEY (RED) SMITH of the *New York Times* for his commentary on sports in 1975 and for many other years.

1977 GEORGE F. WILL, columnist for the *Washington Post* Writers Group, for distinguished comment on a variety of topics.

1978 WILLIAM SAFIRE, columnist for the *New York Times*, for commentary on the Bert Lance affair.

1979 RUSSELL BAKER of the *New York Times*.

1980 ELLEN H. GOODMAN, *Boston Globe*.

CRITICISM

1970 ADA LOUISE HUXTABLE, the *New York Times*, for distinguished criticism during 1969.

1971 HAROLD C. SCHONBERG of the *New York Times* for his music criticism during 1970.

1972 FRANK PETERS, JR., of the *St. Louis Post-Dispatch* for his music criticism during 1971.

1973 RONALD POWERS of the *Chicago Sun-Times* for his critical writing about television during 1972.

1974 EMILY GENAUER of the *Newsday* Syndicate for her critical writing about art and artists.

1975 ROGER EBERT of the *Chicago Sun-Times* for his film criticism during 1974.

1976 ALAN M. KRIEGSMAN of the *Washington Post* for his critical writing about the dance during 1975.

1977 WILLIAM MCPHERSON of the *Washington Post*, for his contribution to "Book World."

1978 WALTER KERR, a drama critic of the *New York Times*, for articles on the theater in 1977 and throughout his long career.

1979 PAUL GAPP, architecture critic of the *Chicago Tribune*.

1980 WILLIAM A. HENRY III, *Boston Globe*.

FEATURE WRITING

[NOTE: *This category was awarded for the first time in 1979.*]

1979 JON D. FRANKLIN, science writer for the *Baltimore Evening Sun*, for an account of brain surgery.

1980 MADELEINE BLAIS, *Miami Herald*, "Zapp's Last Stand."

SPECIAL AWARDS IN JOURNALISM

1958 WALTER LIPPMANN, nationally syndicated columnist of the *New York Herald Tribune*, for the wisdom, perception and high sense of responsibility with which he has commented for many years on national and international affairs.

1964 GANNETT NEWSPAPERS, a special citation for their program, "The Road to Integration," a distinguished example of the use of a newspaper group's resources to complement the work of its individual newspapers.

1976 PROFESSOR JOHN HOHENBERG, a special citation and an antique plaque, inscribed by all the members of the Advisory Board, expressing appreciation for his services for 22 years as Administrator of the Pulitzer Prizes and for his achievements as teacher and journalist.

1978 RICHARD LEE STROUT, for distinguished commentary from Washington over many years as staff correspondent for the *Christian Science Monitor* and contributor to the *New Republic*.

INDEX